Based on New Pattern

# ENGLISH

With

# NIMISHA BANSAL

"The ultimate guide for all competitive exams"

Nimisha Bansal

# 120 RULES OF GRAMMAR

**BY**

## NIMISHA BANSAL

**Updated till APRIL 2026**



Your constructive feedback and suggestions are most important and our team will be highly obliged if you message/mail us your feedback or suggestions at support@nimishabansal.com

First Edition – 2021
Latest Edition – April 2026
Price: ₹399/-
Author: Nimisha Bansal
Published by: Prep Duniya Publishers

**For Distribution:**
Contact Us: support@nimishabansal.com
Call or WhatsApp: +91 9953592800

# DEDICATION

Dedicated to my students

My student, you are the best
Of all the rest
Promise me that you will never admit defeat
Your dedication is visible to everyone you meet
So soothing is your smile
I am amazed for a while
I have students everywhere
But like you are very rare
I can never forget you
Because you are like a drop of shining dew
From a leaf split apart
Your fond memories will always shine in my heart
Yes, I believe in you
Yes, I am proud of you
Don't ever give up
Yes, you can and you will do it

# TABLE OF CONTENTS

## Section - III



## Section – IV

# PREFACE

Dear Students,

***"120 Rules of Grammar"*** is a unique or one of a kind approach to bring all the important concepts and practice questions under one umbrella to assist all the readers in clearing their slightest of doubts regarding this subject. With the diversity of questions based on errors we face in today's competitive examinations, it has become our foremost duty to be self-equipped with proper and relevant solutions. And after going through this book, one can easily find solutions to any type of questions based on errors. This book is solely inspired to make our dedicated readers feel comfortable with the subject so that they can redefine their approach to solve any problem with utmost ease.

Grammar portion of the subject "***English***" plays the most critical role in any competitive examination. With the consistent evolution in the way questions are being asked in the banking, insurance, SSC, railways and defense examinations, maximum efforts have been put to compile ***'Top 120 Rules of Grammar'*** that cover almost every questions based on error part. So, considering all the significance that this book carries, we have divided the book into four sections with each section capable of providing the notable contribution to your skills. The four sections are namely – ***Top 120 Rules, Practice sets, Strategies to solve different types of questions & Mock Tests.*** There are 750+ questions based on spotting errors, duly divided into 15 Practice Sets, to avail our readers with ample opportunities to practice their skills. Moreover, 10 additional mock Tests which contain more than 300+ questions are provided to visualize latest patterns of questions being asked in banking examinations. ***Detailed solutions are provided to every question for a better CONCEPTUAL learning.*** While preparing, all the necessary including minute details have been taken care of. The questions arc preferably selected based on their quality, inculcating different levels and types that will help our readers in getting through any type of new pattern questions with confidence and satisfaction. The book will be extremely helpful in preparing for all the Banking and Insurance examinations like **IBPS, SBI, BANK OF BARODA, SYNDICATE BANK, RBI ASSISTANT, OICL, UIIC, LIC, along with SSC CGL, SSC CHSL, RRB NTPC,** etc.

I express my deepest gratitude to all the aspirants who have chosen this book as their companion to work towards their goal. **I assure that the book is one stop solution to all of them who are looking for a book which can help them gain confidence in "English " and thus score better in all competitive exams.** The innovative, systematic and lucid style adopted in the presentation of this book would definitely delight our readers towards our constructive attempt. The aim of this book is to help students learn, analyze and fathom the pattern of questions being asked especially in the Banking and Insurance exams which will effectively help them in maximizing their overall scores in the most difficult subject of the banking examinations, as considered. I hope that our concerned efforts would find a positive response.

This book is dedicated to all of you My dear students.

All the best for your future endeavors!

Your well wisher

Nimisha Ma'am

# Section – I

# 120 rules of Grammar

## Section - I

**RULE 01**: Difference between "Each" and "Every"

1. They are always followed by a singular verb.

Examples: -

(I) ***Each*** student ***is*** very talented. [Singular verb is used]

(II) ***Each*** of my students ***is*** very talented. [Singular verb is used]

In sentence (I) , "***each***" performs the function of an Adjective (*words used to describe or modify nouns or pronouns*) . The word it describes is the noun "***student***".

In sentence (II) , "***each***" performs the function of a Pronoun (*word that is used instead of a noun or noun phrase*).

In both the cases, we use the singular verb "***is***".

***NOTE**: ***Each*** *refers to a plural number of people or items, but it considers each person or item as an individual or dissimilar unit, it does not consider the group collectively.* **[Individualistic Approach]**

***Every*** *also refers to a multiple number of people or items; but it considers these people or items as part of a similar collective group.* **[General Approach]**

***NOTE**: *"**Each**" can play the role of both a "**Pronoun**" and "**Adjective**". However, "**Every**" is used as an "**Adjective**" only.*

Examples: -

(I) ***Every*** student ***is*** very talented. **[Correct]**

(II) ***Every*** of my students is very talented. **[Incorrect** (X) ]

In sentence (I) , "***Every***" is used as an Adjective. The word it describes is the noun "***student***".

In sentence (II) , "***Every***" is used as a Pronoun which is incorrect.

***NOTE**: *"**Each**" can be used for two or more than two items or people but "**Every**" is used only for more than two items or people. We cannot use "**every**" for exactly two things* (In such case, "***every***" can be replaced by "***both***").

Examples: -

***Each*** person on this earth has to die one day. [more than two persons]

***Every*** person I know has watched the movie. [more than two persons]

He has a book in each hand. [Correct]

He has a book in every hand [Incorrect] (Every cannot be used with two things]

***NOTE**: *"**Every**", but not "**each**", can be used with abstract nouns.*

Examples: -

They have ***every*** reason to be happy with their new home. **[Correct]**

They have ***each*** reason to be happy with their new home. **[Incorrect]**

**RULE 02**: "***Both***" and "***not***" cannot be used together. In such case, we can use "***Neither...nor***" which is used when we want to say that two or more things are not true.

Examples: -

***Both*** Ram and Shyam are ***not*** going to visit this place. **[Incorrect]**

***Neither*** Ram ***nor*** Shyam ***is*** going to visit this place. **[Correct]**

This is a war which ***both*** sides ***cannot*** win. **[Incorrect]**

This is a war which ***neither*** side can win. **[Correct]**

***NOTE**: "***Neither***" allows us to make a negative statement about two people or things at the same time. "***Neither***" goes before singular countable nouns. We use it to say "***not either***" in relation to two things.

**RULE 03**: Usage of Relative Pronouns – ***who, whom, which*** and ***that.***

(1) "***Who***" and "***whom***" are mainly used for people. However, these pronouns can also be used to refer to animals that are mentioned by name and domesticated by people (i.e. Domestic Animals) .

Examples: -

The *witnesses* ***whom*** I interviewed gave conflicting evidence. [Used for people]

The *people* ***who*** just boarded the plane are in a rock band. [Used for people]

The vacuum scared our *dog Rocky*, ***who*** was sleeping on the rug. [Used for a pet]

(2) "***Which***" is used for animals in general or things (i.e. Non- domestic Animals and Non-living things) .

Examples: -

Vinita visited the park with a *dog*, ***which*** likes to chase squirrels. [Used for an animal]

The *bomb*, ***which*** killed 15 people, was the worst of a series of terrorist outrages. [Used for a non-living thing]

(3) "***That***" can be used for people, animals or things (i.e. No restrictions)

Examples: -

The *car* ***that*** Jasprit bought runs on electricity and gas. [Used for a thing]

The *musician* ***that*** won the award is Indian. [Used for a person]

The *dog* ***that*** is chasing the squirrels belongs to Brijesh. [Used for an animal]

***NOTE**: ***All, any, the only, the same, none, much, no, the little, the few, something, anything, nothing and superlative degrees are all followed by "that" only. They cannot be followed by "who" or "which"***

Examples: -

This is the **same** book ***which*** you were reading. **[Incorrect]**

This is the **same** book ***that*** you were reading. **[Correct]**

This is the same person ***that*** I want to marry.

He spent up the little amount ***which he*** had. [Incorrect]

He spent up the little amount ***that he*** had. [Correct]

**Section - I**

This is the ***best that*** I can do for you .

***NOTE**: "***Whoever***" vs. "***Whomever***":

*(1)* ***Whoever*** is a subjective pronoun. It serves as a subject of a verb.

Examples: -

***Whoever*** is hungry can have the leftover pizza. (***Whoever*** is the subject of the verb ***is***, like "He is hungry.")

Give the package to ***whoever*** comes for it. (***Whoever*** is the subject of the verb ***comes***, like "He comes for it.")

I am happy with ***whoever*** wins. (***Whoever*** is the subject of the verb ***wins***, like "He wins.")

***Whoever*** is also correct as a subject complement, with linking verbs such as ***is***, ***are***, and ***will be***.

Examples: -

***Whoever*** it was did not leave her name.

***Whoever*** they are, I like their confidence.

*(2)* ***Whomever*** is an objective pronoun. It serves as an object of a verb or a preposition.

Examples: -

Please invite ***whomever*** you choose. (***Whomever*** is the object of the verb ***choose***, like "You choose him.")

***Whomever*** Kate marries is none of our business. (***Whomever*** is the object of the verb ***marries***, like "Kate marries him.")

I am eager to work with ***whomever*** Dale selects as my partner. (***Whomever*** is the object of the verb ***selects***, like "Dale selects her.")

**RULE04**: There are three types of conditional sentences:

| TYPE | CONDITION |
|---|---|
| I | condition possible to fulfill |
| II | condition in theory possible to fulfill |
| III | condition not possible to fulfill (too late) |

Let's understand their form:

| TYPE | IF–CLAUSE | MAIN CLAUSE |
|---|---|---|
| I | Simple Present | will-future or (Modal + infinitive) or, shall/can/may/must + V1 |
| II | Simple Past | would + V1 or, could/might/should + V1 |
| III | Past Perfect | would + have + past participle (V3) or, could/might/should + have + past participle (V3) |

Examples: -

If I study, I ***will pass*** the exam. **[Type I]**

If I studied, I ***would pass*** the exam. **[Type II]**

If I had studied, I ***would have passed*** the exam. **[Type III]**

If your files are in order you may/can leave at once.

If you want to lose weight you must eat less fat diet.

If I lived near my metro station I would be in time for work.

If I were you, I would plant some saplings around the house.

If we had found him earlier, we could have arrested him and saved the crime.

Had you obeyed the orders this fire accident would have been averted.

***NOTE**: *The given rule is not applicable in the case of universal truths.*

Examples: -

If water reaches 100-degree Celsius, it boils. [Universal truth]

If you heat water, it turns into vapour. [Universal truth]

<u>RULE 05</u>: The general rule for the usage of the phrase "***one of the***" is:

**"One of the + PLURAL NOUN + that/who etc. + SINGULAR/PLURAL VERB"**

So, the noun following the phrase "***one of the***" is always a plural noun

The **RELATIVE PRONOUN (WHO/THAT/WHICH)** is absolutely crucial here:

(1) When the relative pronoun "***who/that***" is not used – i.e. if "***one of the NOUNs***" is actually the SUBJECT of the verb–then we use a singular verb.

Examples: -

There are many birds on the tree. ***One of the birds <u>is</u>*** red. ["***One of the birds***" is used as the Subject]

(2) When the relative pronoun "***who/that***" is used – i.e. if "***one of the NOUNs***" is not actually the SUBJECT of the verb–then we use a plural verb.

Examples: -

(I) That is one of the birds that ***<u>fly</u>*** over my house at night.

(II) She is one of the mothers who ***<u>are</u>*** really working hard to make both ends meet.

In sentence (I) , "***that***" acts as the subject for the verb "***fly***", and "***that***" in this sentence refers to birds (plural noun) and thus, "***fly***" (plural verb) is used.

In sentence (II) , "***who***" acts as the subject for the verb "***are***", and "***who***" in this sentence refers to mothers (plural noun) and thus, "***are***" (plural verb) is used.

(3) If the sentence follows the form, "**The only one of the + PLURAL NOUN + WHO/THAT etc.**", a SINGULAR verb is required.

Examples: -

Rina is the ***only one of the*** girls who ***<u>has</u>*** ever been to India. [Singular verb]

This is the ***only one of the*** novels which ***<u>is</u>*** interesting. [Singular verb]

<u>RULE 06</u>: If there is a combination of "**Number + Unit + Noun**" or, "**Number + Unit + Adjective**"

in a sentence, we always use the singular form of the Unit.

Examples: -

He saw a ten-inch snake. [Unit – Singular]

She gave me two five hundred-rupee notes. [Unit – Singular]

***NOTE**: *If there is a combination of "**Number + Unit**" in a sentence, a singular Unit will be used if the sentence is not self-explanatory , otherwise a plural Unit will be used if the sentence is self-explanatory.*

Examples: -

He had five ***dozen***. [Singular Unit] {Not self-explanatory, hence we have used a singular noun}

I have five ***rupees***. [Plural Unit] {Explanatory; hence we have used a plural noun}

***NOTE**: *In a sentence, if there is more than one Unit, Units are always arranged in ascending order.*

Examples: -

***Thousands*** of ***lakhs*** of students took the test. [Units arranged in ascending order]

Note:

Students take a test and teachers give a test.

***NOTE**: *Use of words like "**handful, glassful** and **fistful**" as measuring units*:

Such units are called arbitrary units

**Singular Plural**

Handful Handfuls

Glassful Glassfuls

Fistful Fistfuls

Spoonful Spoonfuls

Mouthful Mouthfuls

Cupful Cupfuls

Examples: -

He pulled out a ***handful*** of coins from his pocket. [Unit – Singular]

I use two ***handfuls*** of pasta per person. [Unit – Plural]

Drink a ***glassful*** of water with this medicine. [Unit – Singular]

She drank two whole ***glassfuls*** of orange juice. [Unit – Plural]

He has a ***fistful*** of acting awards. [Unit – Singular]

All of a sudden, we just started having ***fistfuls*** of money. [Unit – Plural]

<u>RULE 07</u>: Expressions of time, money, speed, weight, height and distance, when used or covered in one way, usually take a Singular verb. However, when these expressions are used or covered in various ways, a Plural verb is used.

Examples: -

(I) Ten miles ***needs*** to be covered completely <u>*on foot*</u>. [Singular verb]

(II) Ten miles ***need*** to be covered partly <u>*by car*</u> and rest <u>*on foot*</u>. [Plural verb]

In sentence (I) , the complete distance (i.e. ***ten miles***) has to be covered by just one means (i.e. ***on foot***) , thus a singular verb "***needs***" is used.

In sentence (II) , the complete distance (i.e. ***ten miles***) has to be covered by two means (i.e. ***by car and on foot***) , thus a plural verb "***need***" is used.

(III) Five thousand rupees ***is*** his <u>*salary*</u>. [Singular verb]

(IV) Five thousand rupees ***were*** spent on <u>*food*</u> and <u>*entertainment*</u>. [Plural verb]

(V) Six weeks ***is*** not long enough. [Singular verb]

(VI) Five kilograms is his weight.

**<u>RULE 08</u>**: Certain cases of comparisons:

Examples: -

(I) ***Gold*** is more precious than ***<u>all metals</u>***. **[Incorrect]**

(II) ***Gold*** is more precious than ***<u>any other metals</u>***. **[Correct]**

Look at the above two examples carefully; in the first sentence, "***Gold***" is itself a metal and is being compared with all metals that include even gold as a metal. Thus, at a point of time, the meaning of the sentence becomes – "*Gold is more precious than gold*", which makes the sentence wrong.

However, in the second case, gold is compared with any other metals, which means gold is precious than any metal other than gold. This makes the statement meaningful and logical.

(III) ***Diamond*** is more precious than ***<u>all metals</u>***. **[Correct]**

The above sentence is correct as Diamond being a non-metal is compared to all metals.

(IV) ***Kalidasa*** was more famous than ***<u>all English poets</u>***. **[Correct]**

(V) ***Kalidasa*** was more famous than ***<u>all poets</u>***. **[Incorrect]**

In sentence (IV) , ***Kalidasa*** is compared with all English poets, which is correct as Kalidasa was not an English poet.

However, in the sentence (V) , ***Kalidasa*** is compared with all poets, which include even Kalidasa. This makes the sentence wrong or meaningless.

**<u>RULE 09</u>**: Prepositions of Time: "***Since***" and "***For***".

The words "***for***" and "***since***" are used in sentences where the speaker wants to talk about something that started in the past and continues into the present.

The preposition "***for***" is used to talk about an amount of time or space. The amount of time could be seconds, minutes, hours, days, months or even years. The amount of time does not need to be exact.

For is used for "duration"

Since is used to denote "Point of start"

The preposition "***since***" is used to refer to a point of time. "***Since***" can refer to a point after a specific time or event in the past or, it can refer to a particular point beginning sometime in the past and continuing until the present time. The particular point in time could be anything – last Tuesday, 2008 or midnight.

Examples: -

He has been here ***for*** 6 months and still cannot speak a word of German. [for + a period of time]

**Section - I**

I've only known her ***since*** the beginning of last week. [since + a particular point in time]

He has been learning English since childhood.

***NOTE**: *"**for**" is used to specify a period of time while "**since**" is used to specify a particular point in time.*

***NOTE**: *Only the **Perfect Tense** or **Perfect Continuous Tense** is used before "**since**" and **"for"** when they denote time..*

Examples:-

It <u>has been raining</u> ***since*** 8 a.m. [Present Perfect Continuous Tense]

I <u>have had</u> this watch ***since*** 1965. [Present Perfect Tense]

***NOTE**: *"**since**" is always followed by "**Simple Past**" tense.*

Examples: -

I had been waiting for him since the time I ***<u>had completed</u>*** my graduation. [**Incorrect**]

I had been waiting for him since the time I ***<u>completed</u>*** my graduation. [**Correct**]

**<u>RULE 10</u>**: When two actions occurred in past, the action which happened earlier is denoted by using ***Past Perfect Tense*** and the action which happened later is denoted by using ***Simple Past Tense***.

Examples: -

He ***<u>had finished</u>*** the work after we had met him. [**Incorrect**]

He ***<u>finished</u>*** the work after we had met him. [**Correct**]

The patient ***<u>died</u>*** before the doctor arrived. [**Incorrect**]

The patient ***<u>had died</u>*** before the doctor arrived. [**Correct**]

I finished the book after I ***<u>had returned</u>*** from college.

**<u>RULE 11</u>**: We use a Possessive Adjective (***my, our, his, her, their, your***) before a Gerund.

Examples: -

I hope you don't mind ***me*** <u>borrowing</u> your car. [**Incorrect**]

I hope you don't mind ***my*** <u>borrowing</u> your car. [**Correct**]

In the above examples, notice that the only difference is **'*me*'** versus **'*my*'**. "My" is the possessive form of the pronoun **'*I*'** or **'*me*'**. For example, "***my book***" and "***my idea***" are possessives. The book and the idea belong to me.

"Me" is the objective case of the pronoun.

Thus, the second example is correct—the sentence that uses the possessive "***my***" because we use a possessive before a Gerund and "***borrowing***" is a gerund. Here "***borrowing***" plays the role of a noun.

"Gerund" ——————> When V1+ING is used as a noun

I know ***his*** <u>reading</u> every night has helped him pass the test. [Possessive and Gerund – focus is on ***reading***]

I hope you don't mind ***my*** <u>staying</u> with you next week. [Possessive and Gerund – focus is on ***staying***]

My father doesn't like my going outside with Ram.

**RULE12**: Law of Inversion:

Inversion means putting the verb before the subject. It is a literary technique in which the normal order of words is reversed, generally for emphasis or special effect.

Two types of Inversion:

(1) Partial Inversion

(2) Complete Inversion

Structure of Sentence (Normal Sentence) : "***Subject + helping verb + Main verb + ...***"

Examples: -

My students are working very hard. [Normal sentence]

I have never seen such a beautiful place. [Normal sentence]

In case of inversion, we start a sentence with the helping verb instead of the Subject.

Structure of Sentence (Inversion) : "***Helping verb + Subject + Main Verb + ...***"

Examples: -

Never have I seen such a beautiful place. [Inversion]

In the given example, inversion is used to emphasise the fact that in my whole lifetime I have not seen such a beautiful place.

We generally use Inversion when we begin the sentence with an Adverb.

Examples: -

***Rarely*** *did* he go there. [**Adverb + helping verb + subject + main verb + ...**]

***Seldom*** *have* I seen such a beautiful view. [**Adverb + helping verb + subject + main verb + ...**]

Consider the above two examples, whenever we begin a sentence with an Adverb, Law of Inversion is followed, according to which Adverb will always be followed by a helping verb.

And whenever the Adverb is followed by a helping verb, we call that a ***Partial Inversion***.

In the case of ***Complete Inversion***, a main verb is used after the Adverb.

Examples: -

***Here*** *comes* the King! [**Adverb + main verb + ...**]

***There*** *goes* all our money! [**Adverb + main verb + ...**]

***NOTE**: The case of "***No sooner...than...***"

***No sooner*** *had* I entered the class ***when*** it began to rain. [**Incorrect**]

***No sooner*** *had* I entered the class ***than*** it began to rain. [**Correct**]

In the above two examples, "***No sooner***" is used as an Adverb which is followed by a helping verb "***had***". But it is to be noted that "***No sooner***" always comes with "***than***" and not with "***when***".

***NOTE**: Some more examples: -

He never goes to the temple. Neither ***she does***. [**Incorrect**]

He never goes to the temple. Neither ***does she***. [**Correct**]

In the above examples, the first part of the sentence is complete. In the second part, the sentence is starting with an adverb "***Neither***" which will follow the law of inversion. Thus, the helping verb "***does***" will come before the subject "***she***".

**RULE13**: Whenever we use normal places like ***school, college, church, bed, table, hospital, market,***

***prison, jail, court, temple, mosque, university etc***. for primary purpose (for which they are made) , the article "***The***" is not used before them. But when these places are used for a secondary purpose, the article "***The***" is used before them.

Examples: -

Children go to school every day. [Primary purpose]

He goes to the temple. [Secondary purpose]

His home is just beside ***the*** temple. [Secondary purpose]

We go to church on Fridays. [Correct]

We go to the church on Fridays. [Incorrect]

The politician was sent to jail. [Correct]

The politician was sent to the jail. [Incorrect]

***NOTE**: *It is important to understand the difference between primary purpose and secondary purpose. The primary purpose refers to work for which the places are made while the secondary purpose refers to any work other than for which are they are made.*

Examples: -

He goes to the temple. [It means he goes there to worship]

He goes to ***the*** temple. [It means he goes there to do any work other than worship]

**RULE14**: Whenever adverbs like "***No sooner***", "***Hardly***", "***Scarcely***", etc. are used in the beginning of a sentence, they are always followed by a helping verb.

Examples:-

***Hardly had*** I begun to speak *when* I was interrupted.

***Scarcely had*** we started our meal *when* the phone rang.

***No sooner had*** I arrived *than* they all started to argue.

***NOTE**: *Note that adverbs "**hardly, scarcely** and **barely**" are always followed by "**when**", while "**No sooner**" is followed by "**than**".*

**RULE15**: Use of Reflexive Pronoun as the Object of a sentence.

The ***object*** of a sentence is the person or thing that receives the action of the verb. It answers the question "***whom***" or "***what***"?

There are certain words which are always followed by an object: ***enjoy, avail, absent, pride, adjust, reconcile, acquit, amuse, resign, avenge, exert, apply, adapt***, etc.

When these words are not followed by an object in the sentence, we use the reflexive pronouns as their objects.

Examples: -

(I) He *enjoyed* **himself** at the party. [Object]

(II) She *availed* **herself** of the opportunity and thus got a promotion. [Object]

(III) They *enjoyed the* **picture** last evening. [Object]

(IV) The former IPS officer ***acquitted himself*** effectively.

(V) He ***absented himself*** from the class

In the first sentence, the reflexive pronoun "***himself***" does the function of an object. It can be understood by finding the answer of, "*He enjoyed whom*?" – "***himself***".

Similarly, in the second sentence, the word "***availed***" is followed by the object "***herself***".

However, in the third example, the word "***enjoyed***" is followed by the object "***picture***". Thus, we do not need to put a reflexive pronoun as its object.

***NOTE**: *There are certain words that are not followed by reflexive pronouns as their object:* "***keep, stop, turn, qualify, bathe, move, rest, hide,*** *etc.*"

Examples: -

He *hid* **<u>himself</u>** in the room. [**Incorrect**]

He *hid* in the room. [**Correct**]

She has *qualified* **<u>herself</u>** for the post. [**Incorrect**]

She has *qualified* for the post. [**Correct**]

**<u>RULE 16</u>**: There are certain words which are never followed by a Reflexive pronoun: ***hide, keep, stop, turn, shave, bathe,*** etc.

Examples: -

He *hid* ***<u>himself</u>*** in the cave and thus saved his life. [**Incorrect**]

He *hid* in the cave and thus saved his life. [**Correct**]

In the given examples, we cannot use the word "***himself***" as the word "***hid***" is not followed by a reflexive pronoun.

**<u>RULE 17</u>**: Whenever two subjects are connected by "***as well as, together with, along with, and not, in addition to, like, unlike, with, rather than, except, no less than, nothing but, more than one***", the verb agrees with the first Subject.

Examples: -

*John*, **<u>as well as</u>** Mary, ***wants*** to drop the course. [Singular verb]

*Ram,* **<u>as well as</u>** his friends, ***keeps*** asking me many questions. [Singular verb]

The publisher, **<u>as well as</u>** the writers, has come. [Singular verb]

The club members, **<u>along with</u>** his owner, was arrested. [Incorrect]

The club members, **<u>along with</u>** his owner, were arrested. [Correct]

He, **<u>and not</u>** his friends, are found guilty. [Incorrect]

He, **<u>and not</u>** his friends, is found guilty [correct]

In the given examples, the Subject prior to "***as well as***" is Singular, so a singular verb "***wants***" is used. Similarly, in the second case, "***Ram***" is a singular Subject that requires a singular verb "***keeps***".

***NOTE**: *We follow the same rule (i.e. the verb agrees with the first Subject) when two subjects are connected by* "***governed by***", "***accompanied by***", "***but***", "***besides***", "***led by***", "***run by***", *etc.*

Examples: -

*California*, **<u>along with</u>** Florida, ***is*** among the most popular US tourist destinations.

**Section - I**

The *teachers*, **along with** the Principal, ***are*** entering the class. [Subject is plural in this case]

**RULE18**: Difference between Noun and Verb for similar sounding words, like

(a) Advice – **Noun**

(b) Advise – **Verb**

(a) Practice – **Noun**

(b) Practise – **Verb**

**(a) Belief— Noun**

**(b) Believe— Verb**

Examples: -

I ***advise*** you to ***practise*** a lot since ***practice*** makes a man perfect.

I'm quite good at tennis but I need to ***practise*** my serve.

**Practice** makes a man perfect

He gave me a piece of **advice**

It is my **belief t**hat my students are very talented.

I **believe** my students.

***NOTE**: *To locate the nouns in the sentence, we generally try to find the answer of **'what'**, **'who'**, or **'whom'**.*

**RULE 19**: There are three cases of pronouns

| The cases of Personal Pronoun | Subjective Pronouns | Objective Pronouns | Possessive Adjectives | Possessive pronouns |
|---|---|---|---|---|
| First person | I<br>we | Me<br>Us | My<br>our | Mine<br>ours |
| Second person | You | You | your | yours |
| Third person | She<br>He<br>It<br>They | Her<br>Him<br>It<br>Them | Her<br>His<br>Its<br>their | Hers<br>His<br>—<br>theirs |

Comparisons are usually done between the same things. So whenever we compare, we compare **Subjective case to Subjective case and**

**Objective case to objective case.**

Examples: -

1. ***My parents*** scold me more than ***he***. **[Correct]**
2. My parents scold ***me*** more than ***him***. **[Correct]**
3. She is taller than ***me*** [INCORRECT]
4. She is taller than ***I*** [Correct]

Consider the above examples; in the first case, the subjective case "***my parents***" is compared with the subjective case "***he***". If we elaborate the meaning of the sentence, it would be – "*My parents scold me more than he does.*"

In the second case, the objective case "***me***" is compared with the objective case "***him***". If we elaborate the meaning of the sentence, it would be – "*My parents scold me more than they scold him.*"

Both sentences 1 and 2 are correct but they have different meanings.

She likes ***chocolates*** more than ***me***. **[Incorrect]**

***She*** likes chocolates more than ***I***. **[Correct]**

In the first sentence, we cannot compare "***chocolates***" with the objective case "***me***".

Chocolates cannot be compared with a person.

So "me" is wrong

However, the second sentence compares a subjective case with another subjective case.

She is compared to I

Hence it is correct.

***He*** is as tall as ***I***. **[Correct]**

***He*** speaks more frequently than she [Correct]

In the above examples, there is no object, so we cannot use an objective case.

**RULE 20**: ***Who vs. Whom***?

"***Who***" is used as a subjective pronoun, and

"***Whom***" is used as an objective pronoun.

That simply means that "***who***" is always used as a subject to a verb, and that "***whom***" is always working as an object in a sentence. As simple and important as that distinction is, many people have difficulty deciding on the proper usage of "***who***" and "***whom***" in sentences.

To clear this doubt, simply substitute the personal pronoun "***he/him***" or "***she/her***" for "***who/whom.***" If he or she would be the correct form, the proper choice is "***who***". If "***him***" or "***her***" would be correct, use "***whom.***"

Examples: -

Mrs. Dixit consulted an astrologer ***whom*** she met in Sonpur. [She met ***him*** in Sonpur.]

Jack is the man ***whom*** I went fishing with last spring. [I went fishing with ***him***.]

Jyoti is the girl ***who*** got the job. [***She*** got the job.]

***Whom*** can we turn to in a time of crisis? [Can we turn to ***her***?]

The delegates differed as to ***who*** they thought might win. [Not "***whom***". Here the entire clause is the object of the preposition. Substitution is particularly helpful in cases such as this. They thought ***he*** might win.]

Some more examples: -

She is one of the professors ***who*** I think is a mathematician.

He is the man ***whom*** everyone admires.

She met the people ***who*** they say are helping all aspirants.

They hired the man ***whom*** we interviewed last week.

**RULE 21**: Certain words like "***separation, excuse, mention, favour, pardon, leave, report, sight***, etc. do not take Possessive case before them.

Examples: -

***Your separation*** pains me a lot and I become sad. **[Incorrect]**

***Separation from you*** pains me a lot and I become sad. **[Correct]**

Consider the above two examples; in the first case, we cannot use "***your***" with "***separation***" as "***your***" is a Possessive Adjective.

However, the first sentence can be rewritten to make it grammatically feasible without altering its meaning, as can be seen in the second sentence.

I want your ***favour***, will you please help me? **[Incorrect]**

I want a ***favour from you***, will you please help me? **[Correct]**

The first sentence is grammatically incorrect as we cannot use "***your favour***". However, it can be written as "***favour from you***", as in the second sentence.

***His mention*** in the story received great applause from the audience. **[Incorrect]**

***The Mention of him*** in the story received great applause from the audience. **[Correct]**

The first sentence is grammatically incorrect as we cannot use "***His mention***" as "***his***" is also a Possessive Adjective.

However, the first sentence can be rewritten to make it grammatically correct without altering its meaning, as can be seen in the second sentence.

At ***his sight*** the robbers fled. **[Incorrect]**

***At the sight of him***, the robbers fled. **[Correct]**

***NOTE**: *Possessive Case:* ***your, his, her, my, their, our, its,*** *etc.*

**RULE22**: We use "***each other***" and "***one another***" to show that each person in a group of two or more people does something to the others. There is very little difference between ***each other*** and ***one another***. "***Each other***" is generally used for two people while "***one another***" is used for more than two people.

Examples: -

All citizens should love ***each other***. **[Incorrect]**

All citizens should love ***one other***. **[Correct]**

In the first sentence, "***all citizens***" refer to more than two people. So, "***each other***" should be replaced by "***one another***", as in the case of second sentence.

Peter and Mary helped ***each other***. [*Peter helped Mary and Mary helped Peter*]

We sent ***one other*** Christmas cards. [*We sent them a Christmas card and they sent us a Christmas* *card]*

***NOTE**: *Difference between "**other**" and "**another**":*

***Other** is an adjective meaning **'different'** or **'the second of two items'**. Other can be used with singular or plural nouns. Other can also be a pronoun to refer to things or people. The plural form is others.*

*However, When we use **'an'** before **'other'**, we write it as one word: another. It means **'additional'** or **'one more'**. **Another** can be used before a plural noun when that noun is preceded by a number, or words/phrases such as **a couple of, few** etc.*

Examples: -

Some children learn quickly but ***other*** children need more time.

Have you got any ***other*** questions?

Only half of the guests have arrived. Where are the ***others***? [Plural]

This cake is delicious. Could I have ***another*** slice please?

The investigation will take ***another*** two weeks/couple of weeks. [Plural]

This place isn't great. Is there ***another*** place we could go to? [***Another*** can also mean '***an alternative***' or '***different'***]

**RULE 23**: The use of "***Seldom or never***":

The word "***Seldom***" is an Adverb and when a sentence begins with "***seldom***", the law of inversion will be followed.

Examples: -

(I) ***Seldom or never*** he comes to my house. [**Incorrect**]

(II) ***Seldom or ever*** he comes to my house. [**Incorrect**]

(III) ***Seldom, if ever,*** does he come to my house. [**Correct**]

(IV) ***Seldom, or never,*** does he come to my house. [**Correct**]

***NOTE**: *We can either use "**Seldom or never**" or "**Seldom, if ever**", but we cannot use "**Seldom or ever**".*

***NOTE**: The use of the phrase "***Little or nothing***":

The phrase "***Little or nothing***" means "***Hardly anything***". In this case also, we can *either use "**Little or nothing**" or "**Little, if anything**", but we cannot use "**Little or anything**".*

Examples: -

I can find ***little or nothing*** on this table. [**Correct**]

I can find ***little, if anything*** on this table [**Correct**]

I can find ***little if nothing*** on this table. [**Incorrect**]

I can find ***little or anything*** on this table. [**Incorrect**]

**RULE24**: Whenever we use "***very***" with Superlative degree, article "***the***" is always used before "***very***" i.e. "***the very superlative***".

"***Very***" modifies present participles used as an adjective, adverbs and adjectives in the positive degree. E.g. It is a very interesting novel.

However, when we use "***much***" with Superlative degree, article "***the***" is used before the superlative i.e. "***much the superlative***".

"***Much***" is used with a comparative degree and past participle.

E.g. He is much interested.

He is much smarter.

Examples: -

He is ***the much best*** student of my class. [**Incorrect**]

He is ***very the best*** student of my class. [**Incorrect**]

He is ***the very best*** student of my class. [**Correct**] {It means really}

He is ***much the best*** student of my class. [**Correct**] {It means decidedly}

He is ***much*** smarter than all other students. [**Correct**]

I was ***very*** exhausted after the match. [**Correct**]

**RULE 25**: The use of "***Enough***":

"***Enough***" plays the role of both Adverb and Adjective. When it is used as an Adverb, it qualifies an adjective, verb, or other adverb or a word group. When it is used as an Adjective, it qualifies a noun or a pronoun.

When "***enough***" plays the role of an ***Adjective***, "***enough***" is placed before the noun or pronoun i.e. "***enough noun***".

When "***enough***" plays the role of an ***Adverb***, "***enough***" is placed after the adjective i.e. "***adjective enough***".

Examples: -

He has ***enough*** *sugar*. [Used as an Adjective]

She is *smart* ***enough***. [Used as an Adverb]

On neither of those trips was there ***enough*** *sun* to get any decent photographs. [Used as an Adjective]

Test reports indicate that it develops ***enough*** *power* for the job and is flexible. [Used as an Adjective]

You are not *big* ***enough*** for basketball. [Used as an Adverb]

A landing between the ground and first floors is *ample* ***enough*** to be used as a study. [Used as an Adverb]

**RULE 26**: The use of Adverb "***as***":

"***as***" can be used as an adverb with these given words – "***treat, define, regard, describe***, respect, depict, portray, ***view***, ***know***, etc."

However, "***as***" cannot be used as an adverb with these two words – "***elect, name, think, consider, call, make, choose***, ***appoint, etc.***"

Examples: -

Biology is ***defined as*** the science of living beings.

He is ***regarded as*** a God in India.

She ***described*** Gary ***as*** shy.

His latest film is ***described as*** a 'romantic comedy'.

She is ***treated as*** a child.

She was ***elected*** Chair of the Board of Governors.

He has just been ***appointed*** director of the publishing division.

He ***thinks*** her a fool.

The teacher ***called*** him stupid.

**RULE 27**: The use of Conjunction "***although***":

"***Although***", meaning "***in spite of something***", is a subordinating conjunction. This means that the clause which it introduces is a subordinate clause, which needs a main clause to make it complete. Sometimes "***although***" as a subordinate clause may take "***yet***" in the main clause. However, "***although***" as a subordinate clause never takes "***but***" in the main clause.

Yet is optional. It can or cannot be used.

Examples: -

***Although*** she is rich, she thinks twice before spending a penny. [**Correct**]

***Although*** she is rich, ***yet*** she thinks twice before spending a penny. [**Correct**]

***Although*** she is rich, ***but*** she thinks twice before spending a penny. [**Incorrect**]

**RULE 28**: There are certain verbs that do not exist in the "***-ing***" form.

These are:

| POSSESSION | PERCEPTION | FEELING |
|---|---|---|
| Own | See | Love |
| Belong | Smell | Know |
| Have | Taste | Think |
| Include | Hear | Hate |
| Possess | Feel | Want |
| Owe | Appear | Need |
| Contain | Seem | Desire |
| Compromise | Resemble | Wish |
| Consist | Notice | Like |

Examples: -

I **am owning** a car. [**Incorrect**]

I ***own*** a car. [**Correct**]

I **am loving** it. [**Incorrect**]

I ***love*** it. [**Correct**]

This sauce **is tasting** strange. [**Incorrect**]

This sauce ***tastes*** strange. [**Correct**]

This perfume **is smelling** like roses. [**Incorrect**]

**Section - I**

This perfume ***smells*** like roses. **[Correct]**

She has always **been hating** jazz. **[Incorrect]**

She has always ***hated*** jazz. **[Correct]**

All the luggage is belonging to me. [Inc**orrect**]

All the luggage belongs to me. **[Correct]**

***NOTE**: *Sometimes the word "**loving**" is used as an adjective, which should not be confused with a verb.*

Examples: -

He is a very ***loving*** person. [Used as an Adjective]

He described his work in ***loving*** detail. [Used as an Adjective]

***NOTE**: *When "**have**" is used in the sense of possession or belongingness or ownership, we cannot use "**having**". However, apart from this, we can use "**having**" as a perfect participle or in other cases.*

Examples: -

(I) I am ***having*** a book. **[Incorrect]**

(II) I ***have*** a book. **[Correct]**

(III) I am ***having*** lunch now. **[Correct]**

(IV) ***Having*** done the work, he went to play. **[Correct]**

In sentence (I) , "***have***" denotes possession, so we cannot use "***having***" and it should be replaced by "***have***" as rightly done in sentence (II) .

In sentences (III) and (IV) , "***have***" is not used in the sense of possession or belongingness or ownership, thus "***having***" is correctly used in these two sentences.

**RULE 29**: There are certain words which are always used in Perfect Tense: "***ever, never, yet, already, now, just now, until, now, always, occasionally, often, lately, recently, so far, up to now, up to the present***"

Examples: -

The concert *had* ***already*** *begun* by the time we arrived. **[Correct]**

I went to Paris last summer. *Have* you ***ever*** *been* there? **[Correct]**

I *have* not *spoken* to her ***yet***. **[Correct]**

He *has gone* ***just now***. **[Correct]**

He **went** there ***already***. **[Incorrect]**

He *had gone* there ***already***. **[Correct]**

Aman completed his work ***up to now*** . [Incorrect]

Aman ***has not*** completed his work ***up to now*** . [Correct]

The train already left. [Incorrect]

The train ***has*** already left. [Correct]

**RULE 30**: Subject-Verb Agreement with ***Collective Nouns***:

When a collective noun denotes that the whole group is working together on the same task, we use a singular verb.

Examples: -

The *audience* ***is*** watching the movie. [*every audience is watching together*]

The *army* ***is*** marching towards the Himalayas. [*whole army (personnel) is moving together*]

The *jury* ***is*** taking a decision. [*all the members of the jury are taking decision together*]

When a collective noun denotes that the whole group is working on different tasks, we use a plural verb.

Examples: -

The audience ***are*** taking the seats.

The army ***are*** changing their dresses.

The jury ***are*** divided in their opinion.

***NOTE**: *Words like "**police, vermin, cattle, clergy, gentry, poultry, folk, peasantry, people, infantry, cavalry, etc.**" are "plural nouns" and not "collective nouns". Plural noun always takes a plural verb.* So, these words always take plural verbs.

Examples: -

The police ***are*** investigating the case.

Cattle ***are*** wandering in the farm.

People ***want to attain all worldly pleasures.***

***NOTE**: Sometimes the word "***people***" is used in the meaning of "***a country***" instead of "***persons***", in that case we use a singular verb. Peoples means countries or people belonging to different nationalities. "Peoples" in that case is correct.

**RULE 31**: There are certain words which are always followed by the preposition "***to***". These are:

| Prefer | Superior | Inferior |
|---|---|---|
| Injurious | Junior | Ancillary |
| Addicted | Senior | Exterior |
| Known | Ulterior | Posterior |

***NOTE**: *Any word suffixed with "**-ior**" will always be followed by the preposition "**to**".*

Examples: -

For babies, breastfeeding is *superior* ***to*** bottle-feeding.

Too much alcohol is *injurious* ***to*** your health.

Would you *prefer* ***to*** pay by cash, cheque, or credit card?

They promoted a man who was *junior* ***to*** me and made him my boss.

Paragraph 19 was merely *ancillary* ***to*** paragraph 16.

I prefer tea to coffee.

***NOTE**: *The words "**marry**" and "**known**" are always followed by the preposition "**to**" in the*

**Section - I**

*Passive voice.*

Examples: -

Rama is *married* ***to*** Sita.

I am *known* ***to*** him.

I am known by him. ————> Incorrect

**RULE 32**: The use of phrase "***as... as***" and "***so... as***":

These blanks are filled up with the adjectives of positive degree.

Examples: -

If we pass on the information, he's ***as*** *good* ***as*** dead.

I'm not ***so*** *desperate* ***as*** to agree to that.

***NOTE**: *"**as... as**" can be used to denote both positive and negative sentences while "**so... as**" can only be used only to denote negative sentences.*

Examples: -

He is ***as good as*** Ram. [**Correct**]

He is not ***as good as*** Ram. [**Correct**]

He is ***not so good as*** Ram. [**Correct**]

He is *so good as* Ram. [**Incorrect**]

**RULE 33**: In a sentence depicting comparison, whenever the word "***times***" comes up, it is never followed by a comparative degree.

Examples: -

(I) This book is three ***times larger*** than that book. [**Incorrect**]

(II) This book is three ***times heavier*** than that book. [**Incorrect**]

(III) It is ***twice cheaper*** than that. [**Correct**] {Times is not written , hence it is correct}

(IV) This book is three ***times as large as*** that book. [**Correct**]

(V) It is ***twice costlier*** than that. [**Correct**]

(VI) It is two times as costly as that. [Correct]

In sentence (I) , the word "***times***" and the comparative degree "***larger***" cannot be used together. The sentence should be rewritten either as sentence (IV) to make it grammatically correct.

In sentences (III) and (V) , there is no use of the word "***times***" and thus we can use the comparative degree to bring up the comparisons.

**RULE 34**: Some common errors of ***NARRATION***:

Indirect Speech is always a statement.

**Structure of a statement**

Subject + Helping Verb + Main Verb +............

**Structure of a question**

**word + Helping verb + Subject + Main Verb +...............**

**Hence a helping verb comes after a subject in the case of a statement and before a subject in the**

**case of a question.**

Examples: -

He asked me where are you going. [**Incorrect**]

He asked me ***where I was going***. [**Correct**]

He asked me what was my name. [**Incorrect**]

He asked me ***what my name was***. [**Correct**]

She says that ***she is a little bit nervous***. [Direct speech was an **Assertive sentence**]

The teacher ordered me ***to shut the door***. [Direct speech was an **Imperative sentence**]

He exclaimed with great joy that ***he had won the match***. [Direct speech was an **Exclamatory sentence**]

We asked him ***if he was ill***. [Direct speech was an **Interrogative sentence**]

He prayed that ***I might live long***. [Direct speech was an **Optative sentence**]

She wished ***she had been rich***. [Direct speech was an **Optative sentence**]

But all the indirect speeches are always statements.

**RULE 35**: If two subjects are connected by the words "***or***," "***nor***," "***neither/nor***," "***either/or***," ***or*** "***not only/but also***", we use the verb according to the nearest subject.

**Examples: -**

Either the *bears* or the *lion* ***has*** escaped from the zoo. [Nearest subject "***lion***" is singular]

Neither the *lion* nor the *bears* ***have*** escaped from the zoo. [Nearest subject "***bears***" is plural]

Not only the *teachers* but also the *Principal* ***is*** happy. [Nearest subject "***Principal***" is singular]

Not only *dogs* but also *cats* ***are*** available at the animal shelter. [Nearest subject "cats" is plural]

**RULE 36**: Comparison between two qualities of an object:

Whenever two qualities of the same object are compared, we always use the word "***more***". We don't use **comparative** degree in that case.

Examples:-

This pen is *redder* than *white*. [**Incorrect**]

This book is *heavier* than *larger*. [**Incorrect**]

This shirt is ***more*** white than red. [**Correct**]

This umbrella is ***more*** beautiful than strong. [**Correct**]

**RULE37**: Whenever "***more than one***" or "***many a***" is used to quantify a noun, it is always followed by a singular noun and a singular verb.

And whenever "**Many, A good many, A *great many***" are used to quantify a noun, they are always followed by a plural noun and a plural verb.

***Example:-***

***A great many*** students ***are*** waiting for the class..

***Many*** tigers ***are*** missing from the national park.

**Structure**:

More than one + singular noun + singular verb

**Section - I**

Many a + singular noun + singular verb

A great many + plural noun + plural verb

A good many + plural noun + plural verb

Examples:-

***More than one*** student ***is*** absent today. [Singular verb]

***Many a*** student ***is*** absent today. [Singular verb]

***NOTE**: *Also consider the following examples*:

***One*** student ***is*** absent today. [Singular verb]

***A great many*** students ***are*** absent today. [Plural verb]

***Many*** students ***are*** absent today. [Plural verb]

**RULE38**: Whenever we get the word "***doubt***" or "***doubtful***" in a sentence, we use the connector either "***if***" or "***whether***". However, in case we get the words "***no doubt***" and "***not doubtful***", we use the connector "***that***".

Examples:-

I have ***no doubt whether*** it will rain or not. **[Incorrect]**

I have ***no doubt that*** it will rain or not. **[Correct]**

There is a ***doubt that*** he goes there or not. **[Incorrect]**

There is a ***doubt whether*** he goes there or not. **[Correct]**

He has ***no doubt if*** Shyam is his best friend. **[Incorrect]**

He has ***no doubt that*** Shyam is his best friend. **[Correct]**

**RULE39**: **NARRATION**, Sequence of Tenses:

The tense of the verb does not change even if the Reporting verb is in the past tense for the following cases:

(1) **Universal Truth**:

Examples:-

(I) He told me that ***honey was sweet***. **[Incorrect]**

(II) He told me that ***honey is sweet***. **[Correct]**

(III) He told me that ***the honey is sweet***. **[Incorrect]**

(IV) He told me that ***the honey was sweet***. **[Correct]**

In sentence (I) , the sentence is incorrect because "***honey is sweet***" is a universal truth and should be written in Simple Present Tense in indirect speech as well. This makes the statement (II) correct.

In sentence (III) , the sentence is incorrect because "***the honey is sweet***" is not a universal truth as "***the honey***" denotes a particular type of honey. Thus, the indirect statement should follow the tense form of main clause as correctly done in statement (IV) .

***NOTE**: *Sequence of Tenses suggests that if the principal clause of the sentence is in Past Tense, subordinate clause will also be in the Past Tense.*

(2) **Historical Facts**:

Examples:-

The teacher said, "Kalidas is the Shakespeare of India." **[Direct Speech]**

The teacher said that ***Kalidas is the Shakespeare of India***. **[Indirect Speech]**

(3) **Proverbs**:

Examples:-

Rohit said, "**Where there is a will there is a way**." **[Direct Speech]**

Rohit said that ***where there is a will there is a way***. **[Indirect Speech]**

(4) **Habitual Facts**:

Examples:-

He said, "**I snooze my alarm every day**." **[Direct Speech]**

He said that ***he snoozes his alarm every day***. **[Indirect Speech]**

**RULE40**: Use of ***little***, ***the little*** and ***a little***:

We use these quantifiers with uncountable nouns according to their following meanings:

(1) **Little**: Hardly any

(2) **A little**: Some but not much

(3) **The little**: All that is available

Examples:-

I cannot make tea since there is ***little*** milk. [Hardly any milk]

***A little*** knowledge is dangerous. [ Some but not much]

He utilised ***the little*** water that was available. [ All that was available]

***NOTE**: *Use of* ***few***, ***a few*** *and* ***the few***:

We use these quantifiers with countable nouns according to their following meanings:

(1) **Few**: Hardly any

(2) **A few**: Some but not many (*It has a positive meaning*)

(3) **The few**: All that are available

Examples:-

***Few*** members attended the meeting. [Hardly any member attended the meeting.]

There were ***a few*** members present. [Some members were present.]

He lost ***the few*** friends he had. [All those he had]

***NOTE**: Use of ***some*** and ***any***:

The general rule is that "***any***" is used for questions and negative sentences while "***some***" is used for positive sentences.

Both may be used with countable and uncountable nouns.

Examples:-

Do we need ***any*** rice?

No, we don't need ***any*** rice.

We have ***some*** rice in the cupboard.

Would you like ***some*** water?

**Section - I**

May I have ***some*** more chocolate?

But in some cases "Some" is used with interrogative sentences

When we know that the answer will be yes, we can use "some" .

Eg. Do you have some water?

It is correct because we know already that the answer will be yes.

**RULE41**: Objective Case of the pronoun comes after the Preposition.

| SUBJECTIVE CASE | OBJECTIVE CASE |
|---|---|
| I | me |
| We | us |
| You | you |
| They | them |
| He | him |
| She | her |
| It | it |

Examples:-

None **but *he*** is going to the party. [**Incorrect**]

None **but *him*** is going to the party. [**Correct**]

All **except *he*** liked the performance. [**Incorrect**]

All **except *him*** liked the performance. [**Correct**]

In the first sentence, "***but***" plays the role of preposition, so it must be followed by a pronoun of objective case. Similarly, "***except***" in the third sentence is a preposition which should be followed by the pronoun of objective case.

***NOTE**: *"**But**" plays the role of both "**Conjunction**" and "**Preposition**".*

A *Verb is also followed by the pronoun of Objective case.*

Examples:-

**Let *him*** do that work. ["***Let***" acts as a verb here]

They agreed to **let *us*** live there rent-free. ["***Let***" acts as a verb here]

Some more examples:-

Ram ***as well as he*** is going to the party. [**Correct**]

There is a good friendship ***between you*** and ***him***. [**Correct**]

It is to be noted that in the first sentence, "***as well as***" is not used as a preposition, so the subjective case "***he***" is correctly used.

In the second sentence, "***between***" is a preposition so objective case is used after it.

**RULE42**: (1) In case of pronouns as the Subject, when all the three persons are used as the Subject of the sentence and are connected by '***and***', the sequence of ***231*** of the Pronouns is followed if they give a Positive Sense to the sentence and a plural verb is used.

We have used the 2nd person, then the 3rd person, and finally the 1st person.

| 1 | Speaker First Person | I |
|---|---|---|
| 2 | Listener Second Person | You |
| 3 | Non-Active Third Person | He |

Examples:-

***You, he*** and ***I*** are good friends. [the sequence of ***231*** of the pronouns]

(2) In case of pronouns as the Subject, when only two persons are used as the Subject of the sentence and are connected by '***and'***, the sequence of **(2,3)** ; **(2,1)** ; **(3,1)** of the Pronouns is followed if they give a Positive Sense to the sentence and a plural verb is used.

Examples:-

***You*** and ***she*** are good friends. [the sequence of **(2,3)** of the pronouns]

**You** and ***I*** are playing chess. [the sequence of **(2,1)** of the pronouns]

***He*** and ***I*** were watching T.V. [the sequence of **(3,1)** of the pronouns]

(3) In case of pronouns as the Subject, when all the three persons are used as the Subject of the sentence and are connected by '***and'***, the sequence of ***123*** of the Pronouns is followed if they give a **Negative** Sense to the sentence and a plural verb is used.They generally talk about some mistake,blame or guilt.

Examples:-

***I, you*** and ***he*** are guilty. [the sequence of ***123*** of the pronouns]

***I, you*** and ***he*** are robbers. [the sequence of ***123*** of the pronouns]

(4) In case of pronouns as the Subject, when only two persons are used as the Subject of the sentence and are connected by '***and'***, the sequence of **(1,2)** ; **(2,3)** ; **(1,3)** of the Pronouns is followed if they give a Negative Sense to the sentence and a plural verb is used.

Examples:-

***I*** and ***you*** have committed a crime. [the sequence of **(1,2)** of the pronouns]

***You*** and ***he*** are sinners. [the sequence of **(2,3)** of the pronouns]

***I*** and ***he*** were guilty. [the sequence of **(1,3)** of the pronouns]

If all the pronouns are plural , we use the order 123 in all cases.

We, you and they are going to watch a movie.

**RULE43**: Some Superfluousness Errors:

Superfluous means that more than required is given in the sentence. It means extra.

Consider these examples:-

(I) India broke all **previous records** in today's match. [**Incorrect**]

The above sentence is Superfluous as "***records***" always specifies "***previous***". Using them together makes the statement superfluous. It should be rewritten as –

India broke all ***records*** in today's match. [**Correct**]

(II) I want **wet water**. [**Incorrect**]

**Section - I**

Water is already wet and we all know it. Hence this sentence contains extra words and superfluous error is there.

I want ***water***. **[Correct]**

In the above example, "***water***" is always "***wet***", so we cannot use these two words together as it will give us the superfluous meaning.

(III) **Suppose if** you won the Oscar, what would you do? **[Incorrect]**

***Suppose*** you won the Oscar, what would you do? **[Correct]**

In the above example, the usage of ***'if'*** with ***'suppose'*** is superfluous. Hence, either ***'suppose'*** or ***'if'*** should be used.

***NOTE**: *Use of "**supposing if**": "**If**" is not needed with "**supposing**". It's a wrong usage. Use only "**supposing**".*

(IV) The army **retreated back** from the conflict zone in Kashmir. **[Incorrect]**

The army ***retreated*** from the conflict zone in Kashmir. **[Correct]**

Again in the above example, ***'back'*** won't be used here. ***'Retreat'*** itself means – to withdraw, retire etc. We use only "***retreat"***.

(V) The sage was **reborn again** in Vijayanagar. **[Incorrect]**

The sage was ***reborn*** in Vijayanagar. **[Correct]**

***NOTE**: *Never use **'again'** after verbs like – **Rebirth/Reborn/rebuild/regain/reiterate/recast** etc.*

(VI) Manu is **equally as good as** Sharma. **[Incorrect]**

Manu and Sharma are ***equally good***. **[Correct]**

Manu is ***as good as*** Sharma. **[Correct]**

In the above example, the usage of ***'as'*** should strictly be discarded. Use only ***'equally'*** or ***'as good as'*** separately.

(VII) The manager and the chairman decided on a **mutual agreement** on profit. **[Incorrect]**

The manager and the chairman decided on an ***agreement*** on profit. **[Correct]**

In this case the usage of ***'mutual'*** is wrong. Hence, use only ***'agreement'***.

"Agreement" is always mutual.

***NOTE**: ***'Mutual friend'*** is wrong to say. Instead we can say ***'common friend'***. Likewise, we should say – ***'common interest'*** instead of ***'mutual interest'***.

(VIII) She **forbade** me **not** to leave her alone. **[Incorrect]**

She ***forbade*** me to leave her alone. **[Correct]**

In the above example, '***Not'*** is never used after ***until/unless/forbid/prohibit/prevent/dissuade/deny/refuse/lest***.

(IX) He's a **coward man/person**. **[Incorrect]**

He is a ***coward***. **[Correct]**

The usage of ***'coward man'*** is wrong because '***coward'*** itself means a person who lacks courage. Hence, the use of ***'man'*** is illogical.

(X) She left the house **with bag and baggage**. **[Incorrect]**

She left the house, ***bag and baggage***. [**Correct**]

***'Bag and baggage'*** is an idiom which means ***'with all belongings'***. Hence, using ***'with'*** with the idiom is wrong.

(XI) **Passing marks** are thirty-three. [**Incorrect**]

***Pass marks*** are thirty-three. [**Correct**]

The usage of ***'passing marks'/'linking language'/'linking network'/'dressing sense'*** is wrong. Instead, we should use ***'pass marks'/'link language'/'link network'/'dress sense'***.

(XII) I **suddenly came across** him on the train. [**Incorrect**]

I ***came across*** him on the train. [**Correct**]

In the above example, omit ***'suddenly'*** as ***'come across'*** itself means to meet suddenly.

Some more superfluous errors:

(1) **Final *destination***. [*Destination* is always final]

(2) **Rough *estimate***. [*Estimate* is always rough]

(3) **Rough *approximation***. [*Approximation* is always rough; not exact]

(4) **Past *history***. [*History* is always past]

(5) ***Return* back**. [*Return* itself means come back]

(6) **Coming *future***. [*Future* is always coming]

(7) ***Reason* because**. [*Reason* itself means cause so]

(8) ***Consensus* opinion**. [*Consensus* itself means collective opinion or agreement]

(9) **Final *conclusion***. [*Conclusion* is always final]

(10) ***Funeral* service**. [*Funeral* itself a ceremony and service]

***NOTE**: *"**enter into**" is also an example of superfluous error. However, when "**enter into**" is used as a phrasal verb, it means "**investigation**".*

**RULE44**: Use of ***Apostrophe*** **('s) :**

Apostrophe **('s)** is not used with non-living things.

Examples:-

Table's legs. [**Incorrect**]

Door's bolt. [**Incorrect**]

Pen's ink. [**Incorrect**]

Book's page. [**Incorrect**]

Chair's legs. [**Incorrect**]

These can be rewritten as:

Legs of the table. [**Correct**]

Bolt of the door. [**Correct**]

Ink of the pen. [**Correct**]

Page of the book. [**Correct**]

Legs of the chair. [**Correct**]

***NOTE**: *There are some exceptions to this rule. When we talk about* ***time, weight,distance,place, idiom, unit, personification, or heavenly body****, we can use Apostrophe ('s) with them.*

Examples:-

One week's vacation. **[Correct]**

Four dollars' worth. **[Correct]**

Today's date. **[Correct]**

The ship's bells. **[Correct]**

The city's parks. **[Correct]**

Malaysia's land. **[Correct]**

Nature's call **[Correct]**

At a stone's throw **[Correct]**

***NOTE**: *The following pronouns are already possessive and do not require apostrophes:* ***yours, ours, its, theirs, his, hers, and whose.***

**RULE45**: Whenever a point of time in the past is mentioned in the sentence (i.e. ***yesterday, 10 days ago***, etc.) , we always use "***Simple Past***" tense.

Examples:-

I **have gone** to the market yesterday to purchase a car. **[Incorrect]**

I ***went*** to the market yesterday to purchase a car. **[Correct]**

The company's shares **have dived** by 90p to 165p on the stock market last week. **[Incorrect]**

The company's shares ***dived*** by 90p to 165p on the stock market last week. **[Correct]**

**RULE46**: There are certain words like "***unique, excellent, perfect, ideal, entire, complete***, etc." which are never used with "***most***".

The table is as follows

| Chief | Round | Unique | Total | Whole | Singular |
|---|---|---|---|---|---|
| Rectangular | Square | Excellent | Spherical | Extreme | Annual |
| Golden | Deaf | Blind | Right | Empty | Circular |
| Wrong | Impossible | Perfect | Solar | External | Ideal |

Examples:-

He is **the most** *excellent* student. **[Incorrect]**

He is ***an*** *excellent* student. **[Correct]**

This is **the most** *unique* product of our company. **[Incorrect]**

This is ***a*** *unique* product of our company. **[Correct]**

He is **completely** *perfect.* **[Incorrect]**

He is *perfect.* **[Correct]**

**RULE47**: Words like "***Quite***" and "***all***" are never used together in a sentence.

Examples:-

He is **quite all** well. [**Incorrect**]

He is ***quite*** well. [**Correct**]

He has done **quite all** the work. [**Incorrect**]

He has done ***all*** the work. [**Correct**]

***NOTE**: *Do not get confused with the similar sounding words like "**Quiet**" and "**Quite**".*

***Quiet*** is a ***Noun*** which means ***the state of being silent.***

***Quite*** is an ***Adverb*** which means ***completely***.

**RULE48**: Determination of tense based on words like "***ago***" and "***before***":

We generally use Simple Past Tense when the word "***ago***" is mentioned in the sentence.

In the case of "before", we use Past Perfect Tense.

Examples:-

He **had gone** two seconds ***ago***. [**Incorrect**]

He ***went*** two seconds ***ago***. [**Correct**]

She **had submitted** the work five hours ***ago***. [**Incorrect**]

She ***submitted*** the work five hours ***ago***. [**Correct**]

The patient **died** ***before*** the doctor came. [**Incorrect**]

The patient ***had died before*** the doctor came. [**Correct**]

In the last sentence, two actions have happened in the past, so for the earlier action we use "***had + V3***" and for the latter action we use "***V2***".

**RULE49**: Use of Possessive sign:

(1) **Common Possession**: When two nouns are closely connected or implying the common possession, the possessive sign is put to the latter(last one) .

Examples:-

1. *Ram and Shyam's car* ***is*** being decorated for Balram's marriage. [**Correct**]
2. *Ram and Shyam's cars* ***are*** being decorated for Balram's marriage. [**Correct**]

Both the sentences are correct

In the first sentence, there is one car which belongs to both Ram and Shyam [Common Possession]

In the second sentence, there is more than one car which belongs to both Ram and Shyam [Common Possession]

(2) **Split Possession**: Each of two or more connected nouns implying separate possession must take the possessive sign.

Examples:-

*Ram's and Shyam's car* ***is*** being decorated for Balram's marriage. [**Incorrect**]

*Ram's and Shyam's cars* ***are*** being decorated for Balram's marriage. [**Correct**]

In the above examples, the possessive sign with each subject denotes that at least two cars are being decorated one of Ram and the other of Shyam (i.e. ***Ram's car*** and ***Shyam's car***) , so a plural noun "***cars***" is used and it will take a plural verb.

<u>**RULE50**</u>: Some common errors of Possession:

We often make mistakes by using "***it's***" in place of "***its***". Both these terms have separate meanings.

"***It's***" denotes "***It is***", while "***its***" denotes ***possession***.

Examples:-

The child is carrying <u>**it's**</u> book. [**Incorrect**]

The child is carrying ***its*** book. [**Correct**]

<u>**Its**</u> called a miracle. [**Incorrect**]

***It's*** called a miracle. [**Correct**]

<u>**RULE51**</u>: Rule for using "***A number of***" and "***The number of***":

We use the following structures with these two:

"***A number of + Plural Noun + Plural Verb***"

"***The number of + Plural Noun + Singular Verb***"

Similar rule is there for "A variety of" and "The variety of"

Examples:-

***A number of*** students <u>***are***</u> waiting here.

***The number of*** students <u>***is***</u> fifty.

***A number of*** tickets <u>***were***</u> sold almost immediately.

***The number of*** employees taking legal action over work-related hazards <u>***is***</u> increasing.

<u>**RULE52**</u>: Use of the phrase "***It is time***" , "***It is high time" or "It is about time"***:

With the phrases like "It is time" and "It is high time", we follow either of the two conditions:

(1) The phrase should be followed by "***to + V1***" if there is no Subject attached to it.

Examples:-

It is time <u>***to work***</u> hard.

It is time <u>***to ask***</u> for a raise.

(2) If the phrase is directly followed by a Subject, we use the verb form "***V2***" (past tense) after the subject.

Examples:-

It is time *he* <u>***worked***</u> hard. [followed by the subject "***he***"]

Gosh! It's almost midnight. It is time *we* <u>***went***</u> home. [followed by the subject "***we***"]

***NOTE**: *We use the expression "**it's time + subject + past verb form**" to refer to the present moment.*

<u>**RULE53**</u>: Use of preposition with the word "***Angry***":

(1) We use the preposition "***with***" with "***angry***" whenever we refer a person or living thing for the purpose.

Examples:-

I got really *angry* <u>***with***</u> her.

I am *angry* <u>***with***</u> Shyam because he did not go to the class.

(2) We use the preposition "***at***" with "***angry***" whenever we refer something other than person or living thing.

Examples:-

The local residents were *angry* ***at*** the lack of parking spaces.

They are *angry* ***at*** the way they have been treated.

***NOTE**: *We follow the same rule with the word "**Annoy**".*

**RULE54**: Whenever the word "***know***" is used in a sentence, it is not directly followed by the infinitive "to". We use the words like "***how, when, why, where***, etc." to make the sentence grammatically feasible.

Examples:-

I do not ***know*** ***what*** all the fuss is about.

I do not ***know*** ***how*** to make tea; hence you should help me out.

I don't know to make tea [Incorrect]

Do you ***know*** ***where*** the Post Office is?

**RULE55**: The adverb "***else***" is always followed by "***but***" while the adverbs "***other***, and ***rather***" are always followed by "***than***".

Examples:-

It is nothing ***else*** ***but*** mere foolishness.

Everybody ***else*** has agreed ***but*** you.

He met no ***other*** person ***than*** Ram.

I think I would rather stay at home this evening ***than*** go out.

**RULE56**: The words like "***sort, type, kind***, etc." are always followed by a Singular verb.

Examples:-

This ***type*** of article ***is*** sold in the market.

This ***sort*** of camera ***is*** very expensive.

Any ***kind*** of racism ***is*** abhorrent to me.

**RULE57**: Use of the prepositions "***in***", "***Inside***" and "***into***":

(1) The preposition "***inside***" implies "***movement***". Whenever we move from outside to inside, we use "***inside***".

Examples:-

I came ***inside*** the class.

He tried to get ***inside*** her mind.

***NOTE**: "**Inside out**" is completely different from "**In**" and "**Inside**". It means if something is inside out, it has the usual inside part on the outside and the usual outside part on the inside.*

There is one more meaning of "Inside out" which is "completely"

Examples:-

I know my husband ***inside out***. [completely]

She had her sweater ***inside out***.

(2) The preposition "*in*" implies "***static***". Whenever something referred is already inside, we use "***in***".

Examples:-

I am ***in*** the class.

The chlorine ***in*** the pool makes my eyes sore.

(3) The preposition "***into***" implies "***coming toward something***". Whenever we move to a position in or inside something, we use "***into***". It is also used to show a change in state.

Examples:-

Come ***into*** the house.

He threw the letter ***into*** the fire.

Can you translate this passage ***into*** German?

The fruit can be made ***into*** jam.

He jumped ***into*** the well.

She wove her ideas ***into*** a story.

**RULE58**: Use of the prepositions "***with***" and "***by***".

(1) We use "***with***" when we refer to non living things.

Examples:-

We write ***with*** a *pen*. [***Pen*** being a non-living thing]

She wiped her lipstick off ***with*** a *tissue*. [***Tissue*** being a non-living thing]

He hit the dog ***with*** a *stick*. [***Stick*** being a non-living thing]

(2) We use "***by***" when we refer to living things.

Examples:-

The motorcycle was driven ***by*** a *tiny bald man*.

The book was translated ***by*** a *well-known author*.

Any painting ***by*** *Van Gogh* is worth a fortune.

***NOTE**: *Whenever we talk about "**watch**", we use "**by**".*

What is the time **by** your watch? [ In your watch is incorrect]

Examples:-

She had promised to be back ***by*** *five o'clock*. [referring time]

I have got to be home ***by*** *seven*. [referring time]

**RULE59**: We do not use the preposition "***from***" with the word "***start***".

Examples:-

My exams *start* **from** Monday. [**Incorrect**]

My exams *start* ***on*** Monday. [**Correct**]

In the first sentence, the preposition "***from***" gives the meaning that my exams will start on Monday, it will again start on Tuesday and it will continue doing so. Thus, an event started once cannot start again and again. To avoid this error, we use the correct preposition "***on***" which implies that the event has started on Monday only.

Some more examples:-

He will *start* his preparation **from** Monday. [**Incorrect**]

He will *start* his preparation ***on*** Monday. [**Correct**]

However, we can rewrite this sentence using "***from***" this way:-

He will prepare for the exams ***from*** Monday. [**Correct**]

***NOTE**: *"**from**" implies **continuation**.*

**RULE60**: In a general case of infinitive we always use the form "***To + V1***". But in certain special cases, we use the form "***To + V1+ing***".

There are certain words which always follow "***To + V1+ing***" form:-

(1) be + used + to + V1+ing

(2) accustomed to + V1+ing

(3) addicted to + V1+ing

(4) with a view to + V1+ing

(5) look forward to + V1+ing

(6) given to + V1+ing

(7) prone to + V1+ing

(8) devoted to + V1+ing

(9) in addition to + V1+ing

(10) confess to + V1+ing

(11) disposed to + V1+ing

(12) come to + V1+ing

Examples:-

She was ***given to staying*** in bed till lunchtime.

These measures have been taken ***with a view to increasing*** the company's profits.

I ***look forward to hearing*** from you.

He is rather ***prone to making*** tactless remarks.

She has ***devoted herself to getting*** justice for her son.

I am not ***accustomed to being*** treated like this.

***NOTE**: *When we use the form "**V1+ing**" as a noun, it is called **Gerund**.*

**RULE61**: The choice between the two indefinite articles – ***'a'*** & ***'an'*** – is determined by sound. Words beginning with consonant sounds are preceded by ***'a'*** and words beginning with vowel sounds are preceded by ***'an'***.

Vowels – ***a***, ***e***, ***i***, ***o***, and ***u***

Consonants – ***b***, ***c***, ***d***, ***f***, ... *z*

Examples:-

***An*** NCC cadet. [Vowel sounding word]

**Section - I**

***A*** UNICEF participating nation. [Consonant sounding word]

***An*** umbrella. [Vowel sounding word]

***An*** M. Tech. graduate. [Vowel sounding word]

***A*** utensil. [Consonant sounding word]

***A*** university. [Consonant sounding word]

***A*** unicorn. [Consonant sounding word]

***A*** year. [exception] [With every word that starts with "y" and "w" we use article "a"]

***A*** European university

***A*** University

***A*** Uniform

***A*** one-rupee note

***A*** Union

***A*** one-eyed girl

***A*** unanimous decision.

**RULE62**: Usage of definite ARTICLE "***The***":

(1) Series of Mountains, Bays/Gulfs,Group of islands, Canals, Aeroplanes, Ships, Planes, Religious books, Government branches, Armed forces, Names of Deserts,Political parties, Musical instrument, Rivers, Oceans, Seas, and things which are "*unique*" in themselves: These nouns are always preceded by a definite article "***The***".

Examples:-

***The*** Sahara. [Name of Desert]

***The*** Pacific. [Name of Ocean]

***The*** Nile. [Name of the river]

***The*** Coral sea. [Name of the sea]

***The*** Himalayas. [Name of mountain range]

***The*** Guitar [Musical Instrument]

One important point to note is that

Names of mountain ranges are preceded by the article "THE" but mountains peaks are never preceded by article "the"

The Himalayas is correct but the Mount Everest is wrong. We only use "Everest"

(2) Names of Newspaper: These nouns are always preceded by a definite article "***The***".

Examples:-

***The*** Times of India.

***The*** Hindu.

***The*** Indian Express.

(3) Names of Countries (Only the ones which are written in *Abbreviated forms*) : These nouns are always preceded by a definite article "***The***".

Examples:-

***The*** USA.

***The*** UK.

***The*** UAE.

***The*** USSR.

(4) Superlative Degree: The nouns of superlative degree are always preceded by a definite article "***The***".

Examples:-

***The*** *best* book.

***The*** *darkest* cloud.

(5) Comparative Case: "***The***" is used in two cases:

**CASE 1**: ***The*** higher you go, ***the*** cooler it is.

***The*** faster you walk, ***the*** sooner you reach.

The more sugar you put in the dish, the sweeter it is.

**CASE2**: He is ***the*** better of the two.

*She is the* poorer *of the two women*

*He is the better candidate of the two for the job*

(6) Metaphor: Sometimes "***the***" is used before a metaphor.

In case of a metaphor one thing is treated as another thing.

Examples:-

He is ***the*** Mahatma Gandhi of our class.

Delhi is ***the*** Paris of India.

(7) For a phrase which is combination of a common and proper noun, ***the'*** is used.

Examples:-

***The*** river Nile,

***The*** Muslim League Party,

***The*** New York City,

(8) '***The'*** is mandatory before a thing which is only one of a kind in the universe.

Examples:-

***The*** moon is shining tonight.

***The*** earth is moving around ***the*** sun.

(9) For the names of the government organisations, ***'the'*** is used.

Examples:-

***The*** Society for the protection of Child's Rights

*The* ***judiciary*** is composed of a supreme court of seven members, a court of chancery, a county court in each county, a probate court in each probate district, and justices of the peace.

**RULE63**: Omission of Article "***The***": We do not use any article before following nouns:

(1) **Names of Cities**: Los Angeles, Alaska, Sydney, etc.

(2) **Names of Countries**: (*except names of countries with abbreviated form*) Australia, Bolivia, England, France, Spain, etc.

(3) **Names of continents**: Asia, Europe, Australia, Africa, South America, North America, Antarctica.

(4) **Names of streets**: George Street, Albion Street, New town Street, etc.

(5) **Names of singular lakes and bays**: Lake Carey, Lake Eyre, Lake Hillier, Shark Bay, etc.

(6) **Names of Mountain Peaks**: Mount Everest, Mount Solitary, Mount Bindo, Mount Fuji, etc.

(7) **Names of single islands**: Easter Island, Bare Island, Bird Island, Fatima Island, etc.

(8) **Names of languages**: Spanish, Russian, English (*When '**the**' precedes these nouns, they refer to the population of those languages.*)

(9) **Names of sports**: cricket, football, basketball, etc.

(10) In normal cases, we do not use any article before these words – season, language, drinks, meals, God, life, money, etc. However, when we use these words to particularise the information, we use the article "***the***".

Examples:-

*Breakfast* should be light but ***the*** *breakfast* I had this morning was heavy. [The second time "***breakfast***" is used , The article is used before it as it refers to a particular breakfast]

**RULE64**: Use of "***the + Adjective***":

Whenever the article "***the***" is used before an adjective, it determines the whole group.

Examples:-

***The*** poor – poor people

***The*** needy – needy people

The brave— brave people

The rich—- Rich people

***The*** honest are respected. ['***The***'+ '***adjectives***' = Plural noun]It means Honest people

***The*** poor are not always dishonest. ['***The***'+ '***adjectives***' – Plural noun] It means poor people

**RULE65**: Whenever same nouns are connected by a preposition, in that case we use both the nouns in a singular form.

Examples:-

**Villages after villages** were destroyed by the terrorists. **[Incorrect]**

***Village after village*** were destroyed by the terrorists. **[Correct]**

**Books after books** had been read by him. **[Incorrect]**

***Book after book*** had been read by him. **[Correct]**

***City after city*** was set on fire. **[Correct]**

***Page after page*** was reviewed multiple times. **[Correct]**

**RULE66**: Certain nouns whose plurals should be known:

| Singular | Plural | Singular | Plural |
|---|---|---|---|
| Dormouse | Dormice | Man | Men |
| Foot | Feet | Mouse | Mice |
| Goose | Geese | Tooth | Teeth |
| Louse | Lice | Woman | Women |

| Singular | Plural |
|---|---|
| Daughter-in-law | Daughters-in-law |
| Hanger-on | Hangers-on |
| Commander-in-chief | Commanders-in-chief |
| Sister-in-law | Sisters-in-law |
| Passer-by | Passers-by |
| Looker-on | Lookers-on |
| Brother-in-law | Brothers-in-law |

Examples where the second word forms the plural :

| Singular | Plural |
|---|---|
| Book-case | Book-cases |
| Class-fellow | Class-fellows |
| Race-horse | Race-horses |
| Step-son | Step-sons |
| Castaway | Castaways |
| Grand-father | Grand-fathers |
| Horse-race | Horse races |
| Maidservant | Maidservants |

Examples where both words make the plural :

| Singular | Plural |
|---|---|
| Man-servant | Men-servants |
| Woman-servant | Women-servants |
| Lord-justice | Lords-justices |

The plural of some compound nouns are below:

**Section - I**

| Singular | Plural |
|---|---|
| Son-in-law | Sons-in-law |
| Brother-in-law | Brothers-in-law |
| Passer-by | Passers-by |
| Major General | Major Generals |
| Lord-Justice | Lord-Justices |
| Man-servant | Men-servants |

***NOTE**: *To show possession in case of Compound Nouns, we always use apostrophe ('s) at the end.*

Examples:-

***Sister-in-law's car***. [Possession of Compound Noun]

**RULE67**: Whenever "***male***" or "***female***" is used before a noun, it means that we are describing its characteristics.

Examples:-

*Female watch* [means the watches specified for females]

*Female doctor* [means the doctors specified for females]

*Male shoes* [means the shoes specified for males]

But whenever we use "***man***" or "***woman***" is used before a noun, it means that we are describing the profession or post of that noun.

Examples:-

*Man soldier* [means the soldier is a man]

*Woman student* [means the student is woman]

*Woman doctor* [means the doctor is woman]

Some more examples:-

She went to a ***female doctor***. [**Correct**]

Raj went to a **female doctor** to get himself treated. [**Incorrect**]

Raj went to a ***woman doctor*** to get himself treated. [**Correct**]

**RULE68**: Antecedent Rule:

The noun or pronoun that comes just before a Relative pronoun is called an Antecedent.

Examples:-

Ram met ***him*** *who* they say has helped us. ["***him***" in this case is an Antecedent]

He saw ***her*** *whom* everyone admires. ["***her***" in this case is an Antecedent]

***NOTE**: *When there is no antecedent in a sentence, we use "**whoever, whomever**, etc." as relative pronouns.*

Examples:-

Ram met ***whoever*** had have helped us. [No Antecedent in the sentence]

He saw ***whomever*** everyone admires. [No Antecedent in the sentence]

**RULE69**: Rule of Question tags:

A small question is added at the end of a statement. This is called Question Tag.

A question tag for a positive statement is always negative and vice-versa.

Examples:-

He has worked very hard on this project, ***hasn't he***? [Negative question tag for a positive statement]

He has not worked hard on this project, ***has he***? [Positive question tag for a negative statement]

**RULE70**: Some typical errors related to the above rule.

Examples:-

I am working very hard for my students, **amn't I**? [**Incorrect**]

I am working very hard for my students, ***aren't I***? [**Correct**]

I am getting better at this, ***aren't I***? [**Correct**]

The first sentence is incorrect because there is no such word "***amn't***". It should be written as "***aren't I***" which means "***am I not***".

**RULE71**: Certain words like "***Seldom, barely, hardly, scarcely, never***" often impart a negative meaning to the statement, thus these should be followed by a positive question tag.

Examples:-

He ***seldom*** comes to my house, ***does he***? [Positive question tag for a negative statement]

They have ***barely*** enough to pay the rent this month, ***have they***? [Positive question tag for a negative statement]

I ***never*** realised you knew my brother, ***did I***? [Positive question tag for a negative statement]

We ***hardly*** ever go to concerts, do we? [Positive question tag for a negative statement]

I ***seldom*** drive my car into the city, do I? [Positive question tag for a negative statement]

I ***scarcely*** registered the fact that he was there, did I? [Positive question tag for a negative statement]

**RULE72**: It is important to note that question tag statement must be in same tense as the main statement.

Examples:-

I am doing the work which you gave me, **don't I**? [**Incorrect**]

I am doing the work which you gave me, ***aren't I***? [**Correct**]

The first statement is incorrect as the main statement is in Present Continuous Tense which the question tag statement doesn't follow.

**RULE73**: When we use "***Each*** or ***Every***" in a sentence, a singular noun or pronoun is followed which is further followed by a singular verb. But in the case of question tag, noun (or, pronoun) following

**Section - I**

"***Each*** or ***Every***" is considered plural and thus we use the plural verb in question tag statement.

Examples:-

Every girl is very talented, **isn't she**? **[Incorrect]**

Every girl is very talented, ***aren't they***? **[Correct]**

Each one has to work hard to make both ends meet, **hasn't he**? **[Incorrect]**

Each one has to work hard to make both ends meet, ***haven't they***? **[Correct]**

**RULE74**: When a collective noun is used in the main statement and depicts that all its units are working together on the same thing or all are behaving similarly, we consider everything to be singular.

However, if all the units are working on different things, we consider everything to be plural.

Examples:-

The *jury* has taken the decision, ***hasn't it***? [Only one decision is taken]

The *audience* took the seats, ***didn't they***? [Audience took their respective seats]

The *army* changed the uniforms, ***didn't they***? [Army changed their respective uniforms]

**RULE75**: When we talk about Imperative Sentences and that also when we talk about proposals, in that case we always use "***shall we***" in question tag statement.

Examples:-

Let us go for a walk, **don't we**? **[Incorrect]**

Let us go for a walk, ***shall we***? **[Correct]**

Let us consider all the possibilities, ***shall we***? **[Correct]**

Let us hear from Sue at our travel desk, ***shall we***? **[Correct]**

Let us go out to dinner, ***shall we***? **[Correct]**

**RULE76**: Use of the Prepositions "***in***, ***on***, and ***at***":

'**In**' refers to towns, cities, and countries in a wider sense while [ In Delhi, in Dubai, in Saudi Arabia ]

'**At**' is used for speaking of comparatively smaller places. [ at Rohini in Delhi, at Laxminagar ]

***CONCEPT***:-

The Preposition "***in***" implies Area/Volume.

The Preposition "***on***" implies Surface.

The Preposition "***at***" implies Point.

Based on the above concept, we use these prepositions in the following order:

***Point of time < day < month < year***

***At < on < in < in***

The above order can be understood by this way as well:

Since "***point***" is smaller than "***surface***" which in turn is smaller than "***volume***", we follow the order of these prepositions in the same manner.

Examples:-

***At*** 4 pm.

***On*** Sunday.

***In*** 1947.

***On*** 15th August.

***In*** April.

***At*** night.

***In*** the morning.

There's a meeting ***at*** 2.30 this afternoon.

Are you free ***at*** lunchtime?

Hair salons don't usually open ***on*** Sundays.

My birthday is ***on*** 30 May.

I started working here ***in*** 2009.

We are going to Italy ***in*** April.

Bye, see you ***in*** the morning.

***NOTE**: *There are certain words before which we don't use any preposition, like "**last Monday, coming Monday, today, tomorrow, yesterday**, etc."*

Examples:-

I am having dinner with Rachel ***tomorrow*** night.

I saw her ***yesterday*** afternoon.

I have a checklist of things that I must do ***today***.

The weather forecast said it would be fine and dry this ***coming Monday***.

**RULE77**: The conjunction "***Both***" is always followed by "***and***" and not "***as well as***".

Examples:-

***Both*** Ram **as well as** Shyam are good at English. [**Incorrect**]

***Both*** Ram ***and*** Shyam are good at English. [**Correct**]

***Both*** men **as well as** women have complained about the advertisement. [**Incorrect**]

***Both*** men ***and*** women have complained about the advertisement. [**Correct**]

I felt ***both*** happy **as well as** sad at the same time. [**Incorrect**]

I felt ***both*** happy ***and*** sad at the same time. [**Correct**]

***NOTE**: *The word "**good**" is always followed by the preposition "**at**".*

Examples:-

She is very ***good at*** geography.

Rohan is ***good at*** football.

**RULE78**: Use of the conjunction "***Lest***":

## Section - I

***Lest*** means ***otherwise***.

The conjunction "***lest***" is always followed either by the verb "***should***" or no helping verb at all.

Examples:-

Work hard, ***lest*** you **would** fail. **[Incorrect]**

Work hard, ***lest*** you fail. **[Correct]**

Work hard, ***lest*** you ***should*** fail. **[Correct]**

He cut the remark out of the final program ***lest*** it ***should*** offend listeners. **[Correct]**

**RULE79**: Use of "***Until***" and "***Unless***":

***CONCEPT***:-

Until – Time Oriented

Unless – Action Oriented

Examples:-

Wait for me ***until*** sunset. [referring ***Time***]

***Unless*** the government reduces the tax, the tax-payer base will not increase. [referring ***Action***]

I was up ***until*** three o'clock trying to get it finished! [referring ***Time***]

***Unless*** you call me to say you're not coming, I will see you at the theatre. [referring ***Action***]

***NOTE**: *There is no difference in meaning between "**till**" and "**until**" as both mean "**up to (the time that)**". However, we cannot use "**till**" at the beginning of the sentence which is not the case with "**until**"*, meaning *"**until**"* can be used at the beginning of sentences.

Examples:-

***Until*** your next birthday, you will have to wait for a new bike.

We did not eat ***till*** past midnight.

**RULE80**: Error of Parallelism:

The rule of ***Parallelism*** explains that sentence elements that are alike in function should also be alike in construction. These elements should be in the same grammatical form so that they are parallel.

Here are some examples of parallel elements:

(I) **Words**: thinking, running, etc.

(II) **Infinitives**: to see, to understand, etc.

(III) **Prepositional phrases**: at the time, in the house, etc.

(IV) **Subordinate clauses**: because I care, after they met, etc.

(V) **Linking words**: not only…but also…, either…or…, neither…or…, if…then…, etc.

(VI) **Nouns**: honesty, originality, goodness, etc.

(VII) **Adjectives**: charming, courteous, beautiful, etc.

Examples:-

I like ***singing***, ***dancing***, and **to walk**. **[Incorrect]**

I like ***singing***, ***dancing***, and ***walking***. **[Correct]**

He asked his mother ***to cook***, ***to rest*** and **prepare the dish**. **[Incorrect]**

He asked his mother ***to cook***, ***to rest*** and ***to prepare*** the dish. **[Correct]**

My friends never judged me by ***my words*** or **what I did**. **[Incorrect]**

My friends never judged me by ***my words*** or ***my actions***. **[Correct]**

The teacher **not only** wants his students ***to keep quiet*** but also ***to do the task***. **[Incorrect]**

The teacher wants his students ***not only to keep quiet*** *but also* ***to do the task***. **[Correct]**

I like **to read books** over ***watching movies***. **[Incorrect]**

I like ***reading books*** over ***watching movies***. **[Correct]**

I would ***rather pay*** for my education **than financial aid**. **[Incorrect]**

I would ***rather pay*** for my education ***than receive financial aid***. **[Correct]**

Tom is known for his ***honesty*** and **original ideas**. **[Incorrect]**

Tom is known for his ***honesty*** and ***originality***. **[Correct]**

***To learn*** is **understanding** the world. **[Incorrect]**

***To learn*** is ***to understand*** the world. **[Correct]**

This task can be done individually, in pairs, or **can be** done in groups of four. **[Incorrect]**

This task can be done individually, in pairs, or in groups of four. **[Correct]**

**RULE81**: Use of proper Prepositions:

It is important to use exact prepositions after the words.

Examples:-

He is *superior* ***to*** and *older* ***than*** me.

This book is *different* ***from*** and *better* ***than*** that book.

In the first example, the word "***superior***" is followed by the preposition "***to***" and "***older***" is followed by "***than***".

Similarly, in the second case, the word "***different***" is followed by "***from***" and "***better***" is followed by "***than***".

Some more examples:-

Nobody seems to have *responsibility* ***for*** the budget.

What's the *reason* ***for*** your unhappiness?

*Changes* ***in*** society have meant that young people leave home earlier.

There's been a steady *increase* ***in*** the value of the euro.

Go to our website to get the *address* ***of*** our nearest branch.

My *reaction* ***to*** it all was to try to forget it.

Her *response* ***to*** the criticism was very strong.

18 is the *age* ***at*** which you are allowed to vote.

**Section - I**

Fisk is making his third *attempt* **at** the world record.

The police *inquiry* **into** the theft continues.

She did some *research* **into** the causes of back pain.

This is an *example* **of** international collaboration.

We need to find another *way* **of** doing things.

Her *response* **to** the criticism was very strong.

I saw an *advertisement* **for** a teaching job in Malawi which looked interesting.

There is a growing *awareness* **of** the impact of climate change among the young.

*Congratulations* **on** your new job!

I'd like to do a *course* **in** computer programming if I could find a good one.

Do you have any previous *experience* **of** working with children?

He seems to have less *interest* **in** everything these days.

Can you give us some *information* **on/about** bus tours, please?

The invitation **to** the *reception* **at** the embassy arrived the next day.

He has an amazing *knowledge* **of** European history.

Can anyone become a *member* **of** your book club?

I was a *newcomer* **to** windsurfing so I was very nervous.

I'd love to show you some of the nice *places* **in** my hometown.

The *visit* **to** the temple was the high point of the holiday.

I need some *lessons* **in** how to set up a website.

*Changes* **in** our diet have meant that more and more people suffer heart disease. [***Changes that happen***]

The director of studies must be informed of any *changes* **to** the timetable. [***Changes that people purposely make***]

**RULE82**: Use of "***too much***" and "***much too***":

We use "***much***" and "***too***" together in two ways:

(1) ***too much*** – we use "***too much***" as an Adjective.

(2) ***much too*** – we use "***much too***" as an Adverb.

"***MUCH***" indicates a big quantity of an uncountable substance or element (one that you can't count) .

If the quantity becomes too big, much is preceded by "***TOO***": **TOO MUCH + uncountable noun** = *an excessive quantity.*

Another construction describing an excessive quantity is less frequent and is built with an adjective: = **MUCH TOO + ADJECTIVE**

In this construction, '***MUCH***' has played the function of '***increasing***', amplifying the adverb '***too***'; it is equivalent to '***far too heavy***'.

Examples:-

He is **too much** strong. [**Incorrect**]

He is ***much too*** strong. [**Correct**]

There is **much too** sugar. [**Incorrect**]

There is ***too much*** sugar. [**Correct**]

In the above examples, it is to be noted that "***strong***" is an Adjective and "***sugar***" is a Noun. Thus, we use the Adjective "***too much***" with the noun.

Some more examples:-

He drank ***too much*** alcohol last night, and this morning he feels ill. [Too much is an adjective here ]

***Too much*** work and not enough play make Jack a dull boy. [Too much is an adjective here]

This car is ***much too*** expensive for me to buy [Much too is an adverb here]

This case is ***much too*** heavy; you can't carry it! [Much too is an adverb here]

**RULE83**: Possessive Case is always followed by a Noun.

Examples:-

***His belongings*** were lost. [**Correct**]

***His earnings*** are not enough. [**Correct**]

***His surroundings*** are not clean. [**Correct**]

In the above examples, all three words following the possessive case "***his***"–"***belongings, earnings, and surroundings" are nouns***

***Some more examples of nouns which are always plural are***

***Riches ,premises, spectacles, Bowels, Valuables, Proceeds, Alms, Billiards, Movables, Wages, Thanks, Annals, Measles, Trousers, Goods, Socks, Fetters, Shorts, Pantaloons, Tidings, Mumps, Eatables, Scissors, Stockings, Surroundings,Breeches, Arms, Tongs***"

***NOTE**: *Some Verbs play the role of Nouns, just by adding '**s**' at the end.*

Examples:-

| VERB | NOUN |
|---|---|
| Belong | Belongings |
| Earning | Earnings |
| Surrounding | Surroundings |

Some more examples:-

*All his goods were sold at throw away prices.*

***Spectacles*** have been broken

Kindly give me a pair of ***scissors***.

**RULE84**: Use of the word "***Politics***":

**Section - I**

When the word "***Politics***" is considered as a field or a subject, it is used as singular.

When the word "***Politics***" is considered as a set of political beliefs, it is used as plural.

Examples:-

*Politics* ***is*** a very dirty game.

His *politics* ***are*** different from mine.

In the first example, "***politics***" is used as a whole field, so it requires a singular verb. In the second example, "***politics***" is used as political beliefs, thus it requires a plural verb.

Some more examples:-

Her *politics* ***have*** become more liberal over the past few years.

His *politics* ***are*** generally considered to be right of centre.

*Politics* is the main subject at Leicester University.

Joe is very active in left-wing *politics.*

**RULE85**: Usage of "***Mathematics***" and "***Statistics***":

When these two words are used as a field or a subject, we consider them uncountable nouns and thus a singular verb is used.

However, when the meaning of the word "***Mathematics***" is "***Calculation***" and "***Statistics***" is "***Data***", we use plural verb in both the cases.

Examples:-

*Mathematics* ***is*** an interesting subject. [Used as a subject]

*Mathematics* ***are*** telling that he has made a lot of money. [Here it means "***calculations***"]

*Statistics* ***is*** difficult to understand. [Used as a subject]

*Statistics* ***tell*** us that it will rain today. [Here it means "***data***"]

***NOTE**: *The word "**Data**" is plural. The singular form of "**Data**" is "**Datum**".*

Examples:-

*Data* **warns** us and we will have to change our strategy. **[Incorrect]**

*Data* ***warn*** us and we will have to change our strategy. **[Correct]**

***NOTE**: *The word "**Summons**" is a singular noun but "**Summon**" is a verb. The plural form of "**Summons**" is "**Summonses**".*

Examples:-

Two **summons** were issued. **[Incorrect]**

Two ***summonses*** were issued. **[Correct]**

**RULE86**: We use the article "***A***" when we mean "***One of many***" and the article "***The***" when we mean "***only one***". Moreover, we use the article "***A***" with the possessive case and "***The***" with the objective case.

Examples:-

***The*** brother of ***me*** is a scientist. [Objective case]

***A*** brother of ***mine*** is a scientist. [Possessive case]

In the first sentence, "***The brother of me***" suggests that there is only one brother. In the second example, "***A brother of mine***" suggests that there are many brothers.

Some more examples:-

***A*** servant of ***theirs*** lives in Delhi.

***The*** servant of ***them*** lives in Delhi.

***NOTE**: *We can rewrite these phrases:*

*My car – The car of me*

*My brother – The brother of me*

*One of my brothers – A brother of mine*

**RULE87**: Usage of "***too***", "***as well***" and "***also***":

When we have to denote some extra thing in a sentence, we use these three words. It is to be noted that "***also***" cannot be used at the end of the sentence. However, "***too***" and "***as well as***" can be used at the end of the sentence.

Examples:-

I have brought a bag ***too***. [**Correct**]

I have brought a bag ***as well***. [**Correct**]

I have brought a bag **also**. {**Incorrect**]

I have ***also*** brought a bag. [**Correct**]

***NOTE**: *In normal cases, "**too**" and "**so**" are used to give negative sense to the sentence. When we use "**too**" with the meaning of "**addition**", we can use it at the end. However, when we use "**too**" with the meaning of "**high intensity**", we cannot use it alone.*

She is **too** beautiful. [**Incorrect** because the sentence is incomplete]

She is very beautiful. [**Correct**]

It is ***too*** hot ***to*** go outside. [**Correct**]

It is ***so*** hot ***that*** I cannot go outside. [**Correct**]

The question was ***too*** difficult ***to*** solve. [**Correct**]

**RULE88**: ***Optative Sentences***:

The sentence which expresses a prayer, keen wish, curse etc. is called an optative sentence. This kind of sentence generally starts with '***may***' and '***wish***'. Sometimes, '***may***' remains hidden.

In the case of optative sentences, whether the subject is singular or plural, we use the base form of the verb (i.e. ***V1***) .

Examples:-

May God ***bless*** you!

Long ***live*** the king.

May the almighty ***help*** in this tragedy!

***Wish*** you a happy journey together.

**RULE89**: Pseudo Subjects:

When in a sentence, irrespective of the presence of main subject, we have to talk about something which is not related to the main subject, in that case we use "***pseudo subject***".

Examples:-

Being a rainy day, I did not go to school. [**Incorrect**]

***It*** being a rainy day, I did not go to school. [**Correct**]

In the above example, there is no Subject of "***rainy day***", "***I***" is the main Subject and has no relation with "***rainy day***". So to add a Subject, we use "***It***" as a Pseudo Subject.

Being ill, he did not come to class. [**Correct**]

In the above example, there is no need of pseudo subject as "***ill***" in the first part refers to the main subject "***he***".

Being vacant, I did not enter the room. [**Incorrect**]

***It*** being vacant, I did not enter the room. [**Correct**]

In the above example, there is no subject of "***vacant***" which has no relation with the main subject "***I***", thus we need a Pseudo subject "***It***" to make the sentence grammatically correct.

**RULE90**: Whenever infinitive (***to + V1***) in a sentence talks about a noun, it is always followed by a preposition.

Examples:-

The child has no bed *to sleep* ***in***. [Infinitive is used to talk about the noun "***bed***"]

I have a pen *to write* ***with***. [Infinitive is used to talk about the noun "***pen***"]

The child wanted a toy *to play* ***with***. [Infinitive is used to talk about the noun "***toy***"]

**RULE91**: When two different helping verbs are required in a sentence, we always use the main verb in both the cases.

Examples:-

I **have never and will never watch** this movie. [**Incorrect**]

I ***have*** never ***watched*** and ***will*** never ***watch*** this movie. [**Correct**]

**RULE92**: Certain words like "***belongings, savings, congratulations, scissors, proceeds, surroundings, regards, pliers, tongs, jeans, pyjamas, pantaloons, shorts, contents, outskirts, glasses, clothes, thanks, goggles, premises, surroundings, belongings, earnings, earrings, tidings*** etc." are considered Plural, so they always take plural verbs.

Examples:-

His *regards* ***were*** conveyed to his parents.

All *proceeds* from the auction ***are*** donated to charity.

His *belongings* ***were*** lost.

These *scissors* ***are*** for cutting paper.

Your *clothes* ***are*** dirty.

Have you seen my ***glasses***? I want to read the newspaper.

The table of ***contents*** should not contain any pictures.

I live on the ***outskirts*** of the city.

My *trousers* ***are*** dirty. I need to wash ***them***.

Her *thanks* ***were*** clearly sincere.

If your *clothes* ***are*** wet you can dry them upstairs.

***Are*** those your *belongings*?

I would like two ***glasses*** of orange juice, please.

Pass me that ***pair of pliers***, please.

You can get rid of that old ***pair of headphones***.

My ***spectacles*** have been broken.

Kindly give me a pair of ***scissors***.

***Riches*** have wings .

**RULE93**: Certain words like "***Mathematics, Physics, Statistics, News, Economics, Innings, Politics, Athletics, Gymnastics, Gallows, Mechanics, Summons, Classics etc***." are always considered Singular and thus they always require singular verbs.

(a) Mathematics are difficult subject. [Incorrect]

Mathematics is a difficult subject. [Correct]

(b) Politics are a game of compromise. [Incorrect]

Politics is a game of compromise. [Correct]

(c) These news were broadcast from All India Radio only yesterday. [Incorrect]

This news was broadcast from All India Radio only yesterday [Correct]

**Note**

Exceptions of Mathematics, Statistics and Politics have been studied earlier.

**RULE94**: Certain words like "***equipment, furniture, jewellery, luggage, machinery, poetry, scenery, information, advice, baggage, hair,*** etc." do not exist in their plural forms because they all are uncountable nouns.

His luggages was booked. [Incorrect]

His luggage was booked. [Correct]

**Furniture** sets off the beauty of a house. [Incorrect]

**Furniture** set off the beauty of a house. [Correct]

He has given me good **information**. [Correct]

**Section - I**

He has given me a good **information**. [Incorrect]

The **poetries** Society was founded in 1909. [Incorrect]

The **Poetry** Society was founded in 1909. [Correct]

Here is a list of stationeries. [Correct]

Here is the list of stationery. [Correct]

**RULE95**: Rules of Conditional Sentences:

Types of Conditional Sentences:

| CONDITION | RESULT |
|---|---|
| Simple Present | will-future or (Modal + infinitive) or, shall/can/may/must + V1 |
| Simple Past | would + V1 or, could/might/should + V1 |
| Past Perfect | would + have + past participle (V3) or, could/might/should + have + past participle (V3) |

Examples:-

As soon as ***he comes***, I ***will ask him*** this question.

When ***he comes***, I ***will ask him*** this question.

***Had he come*** earlier, I ***would have asked*** him this question.

If he studied, he ***would pass*** the exam.

**RULE96**: Use of Possessive case in a sentence:

The possessive case is used after "***all***" and "***both***".

Consider these examples:-

**My** all students are very talented. [**Incorrect**]

All ***my*** students are very talented. [**Correct**]

**My** both friends are very talented. [**Incorrect**]

Both ***my*** friends are very talented. [**Correct**]

In the above examples, the possessive case "***my***" should be placed after "***all***" and "***both***" respectively.

**RULE97**: Superfluous Sentences:

(1) "***As soon as***" is not followed by "***than***". "***than***" is used after "***No sooner***"

Examples:-

***As soon as*** I complete the work **than** I will go to his house. [**Incorrect**]

***As soon as*** I complete the work I will go to his house. [**Correct**]

***No sooner*** had I started mowing the lawn ***than*** it started raining. [**Correct**]

(2) "***As***" is not used with "***so***".

Examples:-

***As*** he was unwell, **so** he didn't come to the class. **[Incorrect]**

***As*** he was unwell, he didn't come to the class. **[Correct]**

(3) "***Due to***" is not used with "***the reason***" and vice versa.

Examples:-

**Due to the reason** that he is not well, he did not come to the class. **[Incorrect]**

He did not come to the class ***due to*** sickness. **[Correct]**

**RULE98**: Usage of the word "***quantity***":

When the word "***quantity***" is used in the sentence, we cannot use "***little***", "***few***", etc. with it. We can only use "***small***" with it.

Examples:-

**Little** *quantity* of food was wasted. **[Incorrect]**

**Few** *quantity* of food was wasted. **[Incorrect]**

A ***Small*** *quantity* of food was wasted. **[Correct]**

**RULE99**: Different forms of some confusing Verbs:

| V1 | V2 | V3 |
|---|---|---|
| Fly | Flew | Flown |
| Flow | Flowed | Flowed |
| Find | Found | Found |
| Found | Founded | Founded |
| Hang(Prisoner) | Hanged | Hanged |
| Hang(Other things) | Hung | Hung |

Examples:-

The water **overflown** from the banks. **[Incorrect]**

The water ***overflowed*** from the banks. **[Correct]**

The secretary has **found** this organisation. **[Incorrect]**

The secretary has ***founded*** this organisation. **[Correct]**

The prisoner was ***hanged*** till death. **[Correct]**

The clock was ***hung*** on the wall. **[Correct]**

In the fourth sentence, it is to be noted that we have used the word "***founded***" to mean that something was established or discovered.

In the second last sentence, we have used the word "***hanged***" to talk about the haning of prisoner. But when we talk about the clock, we use "***hung***" i.e. V2 form of the verb as can be seen in the last sentence.

**RULE100**: Different forms of the verb "**Lie**":

**Section - I**

| S. No. | V1 | V2 | V3 |
|---|---|---|---|
| 1. | Lie | Lied | Lied |
| 2. | Lay | Laid | Laid |
| 3. | Lie | Lay | Lain |

(1) We use this "*Lie*" to say or write something that is not true in order to deceive someone.

(2) We use "*Lay*" to put something, especially in a flat or horizontal position, usually carefully or for a particular purpose.

(3) We use this "*Lie*" to be in or move into a horizontal position on a surface.

Examples:-

(1) I suspect he ***lies*** about his age. [V1]

She ***lied*** to her parents about her new car. [V2]

He has never ***lied*** to me before, so I have no reason to doubt his word. [V3]

(2) He ***lays*** the book on the table. [V1]

She ***laid*** the baby on the bed. [V2]

He has ***laid*** his bag on the ground. [V3]

(3) He ***lies*** awake at night, worrying. [V1]

A pen ***lay*** on the desk. [V2]

The old book had lain on the shelf for years. [V3]

**RULE101**: Use of a preposition with the word "***Die***":

We use either the preposition "***of***" or "***from***" with the word "***Die***".

We use "***Die of***" whenever it is talked about a disease.

We use "***Die from***" whenever it is talked about the reason

We use "***Die in***" To experience death within a specific location or circumstance.

We use "***Die by***" Refers to the cause or means of death

We use "***Die with***" Refers to the circumstances or company at the time of death.

Examples:-

She ***died from*** overwork. [***Reason***]

He ***died of*** cancer. [***Disease***]

He ***died of*** tuberculosis. [***Disease***]

Trees are ***dying from*** acid rain. [***Reason***]

**RULE102**: Difference between "***Beside***" and "***Besides***":

***Beside*** is a **preposition**, which means at the side of, next to.

***Besides*** is a linking **adverb**, which means in addition to; also.

Examples:-

Come and sit here ***beside*** me.

She knelt down ***beside*** the child.

Do you play any other sports ***besides*** basketball?

***Besides*** being a doctor, he is also an actor.

**RULE103**: Certain words like "***friendly, miserly, cowardly, monthly, yearly, weekly, manly, orderly***, etc." are adjectives and can only be used as an adjective. We cannot use them as adverbs.

Examples:-

He behaved **friendly**. [**Incorrect**]

He behaved in a ***friendly*** manner. [**Correct**]

In the first example, "***friendly***" is used as an adverb, which is incorrect. It should be rewritten as the second statement where "***friendly***" is used as an adjective.

This was a particularly brutal and ***cowardly*** attack. [**Adjective**]

The workers are paid a ***miserly*** $2 a day. [**Adjective**]

She put the letters in three ***orderly*** piles. [**Adjective**]

There was a ***weekly*** dance on Wednesdays. [**Adjective**]

One quality she especially likes to reward is thus held to be ***manly*** courage. [**Adjective**]

Newspapers are constrained by a ***yearly*** license required from the Home Ministry. [**Adjective**]

Other than the ***monthly*** meeting, not much is going on at the association. [**Adjective**]

**RULE104**: Position of Adverbs:

We place an adverb generally at three different positions in a sentence:

(a) Starting of Sentence

(b) Between helping verb and the main verb

(c) At the end

***NOTE**: *An adverb can never be placed between the main verb and object.*

Examples:-

He *comes* **often** to my house. [**Incorrect**]

He ***often*** *comes* to my house. [**Correct**]

In the first sentence, "***comes***" is the main verb and "***often***" is an adverb. So we cannot place adverb between the main verb and the object.

The second sentence is the correct order of the sentence structure.

He *tells* **always** the truth. [**Incorrect**]

He ***always*** *tells* the truth. [**Correct**]

In the above example, "***always***" is an adverb and "***tells***" is the main verb. So "***always***" should be placed before the main verb.

**Section - I**

***Suddenly*** the phone rang. [**Correct**]

He was ***probably*** late for the interview. [**Correct**]

There are few exceptions to this rule.

Adverbs like too, even , only can be placed anywhere in a sentence.

**RULE105**: Whenever we place multiple adverbs in a sentence, in that case we follow a particular order:

***Adverb of Manner*** —-> ***Adverb of Place*** —-> **Adverb of frequency** —-> ***Adverb of Time*** [**MPT** order]

Examples:-

I walked **yesterday slowly**. [**Incorrect** order]

I walked ***slowly yesterday***. [**Correct** order]

I have to run ***quickly*** (manner) ***down the street*** (place) ***each morning*** (frequency) ***after breakfast*** (time) . [**Correct** order]

***Impatiently*** (manner) , I waited ***by the bank*** (place) ***yesterday*** (time) for my father to arrive. [**Correct** order]

**RULE106**: Usage of "**very**" and "**much**":

In a sentence, both these terms are used differently.

"***Very***" is preceded by Adjective's positive degree. ***Very*** emphasises the exact identity of a particular person or thing.

"***Much***" means '***large in amount or extent***'. It is followed by comparative degree and past participle or preceded by **"too"** or **" so".**

Examples:-

It is ***very*** interesting.

He is ***much*** weaker than Shyam.

The girl is ***very*** beautiful.

The weather changes ***very*** quickly.

I am ***much*** better now.

They both talk too ***much***.

He is ***much*** interested in the project.

Thank you so ***much*** for your help.

***NOTE**: *We do not usually use* **very** *to modify superlative adjectives. Instead, we use* **much** *or* ***by far****. But note that* **very** *can be used to emphasise superlatives. It is also used with* ***first****,* ***next*** *and* ***last****.*

Examples:-

This is the ***very best*** wine I have tasted in my life.

This is your ***very last*** chance.

**RULE107**: "**Between**" is always followed by "***and***" and not "***to***".

Examples:-

He will distribute these sweets **<u>between</u>** 4 pm **<u>to</u>** 5 pm. [**Incorrect**]

He will distribute these sweets ***between*** 4 pm ***and*** 5 pm. [**Correct**]

He will distribute these sweets ***from*** 4 pm ***to*** 5 pm. [**Correct**]

**<u>RULE108</u>**: Generally, Uncountable nouns cannot be converted into their plural. However, there are certain uncountable nouns that are found with "***s***" or "***es***" added to the end. These nouns do not form their plurals, rather they give a different meaning to the word.

Examples:-

***Advice*** means suggestion.

***Advices*** means information.

***Air*** means the mixture of gases that surrounds the earth.

***Airs*** means arrogance

***Wood*** means timber.

***Woods*** means forest.

***Iron*** means a chemical elem ent.

***Irons*** means fetters, chain.

| The Noun Singular | Its meaning in (two) | The noun in plural | Its meaning (Only one) |
|---|---|---|---|
| Abuse | i) Wrong use<br>ii) Reproach | Abuses | Wrong practices(Evils) |
| Force | i) Strength<br>ii) Body of armed men | Forces | Troops |
| Issue | i) Result<br>ii) Offspring | Issues | Results |
| Wood | i) Timber<br>ii) Forest | Woods | Forests |
| Light | i) Lamp<br>ii) Brilliance | Lights | Lamps |

Section - I

| | | | |
|---|---|---|---|
| Gain | i) Profit<br>ii) Acquisition of wealth | Gains | Profits |
| People | i) Persons<br>ii) Nations | Peoples | Nations |

**Examples**:-

Wood is used in almost all wooden houses. (Timber)

He lives in the woods. (Forest)

Woods are fast disappearing from India. (Forests)

Force should be met with force.(Strength)

A force of ten persons attacked him .(Body of armed men)

The Indian Forces are known for their bravery and loyalty. (troops)

**Examples:-**

He caught the old man by the arm.

He was standing with his arms cigarette between his lips.

Pakistan is buying arms from the USA.

Every letter of a language expresses a particular sound.

Please write your telegram in capital letters.

He is a man of letters.

The spectacle was horrible.

My spectacles have broken.

| The Noun is Singular | Its meanings (Only One) | The noun in plural | Its Meaning (two) |
|---|---|---|---|
| Arm | Upper limb (Part of the body) | Arms | i) Weapons<br>ii) Upper limbs |
| Pain | Ache | Pains | i) Troubles<br>ii) Care |
| Manner | Method | Manners | i) Methods<br>ii) Behaviour |
| Custom | Habit | Customs | i) Habits<br>ii) Duties on goods |

| Letter | Alphabet | Letters | i) Alphabet<br>ii) Learning |
|---|---|---|---|
| Spectacle | Sight | Spectacles | i) Sights<br>ii) Eye-glasses |
| Colour | Hue | Colours | i) Hues<br>ii) Flags |
| Minute | A unit of time | Minutes | i) Units of time<br>ii) The proceedings of a meeting |
| Moral | Lesson | Morals | i) Moral Lesson<br>ii) Conduct |

Examples :-

It is shameful for a man to use force with a woman . (Strength)

The forces on the border have been alerted. (Army)

I shall return within three hours. (Come back)

Iron is a useful metal. (Metal)

The judge ordered that the irons of the under trial should be removed. (Chains)

| Nouns in Singular | Their meaning | Nouns in Plural | Their meaning |
|---|---|---|---|
| Advice | Counsel | Advices | Information |
| Air | Atmosphere | Airs | Proud<br>Behaviour |
| Authority | Command | Authorities | Persons in Power |
| Good | Nice | Goods | Property(things) |
| Iron | Metal | Irons | Fetters, chains |
| Force | Strength | Forces | Army |
| Content | Satisfaction | Contents | Things Contained |
| Respects | Regards | Respects | Compliments |
| Work | Job | Works | Composition<br>factories |

**Section - I**

Examples :-

(a) He is my younger brother. ( Brother–a singular Noun )

We are four brothers. (Brothers- sons of same parents)

We are brethren of the same profession .(Brethren- person engaged in the same profession)

(b) The cloth from Ahmedabad is sold everywhere in India. (Cloth- kind of cloth)

A man needs many clothes. (Clothes- garment)

(c) It is not possible to master mathematics without learning formulae that govern it. (Formulae- the rules of mathematics)

A number of formulas were offered. (Modes of Application)

| The Noun Singular | Plural of the Noun I | It's meaning | Plural of the Noun II | It's meaning |
|---|---|---|---|---|
| Brothers | Brothers | Sons of the same parents | Brethren | Members of a community or society |
| Cloth | Cloths | Kind or pieces of a cloth | clothes | Garments |
| Die | Dies | Stamps for Coining | Dice | Small cubes for playing |
| Genius | Geniuses | Talented Persons | Geniuses | Natural abilities or skills |
| Index | Indexes | Table of contents | Indices | Signs of Algebra |
| Shot | Shots | Balls of Iron throw, stroke or hit in certain games. | Shots | Firing from the gun |
| Fish | Fish | Considered collectively | Fishes | Considered separately |
| Penny | Pennies | Separate coins | Pence | A collective noun |

| | Nouns (in pairs) | Their proper use | Examples |
|---|---|---|---|
| 1. | Habit<br>Custom | It belongs to individuals<br>It belongs to a society or country | Mohan is a victim of many bad habits.<br>The Nigerians have strange customs. |
| 2. | House<br>Home | It is a building to live in<br>It is a particular house in which one is living | This house is made of brick and stone.<br>You should go home now. |
| 3. | Cause<br>Reason | 'Cause' produces a result<br>'Reason' explains or justifies a cause | The scientists have not been able to tell the cause of an earthquake .<br>You have good reason for going to the court . |
| 4. | Air<br>Wind | 'Air' is what we breathe<br>'Wind' is what makes the leaves of the trees move. | Water and air sustain life.<br>Everyone longs for a cool wind in summer. |
| 5. | Men<br>People | The plural of man. It is used in ordinary sense<br>persons | Only men of character can make a nation great.<br>Most of the people are superstitious |
| 6. | Man<br>Gentleman | Used in ordinary sense<br>Man of character | The man in the red dress is my cousin<br>Mr. sohanlal is a gentleman |
| 7. | Cost<br>Price | Amount paid by the shopkeeper<br>Amount paid by the customer. | The cost of production in every field have gone up.<br>What is the price of this pen ? |
| 8. | Customer<br>Client | A buyer of goods<br>One who avails oneself of services | Gandhi used to say that a customer is like a God for a shopkeeper.<br>That lawyer has plenty of clients. |

| | | | |
|---|---|---|---|
| 9. | Shade<br>Shadow | A place sheltered from the sun.<br>The shadow of a distinct form or object . | The peepal tree makes a nice shade.<br>The lion saw its shadow in the water and roared at it. |
| 10. | Ground<br>Floor | It is outside the house.<br>It is a part of the room. | The ground was slippery.<br>I saw my books lying on the floor. |

**RULE109**: Consider these errors:

I am an **English teacher**. **[Incorrect]**

He is a **Mathematics teacher**. **[Incorrect]**

All his **family members** were going to the temple. **[Incorrect]**

In the first example, "***English teacher***" denotes "***teacher from England***". In the second case, "***Mathematics teacher***" denotes "***teacher made up of Mathematics***" and in the third example, "***family members***" denotes "***members made up of family***". Thus, all these sentences are not meaningful.

To correct them, we may rewrite these sentences in the following ways:

I am a ***teacher of English***. **[Correct]**

He is a ***teacher of Mathematics***. **[Correct]**

All the ***members of his family*** were going to the temple. **[Correct]**

***NOTE**: *There is no such words "**pick-pocketer, cousin brother, cousin sister**, etc." We use "**pick-pocket**" and "**cousin**" to mean the same.*

**Some important points**

- 'Brother or sister' never follows 'cousin'.
- 'Boarding' is wrong. It should be a 'boarding house'.
- 'Poor people' is wrong. It should be 'the poor'.
- 'Signature' should be used in place of the abbreviation 'sign'
- Food taken once is a meal and not meals. Meals means both lunch and dinner and we cannot take them together.
- 'Alphabet' is generally used in the singular sense. But it can also be used in the plural sense. When different languages are referred to at the same time.
- 'Inning' is no word. The actual word is 'Innings' and is always used in the singular sense.
- 'English teacher' is wrong. It should be 'the teacher of English'.
- 'Agendum' is not used in English. Agenda (Programme-of a meeting) is treated as singular in English.
- 'Mankind' is not used in the plural sense.

- 'Room' in a compartment or on a bench, etc. means 'unoccupied seat'.
- 'Witness' means knowledge brought in proof. 'Evidence' denotes means of proving an unknown or disputed fact.
- 'Family members' is a slang use. The correct form is 'members of the family'.
- 'Goodnight' is a parting salutation, but 'Good evening' is a meeting salutation from evening till midnight.
- 'Wage' when used in the singular form means 'punishment' but when used in the plural sense it means charges for the 'labor'.
- The use of double possessive should be avoided. It is better to write the 'son of my uncle's friend' than 'my uncle's friend's son'.

**RULE110**: Use of 'Possessive Adjectives:

***Possessive adjectives*** refer to words which modify a noun by showing a form of possession or a sense of belonging to a particular person or thing.

Table of Possessive Adjectives and Possessive Pronouns

Examples:-

Everyone should do **one's** duty. [**Incorrect**]

Everyone should do ***his*** duty. [**Correct**]

One should do **his** duty. [**Incorrect**]

One should do ***one's*** duty. [**Correct**]

In the above examples, it is to be noted that words like "***one's***" and "***his***" are not used as possessive pronouns. These are possessive adjectives as they are describing the noun "***duty***" respectively.

We use "***one's***" only when the Subject is "***One***" and if the subject is "***Every, each***, etc.", we use "***his***"or "her" accordingly.

Every girl should do ***her*** duty.

In the above example "***gender***" is clearly mentioned. In such cases, we use "***her***" and when gender is not clear we give the priority to "***his***".

**RULE111**: Use of "***fewer***" and "***less***":

"***Fewer***" is used with Countable subjects.

"***Less***" is used with Uncountable subjects.

Examples:-

No **less** than *50 students* completed the work. [**Incorrect**]

No ***fewer*** than *50 students* completed the work. [**Correct**]

There is no **fewer** than *five liters of water* in the vessel. [**Incorrect**]

There is no ***less*** than *five liters of water* in the vessel. [**Correct**]

**RULE112**: Difference between "***Elder***" and "***Older***":

## Section - I

In a sentence, "*elder*" is used for someone who is in our family.

"*older*" is used for someone who is not in family.

Examples:-

A friend of mine in my company is **elder** than me. **[Incorrect]**

A friend of mine in my company is ***older*** than me. **[Correct]**

The ***elder*** son of King John, Henry was nine when his father died. **[Correct]**

***NOTE**: *Difference between "Later" and "Latter"*:

*We use **later** when referring to time while we use **latter** when referring to the second of two persons or things mentioned previously.*

Examples:-

Bran said that he would call me ***later***.

There are two kinds of worries: those you can do something about and those you can't. Don't spend any time on the ***latter***.

Difference between "***Farther***" and "***Further***":-

In a sentence, "***farther***" is used for physical distances object . "***further***" is used for metaphorical ditances or degrees or extents.

Examples:-

Villagers saw a temple on the ***farther*** side of the river.

Suman has appealed in the high court for ***further*** judgement.

Difference between "***Nearest***" and "***Next***":-

In a sentence, "***Nearest***" is used for space or distance ."***Next***" is used for in order or position

Examples :-

Delhi railway station is ***nearest*** to my house.

Mr. Gupta lives in the ***next*** house.

Difference between "***Latest***" and "***Last***":-

In a sentence, "***Latest***" is used as a word opposite to Earliest and means most recent or new. It denotes time . "***Last***" is a word opposite to first and it denotes order or position.

Examples:-

She is the **last** girl to stay in the office

What is the ***latest*** news today ?

Difference between "***Less***" and "***Fewer***":-

In a sentence, "***Less*** " is used to denote quantity and is used as Singular Uncountable Noun ."***Fewer***" is used to denote number and is used as Plural Countable Noun.

Examples:-

He has **less** money than I . **[Correct]**

He has **fewer** money than I . **[Incorrect]**

**Money is an Uncountable noun. Notes and coins are countable nouns.**

Therefore, we can write.

He has **fewer** notes than 1.

She has **fewer** wins than 1.

Difference between "***Less***" and "***Lesser***":-

In a sentence, "***Less***" is used to denote something smaller in size, measurement, duration, number etc.

***"Lesser"*** is used to denote something not so great as the other one.

Examples:-

Maths is less difficult than Enlgish.

She agreed to plead guilty to a **lesser** charge.

**RULE113**: While making comparisons, it is necessary to look at the things being compared:

Examples:-

The ***weather of Delhi*** is far better than **Mumbai**. **[Incorrect]**

The ***weather of Delhi*** is far better than ***the weather of Mumbai***. **[Correct]**

The ***weather of Delhi*** is far better than ***that of Mumbai***. **[Correct]**

In the above examples, the first sentence is incorrect as we are comparing "***the weather of Delhi***" with "***Mumbai***". The comparisons should be made on common grounds. In this case, it should be compared with "***the weather of Mumbai***" instead of "***Mumbai***".

The ***apples of Shimla*** are tastier than **Ooty**. **[Incorrect]**

The ***apples of Shimla*** are tastier than ***those of Ooty***. **[Correct]**

**RULE114**: The words "***One of the, either of, neither of, and each of***" are always followed by plural nouns.

Examples:-

*One of the* **student** was selected to visit NASA. **[Incorrect]**

*One of the* ***students*** was selected to visit NASA. **[Correct]**

A person can turn on *either of* the **light bulb**. **[Incorrect]**

A person can turn on *either of* the ***light bulbs***. **[Correct]**

Do you go to *each of* the ***meetings***? **[Correct]**

**RULE115**: When "***but, except, or between***" are used as a preposition, it must be followed by the objective case of pronoun (***me, him, her, you, us, them, etc***.) and not the subjective case (***I, he, she, you, we, they, etc***.) .

Examples:-

There is friendship *between* ***you*** and **I**. **[Incorrect]**

There is friendship *between* ***you*** and ***me***. **[Correct]**

All *but* **he** are going to the party. **[Incorrect]**

## Section - I

All *but* ***him*** are going to the party. **[Correct]**

*Let* **he** do the work. **[Incorrect]**// Let is a verb and we use an objective case after a verb

*Let* ***him*** do the work. **[Correct]**

All *except* ***him*** are going to the party. **[Correct]**

**RULE116**: Whenever we use the ***pseudo subject*** in a sentence, the pronoun following the pseudo subject should always be in a subjective case and not in an objective case.

Examples:-

*It* is **him** who should be blamed. **[Incorrect]**

*It* is ***he*** who should be blamed. **[Correct]**

***NOTE**: *Pseudo subject takes the place of subject but cannot perform the role of subject. A subject is the combination of* ***syntax*** *(study of structure) and* ***semantics*** *(study of meaning) . Pseudo subject can only fulfill the requirement of syntax. As Pseudo subject semantically fails, it is called Pseudo subject.*

Examples:-

*It* is a lovely day. **[Correct]**

It is us who have defeated the champion. [In**correct**]

It is we who have defeated the champion . **[Correct]**

It is me who am guilty. [Inc**orrect**]

It is I who am guilty. **[Correct]**

Here the subject is day. So, ***'it'*** which works as an introductory subject, is a Pseudo subject.

**RULE117**: When we use the word "***such***" as a determiner, we will only use "***as***" as its connector.

***'Else'*** should be followed by ***'but'***

***'Other'*** and 'otherwise' is followed by ***'than'***

He is ***such*** a person **that** you mentioned. **[Incorrect]**

He is ***such*** a person ***as*** you mentioned. **[Correct]**

***Such*** a book ***as*** this is referred by a teacher. **[Correct]**

They want nothing ***else but*** to have their honor and dignity . [Correct]

It was nothing ***else but*** sheer madness [Correct]

**RULE118**: While showing possession with a plural noun, we should make sure that we do not put an apostrophe ('*s*) in such a way that it creates a hissing sound. In English, words creating a hissing sound are avoided.

Exception:- **"else's"** is grammatically correct in spite of the hissing sound.

Examples:-

Government **girls's** school. **[Incorrect]**

Government ***girls'*** school. **[Correct]**

In the first case, "***girls's***" is incorrect as it creates the hissing sound. It should be rewritten as "***girls'***".

Some more examples:-

***Jesus'*** sake

***For peace'*** sake

***Residents'*** Welfare Association

***Pythagoras***' theorem

For ***goodness'*** sake

For ***justice'*** sake

**RULE119**: We never use an apostrophe *('s)* with pronouns to show possession. It is only used with nouns.

Examples:-

**Your's** friendly. [**Incorrect**]

***Yours*** friendly. [**Correct**]

The kids are ***yours*** and ***mine***. [**Correct**]

We shall finally have what is rightfully ***ours***. [**Correct**]

The ring is ***hers***. [**Correct**]

The bag is ***theirs***. [**Correct**]

Their mother gets along well with ***yours***. [**Correct**]

**RULE120**: There are certain words which are never followed by Noun. These are "***afraid, asleep, due, ready, unable, alike, aware, glad, sorry, well, alone, ill, sure, worth.*** etc."

Examples:-

We were ***unable*** to contact him at the time.

The army is said to be ***ready*** for action.

I am ***glad*** to know the parcel arrived safely.

He likes being ***alone*** in the house.

Your painting has come out really ***well***.

He has proved his ***worth*** to the team.

# Section – II

## Practice Set – 01

Directions (01-50) : **Read each sentence to find out whether there is any grammatical or idiomatic error in it. The error, if any, will be in one part of the sentence. The number of that part is the answer. If there is 'No error', the answer is (e) . (Ignore errors of punctuation, if any.)**

Q1. Stressing the need to have anti-counterfeiting solutions (a) /along with adequate awareness and monitoring, the industrial body ASPA has claimed that (b) /counterfeit products across various sectors in India (c) /are causing losses to the tune of over Rs 1 lakh crore each year. (d) / No error (e)

Q2. These paintings may (a) /look like the real thing, (b) /but every one of (c) /them is fake. (d) / No error (e)

Q3. She has each reason (a) /to be unhappy (b) / after losing her job (c) /and her home. (d) / No error (e)

Q4. Will you join me (a) /in wishing (b) /the bride and groom (c) /each happiness? (d) / No error (e)

Q5. Amazon is running an awesome sale (a) / right now that saves (b) /you $15 on every of the two (c) /newest Pokemon games for Nintendo Switch. (d) / No error. (e)

Q6. The teams change ends (a) /at half-time so that (b) /neither side have an (c) /unfair advantage. (d) / No error. (e)

Q7. Traditional ways of classification (a) /get defied due to the fact (b) /that several living organisms (c) /are not both animals and plants. (d) / No error. (e)

Q8. His words to the press (a) /were deliberately equivocal–he didn't (b) /deny the reports but (c) /neither did he confirm them. (d) / No error (e)

Q9. The desperate scrabble for your ticket while running (a) /for a train could be a thing of the past, a manufacturer has claimed, (b) /with sensors potentially replacing ticket barriers what (c) /detect when passengers board trains. (d) / No error. (e)

Q10. They are in a position to forecast (a) /critical economic variables like inflation, (b) /currency values and interest rates (c) /that influences the performance of the stock markets. (d) / No error. (e)

Q11. Hardly the match (a) / started (b) /when the game (c) /was interrupted. (d) / No error (e)

Q12. No sooner had (a) /I started (b) /mowing the lawn, (c) /when it started raining. (d) / No error (e)

Q13. No sooner did (a) /I walk through (b) /the door than (c) /the phone rings. (d) / No error. (e)

Q14. Seldom do we (a) /receive any (b) /apology when mistakes (c) /are made. (d) / No error. (e)

Q15. Barely they had (a) /finished the match (b) /when the rain (c) /started to fall. (d) / No error. (e)

Q16. This is one of the (a) / place (b) /in the world where (c) /the plant is found. (d) / No error. (e)

Q17. One of the richest people in Hong Kong (a) /have lost $1 billion over the course of the 10-week protests, (b) /and now he is joining the chorus of (c) /wealthy citizens calling for the protests to end. (d) / No error. (e)

Q18. After reaching Mecca, where they spent (a) /the night in prayer and supplication, (b) / thousands of hundreds of pilgrims clad in white seamless cloth (c) /headed towards Arafat following Fajr prayers Saturday morning. (d) / No error. (e)

## Section – II

Q19. Chief Minister B S Yediyurappa has announced (a) /five lakhs rupees compensation (b) /for the family of those (c) /killed in the flood and rain. (d) / No error. (e)

Q20. The government has released 100 crore rupee (a) /under the State Disaster Response Fund (b) /to 14 districts, of which Rs 25 crores (c) /will go to the worst-hit Belagavi. (d) /No error. (e)

Q21. Robert Burns is Scotland's most (a) / venerated poet as he is (b) /considered more famous (c) /than all poets. (d) / No error. (e)

Q22. Special attention is given (a) /to vibratory projects (b) /which have been their (c) /main focus since 1993. (d) / No error. (e)

Q23. Alfredo left the house (a) /at six this morning, (b) /and we have not (c) /seen him since then. (d) / No error. (e)

Q24. Mr. Black has been (a) /a client of (b) /this firm since (c) /many years. (d) / No error. (e)

Q25. This is Djokovic's first tournament (a) / after saving two championship points (b) /in the Wimbledon final (c) /and now en route to claiming his fifth title at The Championships. (d) /No error. (e)

Q26. Kashmir celebrates its first (a) /Independence Day after (b) /the scrapping of Article 370 (c) / amid heavy security. (d) / No error. (e)

Q27. She did well to (a) /find the way, considering that (b) /she was been (c) /there only once before. (d) / No error. (e)

Q28. Mary rang John's doorbell (a) /at 8:15 yesterday (b) /but John already (c) /left the house. (d) / No error. (e)

Q29. I had done (a) /my work when (b) /Harish had come (c) /to meet me. (d) / No error. (e)

Q30. When he graduated, (a) /he had (b) /been in London (c) / from six years. (d) / No error. (e)

Q31. It snowed (a) /in the night, (b) /so the bus (c) /did not arrive. (d) / No error. (e)

Q32. Jorge is in favour (a) /of the candidate (b) / being (c) /interviewed Friday. (d) / No error. (e)

Q33. Nataraj objected (a) /to me borrowing (b) / his (c) /hockey stick. (d) / No error. (e)

Q34. Doing this now (a) /will save (b) /him having to do it next week (c) /when he will be much busier. (d) / No error. (e)

Q35. This job entails (a) /yours making (b) / several trips (c) /overseas each year. (d) / No error. (e)

Q36. She had not (a) /anticipated (b) /their arriving (c) /so early. (d) / No error. (e)

Q37. Many borrowers now (a) /find themself (b) /caught in a precarious (c) /financial position. (d) /No error. (e)

Q38. None of the women availed them (a) /of respite care as they felt that the family (b) /was best equipped to deal (c) /with the caring needs of its members. (d) / No error. (e)

Q39. Automatically to debar (a) /availing us of (b) /such services seems to me (c) /to be an unnecessary sacrifice. (d) / No error. (e)

Q40. I'm ready to go (a) /home now but I do not (b) /want to drag you away (c) /if you are enjoying. (d) / No error. (e)

Q41. He has reconciled (a) /himself to the loss (b) /of the election (c) /and is moving on. (d) / No error. (e)

Q42. She must reconcile (a) /to the fact that she must (b) /do some work if she (c) /wants to pass her exams. (d) / No error. (e)

Q43. You cannot (a) /choose to absent (b) /yours

from (c) / work on a whim. (d) / No error. (e)

Q44. The majority of the lighter-men have (a) / accepted the work in loyal observance (b) /of the decision which was taken last night (c) /but an unknown number absented themselves. (d) / No error. (e)

Q45. He is not one of those (a) /officers who follows (b) /orders blindly (c) /and unthinkingly. (d) / No error. (e)

Q46. The only one of the students (a) /who is American (b) /were late (c) / for the assembly. (d) / No error. (e)

Q47. If I knew (a) /about the exam, (b) /I would have paid (c) /more attention in class. (d) / No error. (e)

Q48. We could have had (a) /a longer holiday, (b) /if we had not spend (c) /so much money on the house. (d) / No error. (e)

Q49. If I had found (a) /her address, (b) /I would have sent (c) /her an invitation. (d) / No error. (e)

Q50. I would have travelled (a) /around the world (b) /if I won (c) /the lottery. (d) / No error. (e)

Section - II

## Solutions (Practice Set - 01)

S1. Ans. (d)

Sol. "***each***" should be replaced by "***every***" as we use "***every***" to say how often something happens (every week, every month, every year, etc.)

S2. Ans. (e)

Sol. No error

S3. Ans. (a)

Sol. "***each***" should be replaced by "***every***" as "***every***" is used with abstract nouns.

S4. Ans. (d)

Sol. "***each***" should be replaced by "***every***" as "***every***" is used with abstract nouns.

S5. Ans. (c)

Sol. "***every***" should be replaced by "***each***" as we cannot use "***every***" for exactly two things.

S6. Ans. (c)

Sol. "***have***" should be replaced by "***has***" as "***neither***" is always followed by a singular verb.

S7. Ans. (d)

Sol. "*are not both animals and plants*" should be replaced by "***are neither animals nor plants***". "***Both***" and "***not***" are not used together.

S8. Ans. (e)

Sol. No error.

S9. Ans. (c)

Sol. "***what***" should be replaced by the correct relative pronoun "***which***" as we use "which" for the things in general (non-living things) .

S10. Ans. (d)

Sol. The verb "***influences***" should be replaced by its plural "***influence***" as the subject of the verb, prior to the relative pronoun "***that***", is in plural form ("***economic variables***") .

S11. Ans. (a)

Sol. A helping verb "***had***" should be used before the subject "***match***" as it is the case of Partial inversion. Hardly is followed by ***had/did***.

S12. Ans. (d)

Sol. Replace "***when***" with "***than***" as "***No sooner***" is always followed by "***than***" and not "***when***".

S13. Ans. (d)

Sol. The present form of the verb "***rings***" should be replaced by its past form "***rang***" as the helping verb "***did***" reflects that the sentence should follow the same tense.

S14. Ans. (e)

Sol. No error.

S15. Ans. (a)

Sol. The helping verb "***had***" should be placed before the subject "***they***" as it is the case of Partial inversion.

S16. Ans. (b)

Sol. The word "***place***" should be replaced by its plural "***places***" as the noun following the phrase "***one of the***" is always a plural noun.

S17. Ans. (b)

Sol. "***have***" should be replaced by "***has***" as "***One of the richest people***" acts as the subject of the verb which should be singular.

S18. Ans. (c)

Sol. "***thousands of hundreds***" should be replaced by "***hundreds of thousands***" as when there is more than one unit in a sentence, units are always arranged in ascending order.

S19. Ans. (b)

Sol. The plural "***lakhs***" should be replaced by "***lakh***" as in the combination of "**Number + Unit + Noun**" we always use the singular form of the

Unit.

S20. Ans. (a)

Sol. "***rupee***" should be replaced by "***rupees***".

S21. Ans. (d)

Sol. "***all poets***" should be replaced by "***any other poets***".

S22. Ans. (e)

Sol. No error.

S23. Ans. (e)

Sol. No error.

S24. Ans. (c)

Sol. "***since***" should be replaced by "***for***" as there is no specified time.

S25. Ans. (e)

Sol. No error

S26. Ans. (e)

Sol. No error.

S27. Ans. (c)

Sol. "***was***" should be replaced by "***had***" as the event occurred earlier than the first one.

S28. Ans. (d)

Sol. Put "***had***" before "***already***" as the event has already occurred.

S29. Ans. (c)

Sol. "***had come***" should be replaced by Simple Past "***came***" as the event occurred after the first one. When two actions occurred in past, the action which happened earlier is denoted by using ***Past Perfect Tense*** and the action which happened later is denoted by using ***Simple Past Tense***.

S30. Ans. (d)

Sol. "***from***" should be replaced by "***for***" as the sentence talks about a period of time.

S31. Ans. (a)

Sol. "***snowed***" should be replaced by Past Perfect "***had snowed***" as the action happened first. When two actions occurred in past, the action which happened earlier is denoted by using ***Past Perfect Tense*** and the action which happened later is denoted by using ***Simple Past Tense***.

S32. Ans. (b)

Sol. "***candidate***" should be replaced by its possessive "***candidates'***" as we use a possessive case before a Gerund.

S33. Ans. (b)

Sol. "***me***" should be replaced by "***my***" as we use a possessive adjective before a Gerund.

S34. Ans. (c)

Sol. "***him***" should be replaced by "***his***" as we use a possessive adjective before a Gerund.

S35. Ans. (b)

Sol. "***yours***" should be replaced by "***your***" as we use a possessive adjective before a Gerund.

S36. Ans. (e)

Sol. No error.

S37. Ans. (b)

Sol. "***themself***" should be replaced by "***themselves***", as "***themselves***" is the correct form of plural reflexive pronoun.

S38. Ans. (a)

Sol. "***them***" should be replaced by "***themselves***" as the word "***avail***" is followed by a reflexive pronoun as the object.

S39. Ans. (b)

Sol. "***us***" should be replaced by "***ourselves***" as the word "***avail***" is followed by a reflexive pronoun as the object.

S40. Ans. (d)

**Section - II**

Sol. Put "***yourself***" after "***enjoying***" as the word "***enjoy***" is always followed by an object.

S41. Ans. (e)

Sol. No error.

S42. Ans. (a)

Sol. The word "***reconcile***" should be followed by an object. Put "***herself***" after "***reconcile***" to make the statement grammatically correct.

S43. Ans. (c)

Sol. "***yours***" should be replaced by "***yourself***" as the word "***absent***" should be followed by an object.

S44. Ans. (e)

Sol. No error.

S45. Ans. (b)

Sol. The singular verb "***follow***" should be replaced by its plural "***follows***" as the focus is on the set of officers which is the subject of the verb. ***"One of the + PLURAL NOUN + WHO/THAT + Singular verb etc."***

S46. Ans. (c)

Sol. The plural verb "***were***" should be replaced by "***was***" as the sentence following the form, "***The only one of the + PLURAL NOUN + WHO/THAT etc.***", requires a SINGULAR verb.

S47. Ans. (a)

Sol. "***knew***" should be replaced by the Past Perfect "***had known***" as the condition is not possible to fulfill now (i.e. too late) and thus it requires a Past Perfect tense with if-clause. [Refer rule number – 04]

S48. Ans. (c)

Sol. The word "***spend***" should be replaced by "***spent***" as we require a past participle form of the verb with the helping verb "***had***".

S49. Ans. (e)

Sol. No error.

S50. Ans. (a)

Sol. "***would have travelled***" should be replaced by "***would travel***" as the condition in theory is possible to fulfill and in that case we use "***would + V1***" in the main clause.

## Practice Set – 02

Directions (01-50) : **Read each sentence to find out whether there is any grammatical or idiomatic error in it. The error, if any, will be in one part of the sentence. The number of that part is the answer. If there is 'No error', the answer is (e) . (Ignore errors of punctuation, if any.)**

Q1. As news of police violence spread, (a) / Patel community members, returning to villages (b) / and towns from the rally, (c) /set fire government property. (d) / No error. (e)

Q2. The only silver line to this recent crisis (a) / over reservation was her successful handling (b) / of talks with other OBC groups (c) /who make up 27 per cent of the state's population. (d) / No error. (e)

Q3. A lot of real estate companies may come up (a) / with tempting offers and discounts but buyers should (b) / always keep their eyes open and must check (c) / whether all approvals are in place or not. (d) / No error (e)

Q4. Before investing, you should look after the (a) / overall business dynamics of the company (b) / along with efficient management and (c) / good corporate governance. (d) / No error. (e)

Q5. Considering that a large part of the population in India (a) / does not have access to banking services, (b) / payments banks are expected to reach far-flung areas (c) / extending the umbrella of financial inclusion to everyone. (d) / No error. (e)

Q6. My teacher used to check that we were (a) / on the right track and if any mistake occurred, (b) / he would help us to analyse (c) / and resolve the issues. (d) / No error. (e)

Q7. He always said success is something to be celebrated, (a) / but he also believed that failure is something (b) / that you must concentrate all (c) / your energies on resolving. (d) / No error. (e)

Q8. The centre accepted the report of a judicial commission (a) / that indicted former chief minister (b) / and six of his ministerial colleagues against corruption, (c) / favouritism, nepotism and administrative impropriety. (d) / No error. (e)

Q9. Companies like Infosys are moving fast (a) / on automation to ensure differentiation at a time (b) / where the technology industry and business models (c) / are undergoing rapid changes. (d) / No error. (e)

Q10. With a sharp rise in the number of large-scale financial crimes, (a) / the CBI and Indian Institute of Management have initiated (b) / a first-of-its-kind course to train sleuths (c) / from CBI to probe financial frauds. (d) / No error. (e)

Q11. A year has passed by (a) / since he went to Delhi (b) /and we have not hear (c) /any news of him. (d) /No error (e)

Q12. From the last one month (a) / each of us (b) / have been working (c) / on the same project. (d) / No error. (e)

Q13. When I receive (a) / the letter, the date (b) / for the interview (c) / was already over. (d) / No error. (e)

Q14. We had (a) / helped him (b) / if he had (c) / requested us earlier. (d) / No error. (e)

Q15. We have observed that (a) / many good programmes (b) / suffer of shortage (c) / of funds and other resources. (d) / No error. (e)

Q16. Jagdish met me yesterday (a) / but he did not tell me (b) / that he has (c) / resigned from the factory. (d) / No error. (e)

Q17. It is unfortunate (a) / but still a reality (b) / that poverty and development (c) / goes hand in hand (d) / No error. (e)

Q18. I know whom (a) / this job should be (b) / entrusted to (c) / for smooth handing. (d) / No error. (e)

Q19. The Supervisor noticed that (a) / one of the employees were (b) / involved in (c) / unfair activities outside the office. (d) / No error. (e)

Q20. How well a person (a) / completes his own (b) / assignments depend (c) / upon his skill (d) / No error. (e)

## Section - II

Q21. He is so lazy (a) / that he takes a (b) / large number of time (c) / to complete such a small piece of work. (d) / No error. (e)

Q22. Dileep has spend (a) / six years in Calcutta (b) / but still he does not know (c) / many parts of the city. (d) / No error. (e)

Q23. Last week when (a) / I reach Viru's house (b) / he had already (c) / left for Mumbai. (d) / No error. (e)

Q24. The number of foreign tourists (a) / visiting India are increasing (b) / day by day during (c) / this tourist season. (d) / No error. (e)

Q25. After 50 years of Independence (a) / many social problems (b) / still remaining (c) / to be solved in India. (d) / No error. (e)

Q26. He does not (a) / fail to came (b) / to my help (c) / whenever I am in trouble. (d) / No error. (e)

Q27. My parents (a) / prevented me (b) / in accepting (c) / the invitation. (d) / No error. (e)

Q28. He climbed (a) / from the ladder (b) / to reach (c) / the ceiling. (d) / No error. (e)

Q29. My sister (a) / insists (b) / that she should be allowed to (c) / remain unmarried (d) / No error. (e)

Q30. In another departure from the (a) / post-Deng practice, no potential successor (b) / to Mr. Xi has been included (c) / in the new line-up of the PBSC.(d) / No error (e) .

Q31. They talked for a while (a) / and then they will (b) / continue to play the game (c) / till tomorrow morning. (d) / No error. (e)

Q32.Some skills are (a) / more difficult than others (b) / so it takes a longer time (c) / to master them. (d) / No error. (e)

Q33. The guide told us (a) / that where the island was (b) / and went on (c) / narrating its history. (d) / No error. (e)

Q34. Even after hearing him (a) / for a fairly long time (b) / we failed to understand (c) / that he was harping on. (d) / No error. (e)

Q35. Prabhakar arrives in the office (a) / as fresh as he starts (b) / from home even though (c) / he commutes a long distance. (d) / No error. (e)

Q36. Hardly has she finish (a) / the typing when the (b) / Manager entered the room (c) / with some more work. (d) / No error. (e)

Q37. Truly speaking (a) / there was little merit (b) / in the complaint sent in (c) / by the employee. (d) / No error. (e)

Q38. Ordinarily, when in difficulty (a) / Renuka prefers keeping her counsel (b) / than running about (c) / taking advice. (d) / No error. (e)

Q39. Cricket has become so (a) / popular that even elderly (b) / people are discussing (c) / the game when they meet. (d) / No error. (e)

Q40. Nitin gets so engrossed (a) / in his work that (b) / he does not often hear (c) / the phone ring. (d) / No error. (e)

Q41. Within an hour's (a) / journey we (b) / will approach near (c) / Patna. (d) / No Error. (e)

Q42. We had swam (a) / across the river (b) / before (c) / the sun set. (d) / No Error. (e)

Q43. Neither Rakesh(a) / nor (b) / I are leaving (c) / for Hyderabad. (d) / No Error (e)

Q44. Death (a) / is (b) / preferable (c) / than life. (d) / No Error (e)

Q45. If (a) / it snowed tomorrow (b) / we'll go (c) / skating. (d) / No Error (e)

Q46. Neither the size (a) / nor the colour(b) / of the gloves (c) / were right. (d) / No Error (e)

Q47. Everyone of (a) / the staffs present here (b) / has given a day's pay (c) / as their contribution to the fund. (d) / No Error. (e)

Q48. The gentleman (a) / together with his (b) / wife and daughter (c) / were drowned. (d) / No Error (e)

Q49. He had looked upon me (a) / level-eyed for (b) / a few moments (c) / before he spoke. (d) / No Error (e)

Q50. The bus was (a) / hired by (b) / the ladies (c) / for its picnic. (d) / No Error (e)

## Solutions (Practice Set - 02)

S1. Ans. (d)

Sol. Replace with 'set government property on fire'

S2. Ans. (a)

Sol. Replace 'line' with 'lining'. ***Silver lining*** means a consoling or hopeful prospect.

S3. Ans. (e)

Sol. No error

S4. Ans. (a)

Sol. Replace 'after' with 'at'.

***Look after*** means to take care of.

***Look at*** means to think about a situation or subject carefully, especially in order to make a decision.

S5. Ans. (e)

Sol. No error

S6. Ans. (c)

Sol. Delete 'to'

S7. Ans. (e)

Sol. No error. A fact is always constructed in Simple Present tense.

S8. Ans. (c)

Sol. Replace 'against' with 'for'

S9. Ans. (c)

Sol. Replace 'where' with 'when' as we are talking of time, not place.

S10. Ans. (e)

Sol. No error

S11. Ans. (c)

Sol. Replace hear by heard.

S12. Ans. (c)

Sol. "Has" will be used in place of "have"

Ex. He has been living with me for the last one year.

S13. Ans. (a)

Sol. 'received' will be used in place of 'receive' as the sentence is in past tense as is indicated by 'already over'.

S14. Ans. (a)

Sol. 'we would have' will be used in place of 'we had' as for unreal situation of past 'Subject + would/ could/ might/ should + have + V3' is used.

Ex. I would have helped you if you had come earlier.

S15. Ans. (c)

Sol. 'from' will be used in place of 'of' as preposition 'from' is used after 'suffer'.

Ex. He is suffering from fever.

S16. Ans. (c)

Sol. 'had' will be used in place of 'has' as the sentence is in past tense. If the principal clause is in past tense, subordinate clause will also be in past. [Sequence of Tenses]

S17. Ans. (d)

Sol. 'go' will be used in place of 'goes' as the subject of 'that- clause' is plural, therefore plural verb is used.

Ex. Oil and water do not mix

S18. Ans. (e)

Sol. The Sentence is grammatically correct.

S19. Ans. (b)

Sol. 'was' will be used in place of 'were' as the subject of 'that- clause' is 'one'.

Ex. One of these girls is very beautiful.

S20. Ans. (c)

Sol. 'depends' will be used in place of 'depend' as the subject of the sentence is singular.

S21. Ans. (c)

Sol. Use 'lot' in place of 'large number' as 'a large number of/ a number of' is not used with uncountable noun 'time'.

S22. Ans. (a)

**Section - II**

Sol. 'spent' will be used in place of 'spend' as 'have/ has/ had/ having+ V3' is used.

S23. Ans. (b)

Sol. 'reached' will be used in place of 'reach' as the sentence is in past tense.

S24. Ans. (b)

Sol. 'is' will be used in place of 'are' as singular verb is used after 'The number of'.

S25. Ans. (c)

Sol. 'still remain' will be used in place of 'still remaining' as verbs that convey state are not used in continuous form.

S26. Ans. (b)

Sol. Use 'come' in place of 'came' as V1 is used after Infinitive (to) . [*to + V1*]

Ex. He does not want to stay here.

She never tries to come here.

S27. Ans. (c)

Sol. 'from' will be used in place of 'in' as preposition 'from' is used after 'prevent, prohibit, abstain, refrain, escape, absent'

Ex. He prevented me from going there.

S28. Ans. (b)

Sol. 'up' will be used in place of 'from' as after 'climb', preposition 'up/ down' is used.

Ex. He climbed up a tree.

S29. Ans. (e)

Sol. The sentence is grammatically correct.

S30. Ans. (e)

Sol. The sentence is grammatically correct.

S31. Ans. (a)

Sol. 'will talk' will be used in place of 'talked' as the sentence contains two actions of future.

Ex. He will go to his sister and then he will go to his friend.

S32. Ans. (e)

Sol. The sentence is grammatically correct.

S33. Ans. (b)

Sol. The use of 'that' before 'where' is superfluous.

S34. Ans. (d)

Sol. Use 'what' in place of 'that'. 'Harping on' means talk or write persistently and tediously on.

S35. Ans. (e)

Sol. The sentence is grammatically correct.

S36. Ans. (a)

Sol. 'had she finished' will be used in place of 'has she finished' as when 'hardly... when' is used in a sentence, then in 'hardly' clause past perfect tense is used and in clause having 'when', simple past tense is used.

Ex. Hardly had she reached the station when the train started.

S37. Ans. (e)

Sol. The sentence is grammatically correct.

S38. Ans. (c)

Sol. 'to' will be used in place of 'than' as if 'prefer' is used in the sentence for comparing two nouns or noun equivalents then preposition 'to' is used after 'prefer'.

Ex. He prefers milk to tea.

S39. Ans. (c)

Sol. Use 'discuss' in place of 'are discussing' as to tell the habit of present, simple present tense is used.

Ex. When the boss comes, everybody stands up.

S40. Ans. (e)

Sol. The sentence is grammatically correct.

S41. Ans. (c)

Sol. The Use of 'near' is superfluous as 'approach' itself means 'to come close'.

S42. Ans. (a)

Sol. 'swum' will be used in place of 'swam' as the past form of 'swim' is 'swam' and its past participle form is 'swum' and moreover after have/ has/ had/ having, past participle form of verb means V3 is used.

S43. Ans. (c)

Sol. Use 'am' in place of 'are' as with 'neither... nor', 'either... or', 'not only... but also', the verb is used according to the subject close to it.

Ex. Either you or he has committed a blunder.

S44. Ans. (d)

Sol. 'to' will be used in place of 'than' as after 'preferable, senior, junior, superior, inferior, prior, anterior, posterior', 'to' is used.

Ex. She is junior to you.

This is preferable to that.

S45. Ans. (b)

Sol. 'snows' is the correct use instead of 'snowed'. There are two incidents of future (tomorrow, we'll go) hence simple present tense should be used with ***If-clause***.

Ex. If it rains, we shall not go out.

S46. Ans. (d)

Sol. 'was' will be used in place of 'were' as the subject of the sentence 'the colour' is singular.

And in case of "Neither...nor" the verb is according to the nearest subject.

S47. Ans. (d)

Sol. Use 'his' in place of 'their' as after 'everyone, everybody, anyone, anybody', 'his' is used as possessive form.

Ex. Everybody should do his duty.

S48. Ans. (d)

Sol. Use 'was' in place of 'were' because if two subjects get connected 'with, along with, together with', then verb is used according to the first subject.

Ex. Mohini together with her parents is...

S49. Ans. (a)

Sol. 'at' is the correct use in place of 'upon' as 'look at' means to glance or gaze in a manner specified.

S50. Ans. (d)

Sol. 'a' will be used in place of 'its'.

## Practice Set – 03

Directions (01-50) : **Read each sentence to find out whether there is any grammatical or idiomatic error in it. The error, if any, will be in one part of the sentence. The number of that part is the answer. If there is 'No error', the answer is (e) . (Ignore errors of punctuation, if any.)**

Q1. He told me (a) / that he wrote a letter (b) / to his superior (c) / for a certain reason. (d) / No Error (e)

Q2. He reminded me (a) / that he has (b) / often told me not to (c) / play with fire.(d) / No Error (e)

Q3. I would have asked (a) / you for dinner (b) / if I had known (c) / that you are staying here tonight. (d) / No Error (e)

Q4. He educated not only (a) / his nephew but also (b) / set him up (c) / in business. (d) / No Error (e)

Q5. As soon as the peon rings (a) / the first bell (b) / then all the students assemble (c) / in the playground for prayer. (d) / No Error (e)

Q6. If the tourists (a) / had come here, (b) / I would certainly have (c) / taken them around. (d) / No Error (e)

Q7. The teacher remarked (a) / very angrily yesterday (b) / that the boys have (c) / done it very badly. (d) / No Error (e)

Q8. Although it was summer, (a) / the weather at the (b) / hill station is (c) / quite pleasant.(d) / No Error (e)

Q9. The lawyer asked me (a) / where I had (b) / kept my clothes (c) / before taking a dip in the river. (d) / No Error (e)

Q10. The plays of Shakespeare (a) / are not only studied (b) / in European countries (c) / but also in the oriental countries. (d) / No Error (e)

Q11. (a) The devastating experiences / (b) of many wars taught some countries / (c) the necessary of pursuing peace / (d) at the expense of nationalist egos. /(e) No error

Q12. (a) The former superstar /(b) recently visit an orphanage, /(c) fueling speculation that / (d) she is planning to adopt a child. / (e) No error

Q13. (a) According to a new study / (b) taking steps to remain healthy and young / (c) may help delay / (d) the onset of Alzheimer's disease. / (e) No error

Q14. (a) Sediment deposit along the coast / (b) may be the primary reason for / (c) the change in conditions, / (d) but a lot more remains to be understand. / (e) No error

Q15. (a) A committee will be set up / (b) to explore the pros and cons by / a common free structure, and will / (c) take a final decision on it within a week. / (e) No error

Q16. (a) The infection which causes / (b) gums to bleed and teeth to fall out / (c) results from the build-up of / (d) a particular bacteria that is common to most mouths. / (e) No error

Q17. (a) More than half the food products / (b) targeted at babies and toddlers have / (c) a high sugar content and are / (d) excessive sweet. / (e) No error

Q18. (a) After forty years of trying to / (b) understand why asbestos causes cancer, / (c) researchers have finally / (d) unraveled the mystery. /(e) No error

Q19. (a) A property dealer was / (b) shoot dead by four unidentified jacket-clad men / (c) while taking a morning walk / (d) in the park. / (e) No error

Q20. (a) The protestors went on a rampaging / (b) and set ablaze three shops / (c) resulting in injuries to thirty people / (d) including women and children. / (e) No error

Q21. If you do not (a) / submit the report (b) / in the next two days (c) / all of us will be punished. (d) / No Error. (e)

Q22. These days Ashok along with (a) / his friends does not go (b) / to a walk (c) / in the morning. (d) / No Error. (e)

Q23. I have been visiting your office (a) / since last several years (b) / but have never met (c) / such a hopeless clerk as this. (d) / No Error. (e)

Q24. As there was no time (a) / the remaining items (b) / were deferred into (c) / the next meeting. (d) / No Error. (e)

Q25. We demonstrated (a) / to them how (b) / we were prepared (c) / the artistic pattern. (d) / No Error. (e)

Q26. She had offered (a) / a temporary assignment but (b) / she turned it down saying that (c) / she would accept only a permanent one. (d) / No Error. (e)

Q27. All the parties (a) / whose presidents were asked to resign (b) / were involved in (c) / anti-national activities. (d) / No Error. (e)

Q28. It is true that a sense of duty (a) /render it necessary (b) /for you to do something(c) /which is displeasing to your companions. (d) /No error (e)

Q29. What should we do (a) / is a matter of (b) / our own choice (c) / and desire. (d) / No Error. (e)

Q30. You cannot withdraw (a) / all your money (b) / unless you do not (c) / give a prior notice. (d) / No Error. (e)

Q31. Dress in black (a) / several students from the University took part (b) / in a protest march in the city on Thursday as part (c) / of a campaign against female infanticide. (d) / No error (e) .

Q32. The poor experience in (a) / neighbouring countries which have implemented (b) / food stamp programmes should serve as (c) / a deterrent on our country. (d) / No error (e) .

Q33. Closing the doors to a foreign citizen (a) / seeking employment in India, the High Court on Thursday ruled (b) / that its not a foreign national's fundamental right, (c) / to get an employment visa in the country. (d) / No error (e) .

Q34. The consumer Forum directed / the Power Corporation to (a) / compensate a complainant for the inconvenience (b) /and mental agony who he had to suffer, (c) / because of the power officials' irresponsible attitude. (d) / No error (e) .

Q35. The Indian stock market is (a) / one of the worse (b) / performing stock markets (c) / in the recent times. (d) / No error (e)

Q36. These vegetables which are grown (a) / here are (b) / cheap in (c) / cost and rich of vitamins. (d) / No error. (e)

Q37. The orphanages in (a) / the thickly populated cities in India (b) / are founded (c) / by generous donors. (d) / No error. (e)

Q38. Riots, however did not cease (a) / to depress him (b) / and make him to (c) / turn to non-violence (d) / No error. (e)

Q39. I often wonder to whom (a) / does a nation (b) / owes its greatest (c) / debt of gratitude. (d) / No error.(e)

Q40. Pressed by his students (a) / the principal suddenly said (b) / that he was in no way (c) /

responsible for the quarrel. (d) / No error. (e)

Q41. You may rest assured (a) / that Madhav knows (b) / more than I (c) / in this matter. (d) / No Error. (e)

Q42. Every one of us (a) / knows that given (b) / an option he prefers (c) / cold drink than coffee. (d) / No Error. (e)

Q43. He has no affection (a) / with anybody (b) / including the members (c) / of his own family. (d) / No Error. (e)

Q44. I am glad (a) / to hear that (b) / you narrowly escaped (c) / being run over yesterday. (d) / No Error. (e)

Q45. Both the girls (a) / helped one another (b) / when both of them (c) / were in difficulty. (d) / No Error. (e)

Q46. It is universally true (a) / that an honest and hardworking (b) / man is always (c) / a happy man. (d) / No Error. (e)

Q47. I heard that Mohan (a) / as well as his parents were present (b) / in the wedding ceremony (c) / of his brother. (d) / No Error. (e)

Q48. They talked over (a) / the matter for (b) / many hours without (c) / arriving to any decision. (d) / No Error. (e)

Q49. Whenever I see her (a) / I feel that (b) / she resembles to (c) / her deceased mother. (d) / No Error. (e)

Q50. I am accustomed with (a) / hard work and (b) / I generally do not (c) / get tired easily. (d) / No Error. (e)

## Solutions (Practice Set - 03)

S1. Ans. (b)

Sol. 'he had written' will be used in place of 'he wrote' as in Direct Narration, when reporting verb is in past tense and reported speech is in simple past tense then in indirect narration, reported speech is changed to past perfect tense.

Ex. He said to me, 'I wrote a letter' (Direct)

He told me that he had written a letter (Indirect)

S2. Ans. (b)

Sol. 'had' will be used in place of 'has' as past tense is used in reporting verb hence past perfect tense will be used in reported speech.

S3. Ans. (d)

Sol. 'were' will be used in place of 'are' because reporting clause (I had known) is in past perfect tense hence past tense will be used in reported speech.

S4. Ans. (a)

Sol. 'not only' is used before 'educated'. "***Not only...but also...***" are equal ranking words. Thus, same constructions are used after them.

Ex. Not only Ram but also Shyam went there.

S5. Ans. (c)

Sol. The Use of 'then' is superfluous as after 'As, Because, Since, as soon as', 'therefore, so, then' is not used.

Ex. As soon as the bell rang, the students entered the class.

S6. Ans. (e)

Sol. The sentence is grammatically correct.

S7. Ans. (c)

Sol. Use 'had' in place of 'have' as the reporting verb is in past tense.

S8. Ans. (c)

Sol. Use 'was' in place of 'is' as the sentence is in past tense.

S9. Ans. (e)

Sol. The sentence is grammatically correct.

S10. Ans. (b)

Sol. 'not only' will be used after 'studied'. "***Not only...but also...***" are equal ranking words. Thus, same construction will be used after them.

S11. Ans. (c)

Sol. Use 'necessity' in place of 'necessary because 'necessary' is an ADJECTIVE while 'necessity' is a NOUN.

S12. Ans. (b)

Sol. Use 'has visited' in place of 'visit' because we use 'recently' in PRESENT PERFECT or SIMPLE PAST.

S13. Ans. (e)

Sol. No error

S14. Ans. (d)

Sol. Use 'understood' in place of 'understand' because in Passive Voice we use To Be + V3

S15. Ans. (b)

Sol. Use 'of' in place of 'by' because with "pros and cons", we use PREPOSITION 'of'.

S16. Ans. (d)

Sol. Use 'bacterium' in place of 'bacteria' because bacteria is a PLURAL NOUN while 'bacterium' is a SINGULAR NOUN

S17. Ans. (d)

Sol. Use 'excessively' in place of 'excessive' because with 'sweet' we use Adverb.

S18. Ans. (e)

Sol. No error

**Section - II**

S19. Ans. (b)

Sol. Use 'shot' in place of 'shoot' because in Passive Voice with 'be' we use V3.

S20. Ans. (a)

Sol. Remove 'a' because we use go on + V4

S21. Ans. (c)

Sol. 'within' will be used in place of 'in' because as there are two different meanings when 'in' and 'within' are used for 'period of time'.

He will return in (= at a close of) a week's time.

He will return within (= in less than) a fortnight.

S22. Ans. (c)

Sol. 'for a walk' will be used in place of 'to a walk' because 'go for a walk' is used.

Ex. I go for a walk early in the morning.

S23. Ans. (b)

Sol. 'for the last several years' is used in place of 'since the last several years' as 'last' is an ordinal adjective before which 'the' is used and 'the last several years' is a 'period of time' before which 'for' is used.

Ex. I have been working here for the last several years.

S24. Ans. (c)

Sol. 'for' will be used in place of 'into' as 'defer' means 'delay something until a later time', after which 'for' is used.

Ex. Let's defer the decision for a few weeks.

S25. Ans. (c)

Sol. 'we prepared' will be used in place of 'we were prepared' as active voice will be used in part (c) of the sentence.

S26. Ans. (a)

Sol. 'she had been offered' will be used in place of 'she had offered' as passive voice will be used in sentence (a) of the sentence.

S27. Ans. (e)

Sol. The sentence is grammatically correct.

S28. Ans. (b)

Sol. "Renders" will be used as the noun is singular.

S29. Ans. (a)

Sol. 'what we should do' will be used in place of 'what should we do' as the sentence is 'affirmative' not interrogative.

S30. Ans. (c)

Sol. 'unless you' will be used in place of 'unless you do not' as clauses starting with 'unless/ until/ lest', 'not' is not used for making them 'negative'.

Ex. I cannot do anything for her unless she comes here.

S31. Ans. (a)

Sol. Change 'dress' to 'dressed'.

S32. Ans. (d)

Sol. Change 'deterrent on' to 'deterrent to'.

S33. Ans. (c)

Sol. Change 'that its not a' to 'that it was not a'. "***its***" is a possessive adjective.

S34. Ans. (c)

Sol. Change 'and mental agony who he had to suffer' to 'and mental agony which he had to suffer'.

S35. Ans. (b)

Sol. 'One of the' is followed by superlative degree. So, 'worse' should be replaced by 'worst'.

e.g. He is one of the worst dancers that I have seen so far.

S36. Ans. (d)

Sol. Use 'in' place of 'of' as 'rich in' means 'having much'.

S37. Ans. (e)

Sol. The sentence is grammatically correct.

S38. Ans. (c)

Sol. 'to' will not be used as 'Subject + make + object + V1' is used.

Ex. I made him laugh. (Active)

He was made to laugh. (Passive)

S39. Ans. (b)

Sol. 'does' should not be used here as the sentence is assertive (a statement) not interrogative and 'subject + verb' is used in assertive sentence.

S40. Ans. (e)

Sol. The sentence is grammatically correct.

S41. Ans. (a)

Sol. 'You may be rest assured' will be used in place of 'you may rest assured' as 'may+ V1' is used in active voice whereas 'may +be + V3' is used in passive voice.

Ex. I may assure you that you will succeed. (Active)

You may be assured that you will succeed. (Passive)

S42. Ans. (d)

Sol. Use 'to' in place of 'than' as after 'prefer', preposition 'to' is used not 'than'.

S43. Ans. (b)

Sol. Use 'for' in place of 'with'.

S44. Ans. (e)

Sol. The sentence is grammatically correct.

S45. Ans. (b)

Sol. 'Each other' will be used in place 'one another' as 'one another' is used for more than two whereas 'each other' is used for only two.

Ex. The three sisters love one another.

The two sisters love each other.

S46. Ans. (e)

Sol. The sentence is grammatically correct.

S47. Ans. (b)

Sol. 'was' will be used in place of 'were' as if two subjects get connected with 'as well as', 'in addition to', 'like', 'unlike' then the verb is used according to the first subject.

S48. Ans. (d)

Sol. 'Arriving at' will be used in place of 'arrived to' because 'arrive at a conclusion/ decision' is used.

Ex. He did not arrive at any conclusion.

S49. Ans. (c)

Sol. 'to' will not be used after 'resembles'.

S50. Ans. (a)

Sol. 'accustomed to' will be used in place of 'accustomed with' because after 'accustomed, habituated, addicted, committed, devoted, confined', preposition 'to' is used

## Practice Set – 04

Directions (01-50) : **Read each sentence to find out whether there is any grammatical or idiomatic error in it. The error, if any, will be in one part of the sentence. The number of that part is the answer. If there is 'No error', the answer is (e) . (Ignore errors of punctuation, if any.)**

Q1. One of my friend (a) / is both a novelist (b) / and a poet (c) / of repute (d) / No error. (e)

Q2. No sooner he left the office (a) / than it started (b) / raining heavily (c) / to make him completely wet. (d) / No error. (e)

Q3. While Xi said China (a) / was committed to the denuclearisation of (b) / the Korean peninsula, he did not announce (c) /any new steps to squeeze the reclusive regime(d) . No error (e) .

Q4. If one of the candidates choose (a) / to leave before the examination is over (b) / allow him (c) / to do so. (d) / No error. (e)

Q5. Whom (a) / do you plan to invite (b) / to your party besides (c) / Mr. Rao and I? (d) / No error. (e)

Q6. The ongoing merger among (a) /the two companies will (b) /have an adverse(c) /impact on consumers.(d) /No error(e) .

Q7. It is evident that (a) /the banking sector has underwent (b) /tremendous change during(c) /the past two decades.(d) /No error(e) .

Q8. According to the consultant (a) / a more detail analysis of (b) /customer needs (c) /and product pricing is required.(d) /No error(e) .

Q9. Over the next five years (a) /the government needs to invest (b) / at less 350 billion dollars (c) /in rural infrastructure .(d) /No error (e) .

Q10. The lack of no funds (a) / has resulted in several (b) /delays in launching our (c) /new products in India .(d) /No error(e) .

Q11. Sheela had to travel all the way back (a) / when she remembered that (b) / she had forgot to take (c) / important documents with her. (d) / No error (e)

Q12. The party is holding a meeting (a) / in order to begin the (b) / painful and difficult process (c) / of rethink its political strategy. (d) / No error (e)

Q13. The only bad thing about (a) / these flowers are the (b) / pollen which causes (c) / allergy in many people. (d) /No error (e)

Q14.Arun is not only eminent (a) /for his writings in English (b) /but also for his (c) /paintings on spiritual themes. (d) / No error (e)

Q15. This is the only organization (a) / which could somehow continue (b) / to making profits (c) / in the face of recession. (d) / No error (e)

Q16. If the teacher is good (a) /the students (b) / will respond (c) / positively to them. (d) / No error (e)

Q17. As it was Rajan's (a) / first interview, he dressed him (b) / in his most (c) / formal suit. (d) / No error (e)

Q18. Whatever be the work (a) / that which you undertake (b) / put your best efforts (c) / in it. (d) / No error (e)

Q19. All the doctors were (a) / puzzled on the (b) / strange symptoms (c) / reported by the patient. (d) / No error (e)

Q20. He has been working on (a) / the problem from a long time (b) / but is still not (c) / able to solve it. (d) / No error (e)

Q21. They stayed in Kashmir (a) / for a very short (b) / period of time and then (c) / they returned home. (d) / No error. (e)

Q22. Despite of the best efforts (a) / made by the government (b) / the condition of the country is (c) / going from bad to worse. (d) / No error. (e)

Q23. The college library is (a) /not only equipped with (b) /very good books, but also (c) /with the latest journals.(d) /No error (e)

Q24. Numerous people in India (a) / are dying from cancer (b) / but the government seems (c) /

to be ignorant of this fact. (d) / No error. (e)

Q25. The sum and substance (a) / of the speech of the leader was (b) / that the country's (c) / future was bleak. (d) / No error. (e)

Q26. The issues were complex (a) / and especially the members (b) / of the committee (c) / have made them obscure. (d) / No error. (e)

Q27. I thought that he (a) / would come and give (b) / me the latest information (c) / about the patient. (d) / No error. (e)

Q28. I was surprised (a) / to know why had he turned (b) / down such a good offer (c) / of marriage. (d) / No error. (e)

Q29. Mohan said that he was going to (a) / the library and wanted to (b) / know that I could (c) / accompany him. (d) / No error. (e)

Q30. All of us (a) / surprised (b) / to see an old man of (c) / sixty taking part in the Marathon held last month. (d) / No error. (e)

Q31. He told her (a) / that he had never seen (b) / her with his (c) / mind's eye. (d) / No error. (e)

Q32. All the flowers (a) / in his garden will surely die (b) / before the rains (c) / will fall. (d) / No error. (e)

Q33. The dog (a) / I have bought (b) / looks more ferocious (c) / than you have. (d) / No error. (e)

Q34. Everybody (a) / who was working in that office gave (b) / a day's pay as their contributions (c) / to the dependants of Dr. Sonu who had died on duty. (d) / No error (e)

Q35. This book is (a) / undoubtedly preferable than (b) / that in many respects and its printing (c) / is also comparatively good. (d) / No error. (e)

Q36. The audience will flock (a) / to his concerts to hear him to sing (b) / as they perceive a sense of purity and piquancy in his music that is hard (c) / to come by today. (d) / No error. (e)

Q37. It is better to stay at home (a) / than to walk in the street (b) / when there erupts (c) / a communal riot in the town .(d) / No error. (e)

Q38. 'Under no circumstances (a) / we can help (b) / you in this illegal (c) / work', said the Manager. (d) / No error. (e)

Q39. Not only we lost (a) / what he had on our disposal, (b) / but we also (c) / lost our patience. (d) / No error. (e)

Q40. Under a tree (a) / was sitting the saint (b) / whom we had seen (c) / somewhere else. (d) / No error. (e)

Q41. Having worked (a) / for the whole day (b) / you could have taken some rest (c) / and start work tomorrow. (d) / No error. (e)

Q42. Scarcely had he (a) / gone a few steps (b) / that he was told by someone (c) / that his mother was no more. (d) / No error. (e)

Q43. Seldom or (a) / ever have I tried my (b) / best to defend my friends, who are after (c) / all guilty to some extent. (d) / No error. (e)

Q44. Dogs soon know (a) / the person whom (b) / they are (c) / kindly treated. (d) / No error. (e)

Q45. If she had told me that (a) / her husband never lived (b) / within his means, I would not (c) / have lent him the money. (d) /No error. (e)

Q46. More than one student (a) / have passed the examination (b) / of the first terminal test (c) / of pronoun. (d) / No error (e) .

Q47. When the doctors found (a) / that the player has taken (b) / prohibited medicines, he reported (c) / the matter to the team manager. (d) / No error (e) .

Q48. No other (a) / typist in this (b) / office is as (c) / slow as her. (d) / No error (e) .

Q49. The director (a) / asked from me (b) / what I was (c) / doing in the cabin. (d) / No error (e) .

Q50. People who intend (a) / to visit the tourist spots (b) / are always thrilling (c) / to see the scenario here. (d) / No error (e).

Section - II

## Solutions (Practice Set - 04)

S1. Ans. (a)

Sol. Use 'friends' in place of 'friend' as after 'one of', 'either of', neither of', 'every one of', noun or pronoun is always plural but verb is always singular.

Ex. One of the books is new.

S2. Ans. (a)

Sol. 'had' will be used after 'No sooner' or 'No sooner did he leave' will be used as sentence starting from 'No sooner', supporting verb is used before the subject.

Ex. No sooner did he reach the office than his friend arrived.

S3. Ans. (e)

Sol. There is no error in the statement.

S4. Ans. (a)

Sol. Use 'chooses' in place of 'choose' because noun or pronoun is used as plural after 'one of' but verb is always used as singular.

S5. Ans. (d)

Sol. 'me' will be used in place of 'I' as pronoun used after preposition is always in objective case.

Ex. He likes Ram besides you and me.

S6. Ans. (a)

Sol. Replace 'among' with 'between' as we use among to talk about things which are not clearly separated but here there is talk for two companies. "***Between***" is used for two individuals or two groups but "***among***" is used for more than two.

S7. Ans. (b)

Sol. Replace 'underwent' with 'undergone' as third form of the verb is to be used here with has.

S8. Ans. (b)

Sol. Replace 'detail' with 'detailed'.

S9. Ans. (c)

Sol. Replace 'less' with 'beacause', we need adjective to describe 'analysis' here the use of beacause will be correct because 350 billion is the minimum requirement.

S10. Ans. (a)

Sol. In place of 'no' use 'any' as the use of lack is already negative.

S11. Ans. (c)

Sol. Substitute 'forgotten' in place of 'forgot'.

S12. Ans. (d)

Sol. Substitute 'rethinking' in place of 'rethink'.

S13. Ans. (b)

Sol. Substitute 'is' in place of 'are' as the main subject is "***the only bad thing***" which is singular.

S14. Ans. (a)

Sol. Use 'eminent' before not only. "***Not only... but also..., either...or..., neither...nor...***" are equal rank words. The construction after "***not only***" should be similar to the construction after "***but also***".

S15. Ans. (c)

Sol. Substitute 'make' in place of 'making'. To + V1 will come here.

S16. Ans. (d)

Sol. 'Them' should be replaced by 'him or her' (singular) to agree with the singular 'teacher'.

S17. Ans. (b)

Sol. One dresses 'oneself'. So, Rajan dressed 'himself'. 'Himself' is a compound personal pronoun of the reflexive kind. It refers back to the subject or turns back the action of the verb upon the doer.

S18. Ans. (b)

Sol. 'That which' is redundant; simply 'that' will do.

S19. Ans. (b)

Sol. The correct preposition is to be used. One is puzzled 'by' something, and not 'on' it.

S20. Ans. (b)

Sol. The correct preposition is to be used. We work on something 'for' some time.

S21. Ans. (c)

Sol. The use of 'of time' is superfluous because 'for a short period' or 'for a short time' is used.

Ex. He stayed here for a short period.

S22. Ans. (a)

Sol. After 'despite', 'of' will not be used because 'Despite = In spite of'.

Ex. Despite his good performance, he was not selected.

In spite of his good performance, he was not selected.

S23. Ans. (b)

Sol. 'Not only' should be placed after 'equipped'. "***Not only…but also…, either…or…, neither… nor…***" are equal rank words. The construction after "***not only***" should be similar to the construction after "***but also***".

S24. Ans. (b)

Sol. In place of 'from', 'of' will be used because we use "***Die of***" whenever it is talked about a disease.

We use "***Die from***" whenever it is talked about the reason.

Ex. The old woman died of malaria.

S25. Ans. (e)

Sol. The sentence is grammatically correct.

S26. Ans. (d)

Sol. Use 'had' in place of 'have' as from "The issues were complex", we come to know that the incident occurred in the past.

S27. Ans. (e)

Sol. The sentence is grammatically correct.

S28. Ans. (b)

Sol. Use 'why he had' in place of 'why had he' because indirect speech is always a statement. It means helping verb comes after the subject.

S29. Ans. (c)

Sol. Use 'if' or 'whether' in place of 'that' because 'if' or 'whether' is used in indirect narration. Whether is used while converting questions whose answer is supposed to be yes or no in indirect narration.

S30. Ans. (b)

Sol. Use 'were' before 'surprised' because the sentence is in passive voice.

S31. Ans. (e)

Sol. The sentence is grammatically correct.

Always remember that the mind's eye, the heart's content, the soul's delight etc. are idiomatic.

S32. Ans. (d)

Sol. In place of 'will fall', only 'fall' will be used because future tense is not used if a clause starts with 'before, if, when', simple present tense is used in such cases.

S33. Ans. (d)

Sol. Add 'the one' after 'than' because comparison is between the two dogs that means comparison is between 'the dog I have' and 'the dog you have'. Therefore other 'the dog' must be replaced by 'the one'.

**Section - II**

Ex. These new books are better than those old ones. (Here ones= books)

S34. Ans. (c)

Sol. Use 'his' in place of 'their' because the subject of the sentence is 'Everybody', hence possessive pronoun 'his' and reflexive pronoun 'himself' is used for that.

S35. Ans. (b)

Sol. In place of 'than', 'to' will be used. Always remember preposition 'to' is used after preferable/ prefer and not conjunction 'than'.

S36. Ans. (b)

Sol. 'to' will not be used because the correct syntax 'hear + object + V1' is used.

Ex. I heard him sing.

S37. Ans. (b)

Sol. Remove 'to' after 'than' as in the case of comparison between two infinitives, infinitive 'to' is not used after 'than' in the later one, V1 is used.

Ex. You had better to do some work than wander.

S38. Ans. (b)

Sol. Put 'can' before 'we' because sentences starting from 'Under no circumstances', auxiliary verb is used before the subject.

Ex. I can do it under no circumstances,

Or, Under no circumstances can I do it.

S39. Ans. (a)

Sol. 'did' will be used after 'not only' and 'lost' will be converted to 'lose' because the sentence is starting with an adverb "***Not only***" which will follow the law of inversion. Thus, the helping verb "***did***" will come before the subject "***we***".

Ex. He not only came but also stayed here.

Or, Not only did he come but he also stayed here.

S40. Ans. (e)

Sol. The sentence is grammatically correct.

S41. Ans. (d)

Sol. Replace 'start' by 'started' as part (c) of the sentence uses 'could have'. "Have/has/had" is followed by V3 form of the verbs. Hence "could have taken ...... and started..." is the correct usage.

S42. Ans. (c)

Sol. Use 'when' in place of 'that' as "Scarcely/ Hardly" is followed by 'when' in correct grammatical usage.

S43. Ans. (a)

Sol. Replace 'or' by 'if' as "seldom if ever" and 'seldom' or 'never' are the correct usage.

S44. Ans. (b)

Sol. Use 'by' before 'whom' to make the sentence grammatically correct. Look at these sentences;

I know the man by whom he was helped. [Passive]

I know the man who helped him. [Active]

S45. Ans. (e)

Sol. The given sentence is grammatically correct. ***Within (one's) means*** is an idiom which means without exceeding one's budget; without going into debt or spending more money than one has.

S46. Ans. (b)

Sol. Use 'has' in place of 'have' because 'More than one+noun" always takes singular verb.

S47. Ans. (b)

Sol. Use 'had' in place of 'has' because the sentence is in the past tense.

S48. Ans. (d)

Sol. Use 'she' in place of 'her' because comparison has been made between two subjects. Subjective case of pronoun is compared to subjective case.

S49. Ans. (b)

Sol. Remove 'from' because no preposition is used between 'ask' and its object, when it means 'say' or 'enquire'.

S50. Ans. (c)

Sol. Use 'thrilled' in place of thrilling. This part of the sentence is in passive form. [Be+V3]

Section - II

## Practice Set – 05

Direction (01-50) : **Read each of the following sentences to find ouVt whether there is any error in it. The error, if any, will be in one underlined part of the sentence. The alphabet of that part is answer. If there is no error, the answer is 'e'. (Ignore the error of punctuation, if any) .**

Q1. I could not recall (a) /what she has told (b) /me about her (c) /concern with Moti. (d) /No error. (e)

Q2. There were only two (a) / soldiers but each and every (b) / soldier was equal (c) / to five policemen. (d) / No error. (e)

Q3. The boy was trembling (a) / with anger when she drowned (b) / all his books (c) / and articles. (d) / No error. (e)

Q4. When asked, he (a) / took tea (b) / and said that it (c) / tasted sweetly. (d) / No error. (e)

Q5. Don't talk to (a) / him, he always (b) /remains in temper (c) / these days. (d) / No error (e)

Q6. People in Darwin (a) / had become so accustomed to cyclone warnings (b) / that few of them paid any attention to the radio warnings (c) / which began this morning. (d) / No error (e)

Q7. This is (a) / thc most important (b) / question which you have (c) / to prepare very carefully. (d) / No error (e)

Q8. Brahmaputra is (a) / one of the longest rivers (b) / that originate (c) / in the Himalayas. (d) / No error (e)

Q9. The trees in a forest (a) / must be properly counted and numbered (b) / and proper entries be made (c) / in the register. (d) / No error. (e)

Q10. The majority of the woman (a) / teachers are persuading (b) / the principal to consider (c) / their demands. (d) / No error (e)

Q11. These type of books (a) / are certainly helpful to the students (b) / preparing for the banking (c) / service examinations. (d) / No error. (e)

Q12. I have been adoring (a) / her for (b) / the voice with (c) / which she is gifted (d) / No error. (e)

Q13. Our leaders should (a) / not let the criminal (b) / activities to grow (c) / in our country. (d) / No error (e)

Q14. Going towards them (a) / with some cups of (b) / tea in the tray, somebody knocked (c) / at the door. (d) / No error. (e)

Q15. He is almost quite competent (a) / for the post of Manager; (b) / so when given a chance, (c) /he can lead the company to its goal (d) / No error. (e)

Q16. He asked me (a) / that why I was (b) / not preparing for the (c) / Civil service Examinations (d) / No error. (e)

Q17. It was almost (a) / ten years ago since he wrote (b) / a letter to me to (c) / remind me of my lapses (d) / No error (e)

Q18. By whom (a) / was he helped (b) / when he seriously wounded(c) / by a terrorist? (d) / No error (e)

Q19. She held something (a) / at her side which (b) / was totally hiding (c) / by the folds of her sari. (d) / No error. (e)

Q20. Accepting (a) / all sorts of challenges (b) / that life offers is (c) / a pleasure to the brave (d) / No error (e)

Q21. Even as the situation on the border (a)/ poses a tricky challenge for India, its geopolitical(b)/ concerns have been ameliorated by the devastation(c)/ caused by the mismanagement of COVID-19. (d)/ No error(e).

Q22. He was determined to (a) / participate in the car race (b) / even though he knew (c) / that he will not succeed. (d) / No error. (e)

Q23. The father forbade his son (a) / to walk in the sun (b) / and play with (c) / his friends on the road (d) / No error (e)

Q24. They exclaimed with delight that it (a) / was a very beautiful picture (b) / and said that they have never seen (c) / such a beautiful picture before (d) / No error (e)

Q25. No Porter being (a) /available he (b) / carried (c) /all his luggages himself. (d) / No error. (e)

Q26. The interrogation made by (a) / him hardly yield (b) / any concrete conclusion (c) / about the crime. (d) / No error (e) .

Q27. What you had said (a) / about the employees was (b) / found to be correct (c) / but it could not be proved. (d) / No error (e) .

Q28. When you had started (a) / the work, you should (b) / ensure that you (c) / concentrate on it. (d) / No error (e) .

Q29. If you have good (a) / control over breathing, (b) / you can float (c) / on water effortlessly. (d) / No error (e) .

Q30. The way to the fort (a) / was too difficult that (b) / we could not reach (c) / the farthest point. (d) / No error (e) .

Q31. I am not patient (a) / to people who (b) / indulge in silly talk (c) / and uncivilized behaviour. (d) / No error (e)

Q32. On my request (a) / Lalit introduced me (b) / to his friend (c) / who is singer and a scientist. (d) / No error (e)

Q33. In spite of her craving (a) / for hot food and soft drinks, (b) / Sushila abstained with (c) / them for a long duration. (d) / No error (e)

Q34. There is no denying the fact (a) / that he is one (b) / of the best players (c) / that has ever lived. (d) / No error (e)

Q35. He paid no heed (a) / to the charges levied against him (b) / and proceeded to behave (c) / in the same way. (d) / No error (e)

Q36. In emerging economies, (a) / the private credit market (b) / remains highly segmented and thus (c) / weaken power of monetary policy. (d) / No error (e)

Q37. His industrious nature (a) / and calm temperament (b) / have endeared him(c) / to his colleagues and one's superiors. (d) / No error(e)

Q38. According to government estimates (a) / at least four million tonnes of sugar (b) / will have to be imported (c) / this year because of a poor monsoon. (d) / No error (e) .

Q39. Migraines may doubles (a) / the risk of a (b) / a nervous system condition that (c) / causes facial paralysis. (d) / No error (e)

Q40. It is better (a) / to keep one's head in the (b) / face of danger than (c) / losing one's courage (d) / No error(e) .

Q41. He heard the guard (a) / blowing whistle and knew (b) / it is time for him (c) / to enter the train. (d) / No Error. (e)

Q42. If you would have read (a) / the instructions carefully (b) / you would not have (c) / answered the questions wrongly. (d) / No Error. (e)

Q43. Many People accused (a) / him of negligent (b) / but there is no evidence (c) / to substantiate that (d) / No error. (e)

Q44. The rise in prices of food items is (a) / likely

the cause of inflation (b) / to exceed eight percent (c) / during the next quarter (d) /. No error (e) .

Q45. Many people believe that (a) / the nationalization of banks (b) / in the 1960s have protected India (c) / from the current financial crisis (d) /. No error (e) .

Q46. He was asked (a) / to complete (b) / this assignment (c) / before arriving on leave. (d) / No error. (e)

Q47. Mr. Sen was (a) / educated (b) / with the presidency college (c) / in Calcutta. (d) / No error. (e)

Q48. Almost ten years (a) / experience (b) / as a manager is essential (c) / for the post. (d) / No error. (e)

Q49. The fact, as brought out by all the newspapers are (a) / that global (b) / tele- communication (c) / market is not very global. (d) / No error. (e)

Q50. This (a) / train takes perfectly (b) / ten hours (c) / to reach Calcutta (d) / No error (e) .

## Solutions (Practice Set - 05)

S1. Ans. (b)

Sol. Replace 'has' by 'had' as part (a) of the sentence denotes the past event while part (b) signifies past of the past event for which Past Perfect Tense should be used.

e.g. I did not know [Simple Past] when he had come [Past Perfect Tense].

S2. Ans. (b)

Sol. Replace 'each and every' by 'each' as 'each' is used for 'two or more than two' while 'every' or 'each and every' is always used for 'more than two'.

e.g. There were two boys and each boy had a red pen.

There were ten students in the class room and each/every/each and every student had a red pen.

S3. Ans. (a)

Sol. There is no error in the given statement.

S4. Ans. (d)

Sol. Replace 'sweetly' by 'sweet' as "taste, feel, seem, appear, look, smell, remain, etc." are 'Copula Verbs' or Linking Verbs which take Adjective and not Adverb.

e.g. A mango tastes sweet [Adjective].

A rose smells sweet [Adjective].

She looks beautiful [Adjective].

She looks suspiciously [Adverb] at him.

S5. Ans. (c)

Sol. In place of 'in temper', use 'in a temper' which is idiomatic.

"***In a temper***" means if someone is in a temper or gets into a temper, the way that they are behaving shows that they are feeling angry and impatient.

S6. Ans. (e)

Sol. Sentence is grammatically correct.

S7. Ans. (b)

Sol. Use 'a' in place of 'the'. Until there is no comparison between two or more than two persons or things, we don't use adjective of superlative degree. 'The most' is used in superlative degree whereas 'a most' is used in positive degree. In such situation, 'most' means 'very'. Ex. (i) You are the most powerful man in this party. (ii) You are a most powerful man. In the first sentence, 'you' is compared to other members of the party, whereas in second sentence 'you' is not compared to anyone. In this 'a most' means 'a very'.

S8. Ans. (a)

Sol. 'Brahmaputra' is the name of a river. Hence 'The' will be used before 'Brahmaputra'.

S9. Ans. (e)

Sol. Sentence is grammatically correct.

S10. Ans. (a)

Sol. Use 'women' in place of 'woman' as in compound nouns made of 'man' or 'woman', plural form is used in both the parts. Ex.'men conductors', 'man conductor'.

S11. Ans. (a)

Sol. Use 'types' in place of 'type' because after demonstrative adjectives like these/ those/ certain/ other etc. noun is always in plural number.

S12. Ans. (a)

Sol. Use 'have adored' in place of 'have been adoring' because verbs like adore, admire, believe, rely, trust, hope etc. are not used in continuous or perfect continuous tense. These verbs are generally used in simple tense or perfect tense. Ex. I admire her, I have admitted her since I met her.

S13. Ans. (c)

Sol. 'to' will not be used here as 'Let + subject + first form of verb' is used, like 'Let them go'.

S14. Ans. (a)

Sol. 'going' has been used in the form of 'participle' but its 'subject of reference' is not clear. Hence it should be 'While I/ she/ he was going…'

S15. Ans. (a)

Sol. 'almost' will not be used here because Adverb is not used before 'quite'.

S16. Ans. (b)

Sol. 'that' will not be used as in indirect narration before 'Wh-question' words, conjunction is not used.

S17. Ans. (b)

Sol. 'that' will be used in place of 'since' as after 'ago', conjunction 'that' is used, not 'since'. Ex. It was ten years ago that his father died.

S18. Ans. (b)

Sol. 'was' will be used after 'he' as sentence is in passive voice.

S19. Ans. (c)

Sol. Use 'hidden' in place of 'hiding' as in passive voice 'To Be + third form of verb' is used.

S20. Ans. (e)

Sol. The sentence is grammatically correct.

S21. Ans: (c) Ameliorate- Incorrect

Exacerbated/ Aggravated- Correct

Amelioration is something that gives you peace and makes you happy. It is a positive word whereas a negative word will come here.

S22. Ans. (d)

Sol. 'would' will be used in place of 'will' because in starting clause of "even though" 'he knew' is in past tense, therefore in "that-clause" also Past tense will be used.

S23. Ans. (e)

Sol. The sentence is grammatically correct.

S24. Ans. (c)

Sol. Use 'had' in place of 'have' because reporting speech 'said' is in past tense therefore in reported speech, in place of present perfect, past perfect tense will be used.

S25. Ans. (d)

Sol. "luggages" should be replaced by "luggage".

S26. Ans. (b)

Sol. Since the sentence is in the past tense, so replace 'yield' with 'yielded'

S27. Ans. (c)

Sol. When the verb 'found' is followed by an adjective, 'to be' is not used before the adjective. E.g. They were found safe and well. So, the sentence should be like ………… found correct ………

S28. Ans. (a)

Sol. The tense of the sentence is 'Present', so replace 'had started' with 'start'.

S29. Ans. (e)

Sol. No error

S30. Ans. (b)

Sol. Replace 'too' with 'so'. [So ……… that', 'Too ……… to'] E.g. He is so weak that he cannot walk=He is too weak to walk.]

S31. Ans. (b)

Sol. The correct preposition should be used. Note that it is patience 'with' people and not 'to' people.

S32. Ans. (d)

Sol. The same friend is both a singer and a scientist. So it should be 'who is a singer and scientist'.

S33. Ans. (c)

Sol. Incorrect preposition is used. We abstain 'from' something.

S34. Ans. (d)

Sol. 'Have' must replace 'has' as 'best players' are referred to. "***One of the + Plural Noun + who/that + Plural verb***".

S35. Ans. (b)

Sol. Charges are 'levelled' against a person, not 'levied'.

**Levy** means an amount of money that you have to pay, for example as a tax.

S36. Ans. (d)

Sol. Change 'weaken' into 'weakens' as singular subject (market) must be followed by singular verb (weakens) .

S37. Ans. (d)

Sol. Delete 'one's'

S38. Ans. (a)

Sol. Definite article 'the' before 'government' should be used.

S89. Ans. (a)

Sol. Replace 'doubles' with 'double' as modals take plural form of verb.

S40. Ans. (d)

Sol. It should be to lose; as it is the case of parallelism. Refer the rule of parallelism.

S41. Ans. (c)

Sol. Use 'was' in place of 'is' as the sentence is in the past tense.

S42. Ans. (a)

Sol. Use 'had' in place of 'would have'. Refer the rule of conditional sentences.

S43. Ans. (b)

Sol. Use negligence in place of 'negligent' as negligent is an adjective and negligence is noun.

S44. Ans. (b)

Sol. Use 'likely to cause the inflation' in place of 'likely the cause of inflation'.

S45. Ans. (c)

Sol. Use 'has' in place of 'have' as nationalization is singular.

S46. Ans. (d)

Sol. Use 'going' in place of 'arriving' as 'go on leave' is idiomatic.

S47. Ans. (c)

Sol. Use 'at' in place of 'with'.

S48. Ans. (a)

Sol. Use years' (with apostrophe {'}) in place of years.

S49. Ans. (a)

Sol. Use 'is' in place of 'are' as the subject 'the fact' is singular.

S50. Ans. (b)

Sol. Use 'completely', 'totally' or 'exactly' but not 'perfectly' in this sentence.

## Practice Set – 06

**Directions (1-50) : In the following questions, a sentence has been given with some of its parts in bold. To make the sentence grammatically correct, you have to replace the bold part with the correct alternative given below. If the sentence is correct as it is, give (e) as your answer (i.e. No correction required) .**

Q1. **Being recovered from** their astonishment, the explorers realized that the problem was easy to solve.

(a) Being recovered with

(b) Having recovered from

(c) Having been recovered from

(d) Recovering with

(e) No correction required

Q2. Sushma **was hurried** to the station when she dashed against the truck.

(a) was hurrying

(b) had hurried

(c) is hurried

(d) was being hurrying

(e) No correction required

Q3. The marriage ceremony **took place** in this very hotel last Saturday.

(a) was took place

(b) did take place

(c) was taken place

(d) will have taken place

(e) No correction required

Q4. I complimented him **for** his success in the examination.

(a) about

(b) on

(c) at

(d) to

(e) No correction required

Q5. If I **will get** an opportunity, I shall attend the conference without fail.

(a) shall get

(b) get

(c) got

(d) had got

(e) No correction required

Q6. He is a far more serious practitioner now than he **would have to be** in the past.

(a) should have been

(b) used to be

(c) you should need

(d) you should have needed

(e) No correction required

Q7. What he **intends to propose** is not clear from his letter.

(a) intends proposing does

(b) intending to propose is

(c) is intending to be proposed is

(d) intended to be proposed is

(e) No correction required

Q8. Dhanush, which is the flagship indigenous artillery gun, **appear to be** doomed even before its induction and deployment in the artillery.

(a) has appeared to be

(b) appearing to be

(c) appears to be

(d) appeared to be

(e) No correction required

Q9. Although their visas **will expires** in

September they can have them extended for six months.

(a) had expired

(b) expires

(c) can expires

(d) expire

(e) No correction required

Q10. He **is speaking** in such a soft voice that he was not audible even to thepeople who were sitting in the first row.

(a) had spoke

(b) has been speaking

(c) was spoken

(d) spoke

(e) No correction required

Q11. A freezing morning accompanied by a dense cover of frost **set the toning** for the coming weekend.

(a) keeping tone

(b) started the toning

(c) kept the tone

(d) sets the tone

(e) No correction required

Q12. The jail is in the news again **with two of its prisoners** winning the game..

(a) with two of their prisoners

(b) by two of their prisoners

(c) by two of prisoners

(d) by two of their prisoner

(e) No correction required

Q13. The space-crunched city throws up several stories of struggle that school **have had put up with to** win playground for their students.

(a) have had to put up

(b) had put up to

(c) have had to put up with

(d) had to put up to

(e) No correction required

Q14. **Emotions was high** as both families were taken to the police station last night.

(a) Emotions went higher

(b) Emotion become high

(c) Emotionally high

(d) Emotions ran high

(e) No correction required

Q15. Work at all the court complexes was paralysed as lawyers went **on a day-long strike** as a mark of protest.

(a) For a one day strike

(b) For a strike

(c) On a day's long strike

(d) On a day-long striking

(e) No correction required

Q16. As it was a dark and stormy night, Lata was **too scared to** go home alone.

(a) very scary to

(b) much scared to

(c) as scared to

(d) to scared too

(e) No correction required

Q17. Since it was her engagement party, Riya was **dress to kill**.

(a) dresses to kill

(b) dressed to kill

(c) dressed to killings

(d) dressing to killed

(e) No correction required

Q18. Ramesh **worries endlessly** about his son's future as he was so poor in studies.

(a) worry endless

(b) worried endless

(c) worried endlessly

(d) worries endless

(e) No correction required

Q19. Now that the actual criminal had been caught, Kunal was happy that he was finally let **of the hook**.

(a) off the hook

(b) of the hookings

(c) off the hooks

(d) of the hooks

(e) No correction required

Q20. The little boy appeared all of a sudden out of nowhere and **take everyone by surprise**.

(a) took everyone as surprised

(b) take everyone with surprised

(c) took everyone by surprises

(d) took everyone by surprise

(e) No correction required

Q21. The two Koreas were divided along the world's most heavily fortified border **since 1950-53 ending Korean War with an armistice**, not a peace treaty.

(a) since the 1950-53 Korean War ended with an armistice

(b) as the Korean War has ended with an armistice since 1950-53

(c) after Korean War ended during 1950-53 with an armistice

(d) because the Korean War ended to an armistice during 1950-53

(e) No correction required.

Q22. The setting up of territorial nation-states in South Asia on the basis of religious or ethnic identities **cannot bring up any improvements** in the lives of people.

(a) did not bring up any improvement

(b) have not brought about any improvement

(c) has not brought in the improvement

(d) could not bring any of the improvement

(e) No correction required

Q23. The annual election to choose five new non-permanent members of the UN Security Council **produced both an expected and a preposterous event**.

(a) has produced the unexpected and the near preposterous event

(b) has been producing both the expected and preposterous event

(c) is both the expected and near preposterous event

(d) produces both the expectation and near preposterous event

(e) No correction required

Q24. **Despite giving the fact that almost half** the work force in the country is still engaged in farming, farmers' woes are naturally an important electoral plank.

(a) There is a fact that almost half

(b) Giving the fact that despite halving

(c) Given the fact that almost half of

(d) The fact that states almost half of

(e) No correction required

Q25. Tagore's views on nationalism as expressed

in his speeches in the US in 1916 and in China in 1924 **as well were severely criticizing by both these countries**, although they were appreciated by Albert Einstein and Romain Rolland.

(a) had been criticized severely by both the countries

(b) were severely criticized in both these countries as well

(c) was severely criticizing in both these countries as well

(d) were criticizing severely at both the countries as well

(e) No correction required

Q26. Gandhi's non-violent methods **envisage that nature ought to be handled** in a mild manner, much against modern technology's onslaught on nature to help technology achieve its goal.

(a) envisaged how nature should be handle

(b) have envisaged the handling of the nature

(c) did envisage the nature's handling

(d) envisage that nature can be handled

(e) No correction required

Q27. Various forms of traditional wisdom about practical solutions of different problems are considered by environmentalists **as more prudent than offered in** modern technology.

(a) to be more prudent than the ones offered by

(b) more prudent than these offered by

(c) to be prudential as compared to

(d) that it is more prudent than what offered in

(e) No correction required

Q28. Indian agriculture **comes over a long way since Independence**, with chronic food scarcity giving way to self-sufficiency in grain despite a two-and-a-half fold increase in population.

(a) has been coming a long way after Independence

(b) have grown a long way after Independence

(c) had gone a longer way after Independence

(d) has come a long way since Independence

(e) No correction required

Q29. North Korea is believed to be developing an intercontinental ballistic missile (ICBM) **capable of carrying a nuclear warhead** and reaching mainland United States.

(a) which is capable of carrying a nuclear war

(b) which can carry a nuclear warhead

(c) that is capable of carrying out a nuclear war

(d) capable of carrying out a nuclear war

(e) No correction required

Q30. The dramatic decision by Saudi Arabia, the United Arab Emirates, Bahrain, Egypt and Yemen **of suspending diplomatic ties to** Qatar could have far-reaching economic and geopolitical consequences.

(a) suspending the ties of diplomacy with

(b) by suspending diplomatic ties of

(c) to suspend diplomatic ties with

(d) with the suspension of diplomatic ties in

(e) No correction required

Q331. When the police started asking questions, the suspect **clammed up**.

(a) camped down

(b) clamped up

(c) clam out

(d) clamed off

(e) No Correction Required

Q32. The implication is that these may be black funds and they **are to being tracked** and the people

behind them will be caught.

(a) are on track

(b) is being tracked

(c) have been tracked

(d) are being tracked

(e) No improvement is required

Q33. I must **look after** my French before going to Paris next month.

(a) brush in for

(b) catch up

(c) brush up on

(d) bring in on

(e) No Correction Required

Q34. If this is freedom of speech, then it **must been curtailed** immediately.

(a) have being curtailing

(b) must be curtailed

(c) must have been curtailed

(d) have been curtailed

(e) No correction required

Q35. India has suffered from terrorism. So has Pakistan. And **it turns out**, now the first world too is not immune.

(a) turning out to

(b) it turns to

(c) it turned out to be

(d) it turning out

(e) No improvement required

Q36. Even as Indian agriculture witnessed such structural changes, policy **remained unchanged** in its focus on the cereal economy.

(a) remaining unchanged

(b) being unchanged

(c) has been remained unchanged

(d) has remained unchange

(e) No correction required

Q37. Simultaneously there was a shift to horticultural production, **with enhancing risk** of perishability.

(a) provided the enhancing risk

(b) and enhancing risk

(c) with enhanced risk

(d) the enhanced risk

(e) No correction required

Q38. Through the mechanism of loan waivers, agricultural distress is **now morphed into** fiscal dangers for states.

(a) now altered to

(b) morphed to

(c) now morphing into

(d) now changing to

(e) No improvement required

Q39. **An acclivity to six places is substantial because** India is now the only lower-middle income country to have found a place in the top 35 tourist destinations.

(a) An ascent of six places is significant

(b) A climb of sixth place is considerable

(c) A rise to sixth place is trivial

(d) A declension to sixth place is appreciable.

(e) No replacement required

Q40. Terrorism is a hard problem to counter. Only a zero tolerance approach works. To that extent, all our homegrown terror apologists **should have been condemned**.

(a) has been condemend

(b) is been condemned

(c) should be condemned

(d) must have been condemned

(e) No improvement required

Q41. It is a pity that a country that dreams of entering the digital age is now drawn into a debate in Parliament and splitting hairs over ways and means **to sensitise its population to the evils to spitting**.

(a) to sensitise their population to the evils of spitting.

(b) to sensitising its population to the evils of spitting.

(c) to sensitise its population to the evils of spitting.

(d) to sensitise its population of the evils of spitting.

(e) No correction required.

Q42. For long, the Board of Control for Cricket in India has been working in an opaque manner, **almost becoming a den for a few elite**, well-connected individuals.

(a) almost becoming a den to a few elite

(b) almost becomes a den for a few elite

(c) almost became a den for a few elite

(d) almost became a den to a few elite

(e) No correction required.

Q43. There is a marked mismatch between the understanding of the Constitution of the Governor as the dignified head of the State executive and the regular turnover of Governors **depending on the party in power in the Centre**.

(a) depending on the party in power at the Centre.

(b) depends on the party in power at the Centre.

(c) depends on the party at power at the Centre.

(d) depends on the party at power of the Centre

(e) No correction required.

Q44. Consecutive sentences are still permissible if one is a fixed term and the other is one of life, **provided the term sentence is completed before** and the life sentence begins later.

(a) provided the term sentence was completed first

(b) provided the term sentence has completed first

(c) provided the term sentence has completed before

(d) provided the term sentence is completed first

(e) No correction required.

Q45. The party led by Boris Johnson has **taken to itself for the noble duty** of giving England its identity.

(a) given itself for the sake of dedicated task

(b) appointed for the worthy duty

(c) taken on itself the sacred duty

(d) taken into employment by the consecrated duty

(e) No replacement required

Q46. I advised my son to engage two coolies instead of one because **the luggage was too much heavy for** a single coolie.

(a) the luggage was much too heavy for

(b) the luggage was too much heavy to

(c) the luggage was too heavier for

(d) the luggage was heavier for

(e) No improvement required

Q47. Sheila Chandra began her concert by

chanting Om turning it finally **into an experience close with prayer**.

(a) to an experience close with prayer

(b) into an experience close to prayer

(c) into an experience closing by prayer

(d) to an experience closed by prayer

(e) No improvement required

Q48. **Simplest solution than this expensive** method which you are suggesting should be found out.

(a) Simpler solution than this expensive

(b) The simplest solution than this expensive

(c) A simpler solution than this expensive

(d) A simplest solution than this expensive

(e) No improvement required

Q49. **The two leaders had taken an unreserved** common position on terrorism, and the joint statement released after the meeting has pledged enhanced India-US cooperation in the Indo-Pacific region.

(a) The two leaders take an unreserved

(b) The two leaders has taken an unreserved

(c) The two leaders took an unreserved

(d) The two leaders have taken an unreserved

(e) No improvement required

Q50. Trump extracted his pound of flesh by insisting on a "fair" and "balanced" trade relationship between the two nations, **indicating a mercantilist approach which can** in the end limit trade and therefore prosperity in both nations.

(a) indicates a mercantilist approach which can

(b) indicate a mercantilist approach that can

(c) that indicates a mercantilist approach that can

(d) indicating the mercantilist approach which could

(e) No improvement required

## Solutions (Practice Set - 06)

S1. Ans. (b)
Sol. 'Having recovered' will be used.
'Having + V3' is Active Perfect Participle whereas 'Having + been + V3' or 'Being + V3' is Passive Perfect Participle.
S2. Ans. (a)
Sol. 'was hurrying' is the correct choice as 'Be + V4' is used in Active Voice but 'Be + V3' is used in Passive Voice'.
Ex. She was writing a letter. (Active)
The thief was caught. (Passive)
S3. Ans. (e)
Sol. No correction is required.
S4. Ans. (b)
Sol. 'on' will be used in place of 'for' as preposition 'on' is used with 'compliment'.
Ex. I complimented him on his skill.
S5. Ans. (b)
Sol. 'get' is the correct use as if two incidents of future has been used, then clause starting with 'if, when, as long as, as soon as, before, after' take simple present tense while future tense is used for the main clause of the sentence.
Ex. If he comes here, I will help you.
S6. Ans. (b)
Sol. 'used to ' is the correct usage for past habit.
S7. Ans. (e)
Sol. No correction is required.
S8. Ans. (c)
Sol. 'appears to be' is the correct use as the subject of the sentence is singular which is "Dhanush".
S9. Ans. (d)
Sol. 'expire' is used as for fixed programme of future, simple present tense is used.
S10. Ans. (c)
Sol. 'was speaking' is the correct use as the sentence is in past tense.
S11. Ans. (d)
Sol. 'sets the tone' fits the sentence appropriately as it conveys the proper meaning of the sentence. "Sets the tone" is an idiom which means "to establish a particular mood for something"
S12. Ans. (e)
Sol. No correction required.
S13. Ans. (d) had put up to
Sol. 'had to put up to' fits the sentence appropriately as it makes the sentence structure grammatically correct.
S14. Ans. (d)
Sol. 'Emotions ran high' fits the sentence appropriately and it is an idiom which means to be in a state of excitement or anger.
S15. Ans. (e)
Sol. No correction required.
S16. Ans. (e)
Sol. Here, too is used as emphatic word. Lata was so scared that she could not go home alone. Hence, no correction is required.
S17. Ans. (b)
Sol. The structure of sentence is subject + was/were + third form of verb + object. Thus, Riya was dressed to kill.
S18. Ans. (c)
Sol. The given sentence is the statement of simple past tense. Hence it should be 'worried' instead of worries.
S19. Ans. (a)
Sol. The phrase 'let off' means to give them only a light punishment.
S20. Ans. (d)
Sol. It should be 'took' instead of 'take'.
**S21. Ans. (a)**
Sol. "since the 1950-53 Korean War ended with

an armistice" is the correct phrase to replace the bold part as 'since' in this case is used to describe the reason. Hence (a) is the correct option.

S22. Ans. (b)

Sol. "have not brought about any improvement" is the correct phrase replacement as the phrase "bring about" means to make something happen, especially to cause changes in a situation. Hence (b) is the correct option.

S23. Ans. (e)

Sol. The given sentence is grammatically correct.

S24. Ans. (c)

Sol. "Given the fact that almost half of" is the correct phrase replacement as it makes the sentence grammatically correct. Other options are grammatically incorrect. So (c) is the correct choice.

S25. Ans. (b)

Sol. As the sentence is in passive form, "were severely criticized in both these countries as well" is the correct phrase to make the sentence grammatically correct.

S26. Ans. (e)

Sol. The given sentence is grammatically correct.

S27. Ans. (a)

Sol. "to be more prudent than the ones offered by" is the correct phrase replacement to make the sentence grammatically correct.

S28. Ans. (d)

Sol. "has come a long way since Independence" is the correct phrase replacement as the sentence is in Present Tense. Hence (d) is the correct option.

S29. Ans. (e)

Sol. The given sentence does not require any correction as it is grammatically correct.

S30. Ans. (c)

Sol. "to suspend diplomatic ties with" is the correct phrase replacement to make the sentence grammatically correct.

S31. Ans. (e)

Sol. Clam up means to refuse to speak.

S32. Ans. (d)

Sol. "are being tracked" is the correct phrase replacement.

S33. Ans. (c)

Sol. brush up on means to improve, refresh one's knowledge of something.

S34. Ans. (b)

Sol. Curtail means reduce in extent or quantity; impose a restriction on.

S35. Ans. (e)

Sol. The sentence is grammatically correct.

S36. Ans. (e)

Sol. The sentence is grammatically correct.

S37. Ans. (c)

Sol. "with enhanced risk" is the correct phrase replacement.

S38. Ans. (c)

Sol. Morphing means change smoothly from one image to another by small gradual steps using computer animation techniques.

S39. Ans. (A)

**A. An ascent of six places is significant**

**ascent** - climb; acclivity; rise; upward movement.

**significant** - considerable or substantial.

**An acclivity to six places is substantial** - the preposition 'to' is wrongly used here. It should have been 'to sixth place' to make the sentence grammatically correct.

**B** - The preposition 'of' is wrongly used.

**C** - **'trivial'** means insignificant. So, it's contextually wrong.

**D** - **'declension'** means 'decline'. How can decline be appreciable?)

S40. Ans. (c)

Sol. "should be condemned" is the correct phrase replacement.

S41. Ans. (c)

Sol. Replace 'to sensitise its population to the evils to spitting' with 'to sensitise its population to the evils of spitting.'

S42. Ans. (e)

Sol. No correction required.

S43. Ans. (a)

Sol. Replace 'depending on the party in power in the Centre' with 'depending on the party in power at the Centre'.

S44. Ans. (d)

Sol. Replace 'provided the term sentence is completed before' with 'provided the term sentence is completed first'.

S45. Ans. (c)

Sol. **taken on itself the sacred duty**

**take on itself -** to begin to perform or deal with itself.

**sacred -** worthy; consecrated; dedicated.

**'take to itself'** is grammatically wrong.

**A - 'given itself for the sake of'** is grammatically wrong. Given itself what?

**B - appointed** whom? **'has been appointed'** would've been correct.

**D - take into employment** means **'take responsibility'**. But, the preposition **'by'** makes it incorrect.

S46. Ans. (a)

Sol. 'too much + noun' is used, whereas 'much too +adjective/adverb' is used. In the sentence in place of 'too much', 'much too' will be used.

S47. Ans. (b)

Sol. 'close to' somebody/something is used.

S48. Ans. (c)

Sol. The sentence is in a comparative degree. Hence in place of 'simplest solution', 'A simpler solution' is used.

S49. Ans. (d)

Sol. As verb is in the conditional perfect which requires an auxilliary ('having' in this case,) therefore the past participle (taken) is necessary.

S50. Ans. (e)

Sol. No improvement required.

## Practice Set – 07

**Direction (01-50) : Read each sentence to find out whether there is any grammatical or idiomatic error in it. The error, if any, will be in one part of the sentence. The number of that part is the answer. If there is 'No error', the answer is (e) . (Ignore errors of punctuation, if any)**

Q1. The old man asked me (a) / if there was any (b) / place in (c) / the compartment. (d) / No error. (e)

Q2. He was (a) / very friendly enough (b) / to help me when (c) / I was in distress (d) / No error. (e)

Q3. Being unable to (a) / cope with (b) / the syllabus (c) / he discontinued the course. (d) / No error. (e)

Q4. The college is (a) / holding special lectures for their students (b) / and teachers so that they (c) / may get enlightened about the economic problems. (d) / No error. (e)

Q5. Had they have anything like (a) / my condition (b) / they would have felt (c) / miserable and thought of committing suicide. (d) / No error. (e)

Q6. Please explain to me (a) / how is a digital computer (b) / different from (c) / an analogy computer. (d) / No error. (e)

Q7. A cell (a) / is the smallest (b) / identifiable unit of life and cannot be (c) / seen with a naked eye. (d) / No error. (e)

Q8. A Quarrel arose between the five members (a) / and for a time (b) / it appeared as if the party (c) / had been heading for a split. (d) / No error. (e)

Q9. The smuggler yielded (a) / for the temptation (b) / and fell into (c) / the police trap. (d) /No error. (e)

Q10. Found guilty (a) / on murder (b) / the accused was (c) / sentenced to death. (d) / No error. (e)

Q11.The Ministry was considered (a) / several proposals for the (b) /development of small and medium (c) / enterprises during Budget discussions. (d) / No error (e)

Q12. Households across the state are either opting for (a) /a more modest lifestyle or compromising on (b) /the nutritional value of their food in on effort to negate (c) /the price rise of essential commodities, cereals, vegetables and fruits. (d) /No error (e)

Q13. Young school students (a) /now-a-days are subjected to intense pressure (b) / from peers and parent alikly to fetch (c) / high marks in public examinations. (d) /No error (e) .

Q14. Most people like (a) /to rest after a day's work (b) / but he seemed (c) / to have an inexhaustive supply of energy. (d) / No error. (e)

Q15. On accounts of the(a) / rising costs many people (b) / are finding it difficult (c) / to feed their families. (d) / No error (e)

Q16. In our experience people usually (a) / value things that they have to (b) / pay off more than those that (c) / they receive free of cost. (d) / No error (e)

Q17. The manager of that city branch (a) / cannot handle it with the help of (b) / only two personnel as (c) / business has increased substantially. (d) / No error (e)

Q18. With the literacy rate in this (a) / region as low as ten per cent (b) / we need to encourage (c) / local people to build schools. (d) / No error (e)

Q19. The cascading effect of economic slowdown

(a) / has brought a much unnerving gloom (b) / to the real estate industry last-year (c) / but the industry is growing this year. (d) / No error (e)

Q20. Bharatpur is transforming into (a) / India's most fastest growing bird sanctuary (b) / attracting thousands of rare migratory birds (c) / from Europe and Siberia. (d) / No error (e)

Q21. At presently the global (a) /supply of wheat is (b) / the lowest of what it has been (c) / for the past fifty

years. (d) / No error (e)

Q22. It goes to his credit (a) /that he was a clean man (b) /in politics as well as (c) / his person dealings. (d) / No error (e)

Q23. It is better (a) / to keep one's head in the (b) / face of danger than (c) / losing one's courage (d) / No error (e) .

Q24. There are ways and measures (a) / to be followed if we (b) / really mean to enhancing agricultural (c) / growth in the years to come. (d) / No error (e)

Q25. In emerging economies, (a) / the private credit market (b) / remains highly segmented and thus (c) / weaken power of monetary policy. (d) / No error (e)

Q26. As soon as he reached the venue, (a) / he asked to the supervisor (b) / about the closing time (c) / of the examination. (d) / No error. (e)

Q27. We did not (a) / participate in the (b) / programme yesterday (c) / due to this reason. (d) / No error. (e)

Q28. No effort has been made at all (a) / to cash on (b) / the refurnished image (c) / of Indian tennis. (d) / No error. (e)

Q29. Political education in real sense (a) / should develop people (b) / who will be committed to (c) / bring social change (d) / No error. (e)

Q30. The police accused him (a) / for setting fire to the building (b) / but he denied having been (c) / in the area. (d) / No error. (e)

Q31. The Police asked (a) / each of us about (b) / his movements (c) / on the night of the crime. (d) / No error. (e)

Q32. Never before have (a) / the achievements of technology so conspicuous (b) / as today when man (c) / has set his foot on the moon. (d) / No error. (e)

Q33. I will encourage (a) / every one of my students (b) / to pursue the path of honesty (c) / in their lives. (d) / No error. (e)

Q34. How to solve the problem (a) / is the main concern (b) / of the organisers (c) / at the moment. (d) / No error. (e)

Q35. After toiling very hard (a) / over a long period (b) / he found he had hardly (c) / made no profit at all. (d) / No error. (e)

Q36. What children (a) /cry with (b) /the slightest (c) /provocation is still not known. (d) /No error (e)

Q37. It took ten long (a) /years for (b) /them to realisation (c) /that there are several problems. (d) /No error (e)

Q38. I watched (a) /the other patients' (b) / progress with a mixture of faccination (c) /and horror (d) /No error (e)

Q39. A new study suggests (a) /that alcohol boosts (b) /the ageing (c) /process and harm the system. (d) /No error (e)

Q40. People have the right (a) /to demand (b) / protection for (c) /their business against a bandit group trying to grab it. (d) /No error (e)

Q41. For he cannot do (a) / a lot of work (b) /

at a time, he rejects (c) / many offers. (d) / No error. (e)

Q42. Bobby intends (a) / to leave (b) / the city (c) / with bag and baggage. (d) / No error. (e)

Q43. Avinash is not so (a) / good a batsman to (b) / be selected for the (c) / national cricket team. (d) / No error. (e)

Q44. The patient recover (a) / so fast that (b) / the expert doctors (c) / also were surprised. (d) / No error. (e)

Q45. The book is written (a) / in a simple and (b) / lucid manner with a (c) / number of well-drawned illustrations. (d) / No error. (e)

Q46. All of a sudden (a) / Sudhir remembered that (b) / he has not (c) / locked the office. (d) / No error. (e)

Q47. I am sure that (a) / all my monthly expenses (b) / would exceed the income (c) / if I do not economise. (d) / No error. (e)

Q48. Although their visas (a) / expires in September (b) / they can have them (c) / extended for six months. (d) / No error. (e)

Q49. Hardly as I stepped (a) / out of my house when (b) / I saw some policemen (c) / coming towards my house.(d) / No error. (e)

Q50. The last of the Mughal (a) / emperors of India was imprisoned (b) / and was later sent into (c) / exile by the British. (d) / No error. (e)

## Solutions (Practice Set - 07)

S1. Ans. (c)

Sol. Use 'room' in place of 'place'. "Room" means space.

S2. Ans. (b)

Sol. The use of 'very' is superfluous because 'positive degree adjective + enough' is used. Ex. Lucky enough, tall enough, etc.

S3. Ans. (e)

Sol. The sentence is grammatically correct.

S4. Ans. (b)

Sol. 'its' will be used in place of 'their' because the subject of the sentence 'the college' is in singular number. Hence 'its' is used.

S5. Ans. (a)

Sol. Use 'had' in place of 'have' because after 'have, had, has', verb third form is used.

(V3) . Ex. He has written a book, Had they had me in their team, I would have helped him.

S6. Ans. (b)

Sol. 'is' should be used after 'a digital computer' because the sentence is assertive not interrogative.

And in assertive sentences, helping verb comes after a subject.

S7. Ans. (d)

Sol. In place of 'a', 'the' is used as 'with the naked eye' is the correct expression.

S8. Ans. (a)

Sol. Use 'among' in place of 'between' because 'between' is used for the comparison of two while 'among' is used for the comparison of more than two.

S9. Ans. (b)

Sol. In place of 'for', 'to' will be used because preposition 'to' is used after 'yield'. Ex. She yielded to bribery.

S10. Ans. (b)

Sol. Use 'of' in place of 'on' because preposition 'of' is used after 'guilty'. Ex. "guilty of murder, guilty of theft."

S11. Ans. (a)

Sol. In this sentence 'was' should not be used because 'was' is used with past form of ordinary verb in passive sentences i.e. the proposal was considered by ministry.

S12. Ans. (e)

Sol. No Error.

S13. Ans. (c)

Sol. Replace 'alike' by equally'.

S14. Ans. (c)

Sol. Use 'seems' in place of 'seemed'. Present Indefinite form of verb is required. It is a fact about him.

S15. Ans. (a)

Sol. 'On account of' which means 'because of' is the correct usage.

S16. Ans. (c)

Sol. Use 'for' in place of 'off'.

S17. Ans. (c)

Sol. Substitute 'persons' for 'personnel'.

S18. Ans. (e)

Sol. There is no error in the statement.

S19. Ans. (b)

Sol. Remove 'has' in the sentence. Whenever past point of time is given we use Simple Past Tense.

S20. Ans. (b)

Sol. Remove 'most' as double superlative is

not used and here both 'most' and 'fastest' are superlatives.

S21. Ans. (a)

Sol. 'Present' should replace 'presently'. At present–at this time, or occuring now.

S22. Ans. (d)

Sol. Instead of 'his person dealings' use 'his personal dealings'

S23. Ans. (d)

Sol. Explanation: "To lose", as comparison is made between identical elements, therefore verb forms should be identical.

S24. Ans. (c)

Sol. It should be 'enhance' in place of 'enhancing'.

S25. Ans. (d)

Sol. Change 'weaken' into 'weakens' as singular subject (market) must be followed by singular verb (weakens) .

S26. Ans. (b)

Sol. Remove "to"

Asked is not followed by "to".

S27. Ans. (d)

Sol. In place of 'due to', 'for' will be used. 'due to' or 'owing to' is not used before 'reason' and 'because' is not used before or after 'reason'. Ex. The reason is because is always incorrect, the reason is because of, the reason is due to ...all are incorrect.

S28. Ans. (b)

Sol. 'in' will be used between 'cash' and 'on' because the use of 'cash in on' is idiomatic which means to get benefit.

S29. Ans. (d)

Sol. Use 'bringing' in place of 'bring'. With "committed to" we use V1+ing.

S30. Ans. (b)

Sol. 'of' is used in place 'for' because preposition 'of' is used after 'accuse'. Eg. The teacher accused him of stealing.

S31. Ans. (e)

Sol. The sentence is grammatically correct.

S32. Ans. (b)

Sol. 'been' should be used after 'technology' because the sentence is in passive form.

S33. Ans. (d)

Sol. Use 'his life' will be used in place of 'their lives' because generally for 'Nobody, everybody, anybody, No one, Everyone, Someone, Anyone', 'his' is used. Eg. Everybody should mind his own business. (Not their own business) When 'his' is used, 'life' is used in place of 'lives'.

S34. Ans. (e)

Sol. The sentence is grammatically correct.

S35. Ans. (d)

Sol. Use 'any' in place of 'no' as after "hardly, scarcely, rarely, seldom etc.", 'any' is used and not 'no'. Ex. He hardly feels any problem.

S36. Ans. (a)

Sol. Substitute 'why' in place of 'what'.

S37. Ans. (c)

Sol. Substitute 'realise' in place of 'realisation'.

S38. Ans. (c)

Sol. Substitute 'fascination' in place of 'faccination'.

S39. Ans. (d)

Sol. Substitute 'harms' in place of 'harm'.

S40. Ans. (c)

Sol. Substitute 'of' in place of 'for'.

Sol. 'As', 'since' or 'because' will be used in place of 'for' because 'for' is not used in starting of the sentence in the form of conjunction of reason.

S41. Ans. (e) no error

S42. Ans. (d)

Sol. The use of 'with' is superfluous as the meaning of 'bag and baggage' itself is with bag and baggage. Hence 'with' is not be used before 'bag and baggage'.

S43. Ans. (b)

Sol. Use 'as' before 'to'. ' so... as' is the correct way to use it in a sentence.

Ex. He is not so good as I expected.

S44. Ans. (a)

Sol. 'recovered' will be used in place of 'recover' as 'were' indicates that the incident happened in past tense. Hence 'recovered' is used.

S45. Ans. (d)

Sol. Use 'well- drawn' in place of 'well- drawned' as the past form of 'draw' is 'drew' and past participle form is 'drawn'. Hence there is no need to add 'ed' in 'drawn'.

S46. Ans. (c)

Sol. Use 'had' in place of 'has' because past perfect is used for events that occured before another event in the past.

S47. Ans. (b)

Sol. The use of 'all' is superfluous as 'monthly expenses' includes all types of expenses.

S48. Ans. (b)

Sol. 'expire' will be used in place of expires.

S49. Ans. (a)

Sol. Use 'had' in place of 'as' as the syntax 'Hardly+ had+ Subject+ V3', 'when + Subject + V2' is used.

Ex. Hardly had I gone out when a friend of mine came.

S50. Ans. (c)

Sol. Use 'on' after 'later' as 'later' means 'after' while 'later on' means 'afterwards'.

## Practice Set – 08

**Direction (01-50) : Read each sentence to find out whether there is any grammatical or idiomatic error in it. The error, if any, will be in one part of the sentence. The number of that part is the answer. If there is 'No error', the answer is (e) . (Ignore errors of punctuation, if any)**

Q1. These sort of men (a) / attain worldly success by hook or by crook, (b) / so they deserve to (c) / be looked down upon. (d) / No error. (e)

Q2. She was startled (a) / to see in (b) / her drawing room (c) / a most popular film producer. (d) / No error (e)

Q3. I saw (a) / an anxious pale girl (b) / who when asked let me know (c) / that she was suffering from consumption. (d) / No error. (e)

Q4. Delhi is far (a) / better than any (b) / other metropolis (c) / of Pakistan. (d) / No error. (e)

Q5. Gold is the most precious (a) / of all the metals (b) / that are used in ornaments, (c) / as far as we all know. (d) / No error. (e)

Q6. He works hard (a) / that he should please (b) / his Manager to promote him (c) / to the post of Sales Executive. (d) / No error. (e)

Q7. I hardly ever (a) / see him because (b) / in my opinion he is not (c) / a man to be admired. (d) / No error. (e)

Q8. 'Where else (a) / did you go besides (b) / the office?' she (c) / asked her husband. (d) / No error (e)

Q9. Many of the founding fathers (a) / of our constitution are (b) / so reverend as Ambedkar (c) / if not more. (d) / No error. (e)

Q10. No sooner was the agitation (a) / in Darjeeling silenced,(b) / the Bodo Land activity (c) / in Assam erupted. (d) / No error. (e)

Q11. Your desire to meet the President (a) / without prior appointment (b) / cannot be fulfill. (c) / No error (d) .

Q12. Whenever man attains fame, (a) / his person qualities are (b) / imitated by others who are close to him. (c) / No error (d) .

Q13. Rivers, mountains and deep forests (a) / are the places mostly like by (b) / people living in urban areas. (c) / No error (d) .

Q14. In financial matters (a) /it is important to (b) /get disinterested advice(c) / or no advice (d) /No error (e)

Q15. He had been (a) / saved of (b) / death which (c) /he encountered due to his actions (d) /No error (e)

Q16. He was (a) / of the belief (b) / that the evening news (c) / are worth watching (d) /. No error (e)

Q17. Many believe that (a) / nothing could have (b) / avoided the war (c) / between America and Iraq. (d) /. No error (e)

Q18. Well planned and congestion-free cities of Rajasthan has (a) / strong urban infrastructure with (b) / a variety of accommodation options(c) / wide parks, schools and colleges and recreational facilities. (d) / No error (e) .

Q19.The two stalwarts of Bihar may have accepted each other (a) / to keep his head above water (b) / but both seem to find it difficult (c) / to conceal the silent game of one up manship. (d) /No error (e) .

Q20. Lord Meghnad Desai believes poverty is (a) / the biggest problem and a systematic strategy (b) / for generating rapid, high and inclusive growth (c) / is only solution. (d) / No error (e) .

Q21. While schooling is about to discipline (a) / cadres into certain behaviours (b) / and responses, education is about (c) / building competence. (d) / No error (e) .

Q22. (a) Today, the first task is to grow good teachers (a) / so that it can grow (b) / the next generation to greatness, (c) / which is India's aspiration. (d) / No error (e) .

Q23. He served the country (a) / with heart and soul (b) / but he got only (c) /a few rewards. (d) / No error (e) .

Q24. With the rise in population (a) / man needed more space (b) / for growing crops (c) /and for building houses. (d) / No error (e) .

Q25. Which do you (a) /prefer (b) / more meat (c) / or fish? (d) / No error (e) .

Q26.His strictly discipline (a) /had made (b) / him very unpopular among (c) / all the employees. (d) / No error (e) .

Q27. Jamshedji knew that an (a) /industrial revolution (b) / can only brought in the country (c) / by setting up iron and steel industry. (d) / No error (e) .

Q28. He being the eldest son (a) /has requested us (b) / to look after the problem (c) / faced by his father. (d) / No error (e) .

Q29. We met our (a) /prospective employer (b) / for a briefing session (c) / in the Taj Hotel. (d) / No error (e) .

Q30. Because of the severe snow storm (a) /and the road blocks, (b) / the air force dropped food and (c) / medical supplies close to the city. (d) / No error (e) .

Q31. More than one successful candidate (a) / have taken the interview for one (b) / of the popular magazines (c) / being published from Delhi. (d) / No error (e)

Q32. No less (a) / than fifty audiences are sitting (b) / in the hall and waiting for their (c) / beloved artiste's appearance on the stage. (d) / No error (e)

Q33. Much to his fortune, he (a) / married a girl who was (b) / more tall and lovelier than (c) / her elder sister. (d) / No error (e)

Q34. The company's decision to issue (a) / bonus shares clearly indicates (b) / the management's confident (c) / about the future. (d) / No error (e) .

Q35. Inspite that organizations are aware (a) / of the importance of IT (b) / they often do not know (c) / how to deploy it effectively. (d) / No error (e) .

Q36. Tarun was the one (a) / person who could somehow (b) / manage to working in the department (c) / for such a long time. (d) / No error (e)

Q37. The insurance companies (a) / and the Government is (b) / working on a uniform package (c) / policy for farmers. (d) / No error (e)

Q38. The number of people applying (a) / was so large that (b) / the office had to stop (c) / issuing application form. (d) / No error (e)

Q39. Modern printing techniques (a) / are far superior (b) / than that employed (c) / in the past. (d) / No error (e)

Q40. Much of the dispute over damages (a) / had to do with whether a certain portion (b) / of Apple's chips that were placed in (c) / devices violated the patent. (d) / No error (e)

Q41. Banks in India (a) / cannot open ATMs (b) / except obtaining (c) / approval from the RBI. (d) / No error (e)

Q42. Today the success of (a) / companies

depends on the (b) / quality of their products and (c) /efficient managing staff. (d) /No error (e)

Q43. Ashok has managed to (a) / achieve his sales targets (b) / for the quarter very easily (c) / than we expected. (d) / No error (e)

Q44. He did not grant (a) / their request for a loan (b) / although it would (c) / displease his boss. (d) /No error (e)

Q45. At present oil companies (a) / are making a loss of (b) / rupees five on all (c) / litre of petrol that they sell. (d) / No error (e)

Q46. The three-day trip that India's Prime Minister, Narendra Modi, made (a) / to china is seen in some quarter (b) / as a chance to reset the relationship (c) / between Asia's two giants (d) / No error (e)

Q47. Economic laws typically aims at balancing (a) / competing interests of various stakeholders (b) / as well as the interests of government departments (c) / charged with implementing such laws. (d) / No errors(e)

Q48. On a separate occasion, the High Court rapped (a) / the Director-General of Police for forwarding a complaint (b) / against Raj to the state government (c) / instead ordering an enquiry into it. (d) / No error (e)

Q49. The decision has immediately drawn a sharp response (a) / from the Congress and the SP, who along with (b) / other Opposition parties have been stalling (c) / the Bill's passage in the Rajya Sabha (d) / No error (e)

Q50. Once the demand draft will be deposited (a) / the individual will be eligible (b) / to participate in (c) / the online bidding process (d) / No error (e)

## Solutions (Practice Set - 08)

S1. Ans. (a)

Sol. 'sorts' will be used in place of 'sort' because adjective 'these' has been used before 'sort', hence noun will be used in plural form.

S2. Ans. (e)

Sol. The sentence is grammatically correct.

S3. Ans. (e)

Sol. No error -- Adjective of opinion is used before Adjective of colour 'pale', 'dark' etc. The correct order of adjective is OSASCOMP.

Opinion>Size>Age>Shape>Colour> Origin>Material> Purpose

S4. Ans. (c)

Sol. 'other' will not be used because when a person, place or thing of a group is being compared to person, place or thing of another group in comparative degree, then 'Any+ Singular Noun' is used. Ex. Rajan of this orchestra is better than any artist of that orchestra.

S5. Ans. (e)

Sol. The sentence is grammatically correct.

S6. Ans. (b)

Sol. In place of 'should', 'may' will be used. If the clause used in a sentence is in future tense or present tense then 'may' is used in dependent clause starting from 'that', 'so that' or 'in order that'.

S7. Ans. (e)

Sol. The sentence is grammatically correct. Remember 'hardly ever' is used which means 'very seldom'.

S8. Ans. (a)

Sol. The use of 'else' is superfluous in this sentence.

S9. Ans. (c)

Sol. In place of 'so', 'as' will be used because 'so...as' is used in negative sentence whereas 'as...as' is used in both affirmative and negative. Ex. (i) Ram is not so/as good as Mohan. (negative) (ii) Ram is as wise as Mohan. (Affirmative)

S10. Ans. (c)

Sol. 'than' will be used before 'the' because after 'No sooner', 'than' is used.

S11. Ans. (c)

Sol. Use 'fulfilled' in place of 'fulfill' because 'be' is followed by V3 (Past participle) in the passive voice.

S12. Ans. (b)

Sol. Use 'personal' in place of 'person' because 'quality' is noun and it must be qualified by an adjective and "***personal***" is an adjective.

S13. Ans. (b)

Sol. Use 'most liked' in place of 'mostly like', because this part of the sentence is in the passive form [Be+V3]

S14. Ans. (e)

Sol. No error

S15. Ans. (b)

Sol. Replace 'of' with 'from'

S16. Ans. (d)

Sol. Replace 'are' with 'is' because 'news' is an uncountable noun and we use singular verbs with uncountable nouns.

S17. Ans. (c)

Sol. Substitute 'averted' for 'avoided'. 'Avoid' means 'refrain from doing something' with 'avert' means 'to prevent something unpleasant'

**Section - II**

S18. Ans. (a)

Sol. Replace 'has' with 'have' as the main subject is "***cities***".

S19. Ans. (b)

Sol. Replace 'his head' with 'their heads' as the main subject is "The two stalwarts".

S20. Ans. (d)

Sol. Insert 'the' before 'only'

S21. Ans. (a)

Sol. Replace 'to discipline' with 'disciplining'

S22. Ans. (b)

Sol. Replace 'it' with 'they'.

S23. Ans. (b)

Sol. Remove 'with' because 'heart and soul' is never preceded by Preposition.

***Heart and soul*** means the whole of one's energy and passion.

S24. Ans. (e)

Sol. No error.

S25. Ans. (c)

Sol. Remove 'more' because prefer itself is comparative and never takes more or most before or after.

S26. Ans. (a)

Sol. Replace 'Strictly' with 'strict'. **Adverb never qualifies a Noun.** "***Strictly***" is an adverb.

S27. Ans. (c)

Sol. The passive construction is required here, so use 'be' before 'brought' **[Be+].**

**Modal + be + V3.**

S28. Ans. (c)

Sol. Use 'into' in place of 'after' because 'look into' means 'to investigate' and 'look after' means 'to care'.

S29. Ans. (d)

Sol. 'in' should be replaced by 'at'. Because "at" is used for smaller places

S30. Ans. (e)

Sol. No error

S31. Ans. (b)

Sol. Use 'has' in place of 'have' as with "more than one" we take singular verb.

S32. Ans. (a)

Sol. 'No fewer' should be used in place of 'no less' because we use "***fewer***" with countable nouns.

S33. Ans. (c)

Sol. Use 'taller' in place of 'more taller'

S34. Ans. (c)

Sol. Change 'the management's confident' with 'the management's confidence' as Noun should be used here.

S35. Ans. (a)

Sol. Here, Inspite of the fact that/Despite the fact that… should be used.

S36. Ans. (c)

Sol. Replace 'working' with 'work' as in the case of infinitive, ***to*** + ***V1*** is used.

S37. Ans. (b)

Sol. Replace 'is' with 'are' because when two different subjects are connected by "and", we use a plural verb.

S38. Ans. (d)

Sol. Replace 'form' with 'forms'

S39. Ans. (c)

Sol. Replace 'than that' with 'to those' because "***superior***" is followed by preposition "***to***".

S40. Ans. (e)

Sol. No correction required.

S41. Ans. (c)

Sol. "except" should be replaced by "without"

S42. Ans. (d)

Sol. "the efficiency of" managing staff

S43. Ans. (c)

Sol. "more easily" will be used because "than" is used and we are comparing.

S44. Ans. (e)

Sol. No error.

S45. Ans. (c)

Sol. "each/every" litre instead of "all" litre, because litre is singular. More over in the context each or every litre is right.

S46. Ans. (b)

Sol. Replace "quarter" with "quarters" because we use a plural noun or an uncountable noun after "some".

S47. Ans. (a)

Sol. Replace "aims" with "aim" because "***economic laws***" is a plural subject.

S48. Ans. (d)

Sol. Replace "instead" with "instead of"

S49. Ans. (e)

Sol. No error

S50. Ans. (a)

Sol. Replace "will be" with "is

Section - II

## Practice Set – 09

**Directions (01-50) : Read each sentence to find out whether there is any grammatical error in it. The error, if any, will be one part of the sentence. The number of that part is the answer. If there is no error, the answer is (e) . (Ignore the errors of punctuation, if any)**

Q1. Reports suggest Flipkart is not the (a) /only company from e-commerce (b) / and related sectors to have deferred (c) / the joining dates of their campus hires. (d) / No error. (e)

Q2. Bengaluru-based labs and start-ups are attempting (a) / to design molecules that can be developed (b) / into broad-spectrum drugs (c) / to combat drug-resistant bacteria. (d) / No error. (e)

Q3. A cab driver was attacked allegedly (a) / by refusing to carry more (b) / than four passengers (c) /in his vehicle. (d) /No error. (e)

Q4. The most stunning (a) / and close-up images of Pluto's surface (b) / has been beamed back (c) / to the Earth by NASA's New Horizons space probe. (d) / No error. (e)

Q5. If I would have realised (a) / what a bad shape (b) /our library is in (c) / I would have done something, to check the deterioration. (d) / No error (e) .

Q6. The functioning of Board (a) / was (b) / scrutinized by the Supreme Court, (c) /which have made some extraordinary interventions. (d) / No error. (e)

Q7. She abandoned herself (a) / to the delicacy of the (b) / dessert which her (c) / husband had prepared for her. (d) /No error. (e)

Q8. I watched my (a) / colleagues abasing (b) / themselves before the (c) / board of trustees (d) / No error. (e)

Q9. When I passed by the port (a) / the sound of siren (b) / resonated over (c) / the harbor (d) / No error. (e)

Q10. The work was (a) / completed from (b) / the assistance (c) / of carpenters. (d) / No error. (e)

Q11. Sheela had to travel all the way back (a) / when she remembered that (b) / she had forgot to take (c) / important documents with her. (d) / No error (e)

Q12. The party is holding a meeting (a) / in order to begin the (b) / painful and difficult process (c) / of rethink its political strategy. (d) / No error (e)

Q13. Part of the research programme (a) / involved interviewing (b) /teenagers in (c) /inner city areas. (d) /No error (e)

Q14.Arun is not only eminent (a) /for his writings in English (b) /but also for his (c) /paintings on spiritual themes. (d) / No error (e)

Q15. This is the only organization (a) / that could somehow continue (b) / to making profits (c) / in the face of recession. (d) / No error (e)

Q16. Many more would have died (a) / if they hadn't received (b) / the timely helping from (c) / the relief team. (d) / No error (e)

Q17. A man along with (a) / his wife and two children (b) / were rescued with the help (c) / of an army helicopter. (d) /No error (e)

Q18. I saw the accident (a) /but, fortunately I did not have to (b) /give evidence as there were (c) /a large number of other evidences. (d) /No error (e)

Q19. Neither the ministers (a) / nor the intelligence sources (b) / was aware of the coup (c) / being planned in the country. (d) /No error (e)

Q20. Certain amounts of stress (a) / at work is natural but (b) / it is important that one learns

(c) / to keep it in the right proportion. (d) /No error (e)

Q21. The university has received (a) / about 500 applications for the (b) / course, out of who 50 will be (c) /shortlisted for the programme.(d) / No error.(e)

Q22. If all things go according to plan, (a) / then we see our-self becoming a (b) / publicly listed company (c) / in two to three years. (d) / No error. (e)

Q23.Nobody can gift the other inner peace (a) / at the same time it is only his (b) / own thoughts that can (c) / rob him of him inner peace. (d) /No error. (e)

Q24. The cosy relationship between banks (a) / and big companies can be (b) / end only when there is real (c) / competition in the sector. (d) / No error. (e)

Q25. How can e-governance (a) / taken-off when the government's (b) / readiness to digitize its (c) /document base is pathetic? (d) / No error. (e)

Q26. Motivating the youth of (a) /nation is (b) / the central theme (c) /of the book. (d) /No error (e)

Q27. He have faced (a) /failures and (b) / disappointments without (c) /feeling defeated. (d) /No error (e)

Q28. Since time immemorial, (a) /India's spiritual (b) /wisdom has being (c) /its strength. (d) /No error (e)

Q29. Courage is an (a) /inner fortress (b) /which no enemy can (c) /ever destruction. (d) /No error (e)

Q30. Boldness has (a) /genius, power and (b) / magic in it along (c) /with infinite possibilities. (d) /No error (e)

Q31. The martyrdom (a) /about Sardar Bhagat (b) /Singh created (c) /a stir. (d) /No error (e)

Q32. He is well (a) /known in Hindi, (b) /Urdu and (c) /Arabic languages. (d) /No error (e)

Q33. Ruskin had postulated (a) /the concept of 'social affection' (b) /as the founding principle (c) /of a humane economy. (d) /No error (e)

Q34. His only motive (a) /was to finding (b) /the truth and (c) /follow it. (d) /No error (e)

Q35. On the surfacing (a) /she presented herself (b) /as someone in supreme (c) /control of her life. (d) /No error (e)

Q36. Men of action (a) / like Napoleon and Frederick the Great (b) / had no opinion for history (c) / holding it to be composed of falsehoods. (d) / No error (e)

Q37. For some years (a) / after the treaty of Versailles, it (b) / was assumed by scholars and laymen (c) / alike that Germany had caused World War I by her aggressive acts and encouraging Austria in her aggression. (d) / No error (e)

Q38. For a long time (a) /I had not known who (b) /was sitting besides me (c) /because it was, so dark. (d) /No error (e)

Q39. When one buys tickets in advance (a) / there is no guarantee (b) / that you (c) / will be free to attend the show on the night of performance. (d) / No error (e)

Q40. Ironically, of the four theories (a) / concerning (b) / the structure of the universe, the one (c) / which to date has had the longest life is also the one which is least correct. (d) / No error (e)

Q41. He thinks that (a) / once he paid money (a) / he is relieved of (c) / all his responsibilities. (d) / No error (e)

Q42. Taking care of yourself (a) / cannot be (b) /

and should not be considered(c) / a selfish thing. (d) / No error (e)

Q43. Cleanliness drives will be (a) / conducted in various localities (b) / to opening the drains blocked (c) / with polythene bags. (d) / No error (e)

Q44. The results of the study showed that (a) / if the partners were willing to talk to each other (b) / and arrive at a mutually agreeable decision, (c) / the joint decisions were more better than any one person's judgment. (d) / No error (e)

Q45. Sugar-sweetened drinks does not (a) / pose any particular health risk and (b) / are not a unique risk factor (c) / for obesity or heart disease. (d) / No error. (e)

Q46. Airline management should note (a) / that the ultimate passenger unfriendliness (b) / is to have their plane crashed (c) / due to the adopted of unsafe procedures. (d) / No error (e)

Q47. The actor thinks, (a) / stick to one kind of role (b) / and finds it difficult to (c) / fulfill everyone's expectations. (d) / No error (e)

Q48. A major computer security firm urged (a) / the social networking site to set-up (b) / an early-warning system after-hundreds of users were (c) / hit by a new wave of virus attacks. (d) / No error (e)

Q49. An administrative decision in (a) /any particular situation (b) /need not be correct (c) / under another situation. (d) /No error (e)

Q50. District police arrested (a) / a gang of notorious robbers, (b) / who were planning to strike at (c) / a house in the vicinity. (d) / No error (e)

## Solutions (Practice Set - 09)

S1. Ans. (e)

Sol. No error.

S2. Ans. (e)

Sol. No error.

S3. Ans. (b)

Sol. Replace 'by' with 'for' as 'for' is used to denote something 'as a result of something'

S4. Ans. (c)

Sol. Here, the subject is 'images' so the verb used must agree with it. Hence, replace 'has' with 'have'.

S5. Ans. (a)

Sol. Part 'a' of the statement is wrong. It will be as 'If I had realized'. Refer the rule of conditional sentences.

S6. Ans. (d)

Sol. use 'has' in place of 'have'. Since subject is 'the Supreme Court' which is singular, hence, verb used should also be singular.

S7. Ans. (b)

Sol. 'for' will be used in place of to

S8. Ans. (e)

Sol. No error.

S9. Ans. (c)

Sol. 'resonated across' is correct usage.

S10. Ans. (b)

Sol. 'with the assistance of carpenters' is the correct usage.

S11. Ans. (c)

Sol. Substitute 'forgotten' in place of 'forgot'.

S12. Ans. (4)

Sol. Substitute 'rethinking' in place of 'rethink'.

S13. Ans. (c)

Sol. 'of' should be used in place of 'in'.

S14. Ans. (a)

Sol. Use 'eminent' before not only. "***Not only... but also..., either...or..., neither...nor...***" are equal rank words. The construction after "***not only***" should be similar to the construction after "***but also***".

S15. Ans. (c)

Sol. Substitute 'make' in place of 'making' as in the case of infinitive, ***to + V1*** is used.

S16. Ans. (c)

Sol. Substitute 'help' in place of 'helping'.

S17. Ans. (c)

Sol. Substitute 'was' in place of 'were' as the main subject is "***a man***" which is singular.

S18. Ans. (d)

Sol. Evidence is an uncountable noun while witness is a countable noun and both are used as testimony or proof so 'a large number of' can't be used with evidence so either witness should be used in place of evidence or 'a large number of' should be removed.

S19. Ans. (c)

Sol. Substitute 'were' in place of 'was'.

In case of "Neither....nor" the verb should be according to the nearest subject.

S20. Ans. (a)

Sol. Substitute 'A certain amount' in place of 'Certain amounts'.

S21. Ans. (c)

Sol. Replace who with which. "Applications" is non living . Hence we will use which.

S22. Ans. (b)

Sol. Replace our-self with ourselves.

**Section - II**

S23. Ans. (d)

Sol. Replace him with his.

S24. Ans. (c)

Sol. Replace end with ended. ***Modal + be + V3 is used in Passive voice.***

S25. Ans. (b)

Sol. Replace taken-off with take-off.

S26. Ans. (e)

Sol. No Error.

S27. Ans. (a)

Sol. Use 'has' in place of 'have'.

S28. Ans. (c)

Sol. Use 'been' in place of 'being'. We use "***has/ have + been***" in passive voice while we use "***being***" is used in Continuous Tenses.

S29. Ans. (d)

Sol. Use 'destroy' in place of 'destruction'. It is a noun. A verb will be used here.

S30. Ans. (e)

Sol. No error.

S31. Ans. (b)

Sol. Use 'of' in place of 'about'.

S32. Ans. (b)

Sol. Use 'for' in place of 'in'.

S33. Ans. (d)

Sol. Use 'human' in place of 'humane'.

**Human** means relating to or characteristic of humankind.

***Humane*** means having or showing compassion or benevolence.

S34. Ans. (b)

Sol. Use 'to find' in place of 'to finding' as in the case of infinitive, ***to + V1*** is used.

S35. Ans. (a)

Sol. Use 'surface' in place of 'surfacing'.

S36. Ans. (d)

Sol. Replace "holding it to be" with "and held it to be".

S37. Ans. (e)

Sol. No error

S38. Ans. (c)

Sol. Use 'beside' in place of 'besides'.

S39. Ans. (c)

Sol. Change 'you' to 'one' as the subject is "one".

S40. Ans. (d)

Sol. Use "the least".

S41. Ans. (b)

Sol. Expression should read out as 'once he has paid'. This reflects the effect of an action done in the past to the present.

e.g. Once you have submitted the form then you are to wait for a month.

S42. Ans. (e)

Sol. No error

S43. Ans. (c)

Sol. 'For opening' is the correct expression to be used in this sentence.

e.g. He gave me a hundred rupee note for buying a balloon.

S44. Ans. (d)

Sol. 'More' is superfluous in this case and therefore it should be removed as 'better' alone is enough to show the comparison.

e.g. She has a better attitude than her brother.

S45. Ans. (a)

Sol. The subject is plural in number so the verb should also be in plural number. Replace 'does' by 'do'.

e.g. The patriots don't deface the country.

S46. Ans. (d)

Sol. 'Adopted' should be replaced by 'adoption' that is in sync with the sentence as "***adoption***" is a noun and "***adopted***" is a verb.

e.g. Adoption of unsafe measures lead to poor health.

S47. Ans. (b)

Sol. All the verbs form should be same if they are used continuously. So, 'stick' is to be replaced by 'sticks'.

e.g. She sings, enjoys and cherishes it too.

S48. Ans. (c)

Sol. 'An early warning system' should be replaced by 'a warning system' because warnings are by nature early and using 'early' becomes superfluous to the sentence.

e.g. The warning system that the company issued in the market is taken with a great zeal.

S49. Ans. (e)

Sol. The given sentence is grammatically correct.

S50. Ans. (c)

Sol. Remove 'at' from the expression. With 'at' the meaning comes as 'to' attack someone.

e.g. The batsman strikes the bowler very mercilessly in the last over.

Section - II

## Practice Set – 10

**Directions (01-50) : Read each sentence to find out whether there is any grammatical error or idiomatic error in it. The error, if any, will be in one part of the sentence. The number of part is the answer. If there is no error, the answer is (e) . (Ignore errors of punctuation, if any)**

Q1. He was grateful (a) / to me for the help (b) / that I had extended for him (c) / in the hour of his need. (d) / No error (e)

Q2. While undergoing a (a) / strenuous workout (b) / he suffered a massive heart attack (c) / but luckily survival. (d) / No error (e)

Q3. People express their expectations (a) / that their leaders should not (b) / resorting to (c) / corrupt practices and nepotism. (d) / No error (e)

Q4. There is no one (a) /whom I esteem (b) / highly than (c) /your mother and father. (d) /No error (e)

Q5. But for your help, (a) /no boys would have succeeded in an (c) /All India competition like this. (d) /No error (e)

Q6. Farmhouse owners in the city, (a) / who were till now paid property tax (b) / for only the built-up area of the plot, will soon (c) / have to pay tax to the government for vacant land as well. (d) / No error (e)

Q7. Once, we were dwelt (a) /by the seaside (b) /but now we have (c) /settled ourselves in Mumbai. (d) /No error (e)

Q8. The district authorities are making (a) / a last-ditch attempt to provide (b) / alternative solutions to farmers but (c) / the option is clearly inadequate. (d) /No error (e)

Q9. The smooth and easier (a) / we allow people to navigate (b) / through any device at any place (c) / in the world, the better opportunities knock at their door . (d) / No error (e)

Q10. The problem of soil erosion (a) /is one of the (b) /serious problem (c) /in various countries. (d) / /No error (e)

Q11. The survey conducted reveals (a) / that there is a lack (b) / of adequate healthcare facilities (c) / even in urban areas. (d) / No error (e)

Q12. Some of the world (a) / largest water bodies are (b) / drying up thus threatening (c) / the livelihoods of millions. (d) / No error (e)

Q13. We had made every effort (a) / to ensure that a (b) / compromise is reached and (c) / that deal was signed. (d) / No error (e)

Q14. The questionaire/ (a) reflected/ (b) various phenomena (c) / that are sparingly experienced. (d) / No error (e)

Q15. The process was so simple (a) / and easy to understand (b) / that it hardly took (c) / 5 minutes for us to learn it. (d) / No error (e)

Q16. It is strange that (a) / even after 15 years of experience, (b) / he is still not (c) / able to be performed. (d) / No error (e)

Q17. Some people like (a) / to do some social (b) / work even though (c) / it lacks resources. (d) / No crror (e)

Q18. His qualities include (a) / the ability to take (b) / right and quickly decisions (c) / on important policies. (d) / No error (e)

Q19. The astronomical (a) / calculations done by the astronomer (b) /were admiringly (c) / accurate. (d) /No error (e)

Q20. The ministry was considered (a) / several proposals for the (b) / development of small and medium (c) / enterprises during budget discussions. (d) / No error (e)

Q21. His main aim is (a) / to create an (b) / interest in hockey (c) / among school children. (d) / No error (e)

Q22. India's travel and tourism (a) / industry is poised (b) / on growth at seven (c) / per cent this year alone. (d) / No error (e)

Q23. We have sought (a) / clearance in (b) / additional expenditure incurred (c) / during the project. (d) / No error (e)

Q24. The Reserve Bank of India's decision (a) / to waive ATM charges (b) / have put banks (c) / in a difficult position. (d) / No error (e)

Q25. The two candidates share (a) / a reputation for (b) / competency as well as (c) / for good communication skills. (d) / No error (e)

Q26. His main qualification (a) / on the job is (b) / his extensive experience (c) / in foreign branches. (d) / No error (e)

Q27. Habit of (a) / saving (b) / helps us (c) / during bad times. (d) / No error (e)

Q28. To know how people react to (a) / an unforeseen situation (b) / is very important (c) / to decide our course of action. (d) / No error (e)

Q29. Countrary/ (a) / to popular belief, (b) / ripe fruits are not necessarily (c) / delicious. (d) / No error (e)

Q30. The most ambitious (a) / enterprise (b) / undertaken in the ancient (c) / Egypt was of the construction of pyramids. (d) / No error (e)

Q31. Know he was dying (a) / Morrie visited (b) / his study every Tuesday with Mitch (c) / just as they used to do back in college. (d) / No error (e)

Q32. We are planning (a) / to set up a training college (b) / to train our marketing team (c) / for effective marketing of our products. (d) / No error (e)

Q33. Nobody knew (a) / where I spend my day (b) / and nobody really (c) / seemed to care. (d) / No error (e)

Q34. My father has (a) / always had a curious habit (b) / of consulting astrologers (c) / which I could never understand. (d) / No error (e)

Q35. I stopped at Aurangabad (a) / from where I make excursions (b) / to the Ajanta Caves (c) / and the temple at Ellora. (d) / No error (e)

Q36. I am extremely tired and (a) / I cannot talk to you now (b) / because I was just (c) / returned from office. (d) / No error (e)

Q37. Roopa very much resembles to (a) / Laxmi in looks (b) / as well as figure although (c) / she is Laxmi's step-daughter. (d) / No error (e)

Q38. I am afraid (a) / neither of them are coming (b) / to attend the marriage reception (c) / of my younger sister. (d) / No error (e)

Q39. All of us are aware that (a) / Shankar has been suffering (b) from fever since ten days (c) / and has been resting. (d) / No error (e)

Q40. Both of them genuinely helped (a) / each other when their (b) / families were going (c) / through a bad patch. (d) / No error (e)

Q41. Rekha was trying for admission (a) / in the Engineering College (b) / even though her parents wanted (c) / her to take up medicine. (d) / No error (e)

Q42. He fixed a metal ladder (a) / for the wall below his window (b) / so as to be able to (c) / escape if there were a fire. (d) / No error (e)

Q43. Several prominent figures (a) / involved in the scandal (b) / are required to appear (c) / to the investigation committee. (d) / No error (e)

Q44. He grow up the way (a) / many young

children grow up-(b) / pampered, adored (c) / and inwardly tortured. (d) / No error (e)

Q45. He pulled his lips together, (a) / close his eyes (b) / and I watched the first teardrop (c) / fall down the side of his cheek. (d) / No error (e)

Q46. If the monsoon is delayed (a) / or is insufficient, there is (b) / inevitable failure of the (c) / crops, causing a famine. (d) / No error (e)

Q47. There is no denying the fact (a) / that he is one (b) / of the best players (c) / that has ever lived. (d) / No error (e)

Q48. The headmaster with all (a) /his senior teachers (b) /have come (c) /to attend the meeting. (d) /No error (e)

Q49. The main difficulty was (a) / the barriers which were standing (b) / at the centre (c) / of the crossroads. (d) / No error (e)

Q50. Despite of a good monsoon this year (a) / the production of food grains (b) / in the country (c) / did not go up. (d) / No error (e)

## Solutions (Practice Set - 10)

S1. Ans. (c)

Sol. 'Extended' should be followed by 'to' and not by 'for'.

e.g. I extended my help to everybody.

S2. Ans. (d)

Sol. 'Survival' should make way for 'survived'. 'Survival' is a noun, which is not required her. So, 'survived' which is a verb should be used here.

e.g. Many people survived in the massive earthquake that hit Nepal.

S3. Ans. (c)

Sol. Modal 'should' is followed by V1. So, 'resorting' should be removed and we should use 'resort'.

e.g. One should not resort to robbery or anything else like this.

S4. Ans. (c)

Sol. Replace 'highly' by 'higher' as the word 'than' infers that the sentence is of Comparative Degree.

S5. Ans. (e)

Sol. No error

S6. Ans. (b)

Sol. 'Paid' should be replaced by 'paying' because the sentence is showing progression.

e.g. The people who were paying attention till now are disturbed by a noise.

S7. Ans. (a)

Sol. Remove 'were' from the sentence as the sentence is in Active Voice.

S8. Ans. (e)

Sol. No error.

S9. Ans. (a)

Sol. Use 'smoother' in place of 'smooth'. Co-ordinate connector 'and' uses the same degree to both its sides.

S10. Ans. (c)

Sol. Use 'problems' in place of 'problem'. "One of the" is followed by a plural noun.

S11. Ans. (e)

Sol. No error.

S12. Ans. (a)

Sol. 'World' should be replaced by 'world's' to make it correct possessive.

e.g. A large part of world's population is not getting nutritious food.

S13. Ans. (c)

Sol. The sentence is in past tense so 'is' is to be replaced by 'was'.

e.g. I tried my level best that a treaty was signed and work could be settled.

S14. Ans. (d)

Sol. 'Sparingly' is wrongly used here. We should use 'rarely' to make it correct.

e.g. Rarely do we see a bird unable to fly.

Sparingly means in a restricted or infrequent manner; in small quantities.

S15. Ans. (e)

Sol. No error.

S16. Ans. (d)

Sol. 'Be Performed' is passive structure that is not suitable here we should use to perform which is correct.

e.g. A batsman out of form is not able to perform in the match.

S17. Ans. (d)

**Section - II**

Sol. 'It lacks' is to be replaced by 'they lack' because people is plural in number.

e.g. Many people struggle to get an education because they lack proper infrastructure.

S18. Ans. (c)

Sol. 'Quickly' is an adverb which is not required here, we should use an adjective quick to make the syntax correct.

e.g. He is a learner who is quick and fast.

S19. Ans. (e)

Sol. No error.

S20. Ans. (a)

Sol. 'Ministry' is the subject of the sentence and hence it should take active voice. So, 'was' is to be removed which is making it passive.

e.g. The department considered his case to be a special one.

S21. Ans. (e)

Sol. No error.

S22. Ans. (c)

Sol. 'Poised' is followed by 'to'. Thus, 'growth' should also be changed to 'grow'. e.g. Our intellect poised to grow from the day we start being lazy.

If someone is ***poised to*** do something, they are ready to take action at any moment.

S23. Ans. (b)

Sol. 'Clearance' should be followed by 'of'. e.g. They have sought for clearance of the bills.

S24. Ans. (c)

Sol. 'RBI's decision' is a singular subject hence 'have' should make way for 'has' which is a singular verb.

e.g. IRDA has issued a notification for the smooth regulations of the different in insurance companies.

S25. Ans. (e)

Sol. No error

S26. Ans. (b)

Sol. 'Qualification' should be followed by 'for'.

e.g. he has the desired qualification for this post.

S27. Ans. (a)

Sol. Since habit is specified here so we have to use 'the' before it to make the syntax correct.

e.g. The habit of smoking is always bad.

S28. Ans. (e)

Sol. No error.

S29. Ans. (a)

Sol. 'Contrary' is wrongly spelt as 'countrary'.

e.g. Contrary to my expectation, he came so early to the party.

S30. Ans. (e)

Sol. No error.

S31. Ans. (a)

Sol. 'Knowing' instead of 'know' is correct.

S32. Ans. (e)

Sol. No error.

S33. Ans. (b)

Sol. Past perfect tense form of the verb–'had spent'–should be used. At the time that nobody knew, the other action–that of spending my day–had already happened. [Two actions occurring in the past]

S34. Ans. (e)

Sol. No error.

S35. Ans. (b)

Sol. The past tense verb–'made'–should be used

for verb conformity.

S36. Ans. (c)

Sol. Past tense verb should not be used; 'have' should replace 'was' for verb uniformity (present form) .

We use Present Perfect Tense with "just"

S37. Ans. (a)

Sol. One person simply 'resembles' another. 'Resembles' means 'looks like'. Some verbs like 'resembles' do not take 'to' after them.

S38. Ans. (b)

Sol. With 'neither', meaning 'none of the tow', only a singular verb should be used. So, 'is' coming. Not 'are' coming.

S39. Ans. (c)

Sol. Use 'for', instead of 'since' because we use ***'for'*** to denote duration of time.

S40. Ans. (e)

Sol. No error.

S41. Ans. (e)

Sol. No error.

S42. Ans. (b)

Sol. A ladder is fixed 'to' the wall, not 'for' it. If instead of 'fixed', the word used is 'placed', the preposition would be 'against'.

S43. Ans. (d)

Sol. One appears 'before' an investigation committee, not 'to' it.

S44. Ans. (a)

Sol. "grow up" should be replaced by "grew up" because a past tense should be used in the first part of the sentence to maintain the correct tense form.

S45. Ans. (b)

Sol. Use 'closed', not 'close'. The past tense verb should be used throughout.

S46. (b)

Sol. 'There will be', that is, future tense, should be used as we are talking of something that may happen in future.

S47. Ans. (d)

Sol. 'Have' must replace 'has' as 'best players' are referred to.

S48. Ans. (c)

Sol. Use 'has' in place of 'have' as the subject is "Headmaster" which is singular.

S49. Ans. (e)

Sol. No error.

S50. Ans. (a)

Sol. 'Despite' itself means 'in spite of'. 'Despite' is not followed by 'of'. So "of" should be removed.

Section - II

## Practice Set – 11

**Directions (01-50) : Read each sentence to find out whether there is any grammatical error or idiomatic error in it. The error, if any, will be in one part of the sentence. The number of part is the answer. If there is no error, the answer is (e) . (Ignore errors of punctuation, if any)**

Q1. The players (a) / whom we have selected (b) / for our team (c) / are young and ambitious. (d) / No Error (e)

Q2. He seems to be happy (a) /because his parents (b) /had come from London (c) /to live with him. (d) / No error. (e)

Q3. There is none (a) /who can help you (b) / in this crucial moments (c) / of your career. (d) / No Error (e)

Q4. This is the same (a) /dog which barked (b) / at him but fortunately did not (c) / bite him. (d) / No Error. (e)

Q5. Whomever (a) /comes late will not be allowed (b) /to mark his presence (c) / in the register. (d) / No Error. (e)

Q6. He lent me some (a) / money on the condition (b) / that I should return same (c) / before November. (d) /No Error (e)

Q7. Under no circumstances (a) / have I harmed (b) / him, and he (c) /knows. (d) / No Error. (e)

Q8. The beggar (a) / whom we had suspected (b) / to be guilty turned out (c) / to be innocent. (d) / No Error. (e)

Q9. The candidate (a) / being a graduate (b) / he is eligible for (c) / the post of Probationary Officer. (d) / No Error. (e)

Q10. I don't appreciate (a) /those who laugh (b) /at others without any (c) /apparent reason. (d) / No Error. (e)

Q11. To be a king and (a) / wear a crown are (b) / more glamorous to (c) / see than to bear. (d) / No error (e)

Q12. None of the student (a) / in the class (b) / scored below (c) / the given cutoff marks (d) / No error. (e)

Q13. Ashok is among the (a) / few people in the world (b) / which did not blindly follow (c) /the path of others. (d) / No error (e)

Q14. Most people like (a) /to rest after a day's work (b) / but he seemed (c) / to have an inexhaustive supply of energy. (d) / No error. (e)

Q15. Ancient artifacts are (a) / a part of global heritage (b) / and should not be (c) / sold to the highest bidder. (d) / No error. (e)

Q16. Neither (a) / Rakesh nor (b) / Shakti, presented their (c) / papers before the deadline for doing so. (d) /. No error (e)

Q17. A recent (a) / poll has indicated (b) / that Binny is considered (c) / brighter than any student in the class (d) /. No error (e)

Q18. The company is planning (a) / a training (b) / programme for their (c) / senior officers sometime in December. (d) / No error (e)

Q19. There was only (a) / a loaf of bread and two bottles of milk in the (b) / refrigerator when (c) / we came back after a weekend in Manali. (d) / No error (e)

Q20. Carrying a bag (a) /in his hand, (b) /he slipped (c) /out unnoticed. (d) /No error (e)

Q21. The government is planning to (a) / sanction grants to pharmaceutical companies (b) / for inventing new treatments for (c) / diseases about malaria and tuberculosis. (d) / No error (e)

Q22. She regards (a) /negotiating prices (b) /with

customers as (c) /her special expertise. (d) /No error (e)

Q23. A representative of the (a) / Reserve Bank will provide students an (b) / insight into the (c) / economic future of our country. (d) / No error (e)

Q24. Despite taking steps to (a) / encourage foreign investment (b) / there has been any (c) / substantial improvement in our economy. (d) / No error (e)

Q25. Let's all work (a) / together as like homogeneous (b) / group so that (c) / success would be obvious. (d) / No error (e)

Q26. The aim of the course (a) / will be to cater to students with diverted needs (b) / from basic knowledge(c) / to top end research and publishing skills.(d) / No error(e)

Q27. The reports prompted the chairman of (a) / the organizing committee to address a hurried press conference (b) / where he reprimanded the media (c) /for conducting a "prejudiced campaign".(d) /No error(e)

Q28. I appealed to (a) /her to look (b) /after my children (c) /during my absence. (d) /No error. (e)

Q29. The RBI has proposed to introduce (a) / polymer notes after taking into considering (b) / the cost and longevity (c) / associated with their manufacturing.(d) / No error (e)

Q30. Neither of the (a) /teams are sensible (b) / enough to (c) /do this task. (d) /No error (e) .

Q31. The teacher advised to (a) /the student to borrow (b) /a book from the library (c) /within three days. (d) /No error (e)

Q32. From the last one month (a) / each of us (b) / has been working (c) / on the same project. (d) / No error. (e)

Q33. When I receive (a) / the letter, the date (b) / for the interview (c) / was already over. (d) / No error. (e)

Q34. We had (a) / helped him (b) / if he had (c) / requested us earlier. (d) / No error. (e)

Q35. We have observed that (a) / many good programmes (b) / suffer of shortage (c) / of funds and other resources. (d) / No error. (e)

Q36. Jagdish met me yesterday (a) / but he did not tell me (b) / that he has (c) / resigned from the factory. (d) / No error. (e)

Q37. It is unfortunate (a) / but still a reality (b) / that poverty and development (c) / goes hand in hand (d) / No error. (e)

Q38. We decided that if they (a) /come up with a creditable (b) / programme we would include (c) /them in the scheme. (d) /No error (e)

Q39. The Supervisor noticed that (a) / one of the employees were (b) / involved in (c) / unfair activities outside the office. (d) / No error. (e)

Q40. How well a person (a) / completes his own (b) / assignments depend (c) / upon his skill (d) / No error. (e)

Q41. We have a fantastic car (a) /this year, even better (b) / that in 2014 and it (c) / should suit the track. (d) /No error (e)

Q42. The Finance Minister's view (a) / is that the scheme will ensure (b) / that millions of farmers will be (c) / lifted out of poverty. (d) / No error (e)

Q43. A representative of the (a) / Reserve bank will provide students an (b) / insight into the (c) / economic future of our country. (d) / No error (e)

Q44. As one of the leader (a) / insurance companies in (b) / India they offer (c) / comprehensive financial services. (d) / No error (e)

Q45. The amount of foreign (a) / direct investment

## Section - II

in (b) / the country in 2008 is (c) / doubled the amount received in 1997. (d) / No error (e)

Q46. No sooner he left the office (a) / than it started (b) / raining heavily (c) / enough to make him completely wet. (d) / No error (e)

Q47. Even after hearing the leader (a) / for a long time (b) / the followers could not make out (c) / which he was talking about. (d) / No error (e)

Q48. The principal along with the teachers (a) / were seen boarding a bus (b) / to go to a picnic (c) / on a national holiday.(d) / No error (e)

Q49. With the introduction of the new syllabus (a) / the number of colleges reporting (b) / high results are decreasing (c) / year after year. (d) / No error (e)

Q50. If the monsoon delays (a) / or insufficient, there will be (b) / inevitable failure of the (c) / crops which will cause a famine. (d) / No error (e)

## Solutions (Practice Set - 11)

S1. Ans. (e)

Sol. No error.

S2. Ans. (c)

Sol. Use 'have' in place of 'had' as the essence of the condition in the sentence is in present form.

e.g. He seems to be happy because his father has sent him a suit.

S3. Ans. (b)

Sol. Use 'that' in place of 'who' as after 'none' only 'that' can be used as a relative pronoun.

S4. Ans. (b)

Sol. Use 'that' in place of 'which' for the same reason as explained in the above solution.

S5. Ans. (a)

Sol. Use 'whoever' in place of 'whomever' as 'whomever' is an objective case therefore the verb comes can't be used. Verb is used in subjective case and subjective case of whomever is whoever.

S6. Ans. (c)

Sol. Use 'it' in place of 'same'.

S7. Ans. (d)

Sol. 'it' should be used after 'knows'.

S8. Ans. (e)

Sol. No error

S9. Ans. (c)

Sol. The use of 'he' is superfluous here as the subject is 'The candidate' and therefore 'he' will not be used.

S10. Ans. (e)

Sol. No error.

S11. Ans. (b)

Sol. Use 'is' in place 'are'. The subject is singular and so a singular verb is required. "To be a king" and "wear a crown" is one and the same thing.

S12. Ans. (a)

Sol. Use 'students' in place of 'student'. After one of, each of, none of a plural noun is required.

S13. Ans. (c)

Sol. Use 'who' in place of 'which'. For persons relative pronoun who is used.

S14. Ans. (c)

Sol. Use 'seems' in place of 'seemed'. Present Indefinite form of verb is required. It is a fact about nature.

S15. Ans. (e)

Sol. The sentence is correct.

S16. Ans. (c)

Sol. presented his papers before...'

Singular antecedent (Rakesh and Shakti) joined by or or nor are referred to by singular pronoun (his) . When two subjects are joined by "neither... nor...", the verb follows the nearest subject.

S17. Ans. (d)

Sol. '....brighter than any other student....'

In a comparative construction we must be sure that if A and B are compared, A is not included as a part of B.

S18. Ans. (c)

Sol. '.... training programme for its....'

A singular pronoun-adjective (its, not their) must be used to refer to a collective noun (company) when the members of the collective noun are considered a unit.

S19. Ans. (a)

Sol. '....there were only.....'

The subject of the sentence is plural (a bread

and bottles) . Therefore, the verb must be plural (were, not was) . Here the word there is not the subject.

S20. Ans. (e)

Sol. The sentence is grammatically correct.

S21. Ans. (d)

Sol. 'About' should be replaced by 'like'.

S22. Ans. (e)

Sol. No error.

S23. Ans. (e)

Sol. No error.

S24. Ans. (c)

Sol. 'Any' should be replaced by 'no' that will make the syntax correct.

S25. Ans. (b)

Sol. use either 'as' or 'like' because ***'as'*** and ***'like'*** together are superfluous.

S26. Ans. (b)

Sol. 'Divert' is a verb and it should not be used here in the form of 'diverted'. Instead, we should use 'diversifying' which is an adjective and that qualifies a noun well.

S27. Ans. (e)

Sol. No correction required.

S28. Ans. (e)

Sol. The sentence is grammatically correct.

S29. Ans. (b)

Sol. Considering should be replaced with 'consideration' to make the sense correct.

S30. Ans. (b)

Sol. Use 'is' in place of 'are'.

S31. Ans. (a)

Sol. Remove 'to' from first part.

S32. Ans. (a)

Sol. 'for' will be used in place of 'from' as in present perfect continuous or present perfect tense , 'for' is used to represent the period of time.

Ex. He has been living with me for the last one year.

S33. Ans. (a)

Sol. 'received' will be used in place of 'receive' as the sentence is in past tense as is indicated by 'already over'.

S34. Ans. (a)

Sol. 'we would have' will be used in place of 'we had' as for If + Past perfect we use 'Subject + would/ could/ might/ should + have + V3' in the result clause Refer the rule of conditional sentences.

Ex. I would have helped you if you had come earlier.

S35. Ans. (c)

Sol. 'from' will be used in place of 'of' as preposition 'from' is used after 'suffer'.

Ex. He is suffering from fever.

S36. Ans. (c)

Sol. 'had' will be used in place of 'has' as the sentence is in past tense.

S37. Ans. (d)

Sol. 'go' will be used in place of 'goes' as the subject of 'that- clause' is plural, therefore plural verb is used.

Ex. Oil and water do not mix

S38. Ans. (c)

Sol. Replace "would" with "will". Refer the rule of conditional sentences.

S39. Ans. (b)

Sol. 'was' will be used in place of 'were' as the subject of 'that- clause' is 'one'.

Ex. One of these girls is very beautiful.

S40. Ans. (c)

Sol. 'depends' will be used in place of 'depend' as the subject of the sentence is singular.

S41. Ans. (c)

Sol. Replace "that" with "than".

S42. Ans. (c)

Sol. 'Will be' should be replaced by 'are'. The first part of the clause is in future tense. So, second part needs to be in present tense.

S43. Ans. (e)

Sol. No error.

S44. Ans. (a)

Sol. The expression should read out as 'As one of the leading' instead of 'as one of the leader' to make the syntax correct.

e.g. As one of the leading run scorers he will be a key in this series.

S45. Ans. (d)

Sol. 'Doubled' is the wrong usage. We should use 'double' only to make the syntax correct.

e.g. The marks obtained by me this year is double the marks I obtained in previous year.

S46. Ans. (a)

Sol. Rewrite the part as "No sooner did he leave……." (rule of inversion)

S47. Ans. (d)

Sol. Replace 'which' with 'what'.

S48. Ans. (b)

Sol. Replace 'were' with 'was'. When two nouns are joined by 'along with', verb agrees with the first subject.

S49. Ans. (c)

Sol. Replace 'are' with 'is' as the subject is 'the number'. ***"The number of…"*** takes a singular verb while "***A number of …***" takes a plural verb.

S50. Ans. (b)

Sol. Add 'is' before 'insufficient'.

## Practice Set – 12

**Directions (01-25) : In the question given below, there are four sentences. Choose the sentence which is grammatically incorrect as your answer. If all the given sentences are grammatically correct and do not require any correction, choose (e) i.e. "All are correct".**

Q1. (a) The future effects of science and technological development must not be harmful to mankind in the long run, he cautioned researchers.

(b) He talked about the importance of the Army collaborating with industry to modernize and equip troops.

(c) It have become almost fashionable to predict doom and gloom for high street clothes shops.

(d) Improved medical technology has been one of the spin-offs of the space program.

(e) All are correct.

Q2. (a) The data, recently updated till 2015-16, shows that employment fell in several sectors.

(b) The problem is that productivity in the construction industry has been declining.

(c) These ratios would be much poorer for the eastern and north-eastern parts of the country.

(d) Employment in the total Indian economy shrank by 0.1% in financial year 2015-16 and by 0.2% in 2014-15

(e) All are correct

Q3. (a) Collected the biometric information of a customer is a long and expensive process.

(b) Indians will experience formal banking systems for the first time in their lives.

(c) No sooner had this sentiment expressed more loudly than India's started facing struggles.

(d) India is short of cash and it is, unfortunately, starving its military.

(e) All are correct

Q4. (a) The loan was extended under consortium arrangements, said the bank.

(b) Karnataka Bank became the latest bank exposed to a wider loan fraud involving Gitanjali Gems and owner Mehul Choksi.

(c) All official correspondence of the state government will now refer to Ambedkar with the new name.

(d) He had inspired the Dalit Buddhist Movement and campaigned against social discrimination against "untouchables".

(e) All are correct

Q5. (a) Two other lines in the name of the chief general manager of Chennai Telephones also functioned from Maran's home.

(b) The DMK was a senior partner in the Congress-led United Progressive Alliance government at the Centre.

(c) He said the acquisition would enable Tenor to accelerate improvements to its service.

(d) The publication had to move to the Supreme Court to ask the CBI registering an FIR in the misuse of Chennai Telephone by the Maran brothers.

(e) No error

Q6. (a) Salvaging the Indian demographic dividend must be a key part of India's growth story.

(b) Short duration courses (with no real skills) that provide low pay for suboptimal jobs cannot be called national standards.

(c) India could surely become the world's skill capital yet not with what it is doing right now.

(d) Short-term training should be confined to recognising prior learning of informally trained workers who are already working.

(e) All are correct

Q7. (a) We need an education system where oral or visual communication is not just a medium but also the language of content generation.

(b) The two leaders came together in 2015 and got a mandate from the people for good governance and institutional reform.

(c) The local body poll results have given sufficient indication of the people's concerns over the economy and unemployment.

(d) I have been thinking about something lately, related to languages, medium of communication and the future of the world.

(e) All are correct

Q8. (a) The popular messaging tools have highlighted that if communities are given a chance, and required bandwidth, they can communicate freely even if they can't read or write.

(b) Even though half the world is now connected to the internet and is communicating digitally, the definition of "literacy" has not changed.

(c) A pickup in domestic demand would only accelerate in the second half of the year given the seasonality of consumption during festival months.

(d) The facts that the inflation forecast would be lowered was broadly expected.

(e) All are correct

Q9. (a) Trump had agreed to sell unarmed drones to India so as to enhance India's surveillance capabilities in the Indian Ocean.

(b) We appreciate India is going to review its options and make a choice at some point in the time of their choosing.

(c) Sometimes political parties find dummy candidates with the same name in order to divide the vote.

(d) Sometimes complicated questions for patriotism and identity can be answered with a simple example.

(e) All are correct

Q10. (a) Good Friday or Easter should be seen as opportunities to ponder on the essentials of religion afresh, which bind and bond each person to the other.

(b) The spirituality is by no means the opposite of the scientific; it is actually the opposite of the material.

(c) Clad in saffron clothes, his long, tangled hair falling into curls and knots, he kept gazing at the car with rapt attention for a long time.

(d) The American pavilion was the centre of people's attention, drawing the crowds away from other pavilions because it had a flying car on display.

(e) All are correct

Q11. (a) To win the Lok Sabha re-election of 2019, the BJP needs 272 seats to form a government without depending on an increasingly volatile set of NDA allies.

(b) The BJP needs 272 seats to form a government without counting on NDA allies by winning the Lok Sabha re-election of 2019.

(c) To form a government, the Lok-Sabha re-elections of 2019 can be won by BJP if it gets 272 seats without depending on NDA allies.

(d) On the next Lok Sabha elections of 2019, the BJP needs 272 seats excluding NDA allies to form a government.

(e) All are correct

Q12. (a) The goods and services tax (GST) , especially the IGST or Integrated GST component, has begun to erode the advantage that the IDS was giving to foreign exporters in Indian markets.

(b) The goods and services tax (GST) , especially the IGST or Integrated GST component, has now reduce the benefit that the IDS was giving to foreign exporters in Indian markets.

(c) There is a decline in the benefits given by the IDS to foreign exporters in Indian markets due to the introduction of GST or IGST component.

(d) The IGST or Integrated GST component of Goods and service tax is now eroding the advantage which it was earlier giving to foreign exporters in Indian markets.

(e) All are correct.

Q13. (a) Southern Asia's striking features has been the presence of liberal democracy in India, especially, in a region having non-plural or mixed regimes.

(b) An interesting feature of Southern Asia for decades has been the existence of a liberal democracy in India, in a region inhabited largely by non-plural or mixed regimes.

(c) For decades Southern Asia has remained popular for the existence of a liberal democracy in India, especially in an area populous with non-plural or mixed regimes.

(d) One of the most thought-provoking traits of Southern Asia since decades has been the presence of liberal democracy in India, inhabited largely by non-plural or mixed regimes.

(e) All are correct

Q14. (a) A direct listing is different from an initial public offering (IPO) where shares of a company are first bought by an intermediary such as an investment bank or a brokerage before those shares are offered for sale to retail investors by the intermediary.

(b) A DPO differentiates from initial public offering (IPO) as in that securities, such as stock or debt, are sold to intermediary investors, to raise capital from an investment banking firm or broker-dealer which are later resold by these intermediaries.

(c) The major difference between DPO and IPO is that in direct listing the shares of the company are initially purchased by investment bank or a brokerage before these shares are resold by these intermediaries.

(d) IPO differs from DPO as in DPO the shares are initially purchased by the intermediaries and then these are sold again to the retail investors.

(e) All are correct.

Q15. (a) The sixth bimonthly Monetary Policy Committee (MPC) of Reserve Bank of India (RBI) has decided to maintain status quo in policy rates by keeping repo rate unchanged at 6.0% under liquidity adjustment facility (LAF) .

(b) The monetary policy committee (MPC) kept policy rates and stance unchanged in its sixth bimonthly policy review, in line with consensus expectations.

(c) Keeping the policy rate and stance unchanged in its sixth bimonthly policy review, the monetary policy committee is in line with consensus expectations.

(d) The Reserve Bank of India's Monetary Policy Committee presents its sixth bi-monthly policy review for the current fiscal on Wednesday and kept policy rates and stance unchanged.

(e) All are correct

Q16. (a) The inconvenient truth is that the underlying fundamentals have not changed.

(b) The boy asked his father why he was cutting down the tree.

(c) He has a scheme of his own which he thinks preferable than that of any other person.

(d) I began to tremble when I saw a sharp long knife in my enemy's hand.

(e) A large number of patients in the country are illiterate and even many literate patients are not well-versed with medical terms.

Q17. (a) Hardly did she went out of her house when the postman came with the telegram.

(b) There were only two soldiers but each soldier was equal to five policemen.

(c) He wanted certain boys to make entry into the Principal's chamber.

(d) But for your help, no boys would have succeeded in an All India competition like this.

(e) Once, we dwelt by the seaside but now we have settled ourselves in Mumbai.

Q18. (a) This photograph was comparatively good than that which he had kept in his purse.

(b) He has not only built this big theatre but also a few bungalows in this city.

(c) He felt happy to learn that his younger brother had got a prestigious job in his bank.

(d) Since they were not aware of the consequences, they might have asked you to transgress this social decorum.

(e) Having reached the station, you may buy your ticket and wait for the train for New Delhi.

Q19. (a) All his relatives expect his daughter to go on a month's vacation tour.

(b) Every animal in the zoo is fed regularly and attended on very promptly.

(c) The unskilled class of workers is the most exploited class under the present labour contract system.

(d) He was hard down for money and was being harassed by his creditor.

(e) No sooner did Minati reach the station than it started raining.

Q20. (a) Every leaf and every flower proclaim the glory of god.

(b) These kinds of shoes seem to be expensive but they are relatively easy to care for.

(c) In the absence of clear instructions one cannot be expected to function effectively.

(d) How you eat is as important as what you eat.

(e) The short boy has seven rupees and the fat boy has only a rupee.

Q21. (a) A new set of £2 coins this year will mark the 200th anniversary of the Dr Frankenstein novels by Mary Shelley.

(b) I tried to figure out where I was, and realised with a sinking heart my accommodation was miles away.

(c) Though the book is not yet available in India, previews published in this country suggest that it is a complex study of an extremely complex personality.

(d) If you resist the first temptation the next will be easier to overcome.

(e) All are correct

Q22. (a) For a few minutes, I stood in the living room alone, but it was a welcome chance for me to gather my thoughts.

(b) It is one of many downtown streets and to most people nothing special.

(c) The first 'real' people I would meet in the UK would be my two new flatmates.

(d) The actor, who was playing a detective in the film, alleged to have pushed the director when he asked him to get into his costume as it was getting late.

(e) All are correct

Q23. (a) The government needs to provide specific regulations that create an environment where a trained scientific personnel enjoyed space and freedom to design new products benefitting society.

(b) My friend has been bruised quite badly in a recent accident.

(c) Conventionally speaking, men are supposed to earn while women are supposed to sit at home, do housework and discipline the children.

(d) Banking industry specialists have pointed out that lending is a commercial activity, which is based on an evaluation of the business decisions of borrowers and their assessment of commercial viability.

(e) All are correct

Q24. (a) The movement, which aims to raise awareness about climate change, hopes to bring people together to think about what they can do for reducing harmful pollution.

(b) Satish was advised an operation more than thirty years back, but due to his financial condition he could not undergoes the procedure.

(c) As I told you earlier, I have never been good with introductions, not even in my native language, and this experience wasn't going to change that record.

(d) It costs me more than a meal for two back home, but at least I managed to get rid of the taste of Penelope's tea.

(e) All are correct

Q25. (a) Without feedback people begin assuming the worst and the anxiety that results leads to reactive behavior, which is actually a protective response.

(b) If an individual works only in team efforts, they will seldom receive individual recognition.

(c) Professional suicide, a widespread but rarely studied phenomenon is costing companies not only dollars and cents, but the talents and skills of many bright, creative and committed key employees.

(d) Workers batting to restore power supply to damaged reactors have successful in reaching upto the second reactor.

(e) All are correct

Directions (26–50) : **Read each of the following four sentences to find out whether there is any grammatical mistake/error in it. Choose the sentence with no grammatical error as the correct answer. If all the given sentences are grammatically incorrect, choose (e) as an answer.**

Q26. (a) Mr Modi certainly struck a chord between student preparing for the ordeal that are the boards , yet it is a moot point if the education system at large will reflect that kind of thinking and take affirmative action to de-stress the situation.

(b) It was touching to cite APJ Abdul Kalam and Sachin Tendulkar as exemplifying special qualities, much young folk would have learnt they were children of a lesser God.

(c) Compared to the contiguous emirate of Dubai, Abu Dhabi has been regarded as relatively conservative in social and educational affairs. Its restaurants and places of entertainment are more subdued, its bazars and malls less lively.

(d) There is a wide swathe of vegetation along all the roads and public areas of the emirate where the desert has been induced to bloom, to the points that the land no longer looks like what it has been from the beginning, the domain for sand.

(e) None of these

Q27. (a) Over the year, India has developed especially close relations with the UAE and the GCC as a whole.

(b) When oil prices suddenly rose dramatically in the early 1970s, the Gulf countries became much more closely linked of India from where they drew many of the skills and much of the manpower they needed for the accelerated development now available to them.

(c) The UAE Crown Prince's burgeoning relationship with India is testimony not only to the growing bilateral friendship and economic intermeshing but also to a wide sort of regional cooperation with securities and strategic overtones.

(d) A glimpse of its new priorities was to be seen at the Republic Day parade where soldiers from Abu Dhabi marched in company with Indian counterparts, thereby inviting attention to how their country's military needs and capacity have developed.

(e) None of these

Q28. (a) The waters of the Mahanadi has become choppier still with the BJD government in Odisha rejecting the formula proposed by the Centre to settle the raging dispute over the river with the Bharatiya Janata Party's government in Chhattisgarh.

(b) A river belong to Nature, and ideally must lend no scope for another puerile bout of Centre-State kerfuffle.

(c) The water of the Mahanadi is vital for the farmlands in Odisha, as often as not confronted by droughts.

(d) On closer reflection, there is not scope for such a panel under the Inter-State River Water Disputes Act, which does provide for a tribunal.

(e) None of these

Q29. (a) The Odisha chief minister's refusal to abide by the Centre formula is, therefore, rooted in a legislative enactment.

(b) The fine print of the controversy must be that Odisha has been accorded the short shrifts.

(c) I know the gentleman who travels frequently between the sub-continent to the US.

(d) The laughter of the vindicated, that exhausted audience of the conspicuous consumption of others, could be heard in homes far and wide.

(e) None of these

Q30. (a) Only a few hundred year ago, inherited caste determined all the opportunities that one could access in life.

(b) It's been seated in first class, those plagued by the inferiority of being lesser in some way can lord it over all those who may be better.

(c) They can imagine that sitting in first class on a plane means being first class in life.

(d) Most of the wealthy lot in Pakistan, fat and rich on money they have usurped or inherited, have a solid sense for entitlement

(e) None of these

Q31. (a) Close behind the wealthy are the almost wealthy, who by virtue of jobs abroad or with multinational corporations have ascended to first class

(b) In the South Asian obsession with first class is an equal and opposite disdain for equality, frugality and avoidance of waste.

(c) The others may have to wait longer, eat less, be more cramped, but they knows that they will get to wherever they are going at exactly the same time.

(d) There is no minefields as farmers till their lands almost up to the international border.

(e) None of these

Q32. (a) Many of its reserve formations is deployed on its western borders, battling militancy.

(b) Many of its reserve formations are deployed on its western border, battling militancy.

(c) Many of its reserves formations are deployed on its western borders, battling militancy.

(d) Many of its reserve formations are deployed on its western borders, battling militancy.

(e) None of these

Q33. (a) Decisions for its employment would flow after considerable territory has being lost.

(b) Decisions for its employment would flew after considerable territory has been lost.

(c) Decisions for its employment would flow after considerable territory has been lost.

(d) Decision for its employment would flow after considerable territory has been lost.

(e) None of these

Q34. (a) The structures necessary to ensure this as also the wherewithal need to be in place.

(b) Sufficient rehearsals must be conducted and plans finely tune.

(c) Pakistan's rhetoric of nuclear strike would then remained mere ranting and raving.

(d) Sanyal narrated how seafarers from Odisha and Bengal has started visiting Sri Lanka from the sixth century BC.

(e) None of these

Q35. (a) The Economic Survey presented in the eve of the Union Budget has been dominated by a singular action of the government.

(b) The Economic Survey presented on the eve of the Union Budget has been dominated by a singular action of the government.

(c) The Economic Survey presents on the eve of the Union Budget has been dominated by a singular action of the government

(d) The Economic Survey presented on the eve of the Union Budget have been dominated by a singular action of the government

(e) None of these

Q36. (a) The Survey, emphatically asserts that while there have being short-term costs to the economy, which would need to be expeditiously addressed, there will be long-term benefits.

(b) The Supreme Court accepted most of the recommendations and made them binding in the BCCI.

(c) Many feels the intervention was needed to keep the exploitation of cricket's commercial potential honest, and run the game in accordance with its tradition and values.

(d) There is a undoubted element of public interest in the manner in which the highest court has engaged itself with the game's administration in recent years.

(e) None of these

Q37. (a) The century old model of education system in India needs a critical examination in a rapidly globalized world

(b) The century old model for education system in India needs a critical examination in a rapidly globalized world

(c) The century old model of education system in India needs a critical examination in a rapidly globalising world

(d) The century old model of education system in India need a critical examination in a rapidly globalising world

(e) None of these

Q38. (a) Many commissions and committees since 1948 have examined the higher education system in India and recommended changes.

(b) Many commissions and committees since 1948 has examined the higher education systems in India and recommended changes.

(c) Many commissions and committees since 1948 have examining the higher education system in India and recommended changes.

(d) Many commissions and committees since 1948 have examined the highest education system in India and recommended changes.

(e) None of these

Q39. (a) Governance and policy making in education sector needs urgent attentions and overhaul.

(b) Central government must consider autonomy, quality, competition and regulatory parity as the guiding principle to fast track reforms to bring it at par with best practices of the world.

(c) Devoting a whole chapter to demonetisation, the Survey recommend fast, demand-driven remonetisation, further tax reforms, including bringing land and real estate under the ambit of the Good and Services Tax, and reducing tax rates and stamp duties.

(d) I feel proud of have contributed to an industry.

(e) None of these

Q40. (a) The beauty of immunotherapy is that it can be used in treatment of all type of cancer.

(b) Radiation uses to be five-seven weeks treatment.

(c) The overall treatment cost of immunotherapy is presently high, but it can be definitely come down.

(d) We are doing entire treatment in one or two day without hurting the patient.

(e) None of these

Q41. (a) While borders remain peaceful, transgressions continue although a strong Indian response indicates that India is capable of responding.

(b) While borders remain peaceful, transgressions continues although a strong Indian response indicates that India is capable of responding.

(c) While borders remain peaceful, transgressions continue although a strong Indian respond indicates that India is capable of responding.

(d) While border remain peaceful, transgressions continue although a strong Indian response indicates that India is capable of responding.

(e) None of these

Q42. (a) India has been observing these developments but has unable to match Chinese investments or stem their actions.

(b) India has been observing the developments but has unable to match Chinese investments or stem its actions.

(c) India has been observed these developments but has unable to match Chinese investments or stem its actions.

(d) India has been observing these developments but has unable to match Chinese investments or stem its actions.

(e) None of these

Q43. (a) It is pertinent to mention in this context that Vietnam, the major party to the South China Sea issue has reach out to China to manage maritime differences.

(b) It is pertinent to mention in this context that Vietnam, the major party to the South China Sea issue has reached out to China to manage the maritime differences.

(c) It is pertinent to mention in the context that Vietnam, the major party to the South China Sea issue has reached out to China to manage maritime differences.

(d) It is pertinent to mention in this context that Vietnam, the major party of the South China Sea issue has reached out to China to manage the maritime differences.

(e) None of these

Q44. (a) Last year the country conducted several tests and launches in its quest to develop a nuclear weapon system capable of hitting the US mainland.

(b) Last year the country conducted several tests and launches in its quest to develop a nuclear weapons system capable to hit the US mainland.

(c) Last year the country conducted several tests and launches in its quest to develop a nuclear weapons system capable of hitting the US mainland.

(d) Last year country conducted several tests and launches in its quest to develop a nuclear weapons system capable of hitting the US mainland.

(e) None of these

Q45. (a) Citing the importance of upholding human rights, the law minister appeared to have done well in calling of nationwide judicial and administrative action to ensure that undertrials were not held in custody longer than legally necessary.

(b) Citing the importance of upholding human rights, the law minister appeared to have done well in calling for nationwide judicial and administrative action to ensure that undertrials was not held in custody longer than legally necessary.

(c) Citing the importance of upholding human rights, the law minister appeared to have done well in calling for nationwide judicial and administrative action to ensure that undertrials were not held in custody longer then legally necessary.

(d) Citing the importance of upholding human rights, the law minister appeared to have done well in calling for nationwide judicial and administrative action to ensure that undertrials were not held in custody longer than legally necessary.

(e) None of these

Q46. (a) Politics in India has, in recent years, often become a dirty game and this is one of the reason why many honest and idealistic people take no interest in it.

(b) Politics in India has, in recent years, often became a dirty game and this is one of the reasons why many honest and idealistic people take no interest in it.

(c) Politics in India has, in recent years, often become a dirty game and this is one of the reasons why many honest and idealistic people takes no interest in it.

(d) Politics in India has, in recent years, often become a dirty game and this is one of the reasons why many honest and idealistic people take no interest in it.

(e) None of these.

Q47. (a) Yet a large number of people are averse to political participation or they participate at the lower level.

(b) Yet a large number of people are aversed to political participation or they participate at the lowest level.

(c) Yet a large number of people are averse to political participation or they participate at the lowest level.

(d) Yet a large number of people are averse to political participation or they participates at the lowest level.

(e) None of these

Q48. (a) Hundreds of thousands of people remain away from the polling booths and some others turn up only to cavil that they do not support any candidate fielded in the particular constituency.

(b) Hundreds of thousands of people remain away from the polling booth and some others turn up only to cavil that they does not support any candidate fielded in the particular constituency.

(c) Hundreds of thousands of people remain away from the polling booths and some others turn up only to cavil that they do not support any candidate field in the particular constituency.

(d) Hundreds of thousands of people remain away from the polling booths and some others turn up only to cavil that they does not support any candidate fielded in the particular constituency.

(e) None of these.

Q49. (a) Though details about the missile is yet to be determined, it is said to have flown for about 500 kilometres before plunging into the sea.

(b) Though details about the missile are yet to be determined, it was said to have flown for about 500 kilometres before plunging into the sea.

(c) Though details about the missile are yet to be determined, it is said to have flew for about 500 kilometres before plunging into the sea.

(d) Though details about the missile are yet to be determined, it is said to have flown for about 500 kilometres before plunging into the sea.

(e) None of these

Q50. (a) Sunday's firing of the ballistic missile by North Korea was not wholly unexpected in the context of Pyongyang's nuclear ambition.

(b) Sunday's firing of a ballistic missile by North Korea was not wholly unexpected in the context of Pyongyang's nuclear ambition.

(c) Sunday's firing of the ballistic missile by North Korea was not wholly unexpectedly in the context of Pyongyang's nuclear ambition.

(d) Sunday's firing of a ballistic missiles by North Korea was not wholly unexpected in the context of Pyongyang's nuclear ambition.

(e) None of these

## Solutions (Practice Set - 12)

S1. Ans. (c)

Sol. Sentence (c) contains a grammatical error. The subject '***It***' is always used to refer a singular subject thus, the verb associated to this subject should also be singular to comply with the rule of subject-verb agreement. Hence, to make the sentence grammatically correct **replace "have" with "has".** All the other given sentences are contextually meaningful and grammatically correct. Therefore, **option (c)** is the most suitable answer choice.

S2. Ans. (e)

Sol. All the given sentences are grammatically correct and contextually meaningful. Hence, **option (e)** is the most viable answer choice.

S3. Ans. (a)

Sol. Among all the given sentences, sentence (a) contains a grammatical error. To complement the correct grammatical syntax of the sentence, replace **"collected" with "collecting"** as the verb "**collect**" will be used as a Gerund in this case. As, apart from sentence (a) all other sentences are correct, **option (a)** becomes the most suitable choice.

S4. Ans. (e)

Sol. All the given sentences are grammatically correct and contextually meaningful. Hence, **option (e)** is the most viable answer choice.

S5. Ans. (d)

Sol. There is a grammatical error in the sentence (d) . To make the sentence grammatically and contextually correct replace **"registering" with "to register"** as to-infinitive is used in such sentence constructions, for expressing the purpose of something or someone's opinion about something. All the other sentences are in precise grammatical syntax providing coherence to the sentences. Hence, **option (d)** is the most suitable choice.

S6. Ans. (c)

Sol. All the sentences, except sentence (c) , are correct. Sentence (c) contains few grammatical errors in it. First, to make the sentence grammatically correct and contextually meaningful, replace "could" with "can" as the modal 'might' is the past form of 'may' which is used in reported speech, to express possibility or permission while 'can' is a modal verb which means 'be able to' is used in present tense to express a possibility. Second, the conjunction 'yet' should be replaced with 'but' to make the sentence coherent. As sentence (c) has errors, it becomes the most suitable answer choice.

S7. Ans. (e)

Sol. All the given sentences are grammatically error free and contextually meaningful. Therefore, option (e) becomes the most viable answer choice.

S8. Ans. (d)

Sol. All the sentences except sentence (d) are grammatically correct and contextually meaningful. To make the sentence (d) error free, the noun "facts" should get replaced with its singular form "fact" as in the latter part of the sentence only one fact has been described about the inflation forecast. Hence, option (d) becomes the correct answer choice.

S9. Ans. (d)

Sol. All the sentences except sentence (d) are grammatically correct and contextually meaningful. It is to be noted that the usage of preposition "for" is incorrect. Therefore, to make the sentence contextually correct replace "for" with "of". Hence, option (d) becomes the most suitable answer choice.

S10. Ans. (a)

Sol. Sentence (a) contains a contextual error in it. It is to be noted that the sentence can be made contextually and grammatically correct by replacing the conjunction "or" with "and" as in the latter part of the sentence the phrase [should be seen as opportunities] provides us with a hint that both the subjects [Good Friday] [Easter] should be connected using the conjunction "and". All the other sentences are correct. Hence, option (a) becomes the most suitable answer choice.

S11. Ans. (d)

Sol. Except for ***statement (d)*** all other given options are contextually and grammatically correct. In statement (d) the preposition "On" is incorrectly used. The correct preposition required here is "in". "In" is used to indicate that someone or something belongs to or is included as part of something. However, "on" is used as the part or object by which someone or something is supported. As option (d) fails to be grammatically correct, it becomes the correct answer choice.

S12. Ans. (b)

Sol. All the given options except for ***option (b)*** are correct both grammatically and contextually. The 3rd form of the verb is used with "has". Hence, the *verb "reduce" should be replaced with "reduced"* Hence, among the given options, option (b) contains a grammatical error making it the correct choice.

S13. Ans. (a)

Sol. All the given options are correct except for ***option (a)*** . All the statements are contextually correct catering the similar meaning about the fact that *Southern Asia has liberal democracy especially, in a region having non-plural or mixed regimes*. However, ***statement (a)*** consists a grammatical error. The statement is describing about a single feature of the southern Asia but the plural form of "feature" has been mentioned. *Thus **"features"** should be replaced by **"feature"**.* Therefore, option (a) is the correct choice.

S14. Ans. (e)

Sol. All the given options are grammatically correct and provide a coherent meaning. All the four statements are describing *the difference between the Direct Public Offering and Initial Public offering.* They all are grammatically appropriate as well. Thus, making ***option (e)*** a correct choice.

S15. Ans. (d)

Sol. All the given options are correct except for ***option (d)*** . Every statement is describing *the unchanged rates of monetary policy committee in its sixth bi-monthly policy.* However, ***statement (d)*** is also fulfilling the similar meaning but it fails to be grammatically viable. The sentence is in the past tense therefore, *the verb **"presents"** should be replaced by its past form **"presented"*** to make it grammatically correct. Hence, the error is in option (d) making it the correct answer choice.

S16. Ans. (c)

Sol. Use 'to' in place of 'than' as after 'preferable', preposition 'to' is used.

S17. Ans. (a)

Sol. Use 'go' in place of 'went' because after 'do, does, did', first form of verb is used.

**Section - II**

S18. Ans. (b)

Sol. Use 'has' after 'he' i.e. "...but he has also built a few bungalows in this city."

S19. Ans. (d)

Sol. Use 'hard up' in place of 'hard down' as '**be hard up**' is an **idiom** that means '**be short of money**'. E.g. He is hard up these days.

S20. Ans. (e)

Sol. Use 'one' in place of 'a'; 'seven' is numeral adjective in 'seven rupees', therefore with 'rupee', numeral adjective 'one' will be used, not the article 'a'.

S21. Ans. (e)

Sol. All the given sentences are grammatically correct.

S22. Ans. (d)

Sol. 'was alleged' will be used in place of 'alleged' as here. 'The actor' is a passive subject and the sentence is in the past tense, hence 'be' verb will be used for 'actor' in the form of 'was'.

S23. Ans. (a)

Sol. 'enjoys' is the correct use instead of 'enjoyed' as the sentence is in present tense {'needs', 'create'].

S24. Ans. (b)

Sol. 'undergo' will be used in the place of 'undergoes' as 'could' is a modal and V1 is used with modal used in the sentence.

S25. Ans. (d)

Sol. 'are' is the correct use in place of 'have' as 'successful' is an adjective and verb 'be' is used for any adjective.

S26. Ans. (c)

Sol. Option (c) is true as there is no error in it. In sentence (a) , "***between student***" should be replaced by "***among students***" as we use "between" for two individuals and "among" for more than two individuals. In sentence (b) , "***much***" should be replaced by "***most***" as we are quantifying a countable noun. In sentence (d) , "***points***" should be replaced by "***point***".

S27. Ans. (d)

Sol. Only option (d) is grammatically correct. In sentence (a) , "***over the year***" should be replaced by "***over the years***" as the sentence is referring to progression. In sentence (b) , "***linked of***" should be replaced by "***linked to***", because we require a proper preposition here. In sentence (c) , "***wide***" should be replaced by its comparative degree "***wider***".

S28. Ans. (e)

Sol. None of the given sentences is grammatically correct. In sentence (a) , "***has***" should be replaced by "***have***" as the subject is plural [i.e. "**waters**"]. In sentence (b) , "***belong***" should be replaced by "***belongs***" as the subject "***water***" is singular. In sentence (c) , "***droughts***" should be replaced by "***drought***". In sentence (d) , "***not***" should be replaced by determiner "***no***" as the adverb "***not***" is generally used with an auxiliary verb or 'be' to form the negative.

S29. Ans. (d)

Sol. Only option (d) is grammatically correct. In sentence (a) , "***Centre***" should be replaced by its possessive "***Centre's***". In sentence (b) , "***shrifts***" should be replaced by its singular "***shrift***". In sentence (c) , "***to***" should be replaced by "***and***" as "***between***" is always followed by "***and***".

S30. Ans. (c)

Sol. Only option (c) is grammatically correct. In sentence (a) , "***year***" should be replaced by its plural "***years***" as the quantifier "***a few***" denotes more than one year. In sentence (b) , "***lesser***" should be replaced by "***less***" to make the sentence grammatically correct. The preposition "***for***" should be replaced by "***of***" in sentence (d) .

S31. Ans. (a)

Sol. Only Option (a) is grammatically correct. In sentence (b) the preposition "for" should be replaced by "of". In sentence (c) , the plural pronoun "***they***" should be followed by a plural verb; "***knows***" should be replaced by "***know***". In sentence (d) , "minefields" should be replaced by its singular "***minefield***" as the determiner "***no***" suggests "***hardly any***".

S32. Ans. (d)

Sol. Only option (d) is grammatically correct. Other sentences are incorrect as they should follow the syntax used in sentence (d) .

S33. Ans. (c)

Sol. Option (c) is grammatically correct. Other sentences are incorrect as they should follow the syntax mentioned in sentence (c) .

S34. Ans. (a)

Sol. Only option (a) is grammatically correct. In sentence (b) , "***tune***" should be replaced by "***tuned***" as the rule of parallelism should be followed. In sentence (c) , the modal "***would***" should be followed by ***V1***; "***remained***" should be replaced by "***remain***". In sentence (d) , the singular verb "***has***" should be replaced by "***have***" as the subject is plural.

S35. Ans. (b)

Sol. Option (b) is grammatically correct. Other sentences are incorrect as they should follow the syntax mentioned in sentence (b) .

S36. Ans. (e)

Sol. None of the given sentences is grammatically correct. In sentence (a) , "***being***" should be replaced by "***been***". In sentence (b) , the preposition "***in***" should be replaced by "***on***". In sentence (c) , "feels" should be replaced by its plural "***feel***" as the quantifier "***many***" requires a plural verb. In sentence (d) , article "***a***" should be replaced by "***an***".

S37. Ans. (c)

Sol. Option (c) is grammatically correct. Other sentences are incorrect as they should follow the syntax mentioned in sentence (c) .

S38. Ans. (a)

Sol. Option (a) is grammatically correct. Other sentences are incorrect as they should follow the syntax mentioned in sentence (a) .

S39. Ans. (b)

Sol. Only Option (b) is grammatically correct. In sentence (a) , the word "***attentions***" should be replaced by "***attention***". In sentence (c) , the plural verb "***recommend***" should be replaced by its singular "***recommends***" as the subject "***survey***" is singular. In sentence (d) , "***have***" should be replaced by "***having***".

S40. Ans. (e)

Sol. None of the given sentences is grammatically correct. In sentence (a) , "***type***" should be replaced by "***types***" as the determiner "***all***" requires a plural noun. In sentence (b) , the verb "***uses***" should be replaced by "***used***". In sentence (c) , "***can be***" should be replaced by "***will***". In sentence (d) , "***day***" should be replaced by "***days***" as the quantifier "***two***" suggests plural noun.

S41. Ans. (a)

Sol. Option (a) is true as there is no grammatical

error in it. Other sentences are incorrect as they should follow the syntax used in sentence (a) .

S42. Ans. (d)

Sol. Option (d) is true as there is no grammatical error in it. Other sentences are incorrect as they should follow the syntax used in sentence (d) .

S43. Ans. (e)

Sol. Option (e) is true. None of the statements is true. The correct sentence is "*It is pertinent to mention in this context that Vietnam, the major party to the South China Sea issue has reached out to China to manage maritime differences.*"

S44. Ans. (c)

Sol. Option (c) is true as there is no grammatical error in it. Other sentences are incorrect as they should follow the syntax used in sentence (c) .

S45. Ans. (d)

Sol. Option (d) is true as there is no grammatical error in it. Other sentences are incorrect as they should follow the syntax used in sentence (d) .

S46. Ans. (d)

Sol. Option (d) is true as there is no grammatical error in it. Other sentences are incorrect as they should follow the syntax used in sentence (d) .

S47. Ans. (c)

Sol. Option (c) is true as there is no grammatical error in it. Other sentences are incorrect as they should follow the syntax used in sentence (c) .

S48. Ans. (a)

Sol. Option (a) is grammatically correct. Other sentences are incorrect as they should follow the syntax used in sentence (a) .

S49. Ans. (d)

Sol. Option (d) is true as there is no grammatical error in it. Other sentences are incorrect as they should follow the syntax used in sentence (d) .

S50. Ans. (b)

Sol. Option (b) is true as there is no grammatical error in it. Other sentences are incorrect as they should follow the syntax used in sentence (b) .

## Practice Set – 13

Directions (01-50) : **Find out the error in each of the following sentences, if any. If there is no error, your answer is option (e)** .

Q1. Ritu as well as (a) / some of her friends (b) / have fallen in love with Sonu, who (c) / is the eldest son of an S.D.O. (d) / No error (e)

Q2. More than one successful candidate (a) / have taken the interview for one (b) / of the popular magazines (c) / being published from Delhi. (d) / No error (e)

Q3. The leader as well as (a) / his followers are fatally injured in (b) / the accident which occurred last night (c) / near this railway crossing. (d) No error (e)

Q4. Along the northern frontier (a) / of India is seen (b) / the Himalayas mighty (c) /in their splendor. (d) /No error. (e)

Q5. His politics is not (a) / good, so we have suggested to him (b) / that he should read Gandhi, Nehru (c) / and Karl Marx. (d) / No error (e)

Q6. Just outside (a) / the station is (b) / two shops, extremely beautiful (c) / as well as crowdy. (d) / No error (e)

Q7. Her pugnacious daughter (a) / always do something that may incur insult (b) / on her neighbours who hold a wrong (c) /opinion about her family. (d) / No error (e)

Q8. Our Head of the Department assured (a) / us that a series of lectures on Milton (b) / were to be arranged (c) / the following week and so we should not create any nuisance.(d) / No error (e)

Q9. Each of the students (a) / whom I have chosen to take part (b) / in the cultural programmes to be performed (c) / on the Children's day, are up to the mark (d) / No Error (e)

Q10. Most of the news (a) / pertaining to the sudden demise of Dr. Sen (b) / have been communicated by some of the ruffians (c) / whom I know well. (d) / No error (e)

Q11. He often says that (a) / it are these obscene films (b) / that lead the youth to their moral degradation (c) / and are responsible for (d) / many evils growing in our society. (d) / No error (e)

Q12. The teachers face the (a) / same problems in their day to day lives (b) / as do an ordinary man (c) / of our society. (d) / No error (e)

Q13. The man who cannot (a) / believe his senses and the man who cannot (b) / believe anything else are (c) / insane. (d) / No error (e)

Q14. Shingles are a disease (a) / in which the patient develops (b) / lots of inflamed spots round the (c) / waist. (d) / No error (e)

Q15. Each faculty member as (a) / well as most of the students (b) / were of the view that there should (c) / be many more new course in this college. (d) / No error (e)

Q16. Every man and woman (a) /of the village have come out (b) /to see this strange child (c) /who claims to know everything about his pre-natal existence. (d) /No error (e)

Q17. One of the developing or underdeveloped (a) / countries are not in favour of launching (b) chemical warfare because it trembles to imagine its repercussions. (d) / No error (e)

Q18. Have either of (a) / the two candidates been (b) / selected for the post of Branch Manager (c) / in the Punjab National Bank? (d) / No error (e)

Q19. Where she went (a) / and where she left her purse (b) / are not known to us; so it (c) / is of no use being worried about her. (d) / No error (e)

**Section - II**

Q20. If any proof was needed to show that the United Nations (a) / have lately become a policy tool in the hands of the U.S.A. and that (b) / the world's sole might has a subservient international body, it was provided (c) / by President Bush's angry comment. (d) / No Error (e)

Q21. The Board of directors (a) / want all possible facilities (b) / and allowances for (c) / itself. (d) / No error (e)

Q22. His efforts (a) / will bring him (b) / more success (c) / than your. (d) / No error. (e)

Q23. The Vice-President of India and (a) / the Vie-Chancellor of this university (b) / have given (c) / his consent to join the meeting. (d) / No error

Q24. None (a) / of these two Principals (b) / has been looking (c) / after his college well. (d) / No error. (e)

Q25. Each of (a) / the four great tragedies (b) / of Shakespeare (c) / is worth reading. (d) / No error. (e)

Q26. He was much (a) / more surprised than me (b) / to see the dancing girl (c) / coming towards us. (d) / No error. (e)

Q27. One should (a) / be true to his (b) / word in all (c) / circumstances. (d) / No error. (e)

Q28. If someone has (a) / finished the work, (b) / he may (c) / go home. (d) / No error (e)

Q29. Everybody (a) / who was working in that office gave (b) / a day's pay as their contributions (c) / to the dependants of Dr. Sonu who had died on duty. (d) / No error. (e)

Q30. As a student (a) / of science (b) / you are far better (c) / than him. (d) / No error. (e)

Q31. The players (a) / whom we have selected (b) / for our team (c) / are young and ambitious. (d) / No error (e)

Q32. There is none (a) / who can help you (b) / in this crucial moment (c) / of your career. (d) / No error (e)

Q33. Whomever (a) / comes late will not be allowed (b) / to mark his presence (c) / in the register. (d) / No error (e)

Q34. He is a self-sacrificing (a) /man and (b) / wins everyone's sympathy (c) / and admiration. (d) / No error (e)

Q35. Every of the five children (a) / standing in the corner (b) / of the room is dexterous (c) / in paintings. (d) / No error. (e)

Q36. You and myself (a) / will enjoy the party (b) / to be arranged in honour of (c) / the new Chief Justice. (d) / No error. (e)

Q37. They also help the poor (a) / and really sympathise (b) / with them in their moments (c) / of distress. (d) / No error. (e)

Q38. You say (a) / it's your problem (b) / but I say it's (c) / my also. (d) / No error. (e)

Q39. The articles (a) / published in this magazine (b) / are better than (c) /that magazine. (d) / No error (e)

Q40. She was more (a) / garrulous than (b) / either of her (c) / three sisters. (d) / No error. (e)

Q41. Nobody can deny (a) / that Gandhi's ideas (b) / are different than (c) / Lenin's. (d) / No Error. (e)

Q42. While she was returning (a) / from College, (b) / a ruffian attacked (c) / on her with a dagger. (d) /No Error. (e)

Q43. Two of my intimate friends (a) / called on me (b) / on yesterday when I was (c) / away from home. (d) /No Error. (e)

Q44. The students complained (a) / to the principal against (b) / the warden and the (c) /

poor management of the hostel. (d) /No Error. (e)

Q45. Somebody reported to me (a) / that Suman had fallen in (b) / the well and nobody had (c) / tried to save him. (d) /No Error. (e)

Q46. The plan was to go for (a) / the cinema but (b) / owing to certain hindrances (c) / it failed. (d) /No Error. (e)

Q47. My friends proposed me (a) / that we should go to (b) / the movies and then have (c) / dinner at a hotel. (d) /No Error. (e)

Q48. My brother said that (a) / he preferred the white (b) / shirt than the black one (c) / which I usually wore. (d) /No Error. (e)

Q49. Glimpses to (a) / the religious side of his (b) / nature appear in (c) / the majority of his plays. (d) /No Error. (e)

Q50. There appears (a) / to be very little (b) / liaison among (c) / the two wings of the party. (d) / No Error (e)

**Section - II**

## Solutions (Practice Set – 13)

S1. Ans. (c)

Sol. Use 'has' in place of 'have'. [ In case of "as well as", verb is used according to the first subject ]S2. Ans. (b)

Sol. Use 'has' in place of 'have'[ "More than one" takes a singular verb ]

S3. Ans. (b)

Sol. Use 'is' in place of 'are' [ In case of "as well as" verb is according to the first subject ]

S4. Ans. (b)

Sol. Use 'are' in place of 'is' [political views are being talked about hence plural verb will come]

S5. Ans. (a)

Sol. Use 'are' in place of 'is'

S6. Ans. (b)

Sol. Use 'are' in place of 'is'[The main subject is two shops which is plural ]

S7. Ans. (b)

Sol. Use 'does' in place of 'do'[Daughter is singular hence does will come]

S8. Ans. (c)

Sol. Use 'was' in place of were. [The main subject is "A series" which is singular ]

S9. Ans. (d)

Sol. Use 'is' in place of 'are' [We use a singular verb with "Each"]

S10. Ans. (c)

Sol. Use 'has' in place of 'have'.[News is an uncountable, hence singular verb will be used]

S11. Ans. (b)

Sol. Use 'is' in place of 'are'[ It is always followed by a singular verb ]

S12. Ans. (c)

Sol. Use 'does' in place of 'do' [Ordinary man is singular, hence "does" will come]

S13. Ans. (e)

Sol. No error

S14. Ans. (a)

Sol. Use 'is' in place of 'are' [Shingles is a singular noun]

S15. Ans. (c)

Sol. Use 'was' in place of were. [Singular verb is used with "each"]

S16. Ans. (b)

Sol. Use 'has' in place of 'have'. [We use singular verb with "each" and "every"]

S17. Ans. (b)

Sol. Use 'is' in place of 'are'[One of the + plural noun + singular verb ]

S18. Ans. (a)

Sol. Use 'has' in place of 'have'. [Singular verb is used with "either of" ]

S19. Ans. (e)

Sol. No error

S20. Ans. (b)

Sol. Use 'has' in place of 'have'. ["The United Nations' is a singular subject ]

S21. Ans. (d)

Sol. Use 'themselves' in place of 'itself' [as in the "Board of directors', the directors acting independently ]

S22. Ans. (d)

Sol. Use 'yours' [Possessive pronoun will come here]

S23. Ans. (d)

Sol. Use 'their' in place of 'his' [Two people are being talked about]

S24. Ans. (a)

Sol. Use 'neither' in place of 'none' [We use "Neither" for two people]

S25. Ans. (e)

Sol. There is no error in the statement

S26. Ans. (b)

Sol. Use 'I' in place of 'me' [Subjective case of pronoun is used with subjective case]

S27. Ans. (b)

Sol. Use 'one's' in place of 'his' [One's should be used when the subject is one]

S28. Ans. (e)

Sol. No error

S29. Ans. (c)

Sol. Use 'his' in place 'their'.[Each, every– singular verb/ singular adjective]

S30. Ans. (d)

Sol. Use 'he' in place of 'him' [Subjective case of pronoun is compared to subjective case]

S31. Ans. (e)

Sol. No error

S32. Ans. (b)

Sol. Use 'that' in place of 'who' ["None" is followed by "that"]

S33. Ans. (a)

Sol. Use 'whoever' [Since "whoever" is subjective case of pronoun]

S34. Ans. (e)

Sol. No error

S35. Ans. (a)

Sol. Use 'every one'."Every" cannot play the role of a pronoun.

S36. Ans. (a)

Sol. Use 'I' in place of 'myself'. Subjective case of pronoun will be used which is "I".

S37. Ans. (e)

Sol. No error

S38. Ans. (d)

Sol. Use 'mine' in place of 'my'. "Mine" is a pronoun. " My" is an adjective.

S39. Ans. (d)

Sol. Use 'those published in that magazine'

S40. Ans. (c)

Sol. Use 'any'. "Either" is used for two people only.For more than two , we use "any".

S41. Ans. (c)

Sol. Use 'from' in place of 'than'. "From" is used after the word "Different".

S42. Ans. (d)

Sol. On should not be used.

When "attack" is used as a verb, it is not followed by "on".

S43. Ans. (c)

Sol. On should not be used.

S44. Ans. (b)

Sol. 'About' or 'of' should be used before 'the warden'

S45. Ans. (b)

Sol. use 'into' in place of 'in'

S46. Ans. (a)

Sol. use 'to' in place of 'for'

S47. Ans. (a)

Sol. Use 'to' after proposed.

S48. Ans. (c)

**Section - II**

Sol. Use 'to' in place of 'than'.

"Preferred" is always followed by the preposition "to".

S49. Ans. (a)

Sol. Use 'of' in place of 'to'

S50. Ans. (c)

Sol. Use 'between' in place of 'among'. "Among" is used for more than two.

## Practice Set – 14

Directions (01-50) : **Find out the error in each of the following sentences, if any. If there is no error, your answer is option (e) .**

Q1. Aspiring Athlets from different (a) / regions competed fiercely in the (b) /All India competition to secure (c) / a spot in the national team. (d) / No error (e)

Q2. There were only two (a) /soldiers but each and every (b) /soldier was equal (c) /to five policemen. (d) /No error (e)

Q3. These sort of men (a) /attain worldly success by hook or by crook, (b) /so they deserve to (c) / be looked down upon. (d) /No error (e)

Q4. In spite of facing (a) / much problems, he did not (b) /desert the path (c) /of honesty. (d) / No error (e)

Q5. Whole the chapter (a) /of the book is full of printing (b) /errors which are the outcome (c) /of the proof reader's carelessness.(d) /No error (e)

Q6. Her black long (a) /hair add (b) /glamour to (c) /her looks. (d) /No error (e)

Q7. I saw (a) /an anxious pale girl (b) /who when asked let me know(c) /that she was suffering from consumption. (d) /No error (e)

Q8. At the utmost gate (a) /was standing a guard (b) /holding a gun in (c) /his hand. (d) /No error (e)

Q9. The Principal has great power (a) /of making some useful (b) /plans but the professors (c) / have even the greatest ability to fool them. (d) / No error (e)

Q10. You can trust (a) /this agency (b) /for the last news (c) /of this week. (d) /No error (e)

Q11. Everybody knows (a) /that Ragini (b) /is the most unique (c) / singer of this college. (d) /No error (e)

Q12. She was curious to (a) /know what it was that made (b) /him stronger (c) /and braver than any man of his village. (d) /No error (e)

Q13. A lots of books (a) /on English Grammar are available (b) /in the market but (c) /this one is the best. (d) /No error (e)

Q14. As a collector of unique (a) /artifacts, she had a passion for (b) / acquiring rare and antiques (c) ornaments from different cultures (d) /No error (e)

Q15. No less (a) /than fifty people are sitting (b) /in the hall and waiting for their (c) /beloved artist's appearance on the stage. (d) /No error (e)

Q16. She had no other (a) /hobby than that of (b) / wearing a dress of (c) /the latest design. (d) / No error (e)

Q17. Much to his fortune, he (a) /married a girl who was (b) /more tall and lovelier than (c) / her elder sister. (d) /No error (e)

Q18. It was no (a) /other than Pandit Nehru (b) / who evinced an exceptional ability to lead (c) / the country to fame. (d) /No error (e)

Q19. Ramesh is as good, (a) /if not better than all the (b) / members of the club (c) /which is known as the Lion's club. (d) /No error (e)

Q20. Delhi is far (a) /better than any other (b) / metropolis (c) / of Pakistan. (d) /No error (e) .

Q21. In science the credit goes to a man (a) / who convinces the world. / (b) / not to the man to whom (c) / the idea first occurs. (d) / No Error(e)

Q22. Of the two (a) / answers, this (b) / is definitely (c) / better. (d) /No Error(e)

Q23. There were a number (a) / of pretty girls in the party (b) / but it was Ragini(c) / who remained a centre of attraction. (d) /No Error(e)

**Section - II**

Q24. He is (a) / the best artist (b) / of the time but unfortunately (c) / least recognised. (d) /No Error(e)

Q25. I don't like (a) / that type of a man (b) / who does nothing but (c) / find out faults in others. (d) /No Error(e)

Q26. The remedy lies (a) / in promoting values of humanism / (b) / and democracy so as to combat (c) / the oncoming brand of fascism. (d) /No Error(e)

Q27. A first step (a) / in a rational solution (b) / to any problem is the (c) / recognition of the fact that a problem exists. (d) /No Error(e)

Q28. Don't talk to (a) / him, he always (b) / remains in temper (c) / these days. (d) / No Error(e)

Q29. It was (a) / by a mistake (b) / that the caught (c) / her hand. (d) /No Error(e)

Q30. These orders of (a) / the Manager (b) / may put the lives of (c) / two thousand workers in a danger. (d) / No error(e)

Q31. I inspired him (a) / to take the heart (b) / in all adverse situation (c) / and deserve to be called a real hero. (d) / No Error(e)

Q32. The most happy (a) / marriage would be (b) / a union of a deaf (c) / man to a blind woman. (d) / No Error(e)

Q33. After returning (a) / from the jail, he abandoned (b) / all the criminal activities and is determined (c) / to lead a simple life. (d) /No Error(e)

Q34. His father (a) / forbade him to go (b) / to cinema (c) / late at night. (d) /No Error(e)

Q35. There was little (a) / milk in the bottle and she gave it (b) / to the baby when it (c) / started weeping. (d) /No Error(e)

Q36. Thanks to an insight (a) / and persistence of the local doctor (b) / hundreds of victims have been (c) / able to resume a normal life. (d) /No Error(e)

Q37. He uses (a) / the mock-heroic (b) / style to depict (c) / a violence. (d) /No Error(e)

Q38. One should (a) / be true to one's promises (b) / in order to earn (c) / name and fame in the life. (d) /No Error(e)

Q39. 'Music is science' (a) / but singing is an art' (b) / said the (c) / music teacher. (d) /No Error(e)

Q40. He should mix (a) / his authority with little (b) / of courtesy and (c) / common sense. (d) /No Error(e)

Q41. Found guilty (a) / on murder, the accused (b) / men were sentenced (c) / to life imprisonment. (d) /No Error (e)

Q42. He looked upon me (a) / level eyed for a (b) / few moments before he (c) /started speaking (d) /No Error (e)

Q43. The smuglar yielded (a) / for the temptation (b) / and fell into the police trap from (c) / which escape was impossible. (d) /No Error (e)

Q44. The man who (a) /was blind with the right (b) / eye was a (c) / notorious criminal of this area. (d) /No Error (e)

Q45. The poet describes about (a) / the beauty of a landscape (b) / in a very (c) / attractive way. (d) /No Error (e)

Q46. Rakesh Sharma, the Indian space (a) / hero, is much sought (b) / after by college students and (c) / is invited for various functions. (d) /No Error (e)

Q47. I advised (a) / him to consult a doctor (b) / but he refused (c) / to do so. (d) /No Error (e)

Q48. Those who are (a) / suffering from diabetes

(b) / are advised to substitute (c) / saccharine by sugar. (d) /No Error (e)

Q49. The debacle of the party (a) / admits no other explanation (b) / than its (c) / poor management. (d) / No Error (e)

Q50. My uncle has the reputation for (a) / being the sort of (b) / manager who is at least willing to listen to (c) / anyone who wants to raise a point. (d) /No Error (e)

Section - II

## Solutions (Practice Set - 14)

S1. Ans. (e)

Sol. No error.

S2. Ans. (b)

Sol. Use 'each' in place of 'each and every' [Every is not used for two things]

S3. Ans. (a)

Sol. Use 'sorts' in place of 'sort'. ["These" is plural]

S4. Ans. (b)

Sol. Use 'many' in place of 'much'.[We use "many" with countable nouns ]

S5. Ans. (a)

Sol. Use 'the whole' in place of 'whole the'. ["Article" comes before the "adjective"]

S6. Ans. (a)

Sol. Use 'long black' in place of 'black long'. [The order of adjective is OSASCOMP- Order Size Age Shape Colour Opinion Material Purpose]

S7. Ans. (b)

Sol. A pale anxious girl' is the correct usage. [The order of adjective is OSASCOMP- Order Size Age Shape Colour Opinion Material Purpose]

S8. Ans. (a)

Sol. Use 'outermost' in place of utmost. [the geatest amount possible]

S9. Ans. (d)

Sol. Use 'greater' in place of 'great' [since comparison is bring ]

S10. Ans. (c)

Sol. Use 'latest' in place 'last'. [ "Latest" means most recent ]

S11. Ans. (c)

Sol. 'the 'most' will not be used before 'unique'

S12. Ans. (d)

Sol. Use 'any other man' in place of 'any man'

S13. Ans. (a)

Sol. 'a lot of' should be used. [The correct use is either "lots of" or "a lot of"

S14. Ans. (e)

Sol. No error

S15. Ans. (a)

Sol. 'No fewer' should be used in place of 'no less' [fewer is used for countable nouns]

S16. Ans. (e)

Sol. No error.

S17. Ans. (c)

Sol. Use 'taller' in place of use 'more taller' [Comparative degree of "tall" is "taller"]

S18. Ans. (e)

Sol. No error

S19. Ans. (a)

Sol. Use 'as' after 'as good'.

S20. Ans. (b)

Sol. Use of 'other' is incorrect.

S21. Ans. (a) [Information of man is given ]

Sol. Replace 'a' with 'the'

S22. Ans. (d)

Sol. Use 'the' before 'better'

S23. Ans. (d)

Sol. Replace 'a' with 'the' [the centre of attraction]

S24. Ans. (d)

Sol. Use 'the' before 'least'["the" is used before superlative degree]

S25. Ans. (b)

Sol. Remove 'a'["Type of ,sort of, kind of" are not followed by article "a"]

S26. Ans. (b)

Sol. Use 'the' before values [Information of values is given]

S27. Ans. (a)

Sol. Replace 'a' with 'the' ['In a temper" means in a bad mood]

S28. Ans. (c)

Sol. Use 'a' before 'temper'

S29. Ans. (b)

Sol. Remove 'a'

S30. Ans. (d)

Sol. 'a' should not be used

S31. Ans. (b)

Sol. Don't use 'the' [ to take heart–take something very seriously ]

S32. Ans. (c)

Sol. Replace 'a' with 'the'

S33. Ans. (b)

Sol. Remove 'the' [ the is not used before general words]

S34. Ans. (c)

Sol. Use 'the' before cinema [ circus, cinema, movie -take article "the" before them ]

S35. Ans. (a)

Sol. Use 'a' before 'little' [ because we mean some but not much ]

S36. Ans. (a)

Sol. 'the' should replace 'an'

S37. Ans. (d)

Sol. 'a' should not be used.

S38. Ans. (d)

Sol. 'the' should not be used before 'life'

S39. Ans. (a)

Sol. Use 'a' before 'science'

S40. Ans. (b)

Sol. Use 'a' before little.

S41. Ans. (b)

Sol. Use 'of' in place of 'on'

S42. Ans. (a)

Sol. Use 'at' in place of 'upon'

S43. Ans. (b)

Sol. Use 'to' in place of 'for'

S44. Ans. (b)

Sol. Use 'in' in place of 'with'

S45. Ans. (a)

Sol. 'about' should not be used.

S46. Ans. (d)

Sol. Use 'to' in place of 'for'

S47. Ans. (e)

Sol. No error.

S48. Ans. (d)

Sol. Use 'for' in place of 'by'

S49. Ans. (b)

Sol. Use 'of' after 'admits'

S50. Ans. (a)

Sol. Use 'of' in place of 'for'

## Practice Set – 15

**Directions (01-05) : The following question consists of a sentence, whose certain parts are highlighted in bold. The highlighted portion is grammatically correct. Each sentence is followed by the three expressions which may or may not contain grammatical errors. Choose the most appropriate alternative among the five options which states the incorrect part(s) of the sentence. If the given sentence is grammatically correct and contextually meaningful, choose option (e) i.e., "No error" as your answer**

Q1. School refusal describes **the disorder of a child** who refuses to go to the school on **a regular basis** or has problems staying in school.

(I) School refusal describes

(II) who refuses to go to the school on

(III) or has problems staying in school.

(a) Only (II)

(b) Only (III)

(c) Both (I) and (II)

(d) Both (II) and (III)

(e) No error

Q2. **The American actor and pop singer David Hasselhoff** has admitted to his frustration at the spread of a legend, **according to which** he has taken credit for the Berlin wall's fall.

(I) has admitted to his frustration

(II) at the spread of a legend,

(III) he has taken credit for the Berlin wall's fall.

(a) Only (II)

(b) Only (III)

(c) Both (I) and (II)

(d) Both (II) and (III)

(e) No error

Q3. **He, along with a host of other chefs in both the U.S. and Mexico**, are simply challenging the idea that Mexican **food should be inexpensive and informal**, using high-quality ingredients to make everything from scratch, and paying rent in a recently gentrified neighborhood.

(I) are simply challenging the idea that Mexican

(II) using high-quality ingredients to make everything from scratch,

(III) and paying rent in a recently gentrified neighborhood.

(a) Only (II)

(b) Only (III)

(c) Only (I)

(d) Both (II) and (III)

(e) No error

Q4. If I would have known that you were going **to the movies**, I would have **gone too.**

(I) If I would have known

(II) that you were going

(III) I would have

(a) Only (II)

(b) Only (III)

(c) Only (I)

(d) Both (I) and (III)

(e) No error

Q5. **There has been a discussion** over the last several months on **one method of return filing that Nandan Nilekani had suggested** and another that the officials from the State governments had suggested.

(I) over the last several months on

(II) and another that the officials from

(III) the State governments had suggested.

(a) Only (II)

(b) Only (III)

(c) Both (I) and (II)

(d) Both (I) and (III)

(e) No error

Directions (06-10) : **The sentences given below are divided into five parts. One of the part is given in bold which is grammatically and contextually correct. Identify the combination of two parts that consists of grammatical or contextual error in them. If no such error is there mark option (e) i.e., "No error" as the answer.**

Q6. **The delay in appointing the (A)** / insurance regulator and a deputy governor (B) / to the RBI to steer banking supervision (C) / is baffling, and a telling reflection of poor (D) / succession planning for crucial appointment in the financial sector. (E)

(a) B-D

(b) B-E

(c) B-C

(d) C-E

(e) No error

Q7. As per World Bank Ease of (A) / Doing Business rankings 2018, (B) / **India's entry to the list of top 100 countries suggests(C)** / that business dynamics under the Modi regime is (D) / changing faster than before. (E)

(a) B-E

(b) A-D

(c) B-D

(d) A-B

(e) No error

Q8. Western sanctions on China's quest (A) / for high tech could not be effective, however, (B) / simply because everyone in the West want (C) / a good price for high-tech for rich customers (D) / **who are prepared to pay for it. (E)**

(a) C-D

(b) A-B

(c) B-C

(d) A-D

(e) No error

Q9. Almost a decade and a half ago at the G8 Institute (A) / at the University of Toronto, a paper by John Kirton was to show that (B) / **in Purchasing Power Parity terms, India was already the fifth largest economy (C)** / of the world and in fact, China and India were among the(D) / eight (G8) largest economies of the world. (E)

(a) A-B

(b) B-D

(c) D-E

(d) A-E

(e) No error

Q10. **Instead of waiting for manufacturers (A)** / to come to India with transfer-of-technology, (B) / should we go to the foreign manufacturer in his own country, (C) / as was being done by an Indian company for buying, (D) / owning and manufacture high tech Jaguar-Land Rover automobile. (E)

(a) B-D

(b) C-D

(c) C-E

(d) B-C

(e) No error

Directions (11-20) : **A part of the sentence is underlined below are given alternatives to thee underlined part at (a) , (b) , (c) and (d) which may improve the sentence choose the correct alternative and mark your answer in the answer sheet. In case no improvement is needed, our answer is (e)** .

Q11. Having logged thousands of hours watching felines from tigers to cheetahs, tigers and other felines are no longer thought to be natural-born killers by Dr. Stinson, they are attuned to peacemaking.

(a) tigers and other felines are no more thought to be natural-born killers by Dr. Stinson, they

(b) Dr. Stinson has come to believe that far from being natural-born killers, tigers and other felines

(c) Dr. Stinson has now the belief that far from being natural-born killers, tigers and other felines

(d) tigers and other felines are not longer thought to be natural-born killers by Dr. Stinson, they

(e) No error

Q12. Using it wisely, leisure promotes, health, long life, efficiency, and happiness.

(a) If used wisely, leisure promotes health, long life, efficicncy, and happiness.

(b) Having used it wisely, leisure promotes health, long life, efficiency, and happiness.

(c) If it is used wisely, leisure promotes health, long life, efficiency, and happiness.

(d) If, when using wisely, leisure promotes health, long life, efficiency, and happiness.

(e) No improvement.

Q13. We want the trainer to be him who has the best rapport knowledge about the subject and the most superior communication skills.

(a) we want the trainer to be he who has the best rapport knowledge about the subject and the most superior communication skills.

(b) We want him to be the trainer who has the best rapport knowledge about the subject and the most superior communication skills.

(c) We desire that the trainer be him who has the best rapport knowledge about the subject and the most superior communication skills.

(d) We would want the trainer to be him who has the best rapport knowledge about the subject and superior most communications skill.

(e) No improvement.

Q14. The soldiers were told to take a long arduous hike, pitch their camps, have dinner, and that they should be in bed by 10 p.m.

(a) The soldiers were told to take an arduous hike, pitch their camps, have dinner, and that they should be in bed by 10 p.m.

(b) The soldiers were told to take a long arduous hike, pitch camp, have dinner, and be in bed by 10 p.m.

(c) The soldiers were told to take a long arduous hike, pitching their camps, have dinner, and be in bed by 10 p.m.

(d) The soldiers was told to take a long arduous hike, pitch camp, having dinner and to be in bed by 10 p.m.

(e) No improvement.

Q15. The Indian government's failing to keep its pledges will have the effect of earning distrust from all the other nation in the region.

(a) The Indian government failing to keep it's pledges will have the effect of earning distrust from all the other nations in the region.

(b) The Indian government's failing to keep its pledges will have the effect of earning distrust from all the other nations in the region.

(c) The Indian government failing to keep its pledges will have the effect of earning distrust from all the other nations in the region.

(d) The Indian government's fail to keep its pledges will have the effect of earning distrust of all other nations in the region.

(e) No improvement.

Q16. If he was to decide to go to college,one would recommend that he plan to go to IIM Ahmedabad.

(a) If he were to decide to go to college,one would recommend that he plan to go to IIM Ahmedabad.

(b) Had he decided to go to college,one would recommend that plan to go to IIM Ahmedabad.

(c) In the event that he decides to go to college,one would recommend that plan to go to IIM Ahmedabad.

(d) Had he decided to go to college,one would recommend that he go to IIM Ahmedabad.

(e) No improvement

Q17. When one reads the Hindi literature of the twentieth century,you find a striking contrast between the writings of Munshi Premchand and later day writers of popular Hindi fiction.

(a) When you read the Hindi literature of the twentieth century,one finds a striking contrast between the writings of Munshi Premchand and later day writers of popular Hindi fiction.

(b) When one reads the Hindi literature of the twentieth century,he finds a striking contrast between the writings of Munshi Premchand and later day writers of popular Hindi fiction.

(c) If one reads the Hindi literature of the twentieth century,you find a striking contrast between the writings of Munshi Premchand and later day writers of popular Hindi fiction.

(d) When one reads the Hindi literature of the twentieth century,one finds a striking contrast between the writings of Munshi Premchand and later day writers of popular Hindi fiction.

(e) No improvement

Q18. When one travels by Air Lahara,you often find that the prices are high and that the journey experience is extremely poor.

(a) When you travel by Air Lahara,one often finds that the prices are high and that the journey experience is extremely poor.

(b) As you travel by Air Lahara,you often find that the prices are high and that the journey experience is extremely poor.

(c) If you travel by Air Lahara,you often find that the prices are high and that the journey experience is extremely poor.

(d) When one travels by Air Lahara,the one often finds that the price is higher and that the journey experience is extremely poor.

(e) No improvement

Q19. Because of his tennis elbow injury, Limba Ram has not and possibly never will be able to pick up the bat again.

(a) Because of his tennis elbow injury, Limba Ram has not and possibly will never be able to pick up the bat again.

(b) Because of his tennis elbow injury, Limba Ram has not been and possibly never would be able to pick up the bat again.

(c) Because of his tennis elbow injury, Limba Ram has not been able to and possibly never will be able to pick up the bat again.

(d) Because of his tennis elbow injury, Limba Ram has not and if possible be never able to pick up the bat again.

(e) No improvement

Q20. Had he realized how close he was to failing, he would not have gone to the party.

(a) If he would have realized how close he was to failing, he would not have gone to the party.

(b) Had he had realized how close he was to failing, he would not have gone to the party.

(c) When he realized how close he was to failing, he did not go to the party.

(d) If he would realize how close he was to failing, he should not have gone to the party.

(e) No improvement

Directions (21-30) : **In each sentence below, a group of words has been underlined. From the five answer choices given below each sentence, pick out the one which can substitute the underlined group of words correctly, without changing the meaning of the sentence.**

Q21. This is exactly **what he wanted me** to solve the problem.

(a) how he wanted me

(b) what he wants from I

(c) how does he want me

(d) how did he want me

(e) No correction required

Q22. The Minister said that **he is proud of** the people of his constituency.

(a) he should be proud of

(b) he was proud of

(c) he had pride for

(d) it is he to be proud of

(e) No correction required

Q23. The mob **started pelting stones** on the vehicles which were parked on the street.

(a) started to pelting stones

(b) started stones to be pelted

(c) pelted stones starting

(d) had started to pelting stones

(e) No correction required

Q24. Although scared of heights, she **gather all her courage** and stood atop the 24-storey building to participate in the activities.

(a) gathered all her courage

(b) gathered all courageous

(c) gather all courageous

(d) is gathered all courage

(e) No correction required

Q25. Naturally, with everything **gone so well** for them, it was time for celebration.

(a) go so well

(b) going so well

(c) gone as well

(d) going as well

(e) No correction required

Q26. The ban was imposed by the state's commercial taxes department last Friday after protests by a certain community, which **had threat to burn** cinema halls screening the controversial movie.

(a) had threats of burning

(b) had threated to burn

(c) had threatened to burn

(d) had threatened to burning

(e) No correction required

Q27. Rakesh, an avid football player who captained his team in school and college, **will inaugurate** the match tomorrow in Pune.

(a) will be inaugurating

(b) is inauguration

(c) will inaugurating

(d) is inaugurate

(e) No correction required

Q28. The military has highly sophisticated simulators **on which soldiers train**.

(a) which soldier training on

(b) on which soldier have trains

(c) which the soldier do train

(d) on which the soldiers have been trained

(e) No correction required

Q29. Any policy of social welfare **will be likely to face** resistance from vested interests.

(a) would be like facing

(b) will be likely facing

(c) is likely to face

(d) is likely to be facing with

(e) No correction required

Q30. The key to a competitive economy **is its investment regime**.

(a) in its invested regime

(b) in its investment regime

(c) investment of its regime

(d) investment in its regime

(e) No correction required

Directions (31-40) : **In each sentence below, certain groups of words (phrases) have been underlined. From the five answer choices given below each sentence, pick out the one which can substitute the underlined group of words correctly, without changing the meaning of the sentence**.

Q31. Take a simple regulatory change like **the recent impose on the bans on** non-transparent, discriminatory **prices discounts that are quiet offered to** select customers.

(a) the recently imposed ban on, price discounts that are quietly offered to

(b) for the immediately imposed ban, expenses those are secretly provided to

(c) the recent bans imposed to, prices offered requested to

(d) the bans on the immediate, prices discount which were offered by

(e) No improvement required

Q32. These new initiatives and restructuring **will include setting up** a powerful new financial regulator as well as a super ministry **to deal with the environment.**

(a) was included set up, to dealing with the environment

(b) will be included setting up, to dealing with the environment

(c) would have include set up, has to deal with the environment

(d) will be include setting up, should be dealing with the environment

(e) No correction required

Q33. **Customers can prefers cabs to book** up to seven days in advance or upon reaching the railway station. In addition, the IRCTC outlets at railway stations or Ola's self-serving kiosk **will be also enable commuters to book cabs.**

## Section - II

(a) Customers could make a choice to book cabs, will also force commuters to book cabs.

(b) Customers can choose to book cabs, will also enable commuters to book cabs.

(c) To book cabs customers can choose, would have been forced to book cabs.

(d) Customers can be booked by cabs, has enabled cabs to book commuters.

(e) No correction required

Q34. **It would have been a long** and arduous climb for the Congress that has 44 seats in the Lok Sabha **to get closely to a figure that will help** it be in a respectable position, let alone reach the magical figure of 272.

(a) It isn't a long, to reaching a position that will help

(b) Its a long, to achieve a figure that will help

(c) It will be a long, to get close to a figure that will help

(d) It has a long, for getting close to the figure that will help

(e) No improvement required

Q35. It will not be able **to shake off its life support** as long as Congress leaders **continue to serve workers** with stale slogans and misplaced hopes.

(a) to shake up its life support, continuing to serve workers

(b) to shaken off the support of life, to continue serving workers

(c) to shake of it's life support, continues to serve workers

(d) to shake with the life support, shall continue to serve for worker

(e) No correction required

Q36. Union Minister for Shipping Nitin Gadkari on Tuesday **stressed on needs to improve** waterways in the country to **cutting down the cost of logistics**, which, he said, will boost the economy and tourism sector.

(a) have stressed on the needs for improving, reducing the cost of logistics

(b) stressed the need to improve, cut down the cost of logistics,

(c) stressing on the needs to degrade, reduced the share of conveyance

(d) improved the stressed needs for, cut through the costs from logistics

(e) No correction required

Q37. Investors are apparently shocked that big tech companies **that have long received** political protection **from liberals are suddenly getting** the Big Oil rubdown.

(a) that has been received Long, to liberals are getting

(b) who have long received, since liberals to suddenly get

(c) has received long, for liberals suddenly getting

(d) which will long receive, that liberals are receiving

(e) No correction required

Q38. The US Congress **withdraw support as the** protections provided to American corporations against 'expropriation' of **investments are considered not to be strong** enough.

(a) withdrawing support at the, investments are considering not to be

(b) withheld support for the, investing were considerably not strong

(c) withstand the support for the, investments are considered not to be strong

(d) withdrew support because the, investments were considered not strong

(e) No corrections required

Q39. Former rivals BlackBerry and Microsoft **has announced they are** collaborating **too offer enterprise's a solution** that integrates the latter's expertise in mobility and security with Microsoft's Cloud and productivity apps.

(a) have announced they were, to offer enterprises a solution

(b) are announcing they were, offering enterprise a solutions

(c) had been announcing they were, solutions to offer enterprises

(d) are announcing that they would, an offer to enterprises to solve

(e) No correction required

Q40. Pakistan's failure **to produce and trade deserves** a separate analysis. The interests of the **developing countries would be** best served if they are able to act collectively.

(a) for producing the trade that deserves, developing countries has been

(b) to produce a trade that deserve, to develop countries will be

(c) from trade that produced, developing countries have to be

(d) on producing and trading deserves, to developing countries are

(e) No correction required

Directions (41-50) : **In each of the question below, four different ways of writing a sentence are indicated. Choose the best way of writing the sentence.**

Q41. (a) Visiting Agra for the first time, the TajMahal in moonlight was truly impressive.

(b) Visiting Agra for the first time, I found the TajMahal truly impressive in the moonlight.

(c) Visiting Agra for the first time, I found the TajMahal in moonlight truly impressive.

(d) Visiting Agra the first time, I find the TajMahal the moonlight was truly impressive.

(e) None of the above

Q42. (a) The policeman attempted to tactfully pacify the quarrelling families.

(b) The policeman tactfully attempted to pacify the quarrelling families.

(c) The policeman attempted tactfully to pacify the quarrelsome families.

(d) The policeman attempted to pacify tactfully the quarrelling families.

(e) None of the above

Q43. (a) Modern films have a detrimental effect on child psychology for they make the children think that violence is justifiable.

(b) Modern films have a detrimental effect on child psychology for these films make them think that violence is justifiable.

(c) Modern films have a detrimental effect on child psychology for they make them think that violence is justifiable.

(d) Modern films have a detrimental effect on child psychology for they make those children think that violence is justifiable.

(e) None of the above

Q44. (a) The war victims needed nurses to bandage their wounds badly.

(b) The victims of war needed nurses to bandage

their wounds badly.

(c) The war victims badly needed nurses to bandage their wounds.

(d) The war victims needed nurses badly for bandaging their wounds.

(e) None of the above

Q45. (a) Teacher and parents alike should realize that to say a particular child is better than the other is doing a great injustice to the former.

(b) Teachers and parents alike should realize that to say a particular child is better than the other is doing a great injustice to both of them.

(c) Teachers and parents alike should realize that to say a particular child is better than the other is to do a great injustice to both the children.

(d) Teachers and parents alike should realize that to say a particular child is good than the other is doing a great injustice to both the children.

(e) None of the above

Q46. (a) To move people away from the clutches of militants, the army had adopted a policy of winning hearts and minds, while simultaneously battling militancy.

(b) To move people away from the clutch of militants, the army has adopted a policy of winning hearts and minds, while simultaneously battling militancy.

(c) To move people away of the clutches of militants, the army had adopted a policy of winning hearts and minds, while simultaneously battling militancy.

(d) To move people away from the clutch of militants, the army had adopted a policy of winning hearts and minds, while simultaneously battling militancy.

(e) None of these

Q47. (a) The soldiers are involved in operations not for sacrificing his life, but to eliminate those who threaten the fabric of the country.

(b) The soldier is involved in operations not for sacrificing its life, but to eliminate those who have threatened the fabric of the country.

(c) The soldier is involved in operation not for sacrificing his life, but to eliminate them who threatened the fabric of the country.

(d) The soldier is involved in operations not for sacrificing his life, but to eliminate those who threaten the fabric of the country.

(e) None of these

Q48. (a) It was disappointing that the participants were informed that the revised procurement or offsets policy will be announced shortly.

(b) It was disappointing that the participants were informed that the revising procurement or offsets policy would be announced shortly.

(c) It was disappointed that the participants were informed that the revising procurement or offsets policy would be announced shortly.

(d) It was disappointing that the participants were informed that the revised procurement or offsets policy would be announced shortly.

(e) None of these.

Q49. (a) Notwithstanding the ease with which Pakistani artistes has always had access to an Indian visa either for sashaying a grand entry in the hallowed chamber of fame and success.

(b) Notwithstanding the ease with which Pakistani artistes had always had accesses to an Indian visa either for sashaying a grand entry into the hallowed chamber of fame and success.

(c) Notwithstanding the ease with which Pakistani artistes had always had access to an

Indian visa either for sashaying a grand entry into the hallowed chamber of fame and success.

(d) Notwithstanding the ease with which Pakistani artistes had always had access to an Indian visa either for sashaying the grand entry into the hallowed chamber for fame and success.

(e) None of these

Q50. (a) France having a presidential form of government and all eyes are directed towards the presidential candidates running in the first round.

(b) France has a presidential form of government and all the eyes are directed toward the presidential candidates running in the first round.

(c) France has a presidential form of government and all eyes are directed towards the presidential candidates running in a first round.

(d) France has a presidential form of government and all eyes are directed towards the presidential candidates running in the first round.

(e) None of these

## Solutions (Practice Set - 15)

S1. Ans. (a)

Sol. Option (a) is the correct choice for the given question.

The error is in part (II) of the sentence.

The should not be used before school.

When School, College, Church, Hospital, Prison, Jail, Court, Bed, Market are used for the primary purpose, we don't use article 'the' before it.

S2. Ans. (b)

Sol.

The error is only in part (III) of the sentence.

"He has taken credit for the fall of the Berlin Wall" should be used in place of "he has taken credit for the Berlin wall's fall" as 'wall' is a non-living thing and **we don't use 's with non- living things.**

S3, Ans. (c)

Sol. Option (c) is the correct choice as error is in part (I) of the sentence.

'Is' should replace 'are' **as when two nouns or pronouns** are connected by **"as well as, in addition to, besides, like, unlike, with, along with, together with, accompanied by, led by, headed by, guided by, controlled by, governed by, rather than, and not"** then the **verb agrees with the first noun or pronoun.**

S4. Ans. (c)

Sol. Option (c) is the correct choice.

For part (I) "If I had known" should replace "If I would have known" as for the **"unfulfilled wish, condition, desire"** of the past we use **past perfect** tense with **I wish/as/if** etc.

It is to be noted that "The conditional perfect can only go in the "then" clause — it is grammatically incorrect to use the conditional perfect in the "if" clause:"

Hence there is an error in only part (I) of the sentence.

S5. Ans. (e)

Sol. All the given parts are correct and therefore option (e) is the correct choice for the given question.

S6. Ans. (d)

Sol. The combination of two parts of the sentence where the error lies is ***option (d) i.e., part (C) and (E)*** . To make ***part (C)*** correct, ***replace 'to' with 'at'.*** While for the ***part (E)*** it should be noted that the sentence is describing about ***two appointments at RBI***, therefore here the noun ***"appointment" should get replaced with its plural form "appointments"*** to make the sentence grammatically and logically correct. Hence, option (d) is the most viable choice.

S7. Ans. (b)

Sol. The pair of the erroneous parts of the sentence is ***option (b) i.e., parts (A) and (D)*** . The omission of the article 'The' from the prefix of 'world bank' is the error in ***part (A)*** . Article ***'the'*** is used *to describe specific means that the noun has a defined identity, which can happen for a variety of reasons*. And, in ***part (D)*** , the ***verb 'is'*** is incorrectly used as the noun '***business dynamics'*** is in plural form therefore, to comply with ***subject-verb-agreement*** the verb should also be in its plural form, hence, ***replace 'is' with 'are'*** to make the sentence grammatically and contextually correct. Thus, option (b) is the correct choice.

S8. Ans. (a)

Sol. ***Parts (C) and (D)*** consist errors in them. For

***part (C)*** **, *the verb 'want' which is in present tense should get replaced with its past tense form i.e., 'wanted'.*** Also, in order to correct the ***part (D)*** of the sentence ***use "from" in place of "for"***, as the correct bold part of the sentence is providing a clue for the people who are prepared to pay the price for high-tech, thus, the West wants a good-price for high-tech from rich customers rather than for rich customers. Hence, with the corrections in part (C) and (D) , the sentence becomes grammatically and contextually correct and therefore, ***option (a)*** becomes the most suitable answer choice.

S9. Ans. (e)

Sol. The given sentence is grammatically and contextually correct and doesn't carry errors in any part of it. Hence, ***option (e)*** is the most feasible answer choice.

S10. Ans. (c)

Sol. The erroneous parts of the sentence are ***part (C) and (E)*** **.** There is a contextual error in ***part (C)*** as the correct bold part consists "***instead of***" which is used to represent a contrast in the statement. Thus, to make the sentence contextually correct the phrase "*should we go to the foreign manufacturer in his own country*" should be replaced with "*should we* ***not*** *go to the foreign manufacturer in his own country"*. Moreover, in part (E) of the sentence replace "manufacture" with "manufacturing" as all the objects of sentence joined with a conjunction should be in the similar form. Since, all the objects in the sentence are gerunds thus the verb connected with the conjunction 'and' should also be in its gerund form. Therefore, as the errors are in part (C) and (E) , ***option (c)*** becomes the most viable choice.

S11. Ans. (b)

Sol. The best answer is (b) . The noun that comes directly after the comma is modified by the pharase having logged thousands of hours watching felines from tigers to cheetahs.

S12.Ans. (a)

Sol. One way of correcting a dangling participle is to change the participle phrase to a clause. Choices (a) and (c) substitute clauses substitute clauses for phrase. However choice (c) changes the meaning of the sentence.

S13.Ans. (a)

Sol. 'He' is the subject of the sentence, which takes 'who' as the relative pronoun.

S14.Ans. (b)

Sol.

This choice doesn't violate the parallel structure, neither does it change the original message.

S15.Ans. (b)

Sol. Option (b) corrects error in the possessive form of government (needed before a verbal noun)

S16.Ans. (a)

Sol. Option (a) is the best way of expressing the idea.

S17.Ans. (b)

Sol. The improper use of pronoun 'one' and 'you' is corrected in option (b)

S18.Ans. (c)

Sol. Option (c) is the best way of expressing the idea.

S19.Ans. (c)

Sol. The omission of the past participle 'been' is corrected in choice (c)

**Section - II**

S20.Ans. (e)

Sol. There is no need for improvement in the original sentence.

S21. Ans. (a)

Sol. Replace 'what he wanted me' with 'how he wanted me'.

S22. Ans. (e)

Sol. No correction required

S23. Ans. (e)

Sol. No correction required

S24. Ans. (a)

S25. Ans. (b)

S26. Ans. (c)

S27. Ans. (e)

S28. Ans. (e)

Sol. No correction required

S29. Ans. (c)

Sol. Replace 'will be likely to face' with 'is likely to face'.

S30. Ans. (e)

Sol. No correction required

S31. Ans. (a)

Sol. Both the phrases in bold are incorrect. The first phrase ***"the recent imposes on the bans on"*** doesn't follow the correct grammatical syntax of the sentence. It should be replaced with "***the recently imposed ban on".*** It should be noted that the activity is of past tense hence verb ***[impose]*** should be replaced with ***"imposed***". Moreover, here the sentence requires an adverb rather than an adjective to describe the verb [impose] hence, replace ***[recent]*** with "***recently".*** The second bold expression "***prices discounts that are quiet offered to***" of the sentence is also grammatically incorrect. It should be replaced with "***price discounts that are quietly offered to"*** to make the sentence grammatically and contextually coherent. ***[Prices]*** should be replaced with ***"price"*** as the discounts are given on a single price. Also, again rather than an adjective, an adverb is required with the verb [offered], therefore, replace ***[quiet]*** with [***quietly]*** to make the sentence grammatically viable. All the other options fail to fit into the sentence either grammatically or contextually. Hence, ***option (a)*** becomes the most suitable choice.

S32. Ans. (e)

Sol. The given phrases in bold are correct and don't require any further corrections or replacements. The other alternatives given are either contextually meaningless or grammatically incorrect. Hence, ***option (e)*** is the most feasible choice.

S33. Ans. (b)

Sol. Both the bold phrases of the sentence require corrections and replacements to make the sentence grammatically correct. The first bold expression ***"Customers can prefers cabs to book"*** should be replaced with ***"Customers can choose to book cabs".*** *As the given phrase lacks* ***subject-verb-agreement.*** *Subjects and verbs must AGREE with one another in number (singular or plural) . Thus, if a subject is singular, its verb must also be singular; if a subject is plural, its verb must also be plural.* Therefore, replace the verb ***[prefers]*** with its plural form ***[prefer]*** to make the expression correct. The second bold phrase "***will be also enable commuters to book cabs"*** lacks the correct grammatical syntax of the sentence. The correct structure is ***[Subject + Will + Base form or 1st form of verb +Object].***

Therefore, it should be replaced with ***"will also enable commuters to book cabs***". All the other options fail to be grammatically and contextually correct. Hence, ***option (b)*** is the correct choice.

S34. Ans. (c)

Sol. The first bold phrase should be replaced with ***"It will be a long"*** to make the sentence contextually and grammatically correct. *Would is a past-tense form of will. If the past events are discussed, it is used to indicate something that was in the future at that point in time, but is not necessarily in the future right now.* As, the elections are actions of future ***"will"*** should be used instead of ***[would have been].*** Moreover, the second phrase contains a grammatical error as ***[to get closely]*** should be replaced with ***[to get close]*** to make the sentence grammatically and contextually correct. All the other options fail to make the sentence coherent. Hence, ***option (c)*** is the correct choice.

S35. Ans. (e)

Sol. The given phrases in bold are correct and don't require any further corrections or replacements. The other alternatives given are either contextually meaningless or grammatically incorrect. Hence, ***option (e)*** is the most feasible choice.

S36. Ans. (b)

Sol. The given expressions in bold are incorrect. The correct phrases that shall replace the phrases given in bold are ***"stressed the need to improve"*** and ***"cut down the cost of logistics***" respectively. All the other phrases fail to fill the blanks in a coherent manner. Hence ***option (b)*** becomes the most suitable answer choice.

S37. Ans. (e)

Sol. The given phrases in bold are correct and don't require any further corrections or replacements. The other alternatives given are either contextually meaningless or grammatically incorrect. Hence, ***option (e)*** is the most feasible choice.

S38. Ans. (d)

Sol. The given phrases in bold are incorrect. The phrase **"withdraw support as the"** should be replaced with "***withdrew support because the"*** along with replacing the second phrase **"investments are considered not to be strong"** with ***"investments were considered not strong***" respectively to make the sentence grammatically and contextually correct. *It is to be noted that the given sentence is in the past tense while the bold phrases use the verbs in their present form thus, making the grammatical syntax of the sentence incorrect. All the other options don't fit into the sentence aptly.* Hence, ***option (d)*** is the most viable answer choice.

S39. Ans. (a)

Sol. The given expressions in bold are incorrect. The correct phrases that shall replace the phrases given in bold are "***have announced they were"*** and "***to offer enterprises a solution"*** respectively. All the other phrases fail to fill the blanks in a coherent manner. Hence ***option (a)*** becomes the most suitable answer choice.

S40. Ans. (e)

Sol. The given phrases in bold are correct and don't require any further corrections or replacements. The other alternatives given are either contextually meaningless or grammatically incorrect. Hence, ***option (e)*** is the most feasible choice.

S41. Ans. (c)

**Section - II**

Sol. "The Taj Mahal in moonlight" is the correct usage.

S42. Ans. (c)

Sol. "Attempted tactfully" is the correct usage.

S43. Ans. (a)

Sol. Use of 'they' or 'them' is inappropriate in other options.

S44. Ans. (c)

Sol. "badly needed" is the correct usage.

S45. Ans. (c)

Sol. "to say" will be compared with "to do".

S46. Ans. (a)

Sol. Option (a) is true as there is no grammatical error in it; "from the clutches of militants" is the correct usage.

S47. Ans. (d)

Sol. Option (d) is true as there is no grammatical error in it; "is involved in operations not for sacrificing his life" and "those who threaten the fabric" are the correct usage.

S48. Ans. (d)

Sol. Option (d) is true as there is no grammatical error in it; "the revised procurement or offsets policy would be announced shortly" is the correct usage.

S49. Ans. (c)

Sol. Option (c) is true as there is no grammatical error in it; "entry into the hallowed chamber of fame and success" is the correct usage.

S50. Ans. (d)

Sol. option (d) is true as there is no grammatical error in it; "all eyes are directed towards the presidential candidates running in the first round" is the correct usage

# STRATEGIES TO SOLVE DIFFERENT TYPES OF QUESTIONS

# Section – III

# Reading Comprehension

**Steps For Solving RC:** Most of you are confused whether to attempt the RC or not. Well RC can actually be your saving glory in the exams, as it does not require any grammar rules or guess work, all you need to do is to look for the answers. Now one RC is expected in the exams, well you obviously cannot immediately read long passages due to lack of time. So what do you do?

**So, here are the strategies to follow to get more marks in Reading Comprehension.**

**1.** A complaint which I hear often is that, the **students are unable to understand** the given reading comprehension. If you belong to this category, you need to understand that you don't need to understand each and every word of the comprehension. At the same time, you should find the gist (summary) of it. Both these points above may appear contradictory. But the crucial thing is, you need to eliminate the words, phrases, sentences from the Reading Comprehension that are not useful and need to focus on keywords.

**2. Find your strengths first**: To improve reading comprehension, you need to find your strengths first, read one question and then search for the answer quickly, looking for similar words in the paragraphs.

But make sure you do it really quickly. Once you get the needed lines of the answer in the RC, then compare it with the options given in the question. If you are unable to locate an answer then move to the next question, but do not get stuck on any question!! Using this method you will be able to attempt the RC in a short span of time and it will help you score well too. This method seems odd, but works beautifully in the exams. You still have time before the exams, try it at home as an experiment to see if it works for you. Also stay away from questions like what is the authors view in this passage, or what is the author trying to say, as these questions are usually quite controversial. So basically these exams require you to be really smart. And smartness comes from practice.

**3. Practice a lot**: "Normally, students who believe themselves to be weak in Reading Comprehension, are unwilling to practice. Most of them try to avoid solving at home. They make a lot of excuses. But remember excuses don't bring you success. Success won't be available unless you confront your fears and weaknesses. **Remember,** No one asks you "why didn't you succeed in life?" They only ask you "Did you succeed or not?"

**4. Improve Your Vocabulary**: Why you need to improve your vocabulary? Vocabulary means knowledge of words (meaning of words) . If you do not have a good vocabulary, you have to stop at every new word in the reading comprehension, and be puzzled what does it mean? So, when you don't know the meaning of a word, it becomes very difficult to understand the gist of the Comprehension. Having a good vocabulary, makes you understand the reading Comprehension much easier.

**How to improve your vocabulary?**

Start reading in English, anything....... Newspapers, stories, comics, text books.... anything, that keeps you immersed in

English. New words gradually sink into your subconscious mind and become familiar.

Keep a notebook, Note down the new words you learned today and revise them regularly.

Keep a target and a schedule to learn a certain number of new words every day. You are the better person to decide the number,... I am not. Do not deviate from the schedule at any cost.

**5. Use a pen while reading**: Do not read the Reading Comprehension like a movie novel. While going through the passage, your three body organs should act in collaboration.

**Eyes, Hand, Brain**

**6. Focus**: It is not unusual for any person to wander somewhere while reading something uninteresting. So, when you find the Comprehension dull, difficult and uninteresting, your eyes run through the sentences, but your mind wanders somewhere else. The result.... you complete reading, but you grasp nothing.

**Solution:** Focus on the content. Don't let your mind go away from there. If it starts daydreaming....bring it back into reality. Tell yourself that you have plenty of time to dream after the exam.

**7. Improve reading Speed:** Do not move your lips while reading, it slows you down.

**Types of questions**

The questions asked in reading comprehension can be categorised into the following categories. It is wise to be familiar with these categories so that while giving the test you can identify the type of the question and the appropriate approach to ensure accuracy. They are:

**1. Central Idea Questions:** These types of questions test your understanding of the theme of the passage. These questions include words like, 'the main idea, central idea, purpose, a possible title, theses, and so on.' You may be asked to choose the option which best expresses the author's arguments or conclusion.

• How to solve these types of questions?

While solving these questions you will note that in order to answer the central idea question correctly you need to pay attention to the details. You have to comprehend what these details are trying to emphasize or support. The idea is not specifically stated in the passage but it is what every point will support.

**2. Specified Idea Questions:** As the name suggests, these are the direct questions. The answer of these questions will be specifically given in the passage.

• How to solve these types of questions?

In order to answer these types of questions, you need to read the passage carefully and chose the option wisely because sometimes the facts given in the passage are maneuvered to confuse the candidate.

**3. Inference Question:** These are the indirect questions. Inference questions a candidate to make sustainable inferences based on the facts given in the passage.

• How to solve these types of questions?

In order to answer these types of questions, you need to understand the facts given in the passage, observe the logic used by the author and then decide which option can be inferred from the same.

Sometimes, you may be requires to identify the option that cannot be inferred. In such types of questions same approach is applied.

**4. Tone/ Attitude Questions:** While writing on some topic, every author will have some ideas/ character/ attitude towards it.

• How to solve these types of questions?

In order to answer these ideas/ attitude questions you need to identify the ideas/ character/ attitude he has towards the subject he is dealing with. This 'attitude' can be inferred by a careful reading.

Also, his attitude towards the subject will impart a tone to his writing and will explicitly be shown by his choice of words.

**5. Vocabulary Based Questions:** These questions ask you to choose the **MOST SIMILAR/ MOST OPPOSITE** option among the given options.

• How to solve these types of questions?

There is no hierarchical process which you can follow to answer these types of questions. However, you can refer to the wordlist given in the vocabulary section to improve your vocabulary. Also, try to infer the meaning of the word on the basis of the tone of the sentence.

The genesis of service tax emanates from the ongoing structural transformation of the Indian economy, whereby presently more than one-half of GDP originates from the services sector. Despite the growing presence of the services sector in the Indian economy, it remained out of the tax **net** prior to 1994-95, leading to a steady deterioration in tax-GDP ratio. The service tax was introduced in 1994-95 on a select category of services at a low rate of five per cent.

While the service tax rate and the coverage of services being taxed have increased ever since, the combined tax-GDP ratio of the Centre and States, nevertheless, deteriorated from 16.4 per cent in 1985-86 to 14.1 per cent in 1999-2000. It may be noted that between 1990-91 and 1998-99, the share of industrial sector in GDP dropped by 6.4 percentage points whereas almost 64 per cent of the tax revenue was generated by indirect taxes for which industrial sector continues to be the principal tax base. On the other hand, during the same period, the share of services sector in GDP has increased by 10 percentage points and this sector has still remained poorly taxed.

The rationale for service tax, therefore, lies not only in arresting the falling tax-GDP ratio but also in ipso facto improving allocative efficiency in the economy as well as promoting equity. Against this back-drop, the service tax needs to be designed taking into account the fact that (i) the share of services in GDP is expanding; (ii) failure to tax services distorts consumer choices and encourages spending on services at the expense of goods; (iii) untaxed service traders are unable to claim value added tax (VAT) on service inputs, which encourages businesses to develop in-house services, creating further distortions; and (iv) most services that are likely to become taxable are positively correlated with expenditure of high income households and, therefore, service tax improves equity.

In the Indian context taxation of services assumes importance in the wake of the need for improving the revenue system, ensuring a measure of neutrality in taxation between goods and services and eventually helping to evolve an efficient system of domestic trade taxes, both at the Central and the State levels.

The coverage of services under tax net has been **progressively** widened over the years. With effect of the Finance Act, 2004, 71 services are presently contributing to the service tax collections.

The services tax is applicable to all parts of India except the State of Jammu and Kashmir and is leviable on the gross amount charged by the service provider from the client. The rate of service tax was increased from 5 per cent since September 10, 2004. With the increase in tax rate and base of service tax, the collections from the service tax have shown a steady rise from Rs. 410 crores in 1994-95 to Rs. 8,300 crores in 2003-04; however, they accounted for only 4.4 per cent of the total tax receipts of the Centre (0.3 per cent of GDP) in 2003-04.

Service tax is **envisaged** as the tax of the future. The inclusion of all value added services in the tax net would yield a larger amount of revenue and make the existing tax structure more **elastic**. Once the service sector is adequately covered under tax net, the buoyant services sector will enable the reversal of declining trend in tax buoyancy. Besides raising the revenue buoyancy, appropriate taxation of services sector would also provide equity, efficiency and consistency in the tax administration as well as neutrality for various economic activities. Integration of services sector to the tax net would be the prelude to the introduction of a full-fledged VAT system.

**1.** The origin of service tax is attributed to

(a) Increase in Gross Domestic Products (GDP)

(b) Existence of service sector

(c) Tax of the future

(d) Metamorphosis of our country's economy

(e) Enormous growth potential of industrial sector

**Sol. (d)** ; The first line of the passage 'The genesis (origin) of service tax emanates from the ongoing structural transformation of the Indian economy' enables us to infer that the origin of service tax is attributed to the transformation of the Indian economy. Hence (d) is the correct option.

**Main Idea Question**

**2.** When the author mentions that the service taxes constitute 0.3 percent of GDP, he implies that-

(a) It is a substantially high amount

(b) The service taxes show a very progressive trend

(c) It is a very small amount

(d) There is no scope for further increase

(e) None of these

**Sol. (c)** ; In the second last paragraph it is given that 'they accounted for only 4.4 per cent of the total tax receipts of the Centre (0.3 per cent of GDP) '. Here, the usage of the word 'only' suggests that 'It is a very small amount'. Hence, (c) is the correct option.

**Inference Question**

**3.** Levying service tax is most likely to achieve which of the following ?

1. Check on reducing Tax-GDP ratio.

2. Enhancement in allocative efficiency.

3. Promoting equity.

(a) (a) and (b) only (b) (b) and (c) only (c) (a) and (c) only

(d) All the three (e) None of these

**Sol. (d)** ; From the figures given in the first paragraph and the statement

'The rationale for service tax, therefore, lies not only in arresting the falling tax-GDP ratio but also in ipso facto improving allocative efficiency in the economy as well as promoting equity' we can conclude that (a) ,(b) and (c) are true. Hence, (d) is the correct option.

**Tone/ Attitude Question**

**4.** The author of the passage seems to be having-

(a) An antagonistic attitude about levying service tax

(b) A favourable attitude towards levying service tax

(c) A sympathetic and lenient view regarding untaxed service traders

(d) A distorted view about equity

(e) A soft corner for the tax payers brought under service tax net

**Sol. (b) ;** In the entire passage, the author discusses the positive impact of service tax, so we can infer that he has a 'A favourable attitude towards levying service tax'. Hence, (b) is the correct option.

**Vocabulary Based Questions**

**5.** Choose the word/group of words which is most nearly the SAME in meaning to 'NET'.

(a) Actual amount (b) Amount after tax (c) Governance

(d) Coverage (e) Mesh

**Sol. (d) ;** 'Coverage' is the word which is most nearly the same in meaning to 'NET'.

**6.** Choose the word/ group of words which is most OPPOSITE in meaning to PROGRESSIVELY.

(a) Gradually (b) Abruptly (c) Occasionally

(d) Narrowly (e) Ineffectively

**Sol. (b) ;** 'PROGRESSIVELY' means 'gradually'. Hence 'Abruptly' is the word which is most nearly the opposite in meaning to it.

Section - III

# Cloze Test

A cloze test is an exercise in which there is a passage with certain blanks, each of which is numbered. These numbers are printed below the passage and against each, four or five words are suggested, one of which fits the blank correctly.

So, cloze test is there to test the grammar skills, vocabulary and English command of a candidate.

**How to approach such questions:**

**1. Some important points:**

**(a)** First of all go through the complete passage and get a rough idea about the content and theme of the passage. The correct understanding of the content will make you think in the right direction and thus help you make the right decision and the right choice among the given words.

**(b)** Logically analyze each sentence and try to understand the grammatical construction of it because some word-choices are based on grammar.

**2. Eliminate the less Probable option:**

**(a)** Eliminate the less probable option and get the correct one.

**(b)** In case if you have multiple correct options then first mark options of this kind and try fitting them in blank one by one, then use the one which fits perfectly with the given sentence.

**(c)** It may happen sometimes that you are unable to decide between two words. In such case use that one from options which is used frequently with the words around the blank.

**Ex – (1) Did you find him ___________ for matrimonial purpose?**

**(a) Compatible (b) Perfect (c) Good**

In this case almost all the words seem synonymous but the words 'compatible' and 'matrimonial' are interlinked. Hence (a) is answer.

**(2) Can we have a ___________ chat?**

**(a) Swift (b) Quick (c) Prompt**

Here all three options are synonyms of each other so it may be difficult to decide which one is the correct answer. Here, the word 'quick' and chat are used more frequently as a combination rather than 'swift chat' or 'prompt chat'.

So (b) is the answer.

**3. Think like the Author:**

Each passage is written in a certain tone, humor, serious, narrative and so on. Identify the tone and pick the words accordingly. If the tone is funny/humorous, try and use words which evoke fun and vice-versa.

**Ex** – Jonah ___________ down the stairs, bumping along like a quarter in a tumbling dyer.

**(a) tumbled (b) fell (c) dropped**

Clearly, you can use either 'tumbled' or 'fell' in this blank but the rest of the sentence is written in a humorous vein. So we try to maintain the tone of the sentence. This is best accomplished by the use of the word 'tumbled'.

**4. Decide the correct part of speech:** Read the sentence carefully and see which part of speech is required to be filled. To decide the right part of speech, you need to keep the following things in the mind.

**(a) Noun/ Pronoun:** A noun will be required if—

(i) The blank is at the position of subject or

object.

**Ex** – Every leader should perform his duty.

Noun Pronoun

(ii) If the blank is after an adjective

**Ex** – A little knowledge is a dangerous thing.

(iii) Blank is after preposition.

**Ex** – He sat beside me.

**(b) Adjective:** An adjective will be required if

(i) the blank requires a qualifier for a preceding or following noun or pronoun.

(ii) the blank is just before a noun.

**Ex** – Do you have any problem?

**(c) Adverb:** An adverb is required if

(i) The blank is after a verb

**Ex** – He works hard

(ii) A blank is before the subject at the beginning of a sentence.

**Ex** – Only I know the truth.

**(d) Conjunction:** A conjunction is required if

The blank required a word to combine two words or sentences

**Ex** – You must run fast else you will miss the train.

**(e) Article:** An article is required if

(i) The blank is before a noun.

**Ex** – He is an heir to the throne.

(ii) The blank is before a comparative or superlative degree.

**Ex** – He is the better of the two wrestlers.

He is the best student of our class.

**(f) Preposition:** A preposition is required if

(i) The blank required a word to relate two words.

**Ex** – The bill was passed amid pandemonium.

The cat jumped upon the rat.

**(g) Verb:** A verb is required if

(i) The blank is after a subject.

**Ex** – They played very well.

(ii) The blank after a helping verb.

**Ex** – We have to make the system work.

(iii) The blank required a linking verb

(iv) The blank required a word that describes the action of a noun or pronoun.

**Ex** – Swimming is a good exercise.

**(h) Phrasal Verb:** Sometimes a phrasal verb is required to fit in the sentence.

**Ex** – The meeting was put off due to agitation held by union leaders of the company.

Corruption is eating into our country.

**5. Commonly used phrases:** You have to give preference to those words which commonly precede or follow the word around the blank.

Consider the following example:

**Ex – Tens of thousands of demonstrators in Malasiya defied police orders on Saturday, amassing in the capital in a __________of anger at the government prime minister Najib**

**Razak.**

**(i) Show (ii) Display (iii) Expression (iv) Plainness**

You cannot use 'expression' here as it needs article 'an' before itself.

Plainness is inappropriate here, show of anger is not correct but display of anger is commonly used. Hence (ii) is the answer.

**6. Enhance your vocabulary and**

## Section - III

**comprehension of language: –**

Read as much as you can to improve your language. When you read more, you tend to have a better idea of which word goes with the other words.

**7. Solve plenty of cloze tests to attain perfection:** By solving a large number of cloze tests, you will not only enhance your vocabulary but also learn how and where words should be used. This will surely help in building up your language skills.

Now let's consider an example:

Whenever I (**1**) at the moon, my heart (**2**) with pleasure. I wish I have (**3**) to fly up to the moon. I know if I could (**4**) to become an (**5**) . I would be able to go to the moon.

**1.** (a) looked (b) saw (c) viewed (d) gaze

**2.** (a) fills (b) filled (c) field (d) feels

**3.** (a) hands (b) wings (c) legs (d) courage

**4.** (a) grow up (b) mow (c) blow (d) show

**5.** (a) astrology (b) astronomy(c) astronaut (d) aristocrat

**Ans.**

**1.** (a) **2.** (b) **3.** (b) **4.** (a) **5.** (c)

**Explanation:**

**1. (a)** ; By reading sentence, two options would be eliminated. Now you have two words 'looked' and 'gazed'.

But gaze means looking continuously for a time so the answer here is (a)

**2. (a)** ; Here we are talking in present so option (a) fits the blank correct.

**3. (c)** ; You can fly only if you have wings

**4. (a)** ; Author is talking about his ambitions. So only option (a) fits the blank

**5. (c)** ; Astronaut is one who goes into space other options are irrelevant.

# Fillers

**How to solve filler Questions –**

These are the following steps to be followed.

**Step 1:** Read the statements carefully and first try to fill the missing word without looking at the options.

**Step 2**: Do check the tense i.e. present tense, past tense or future tense in the sentence provided.

Secondly, check for the tense of answer provided in option.

**Step 3**: Choose the word from the options.

That best replaces the word that you had thought of initially.

**Note: you must ensure that the word inserted in the blank enables you to read the sentence smoothly and correctly.**

**Step 4:** Check whether the sentence actually makes sense or not.

**Points to remember**

**1.** To be able to solve such question correctly. You must have a very good vocabulary.

**Ex.** The villagers ___________the death of their leader by keeping all the shops closed.

(a) announced (b) protested

(c) mourned (d) consoled

**Ans.:** (c)

Shops were closed by villagers on the death of their leader which shows their feeling of sadness.

**Ex.** Man is ___________, however he is more in need of mental companionship than of physical companionship.

(a) biological (b) physical (c) egoistic

(d) Gregarious (e) democratic

Companionship indicate togetherness so only option (d) Gregarious fits here.

**2.** Do check noun, pronoun, adverb, adjective, preposition, conjunction etc.

**Ex.** We met ___________the party.

(a) in (b) at (c) on (d) to

**Ans.**(b) 'at'

**Ex.** We all are very indignant ___________ the injustice done to him.

(a) For (b) of (c) to (d) at

**Ans.**(d) 'at

**3. Double Blanks**

**Ex.** You ___________ have thanked him for his ___________ help.

(a) must ............ Negligible (b) would ............ Needful

(c) should ............ Timely (d) better ............ Immense

(e) often ............ Great

**Ans.** (c) ; The option 'must', 'would', 'should', 'better', 'often' all are model verbs and (a) & (c) could be possibilities but keeping in mind the second blank we select the option accordingly. Now understand the context of question. Negligible cannot be a possibility so we will eliminate it.

Now option (E) cannot be considered for its first option similarly

D & B cannot be considered. So the left out option is C.

**4. Phrasal Verb**

**Ex.** Once he has signed the agreement, he won't be able to _______.

(a) back out (b) back at (c) back in (d) back up

**Sol. (a) ;** Back out – to retreat

**5. Conjunction**

**Ex.** He will not work ____________ he is compelled

(a) till (b) if (c) after (d) unless

**Ans. (d) ;** unless

**6. Idioms**

**Ex.** Take this medicine and you will get rid ____________ this disease.

(a) from (b) of (c) over (d) at

**Ans. (b) ;** of (get rid of – to dispense with)

In above questions your knowledge and understanding of common idioms & phrases in English language may be tested. Hence make sure to have such good skill of such phrases.

**7. Try to determine the tone of the missing word** – whether the required word is positive or negative in the meaning.

**Ex.** ____________to popular belief that red meat makes human aggressive, scientist have found that it actually has a calming effect.

(a) sticking (b) Similarly (c) opposite (d) Contrary

**Sol.** On examining the sentence carefully it would be found that the blank needs a word that makes the first statements opposite to second.

Hence only (c) & (d) satisfies this condition. But contrary fits more

correct than opposite, so answer is (d)

**8. In case you are confused between two or more options you can also**

**apply the hit and trial method** – one by one place each of the likely options in place of missing word in the sentence. The option which credits maximum meaning to the sentence should be the correct answer.

**Ex.** Our rich culture inspires us to take ____________ in our heritage

(a) prided (b) proudly (c) pride (d) proud

**Ans.** (c) pride

**Ex.** After initial set back, all ____________ programmes were successful due to the initiative of the new dynamic team.

(a) consequent (b) subsequently

(c) consequently (d) subsequent

**Ans.** (d) Subsequent

**Ex.** The car broke down and we ____________ get a taxi.

(a) were to (b) are to (c) had to (d) have to

**Ans.** (c) 'had to'

# Paragraph Completion

Paragraph completion questions follow a clear line of reasoning. These questions in the exams are based on paragraphs excerpted from Newspapers, Magazines, Journals, etc. They are rarely original paragraphs written specially for the exam. Hence the methodology that good writers use to complete their paragraphs holds true for the answer choice; your duty, therefore is to understand the line of reasoning used by the writer.

If followed appropriately then scoring becomes easier.

A paragraph is a short composition or note on an idea that is complete in itself. Hence the last sentence of a paragraph will have the following characteristics:

- It fulfills the purpose of the paragraph.
- It brings the paragraph to a smooth closure.
- It does not introduce (contain) any new ideas.
- It is not an inference.

You need to not only read the paragraph actively and carefully, but also identify its purpose as you read. The last sentence will merely fulfill this purpose and bring the paragraph to a smooth closure. The last sentence, hence, arises from the paragraph itself and not from outside it. If required, you must read the paragraph several times or until you have identified the purpose for which it is written. The operative idea in the directions to the questions is "... choose the one that completes the paragraph". A sentence that completes the paragraph hence cannot logically introduce any new ideas. That is why the last sentence will contain nothing that requires further clarification. The paragraph needs to be closed with the last sentence; it should not leave loose ends to be closed or explained further.

**What does a smooth conclusion mean?**

When we say that "The last sentence concludes the paragraph", the word 'conclude', in this context, merely means to bring to an end. It does not mean that you have to reason out on the basis of the given facts and reach a judgment or decision or an inference. You —as a test taker—have to merely notice the direction in which the paragraph is moving and choose the best sentence that brings it to an end. The reader hence is not actively involved in the paragraph, except in identifying the writer's purpose in writing the paragraph. If you are able to unravel, by looking at the details given in the paragraph, the direction and purpose of the writer, the scoring option stands out from the other options very clearly and conspicuously.

You must spend sufficient time with the paragraph before going to the options to evaluate them for the answer. Some of these questions can be, at times, prove themselves to be extremely tricky if you haven't understood the purpose of the paragraph. Then, all options can appear right.

Another point to bear in mind is that the task in these questions is to complete the paragraph and not merely continue it. The difference between an option that completes the paragraph and an option that continues the paragraph is that the former fulfils the purpose of the paragraph whereas the latter merely continues one or the other of the ideas mentioned in the paragraph. However, in certain questions an option that continues the paragraph may be accommodated as the last sentence (answer) if a sentence (option) that brings the paragraph to a logical closure is not available.

Look at the following example.

"I am sometimes attacked for imposing "rules." Nothing could be further from the truth. I hate rules. All I do is report on how consumers react to different stimuli. I may say to a copywriter, "Research shows that commercials with celebrities are below average in persuading people to buy products. Are you sure you want to use a celebrity?" Call that a rule? Or I may say to an art director, "Research suggests that if you set the copy in black type on a white background, more people will read it than if you set it in white type on a black background................"

What is the purpose of the above paragraph? The writer is at pains to explain to us that he does not want to be seen as framing rules for anyone.

He hates rules. He tells us the different situations which had led to this (erroneous) belief, among others, that he is laying down rules; but he was merely 'reporting' consumer behaviour. He tells us those examples are not rules. So, the purpose of the paragraph is to tell us that whatever he says to others are not rules. They are merely reports, in order that the other may reconsider his or her stand in relation to consumer behaviour.

Now we need to close this paragraph without leaving any loose ends.

**Options:**

**A.** Guidance based on applied research can hardly qualify as "rules."

**B.** Thus, all my so called "rules" are rooted in applied research.

**C.** A suggestion perhaps, but scarcely a rule.

**C.** Such principles are unavoidable if one wants to be systematic about consumer behaviour.

**D.** Fundamentally it is about consumer behaviour — not about celebrities or type settings.

**E.** The findings of research done by London Business School reveal an interesting fact.

Options A and B. "Guidance based on applied research can hardly qualify as 'rules'" and, "Thus, all my so called 'rules' are rooted in applied

research." ring completely untrue because "guidance based on applied research" only reinforces the claim of others that those are strict and rigid principles that no one can refute—by implication stricter than rules. Option

D, "Such principles are unavoidable if one wants to be systematic about consumer behaviour," is in not related to the purpose of the paragraph which is not about how to be systematic about consumer behaviour. In the same vein option E is also far away from the purpose of the writer as it introduces a new topic (research work of London Business School) . Option

C. "A suggestion perhaps but scarcely a rule," fulfils the writer's purpose that they are not rules but merely suggestions. This sentence, read in conjunction with the following "I am sometimes attacked for imposing 'rules'. Nothing could be further from the truth. I hate rules. .... Call that a rule? Or I may say to an art director ..." makes the paragraph a logically complete unit. Hence Option C is the answer.

Now try to solve the questions given in the exercise and read newspapers, magazines, journals, etc. as much as you can in order to improve your reading skills.

# Sentence Improvement

Sentence improvement is one of the most important topics from examination point of view. At an average, 5-10 questions are asked from this particular topic in the examination. Even though there are no hard and fast rules for mastering Sentence Improvement, yet a good knowledge of rules of Grammar and vocabulary can be proved fruitful in this particular section. Generally, there can be two types of questions from this topic. The first one is Grammar based and the second one is vocabulary based.

Obviously, for grammar based questions you need to read the Grammar section diligently and for vocabulary based questions the vocabulary section of this book would definitely be proved out to be helpful to you.

Consider the following example and the solution given in order to comprehend the approach you can adopt while solving Grammar based questions of sentence improvement in the exam.

**1.** *The three names have reached the Ministry of Law and Justice,* ***who has been processing the files****, ministry sources said.*

(a) who is processing the files (b) which was processed

(c) which is processing the files (d) who was processed the files

(e) No replacement required

**Sol.** In the above example relative pronoun 'who' has been used after

'Ministry of Law and Justice' which is not a human being. Hence, the usage of 'who' is incorrect. Now, we know that the relative pronoun which follows 'non-living things' is 'which'. Hence, either (c) or (b) is the correct option. Now, the question is not in passive voice, hence, (b) is not the correct option. Hence, (c) is the correct option.

As you can see, it becomes quite easier to choose the correct option if you are well versed with the rules and basics of grammar. Now, look at the following example based on vocabulary.

***2. To cover the gap between rainfall and water*** *scarcity, govt. will have to invest in desilting water storage in canals and minor water bodies.*

(a) To bridge the gap between rainfall and water

(b) To take down the gap between rainfall and water

(c) To make for the gap between rainfall and water

(d) To make up the gap between rainfall and water

(e) No replacement required

**Sol.** To cover something means 'put something on top of or in front of (something) in order to protect or conceal it'. Hence, it does not go with the meaning of the sentence. Now, 'to take down' means 'to lower without removing' hence, (b) is also not the appropriate option.

Again, 'to make for' means' to move or head towards something' whereas, 'to make up for' means 'compensate for something lost, missed, or deficient.' Hence, (c) and (d) are also not the correct option. 'To bridge the gap' means 'to make the difference between two things smaller'. Hence, (a) is the most appropriate option.

Section - III

# Sentence Rearrangement

Sentence rearrangement or parajumbles are one of the trickiest sections to attempt in English Section. It is a difficult and time consuming question asked in banking exams and other competitive exams. It consists of a group of jumbled up sentences. The goal is to rearrange the sentences in the original sequence. One sentence rearrangement question is usually followed by 5 questions and that means if your arrangement is right, your score increases by 5 marks. Here we are providing you with some simple tips that can save your valuable time and help you solve these questions quickly.

**1.** Just scan all the sentences, try to get the feel of what the passage is about. If you get the tone of the paragraph then it becomes easy for you to guess the opening and closing sentence.

**2.** Try to find out the first sentence. If you can see any chronological order in the given paragraph, then it is easy to solve that question. You should try to find out the linkage how the events occur in the paragraph. If you are able to find out the last sequence then it will also help you in coming to the right sequence of paragraph.

**3.** Generally the first sentence will introduce the theme of the paragraph and will not begin with a conjunction like because, so, but etc.

**4.** Questions where first and last sequence is given can be solved quite easily. Just try to find out the sentence which has the linkage to the first sequence's event. Eliminate all those options of whom you have found the order.

**5.** Finding linkage between parts is more important in these questions in order to make the paragraph more meaningful. The things that are going to help you in these type of questions is only your command over vocabulary, your knowledge of English grammer, preposition, conjunctions, etc. There are some transition words that can help you in identifying the links among the sentences, simultaneously, hence, besides etc.

**Look out for:**

**Relative pronouns** (who, whom, whose, which, that)

**Demonstrative pronouns** (this, that, these, those)

**Personal Pronouns** (he, she, it, him, her, you, they)

If a sentence has these pronouns, make a note of it and scan the paragraph again for the original person, place or object that it refers to.

**6.** Look for cause and effect.

Look for words or phrases explicitly indicating that one thing causes another or logically determines another.

Accordingly In order to

Because So..... that

Consequently Therefore

Given Thus

Hence When.....then

If.....then

**7.** After you are finished with the rearrangement, check it again and make sure that it is coherent and makes sense.

**8.** Article based approach–Indefinite articles (a, an) introduces new and general ideas and definite article (the) points out towards already explained idea. A sentence with definite article (the) cannot be the first sentence of the paragraph.

**9.** Acronym based approach–If two sentences are given and in the first sentence full form is given, i.e. World Trade Organization and if in the second sentence short form is given i.e. WTO. Then the sentence with full form will come first in the paragraph.

**Some more tips**

**1.** Practice as much as you can of these questions to make yourself more familiar with these type of questions. Never think that these questions are easy but you can do them with a bit of practice if you have a little command over English.

**2.** Focus on improving your skills. Read more books, more articles on internet, editorials in the newspaper. Good reading skills will not only help you in these questions. It will also be very helpful when you solve **Double fillers, Comprehension and cloze Test.**

**3.** Practice!! Practice!! Practice!!

**Just to make it more clear. Here is an example**

**A.** Hence, the meal that is taken in the morning is breakfast.

**B.** The word originated from the fact that after dinner, we don't eat the whole night and this is a long time for the body to go without food.

**C.** During day time, we keep on eating and munching after every 3-4 hours.

**D.** People often ask as to why breakfast is important.

**E.** But the duration between dinner and breakfast is pretty long, sometimes may be equivalent to a fast.

**F.** The answer lies in the word 'breakfast' itself.

**Steps:** Scan all the sentences, you get the main theme. It's about Breakfast and the origin of the word.

Now, what can be the opening sentence?

From all the sentences

First sentence can't be the opening sentence as it has a Linking word "HENCE"

Second sentence can't be the opening sentence as it has THE. "THE" as an article, here is used to refer to something.

Third sentence also has a transition word "DURING"

Fifth sentence has a transition word "BUT"

Sixth sentence is not giving the sense of an opening sentence.

Therefore, D is the most apt opening sentence.

What can be the closing sentence?

By just scanning all the sentences, the sentences which are giving the feel of closing sentences are F and A.

**Don't get confused, we will get our last sentence with the help of elimination.**

D is linked to F as there is a link. A question is asked and answer is given. Here A gets eliminated so the probable last sentence is going to be F. F is linked to B as it is giving the explanation to the answer.

As we said look out for transition words But and Hence, To get the theme right, C is linked to E with the help of "But" and then E is linked to A with the help of.

Hence, the correct sequence is: **DFBCEA**

# Section – IV

# Mock Test – 01

Directions (01-08) : **Read the following passage carefully and answer the questions given below it. Certain words have been printed in bold to help you locate them, while answering some of the questions.**

As the world continue to discover the economics of Indian talent. Indian business leaders increasingly worry about hanging on to their key "breadwinners" or perhaps we should say "cake earners". With the continuing strong economic growth in many sectors, the buoyancy in hiring has improved and correspondingly the level of attrition has increased. Retention of employees is again the subject of concern in all our buoyant industries: IT, BPO, auto, components, pharmaceuticals, and research and development.

Attrition figures depending on the industry and level vary from 10 per cent to as high as 50, in some of the BPO segments. But figures of 20 per cent attrition especially at junior to middle levels (the one-year to five year experience levels) are pretty common across a wide spectrum of industries. For most companies the cost of attrition in terms of the attendant hiring costs, training costs and discontinuity costs are often about 30 per cent of the manpower costs! The search for the right retention tool and insights in this respect is an industry in itself!

Employee satisfaction surveys and compensation surveys are all tailored to address the issue of retention by providing "insights". On what the "Employee wants" and how to keep up with the Joneses next door or in our industry. Most often companies look for quick fixes; and the answers are usually in compensation, stock programmes, complex golden handcuff programmes, feel god programmes; retreats in Singapore or Zurich large brand building and induction and orientation programmes! All of which are vitally important, but do not necessarily address the retention problem in isolation.

While stock programmes were seen to be the most effective retention for a long time, the crash and **volatility** in the stock markets have reduced the relevance of this favourite tool. But they have also shown us that employers of substance have a lot more "fundamentals" that work for them!

I do not know the importance of either the surveys or the **consequent** HR initiatives including the compensation and stock programmes but feel that often organizations miss the basic points that build a great organization and employee "stickiness".

I have seen many organizations with fairly modest compensation (not low) continue to attract excellent people. Take the HDFC group for example, or TCS or Infosys. While us often search to uncover the hidden "incentives" in these organizations: is their stock working for them, do they have great benefits, do they send them abroad, do they make extraordinary investments or training? Are they lucky to have great performance? Or be in the right sector?

Yes, many of them do all of these and yet there are many other organizations that do the same, but do not inspire the same amount of loyalty.

## Section - IV

It is important to remember that most employees are simple people wanting the comfort of a secure supportive environment and a decent (not super) compensation and with reasonable opportunities to grow. But, what they often look for in addition, is inspirational or strong leadership that the you can 'trust" and believe, when gives them comfort that their affairs are in good hands even in bad or tough times, and who they believe will be "fair".

"Fairness" is always the toughest issue because it is often in the eyes of the beholder. As several of our companies turn in good results, there is often the question of what they must share with the shareholder and the employee. When a company needs to restructure for better performance the same debate can be in the reverse. The fairness and consistency of leadership usually comes through at such times and is not lost on employees in the long run.

Our surveys therefore need to lose track more strongly the **perceived** fairness and trust our leaders **evoke** their 'connect with people". And not just their business vision and acumen.

And lastly in India where the work we do is virtually our only identity employees' look to be part of an organization that they are proud of in all respects. No retention programme can afford to ignore this reality.

Q1. Why does the author say that most companies look for quick fixes as far as retention is concerned?

(a) Because there is non-availability of any research based study on the problem of retention, companies do not have fare idea to deal with this problem.

(b) Because of the cut-throat competition in today's globalised world, retention is not a major issue for companies so they take it lightly.

(c) Since most of the companies can afford the losses due to attrition therefore they are least bothered.

(d) because of the focus on short term solution thereby missing the finer retails of underlying basis of retention.

(e) None of the above

Q2. What are the shortcomings of compensation surveys and stock programmes according to the author?

(a) Most of the surveys favour employers and hence are partisan in nature.

(b) At times companies forget to examine the benefits of compensation surveys and stock and try to implement them quickly

(c) These are the parts of traditional ways of dealing with the problem therefore these methods are useless.

(d) Most of the compensation surveys and stock miss the basics and also they do not focus employees stickiness.

(e) None of the above

Q3. What are the key elements of employee satisfaction according to the author?

(a) High growth and decent salary.

(b) Good H.R. initiatives and grievance policy

(c) Good training and recreational facilities

(d) Trust and fairness

(e) None of the above

Q4. What is the advice that the author gives for

retention of employees?

(a) Companies must analyze the humanitarian aspect of this problem.

(b) Since it is one of the problems in corporate sector therefore it is to be solved by tried and tested ways.

(c) Companies must consider that "money is cure to all ills" so they should focus on giving monetary incentives to their employees in order to retain them

(d) That companies should focus not on short term but on long term measures

(e) None of the above

Directions (05-07) : Choose the word which is **MOST OPPOSITE** in meaning to the word printed in bold as used in the passage.

Q05. **VOLATILITY**

(a) Fickleness

(b) Impulsive

(c) Fragility

(d) Certitude

(e) Fluctuation

Q06. **CONSEQUENT**

(a) Subsequent

(b) Collateral

(c) Resultant

(d) Effectuate

(e) Concomitant

Q07. **PERCEIVED**

(a) Cognize

(b) Ascertain

(c) Apprehend

(d) Intuit

(e) Confound

Direction (08) : Choose the word which is **MOST SIMILAR** in meaning to the word printed in bold as used in the passage.

Q8. **EVOKE**

(a) Assuage

(b) Indict

(c) Kindle

(d) Regality

(e) Indignation

Directions (09-13) : **In each of the following sentences there are blank spaces. Below each sentence there are five set of words denoted by the alphabets (a) , (b) , (c) , (d) and (e) . Find out which set of words can be filled up in the blanks in the sentence in the same sequence to make it grammatically correct.**

Q9.It is said in the budget that ____________ changes would be made in the law to bring down prices of essential drugs and health equipment. Production of generic drugs would be___________.

(a) Dispensable, stimulated

(b) Imperative, dissuaded

(c) Requisite, encouraged

(d) Superfluous, incited

(e) Essential, deterred

Q10. Many of the renowned off-shore universities are willing to invest in campuses abroad, and, in practice, it is hard to ___________the standards of the home country in some other country. Other related problems are: returns from the investment made in _________ and running of campuses, non-repatriation of profits as mentioned, the regulatory mechanism of the host country in regard to the fee-structure, faculty salaries, curriculum to be offered, and issues pertaining to research and intellectual property rights etc.

(a) Replicate, establishing

(b) Copy, nullify

(c) Concurring, determining

(d) Duplicate, annihilate

(e) Avowal, setting up

Q11. Mr. Trump could either fight back or make peace. Two days after Mr. Flynn's resignation, he has signaled both. He attacked the intelligence agencies on Twitter on Wednesday, while the White House_________ that the promised détente with Russia was over. But Mr. Flynn has set in motion a process that is unlikely to be controlled by a seemingly __________ administration like Mr. Trump's.

(a) Imply, efficient

(b) Denoted, ability

(c) Abrogated, ineptitude

(d) Indicated, incompetent

(e) Refute, Inadequacy

Q12. It takes singular skill and acertain ruthlessness, however, to make capital of the smallest advantages, and Federer and Serena, and to a marginally_________ extent Nadal and Venus, did precisely that. Federer, who missed six months last year with an injury, knew he could not allow Nadal time and space. With his opponent looking in excellent physical condition, Federer could not ________to be drawn into long, bruising rallies;

(a) minute, reject

(b) auxiliary, sustain

(c) larger, manage

(d) lower, refuse

(e) lesser, afford

Q13. India's Railways serves the __________ function of providing travel access to millions, and, as Mahatma Gandhi wrote in his article 'Third Class in Indian Railways', have the _________of making it equitable and comfortable. It must also be safe.

(a) Lethargic, obligatory

(b) Important, liability

(c) Vital, responsibility

(d) Essential, irresponsibility

(e) Indispensable, duty

Directions (14-18) : **In each of the question given below a/an idiom/phrase is given in bold which is then followed by five options, which then tries to decipher its meaning as used in the sentence. Choose the option which gives the meaning of the phrase most appropriately in thc context of the given sentence.**

Q14. The dating applicant **spelled out** exactly what she wanted in a man.

(a) respected

(b) favoured

(c) sanctioned

(d) rejection

(e) deciphered

Q15. Young people used to **look down** on the rules of society.

(a) disparate

(b) fabricate

(c) neglect

(d) consider

(e) investigate

Q16. He's too fat, he'd better **cut bread and sugar out** of his diet and do more exercise.

(a) manifest

(b) split

(c) displace

(d) eliminate

(e) migrate

Q17. I thought I'd **hang around** for a while and see if she comes.

(a) unravel

(b) resolve

(c) linger

(d) attend

(e) anticipate

Q18. The customer service representative couldn't help me, so he **put me through** to a manager.

(a) pass

(b) persist

(c) operate

(d) manage

(e) supervise

Direction (19-23) : **Which of the following phrases (I) , (II) , and (III) given below each sentence should replace the phrase printed in bold letters to make the sentence grammatically correct? Choose the best option among the five given alternatives that reflect the correct use of phrase in the context of the grammatically correct sentence. If the sentence is correct as it is, mark (e) i.e., "No correction required" as the answer.**

Q19. From the low 'Hindu' rate of growth of 3.5 per cent **that has been persisted during the period from** the 1950s to the mid-80s, the Indian economy has come a long way to post almost double-digit growth.

(I) which had been persisted during the period from

(II) as persisted during the period from

(III) that persisted during the period from

(a) Only (I) is correct

(b) Only (III) is correct

(c) Both (I) and (II) are correct

(d) All are correct

(e) No correction required

Q20. The system of accountability, checks and balances in the delivery system, **must be incorporating for paving the way for equal opportunities** and shared prosperity for Indians irrespective of caste, class, gender and region.

(I) must incorporated to pave the way for equal opportunity

(II) must be incorporated to pave the way for equal opportunities

(III) must be incorporated for paving the way for equal opportunities

## Section - IV

(a) Only (I) is correct

(b) Only (III) is correct

(c) Both (II) and (III) are correct

(d) All are correct

(e) No correction required

Q21. **In many social indicators**, some of India's leading states are lagging behind Sub-Saharan African nations.

(I) As many social indicators

(II) Besides many social indicators

(III) Although many social indicators

(a) Only (I) is correct

(b) Only (III) is correct

(c) Both (II) and (III) are correct

(d) All are correct

(e) No correction required

Q22. When they brought the Wage Code, **unions had extensively discussed among themselves**, and then we took a joint position before the government.

(I) unions had been through extensive discussions among themselves

(II) unions had extensive discussions among themselves

(III) unions have been made extensive discussions among themselves

(a) Only (I) is correct

(b) Both (I) and (II) are correct

(c) Both (II) and (III) are correct

(d) All are correct

(e) No correction required

Q23. **Besides an open relationship**, India has also decided to have a more honest conversation with Israel on the peace process.

(I) With a relationship that is more open

(II) As the relationship is very open

(III) while the most open relationship

(a) Only (I) is correct

(b) Both (I) and (II) are correct

(c) Both (II) and (III) are correct

(d) All are correct

(e) No correction required

Directions (24-30) : **In the following passage there are blanks, each of which has been numbered. These numbers are printed below the passage and against each, five words/ phrases are suggested, one of which fits the blank appropriately. Find out the appropriate word/phrase in each case**.

There was a time when people thought of the environment, they thought of its beauty; but now as the natural beauty of the earth that **(24)** , many people around the world have **(25)** up to the realities of just how fragile our earth actually is. Central to this issue is pollution, which involves the introduction of **(26)** substances into the air, land, and water. Although pollution has been occurring **(27)** the earth's history, the rate by which the human species have **(28)** to the amount of pollution that has entered our environment over the **(29)** several hundred years far **(30)** the earth's inherent ability to heal itself.

Q24. (a) disappears

(b) demolishes

(c) stops

(d) destroys

(e) remains

Q25. (a) backed

(b) built

(c) broken

(d) awoken

(e) realized

Q26. (a) adverse

(b) evil

(c) insecure

(d) worse

(e) harmful

Q27. (a) never

(b) throughout

(c) always

(d) forever

(e) everywhere

Q28. (a) evolved

(b) promoted

(c) contributed

(d) encouraged

(e) imparted

Q29. (a) recent

(b) ancient

(c) departed

(d) past

(e) coming

Q30. (a) exceeds

(b) outnumbers

(c) continues

(d) expands

(e) matches

## Solutions (Mock Test – 01)

S1. Ans. (d)

Sol. After reading paragraphs 3& 4, (d) is the best option. The answer (c) is factually wrong as in the passage it is mentioned that cost is generally high and this shows that companies are not in position to bear this cost. Option (a) and (b) do not fit in the theme and hence are rejected.

S2. Ans. (d)

Sol. After reading the last line of paragraph 5, option B seems to be right answer. In the passage, Nothing has been given regarding the time or speed of the implementation of survey and stock options so (b) rejected (a) and (c) are irrelevant to the questions and are therefore rejected.

S3. Ans. (d)

Sol. Refer to paragraph 8 and 9 where author has mentioned the value of trust and fairness.

S4. Ans. (d)

Sol. Read paragraph 3 option (c) is factually wrong. Rests of the choice are out of context. Option (d) is correct as he says that short term fixes can be vital but do not necessarily address the retention problem in isolation.

S5. Ans. (d)

Sol. Volatility means liability to change rapidly and unpredictably, especially for the worse hence certitude is the word most opposite in meaning.

S6. Ans. (d)

Sol. Consequent–following as a result or effect. Effectuate is most opposite as it means to put into force or operation.

S7. Ans. (e)

Sol. Perceived means become aware or conscious of (something) ; come to realize or understand hence confound is the word most opposite in meaning.

S8. Ans. (c)

Sol. Evoke means to bring or recall (a feeling, memory, or image) to the conscious mind hence kindle is the word most similar in meaning.

S9. Ans. (c)

Sol. Option (c) is true.

Requisite means which is necessary or required.

Superfluous means redundant, surplus

S10. Ans. (a)

Sol. Option (a) is true.

Replicate means make an exact copy of; reproduce.

Concurring means be of the same opinion; agree.

S11. Ans. (d)

Sol. Option (d) is true.

Refute means disapprove.

Abrogate means to evade.

S12. Ans. (e)

Sol. 'lesser, afford' fits the two blanks perfectly. Meaning of some other words are:

Auxiliary means providing supplementary or additional help and support.

Sustain means strengthen or support physically or mentally.

S13. Ans. (c)

Sol. 'Vital, responsibility' fits the two blanks perfectly. Meaning of some other words are:

Indispensable means absolutely necessary.

lethargic means sluggish and apathetic.

S14. Ans. (e)

Sol. 'Spelled out' means to explain something explicitly, so that the meaning is unmistakable.

S15. Ans. (c)

Sol. 'Look down' means to regard with contempt.

S16. Ans. (d)

Sol. 'cut out' means delete, remove or leave out.

S17. Ans. (c)

Sol. 'hang around' means loiter, wait around.

S18. Ans. (a)

Sol. 'Put through' means transfer or connect somebody on the telephone.

S19. Ans. (b)

Sol. 'that persisted during the period from' is the correct phrase for the sentence. The sentence is talking about certain time period, for that past indefinite tense is used.

S20. Ans. (c)

Sol. Both the sentences (II) and (III) are correct. For showing the intention, we can use infinitive verb ('to + V1') and 'for +Ving'.

Sentence (I) is incorrect as the sentence must be in passive form.

S21. Ans. (e)

Sol. No correction is required here. Here social indicators refer to statistical measures that describe social trends and conditions impacting on human well-being.

S22. Ans. (b)

Sol. Both the Sentences (I) and (II) are correct.

Sentence (III) is incorrect as 'made' is not correct here as 'discussions' are never been made. It is done by us.

S23. Ans. (a)

Sol. Only sentence (I) is correct.

'while' should not be used as it is used to talk about two things that are happening at the same time.

S24. Ans. (a)

S25. Ans. (d)

S26. Ans. (e)

S27. Ans. (b)

S28. Ans. (c)

S29. Ans. (d)

S30. Ans. (a)

# Mock Test (Pre-Level) Set–02

**Directions (01 – 10) : Read the following passage carefully and answer the questions given below it. Certain words/phrases have been printed in bold to help you locate them while answering some of the questions.**

What do we mean by fear? Fear of what? There are various types of fear and we ne ed not analyse every type. But we can see that fear comes into being when our comprehension of relationship is not complete. Relationship is not only between people but between ourselves and nature, between ourselves and property, between ourselves and ideas; as long as that relationship is not fully understood, there must be fear. Life is relationship. To be is to be related and without relationship there is no life. Nothing can exist in isolation; so long as the mind is seeking isolation, there must be fear. Fear is not an abstraction; it exists only in relation to something.

The question is, how to be rid of fear? First of all, anything that is overcome has to be **conquered** again and again. No problem can be finally overcome, conquered; it can be understood but not conquered. They are two completely different processes and the conquering process leads to further confusion, further fear. To resist, to dominate, to do battle with a problem or to build a defence against it is only to create further conflict, whereas if we can understand fear, go into it fully step by step, explore the whole content of it, then fear will never return in any form.

As I said, fear is not an abstraction; it exists only in relationship. What do we mean by fear? Ultimately we are afraid, are we not, of not being, of not becoming. Now, when there is fear of not being, of not advancing, or fear of the unknown, of death, can that fear be overcome by determination, by a conclusion, by any choice? Obviously not. Mere suppression, **sublimation**, or substitution, creates further resistance, does it not? Therefore fear can never by overcome through any form of discipline, through any form of resistance. That fact must be clearly seen, felt and experienced: fear cannot be overcome through any form of defence or resistance nor can there be freedom from fear through the search for an answer or through mere intellectual or verbal explanation.

Now what are we afraid of? Are we afraid of a fact or of an idea about the fact? Are we afraid of the thing as it is, or are we afraid of what we think it is? Take death, for example. Are we afraid of the fact of death or of the idea of death? The fact is one thing and the idea about the fact is another. Am I afraid of the word 'death' or of the fact itself? Because I am afraid of the word, of the idea, I never understand the fact, I never look at the fact, I am never in direct relation with the fact. It is only when I am in complete communion with the fact that there is no fear. If I am not in communion with the fact, then there is fear, and there is no communion with the fact so long as I have an idea, an opinion, a theory, about the fact, so I have to be very clear whether I am afraid of the word, the idea or of the fact. If I am face to face with the fact, there is nothing to understand about it: the fact is there, and I can deal with it. If I am afraid of the word, then I must understand the word, go into the whole process of what the word, the term, implies.

For example, one is afraid of loneliness, afraid

of the ache, the pain of loneliness. Surely that fear exists because one has never really looked at loneliness, one has never been in complete communion with it. The moment one is completely open to the fact of loneliness one can understand what it is, but one has an idea, an opinion about it, based on previous knowledge; it is this idea, opinion, this previous knowledge about the fact that creates fear. Fear is obviously the outcome of naming, of terming, of projecting a symbol to represent the fact; that is fear is not independent of the word, of the term.

I have a reaction, say, to loneliness; that is I say I am afraid of being nothing. Am I afraid of the fact itself or is that fear awakened because I have previous knowledge of the fact, knowledge being the word, the symbol, the image? How can there be fear of a fact? When I am face to face with a fact, in direct communion with it, I can look at it, observe it; therefore there is no fear of the fact. What causes fear is my apprehension about the fact, what the fact might be or do.

It is my opinion, my idea, my experience, my knowledge about the fact that creates fear. So long as there is verbalization of the fact, giving the fact a name and therefore identifying or condemning it, so long as thought is judging the fact as an observer, there must be fear. Thought is the product of the past, it can only exist through verbalization, through symbols, through images; so long as thought is regarding or translating the fact, there must be fear.

Thus it is the mind that creates fear, the mind being the process of thinking. Thinking is verbalization. You cannot think without words, without symbols, images; these images, which are the prejudices, the previous knowledge, the **apprehensions** of the mind, are projected upon the fact, and out of that there arises fear. There is freedom from fear only when the mind is capable of looking at the fact without translating it, without giving it a name, a label. This is quite difficult, because the feelings, the reactions, the anxieties that we have, are promptly identified by the mind and given a word. The feeling of jealousy is identified by that word. Is it possible not to identify a feeling, to look at that feeling without naming it? It is the naming of the feeling that gives it continuity, that gives it strength. The moment you give a name to that which you call fear, you strengthen it; but if you can look at that feeling without terming it, you will see that it withers away. Therefore if one would be completely free of fear it is essential to understand this whole process of terming, of projecting symbols, images, giving names to facts.

Q1. Which statement best expresses the meaning of fear as explained in the passage?

(a) Fear is experienced because we do not form and understand relationships.

(b) Fear occurs in the mind and needs to be confronted.

(c) Fear is caused when we engage more closely with ideas about a fact, than with trying to understand the fact.

(d) Fear is an act of suppression of understanding of facts.

(e) None of the above

Q2. Human beings are victims of ............. because of which they experience fear. (Choose an option to fill the blank)

(a) Conditioning

(b) Deconditioning

(c) Suppression

(d) Isolation

(e) Intelligibility

Q3. We can eradicate fear if we do any one of the following:

(a) Verbalize and think about the fact that causes fear

(b) Look at the fact that causes fear and experience it fully

(c) Withhold judgements about a fact or situation while experiencing it

(d) All of the above

(e) None of the above

Q4. Which set of key words, when put to practice will help us overcome fear?

(a) Minimise: suppression, sublimation, substitution

(b) Avoid: naming, terming, projecting facts

(c) Build: relationships, understanding, judgement of facts

(d) Engage in: communion, experiencing facts, withholding judgement

(e) None of the above

Q5. Which of the following can be concluded from the passage?

(a) As long as there is any relationship, there must be fear of losing it.

(b) As long as our thoughts can identify and judge a fact as an observer, there would be no fear.

(c) Previous knowledge about a fact hinders dealing with the fact when it arrives.

(d) Fear can be best diminished by fighting it and building a defence against it.

(e) None of the above

Q6. Which of the following can be concluded from the passage?

(a) If one is in complete communion with a fact, there is little chance of fear.

(b) Ideas of a fact aid us in making a communion with the fact.

(c) Fear is a feeling that is independent of the tag or the symbol representing the fact.

(d) All of the above

(e) None of the above

Q7. Which of the following can be concluded from the passage?

(a) Fear can be overcome by conquering it once and for all.

(b) Fear of unknown can be overcome by determined resistance.

(c) Freedom of fear can be achieved by a simple intellectual explanation of the phenomenon.

(d) All of the above

(e) None of the above

**Directions (08–09) : Choose the word/group of words which is MOST SIMILAR in meaning to the word/ group of words printed in bold as used in the passage.**

Q8. **Conquered**

(a) liberate

(b) extricate

(c) disencumber

(d) emancipate

(e) vanquish

Q9. **Sublimation**

(a) plebeian

(b) proletarian

(c) utter

(d) obscure

(e) inferior

Direction (10) : Choose the word/group of words which is **MOST OPPOSITE** in meaning to the word/ group of words printed in bold as used in the passage.

Q10. **Apprehensions**

(a) credence

(b) trepidation

(c) dread

(d) cognizance

(e) angst

Directions (11- 15) : **Rearrange the following sentences (A) , (B) , (C) , (D) and (E) in the proper sequence to form a meaningful paragraph and then answer the questions given below it.**

A. Neither cinema nor the press are separately listed in the Constitution, though they are derived from Article 19 (1) A, which lists the freedom of speech and expression.

B. The issue of censorship comes up when we debate whether there should be restrictions to freedom of expression.

C. India is a very vast and complex country and the same freedom enshrined in the Constitution applies to cinema as well.

D. And the answer is that a total censorship and absolute freedom can both be problematic.

E. Citizens of the country as complex as ours have varying needs, requirements and sensibilities and one has to strike a balance.

Q11. Which of the following would be the THIRD sentence after rearrangement?

(a) A (b) B (c) C (d) D (e) E

Q12. Which of the following would be the FIRST sentence after rearrangement?

(a) D (b) C (c) A (d) B (e) E

Q13. Which of the following would be the FOURTH sentence after rearrangement?

(a) C (b) D (c) A (d) E (e) B

Q14. Which of the following would be the SECOND sentence after rearrangement?

(a) E (b) D (c) A (d) C (e) B

Q15. Which of the following would be the FIFTH (LAST) sentence after rearrangement?

(a) E (b) A (c) B (d) D (e) C

Directions (16-20) : **In each of the questions given below a sentence is given with one blank. Below each sentence FOUR words are given out of which two can fit into the sentence. Five options are given with various combinations of these words. You have to choose the combination with the correct set of words which can fit into the given sentence.**

Q16. If you ever have the _____________ to see some of these beautifully made teapots, they will certainly put a smile on your face.

(A) scenario

(B) possibility

(C) determination

(D) opportunity

(a) A-C

(b) A-D

(c) B-C

(d) C-D

(e) B-D

Q17. If you have not seen a samovar, please take the time to ___________ this beautiful piece of functional artistic equipment.

(A) investigate

(B) vindicate

(C) explore

(D) interrogate

(a) A-C

(b) A-D

(c) B-C

(d) C-D

(e) B-D

Q18. For some odd reason people keep a slight distance from couples and groups, probably because they seem so self-contained and______________.

(A) flamboyant

(B) exclusive

(C) restrictive

(D) selective

(a) A-C

(b) A-D

(c) B-C

(d) C-D

(e) B-D

Q19. The sharp rise in bond yields has hit banks with losses on treasury operations ___________ by sovereign bond holdings.

(A) preferred

(B) dominated

(C) spirited

(D) influenced

(a) A-C

(b) A-D

(c) B-C

(d) C-D

(e) B-D

Q20. The present fall in potato prices comes against the ___________of a slowdown in the rural economy.

(A) capacity

(B) support

(C) situation

(D) Backdrop

(a) A-C

(b) A-D

(c) B-C

(d) C-D

(e) B-D

Directions (21-25) : **In the following passage, some of the words have been given in bold, each of which is indicated by a number. The words given in bold may be or may not be suitable in the context of the sentence. Choose the most appropriate word from the four options given against each number that should replace the existing word to make the paragraph meaningful. If the given word doesn't require any replacement, choose option (e) i.e. "No improvement required" as your answer.**

The selection of a US vice president is always a **difficult (21)** business. Every president hopes to find a person who can complement, not **supplant (22)** him. Invariably, the choice falls on someone with more **credence (23)** than ambition, on a man who can be trusted to remain a patient Prince of Wales than a restless heir apparent in **hold (24)** . Some US presidents suffered the same disease that the Guelph Georges did: they hated their potential **descendants (25)** . President Dwight Eisenhower disliked his vice president Richard Nixon, refusing on one occasion to defend him during a corruption investigation.

Q21. (a) Tricky

(b) Delicate

(c) Precarious

(d) Complex

(e) No improvement required

Q22. (a) Overthrow

(b) Rescind

(c) Override

(d) Alienate

(e) No improvement required

Q23. (a) Conviction

(b) Experience

(c) Patience

(d) Wisdom

(e) No improvement required

Q24. (a) Waiting

(b) Pause

(c) Rest

(d) Anticipation

(e) No improvement required

Q25. (a) Forbearers

(b) Beneficiaries

(c) Successors

(d) Brood

(e) No improvement required

Directions (26-30) : **There are three sentences given in each question. Find the sentence(s) which is/are grammatically correct and mark your answer choosing the best possible alternative among the five options given below each question. If all the sentences are correct, choose (e) as your answer.**

Q26.

(i) One of my brother told me about the sad demise of your uncle.

(ii) He emphasised the role technology was playing in India's development.

(iii) The proposal to extend trading hours in order to attract investors too has failed to take off.

(a) Only (i) is correct

(b) Only (iii) is correct

(c) Both (ii) and (iii) are correct

(d) None is correct

(e) All are correct

Q27.

(i) The temple will be a replica of the one in New Delhi and another under construction in New Jersey.

(ii) All the people living in the house including the servant was invited here.

(iii) There has not been any rainfall in this part of the country since the last two years.

(a) Only (i) is correct

(b) Only (ii) is correct

(c) Both (i) and (ii) are correct

(d) None is correct

(e) All are correct

Q28.

(i) People who enjoy these kind of activities can be very useful for your company.

(ii) The recent changes in the monetary policy has enabled us to aggressively work in this area.

(iii) The BJP has occupied the non-Left political space of the State to fulfil the wishes of the people.

(a) Only (i) is correct

(b) Only (iii) is correct

(c) Both (i) and (ii) are correct

(d) None is correct

(e) All are correct

Q29.

(i) Your suggestion is no different from the other employees.

(ii) This is despite enthusiastic calls by several members of the Indian strategic community to adopt harder measures to resolve the crisis.

(iii) The author supported his arguments with the findings of a recently concluded research study.

(a) Only (i) is correct

(b) Only (ii) is correct

(c) Both (i) and (ii) are correct

(d) None is correct

(e) All are correct

Q30.

(i) We are quite fond of this house because we are living in it for the last five years.

(ii) The purchase made by him brought with him a number of prizes.

(iii) The advocate declared in the court that his client has prepared to surrender.

(a) Only (i) is correct

(b) Only (iii) is correct

(c) Both (i) and (ii) are correct

(d) None is correct

(e) All are correct

## Solutions (Mock Test – 02)

S1. Ans. (c)

Sol. Refer the fourth paragraph of the passage which best expresses the meaning of fear through the concepts of "ideas' and 'facts'.

S2. Ans. (d)

Sol. Refer the second-last sentence of the first paragraph, "Nothing can exist in isolation; so long as the mind is seeking isolation, there must be fear. Fear is not an abstraction; it exists only in relation to something". Hence option (d) is the correct choice.

S3. Ans. (b)

Sol. Refer the last sentence of the second paragraph, "To resist, to dominate, to do battle with a problem or to build a defence against it is only to create further conflict, whereas if we can understand fear, go into it fully step by step, explore the whole content of it, then fear will never return in any form". Hence option (b) is the correct choice.

S4. Ans. (d)

Sol. Engage in: communion, experiencing facts, withholding judgement is the one which will help us when put to practice overcome fear. Hence option (d) is the correct choice.

S5. Ans. (c)

Sol. Refer the fifth paragraph, "The moment one is completely open to the fact of loneliness one can understand what it is, but one has an idea, an opinion about it, based on previous knowledge; it is this idea, opinion, this previous knowledge about the fact that creates fear".

S6. Ans. (a)

Sol. Stated directly in the fourth paragraph

S7. Ans. (e)

Sol. None of the given options is correct.

S8. Ans. (e)

Sol. Conquered means successfully overcome (a problem or weakness) and vanquish means defeat thoroughly.

S9. Ans. (c)

Sol. Sublimation means (of a person's attitude or behaviour) extreme or unparalleled and utter means complete; absolute.

S10. Ans. (a)

Sol. Apprehensions means anxiety or fear that something bad or unpleasant will happen and credence means belief in or acceptance of something as true and something good.

For questions (11-15) : The correct sequence is **CABDE**

S11. Ans. (b)

S12. Ans. (b)

S13. Ans. (b)

S14. Ans. (c)

S15. Ans. (a)

S16. Ans. (e)

Sol. 'opportunity, possibility' best suits here. They both are similar in meanings.

S17. Ans. (a)

Sol. Here explore, which means travel through (an unfamiliar area) in order to learn about it, is going appropriately with the sentence. It is similar in meaning as 'investigate'.

Vindicate means show or prove to be right, reasonable, or justified.

S18. Ans. (c)

## Section - IV

Sol. 'exclusive/restrictive' goes correctly as they are similar in meaning with 'self- contained'.

S19. Ans. (e)

Sol. Dominated means have power and influence over. It has the similar meaning as 'influenced'.

S20. Ans. (d)

Sol. Backdrop means accomplishment or atmosphere, which is similar in meaning to 'situation'.

S21. Ans. (a)

Sol. Precarious means dependent on chance; uncertain.

S22. Ans. (e)

Sol. No improvement is required here.

S23. Ans. (b)

Sol. Here quality of vice president has been discussed.

S24. Ans. (a)

Sol. Anticipation means expectation or prediction.

S25. Ans. (c)

Sol. Vice president is an executive ranking below and deputizing for a president.

S26. Ans. (c)

Sol. Option (i) is grammatically incorrect. Use 'brother' in place of 'brothers' as after 'One of' we use a plural noun.

S27. Ans. (a)

Sol.

(ii) Use 'were' in place of 'was' as the subject is 'all the people' which is plural.

(iii) Use 'since' in place of 'for' as 'since' is used for 'point of time' and 'for' is used for 'period of time'.

S28. Ans. (b)

Sol.

(i) Use 'these kinds' in place of 'these kind' as 'these' is plural after which plural noun must be used.

(ii) Use 'have' in place of 'has' as the subject "the recent changes" is plural.

S29. Ans. (b)

Sol.

(i) 'not different from that of' will be used as the comparison is not between two people but with their suggestion.

(iii) The use of 'study' is superfluous.

S30. Ans. (d)

Sol.

(iii) 'was prepared to' will be used in place of 'has prepared to' as the given sentence is an indirect narration whose reporting verb 'declared' is in past tense and therefore the reported speech will also be in past tense.

(ii) Use 'brought him' in place of 'brought with him'.

Bring, buy, give + Indirect Object + Direct Object.

(i) Use 'have been living' in place of 'are living' as the sentence must be in the present perfect continuous tense due to the use of "for the last five years."

# Mock Test (Pre-Level) Set – 03

Directions (01- 10) : **Read the following passage carefully and answer the questions given below them. Certain words/phrases have been printed in bold to help you locate them while answering some of the questions.**

The Arms Trade Treaty (ATT) is the first multilateral treaty to regulate the international trade in conventional arms. In this respect, it is a landmark treaty for the international community, focusing on an issue that is of highest importance for many Asia-Pacific countries – trying to find and establish mechanisms to control unregulated flows of arms. Since its entry into force on December 24, 2014, 130 states have signed the treaty and so far 92 became State Parties. However, when looking at the regional divide of ratifications and accessions on a world-wide scale, the Asia-Pacific shows by far the lowest numbers in global comparison. The past years didn't result in much progress; efforts to tighten arms transfer controls in the region seem to be at a **stalemate**. What is the reason for this inactivity, given so many countries in the region face significant small arms proliferation problems which pose threats to both national and regional security? Which incentives could help to pave the way for this new security and counter-terrorism tool to take full effect?

The ATT is to be seen in the greater scope of what is commonly known as export control, or, more positively **connoted**, Strategic Trade Control (STC) . The main security-enhancing effect of the treaty is to be found in the requirement to introduce comprehensive control systems to make sure that exports, imports, transits, and transshipments of conventional weapons will not be diverted and end up in the hands of **illicit** actors. Thus, the ATT can serve as another instrument inside the global anti-terrorism toolbox. The treaty scope requires states to introduce legislation and establish comprehensive control systems to perform case-by-case risk assessments. To do so, states must have competent national licensing authorities that check relevant control lists of military items. Questions of the end-use and the end-user of weapons shipments are thus essential for such authorities to consider when reviewing applications for arms transfer licenses. Possible cases when a license must be denied include those where arms might end up in situations where crimes against humanity occur.

Comparing the Asia-Pacific to other developing regions, such as Latin America, the Caribbean, and Africa, it becomes obvious that acceptance and popularity of the ATT has progressed rather slowly. Up to date the number of ATT ratifications within the Asia-Pacific remains at an absolute low of only six out of 53 countries. In Oceania, these supporters are Australia, New Zealand, Tuvalu, and Samoa. It is within the Pacific Islands where one can see probably the most forward movement in putting the ATT in practice on a regional basis. This is mainly due to the work of the Pacific Island Forum Secretariat, with the help of the government of New Zealand. The Secretariat published an ATT blueprint legislation in an effort to support the Pacific states in their ambitions to ratify and implement the treaty framework. Amongst its 18 member countries, ratifications by Tuvalu, Samoa, and signatures to the treaty by Kiribati, Nauru, and Palau prove these regional efforts to be at least partly successful. Australia and New Zealand as strong ATT supporters also played a major role in these efforts to make ATT gain momentum in the region.

In eastern Asia, Japan and South Korea are the sole active supporters of the treaty. For many years, South Korea has viewed STC as an important security instrument, mainly preventing North Korea from **acquiring** products that may add to its conventional and unconventional weapons arsenal. After the Tokyo subway sarin gas attack in 1995, Japanese authorities started to give the overall topic of STC ever more emphasis and also began to promote the goal of establishing a tight regional network of sensitive items controls amongst their neighbors. For both countries, ratifying and implementing the ATT was an easy and logical next step that fit in their overall security strategy.

Q1. According to the passage, How Arms Trade Treaty can be referred as Strategic Trade Control?

(a) The Arms Trade Treaty ensures the tightening of the exports, imports, transits and transshipments of conventional weapons controls.

(b) The Arms Trade treaty ensures the national and regional security.

(c) The Arms Trade Treaty is introduced to ensure that the haulage of the weapons will not fulfill some illegal purpose.

(d) Both (a) and (c)

(e) All are correct.

Q2. Which of the following cannot be inferred from the passage?

(a) There are many countries which face small arms proliferation problems posing threat to national and regional security.

(b) The purpose and success of the treaty made many other countries to join this agreement.

(c) Arms Trade Treaty is a multilateral treaty in which there are 92 State Parties.

(d) The Arms Trade Treaty is signed among the countries to control unregulated flows of arms and hence ensuring national security.

(e) All the sentences are correct

Q3. According to the passage, how can the purpose of the arms trade treaty be fulfilled?

(I) By issuing limited number of arms for avoiding illegal use.

(II) By keeping check on the control lists of military items that were transported.

(III) The purpose can be fulfilled by evaluating the risks.

(a) Only (I) is correct

(b) Only (II) is correct

(c) Both (I) and (III) are correct

(d) Both (II) and (III) are correct

(e) All are correct

Q4. According to the passage, what had made the Arms Trade Treaty ratification progress?

(a) The legislation published by the developed country in order to make the treaty implemented and ratified by the pacific states.

(b) The advantages of the treaty towards national security attracted many other countries for the treaty ratification.

(c) The supporters of the treaty like Australia and New Zealand had played a major role in making the treaty ratified by other member nations.

(d) Both (a) and (c)

(e) All of the above

Q5. Which of the following is the appropriate title of the passage?

(a) Arms proliferation problems

(b) Peace among nations

(c) National and regional security

(d) The Arms Trade Treaty in the Asia- Pacific

(e) Regulating the conventional arms

Q6. According to the passage, what is/ are the perspective(s) of the east Asian countries regarding the treaty?

(I) Despite increased counter terrorism attacks, east Asian countries has not taken any further step towards signing the treaty.

(II) East Asian countries like Japan being the active supporter check relevant control lists of military items among its neighbours.

(III) South Korea support the treaty as it prevents other countries from acquiring products.

(a) Only (I) is correct

(b) Only (II) is correct

(c) Both (I) and (III) are correct

(d) Both (II) and (III) are correct

(e) All ae correct

Direction (07-08) : **Choose the word which is MOST SIMILAR in meaning to the word printed in bold as used in the passage.**

Q7. **Stalemate**

(a) evitable

(b) impasse

(c) regulation

(d) edict

(e) precept

Q8. **Connoted**

(a) implied

(b) interdicted

(c) confiscate

(d) procure

(e) seize

Direction (9- 10) : **Choose the word which is most opposite in meaning to the word printed in bold as used in the passage.**

Q9. **Illicit**

(a) rupture

(b) munificent

(c) arrogate

(d) collocate

(e) authorised

Q10. **Acquiring**

(a) cessation

(b) forfeit

(c) divulge

(d) conceal

(e) acquaint

Directions (11-15) : **The following question consists of a sentence which is divided into five parts which contain grammatical errors in one or more than one parts of the sentence. The portions specified in bold suggest that they are grammatically correct and do not require any correction or replacement. If there is an error in any rest parts of the sentence, find the correct alternatives to replace those parts from the three options given below each question to make the sentence grammatically correct. If the given sentence is grammatically correct or does not require any correction, choose (e) , i.e., "No correction required" as your answer.**

Q11. **The recent decision of the J and K government** (I) /to condone stone throwers, many of whom were habitual offenders, (II) / while charging army personnel who were victims of stone throwing (III) /**and opened fire in self-defence in an FIR** (IV) /was the latest confused news emanates from the valley. (V)

(II) condoned stone throwers, many of who were habitual offenders

(III) but charging army personnel were victims of stone throwing

(V) is the latest confused news emanating from the valley

(a) Only (III)

(b) Only (V)

(c) Both (II) and (III)

(d) All (II) , (III) and (V)

(e) No correction required

Q12. The desires for political stability (I) /**has become important** (II) /**precisely because of the perpetual political instability** (III) /that Nepal has undergoing (IV) /from more than half a century. (V)

(I) The desire for political stability

(IV) that Nepal has been undergoing

(V) for more than half a century

(a) Only (I)

(b) Both (I) and (IV)

(c) Both (I) and (V)

(d) All (I) , (IV) and (V)

(e) No correction required

Q13. Political stability also depends (I) /**on the state of mind of the people** (II) /residing in a certain geographical location, (III) /and its capacity to resist (IV) /**various internal and external shocks**. (V)

(I) Political stability also depend

(III) who resides in a certain geographical location

(IV) and their capacity to resist

(a) Only (I)

(b) Only (IV)

(c) Both (I) and (III)

(d) Both (III) and (IV)

(e) No correction required

Q14. The endless chatter of GDP growth (I) / misses the cardinal aspect (II) /of the country's cherished idealism and vision, (III) /**societal values of civility, gentleness** (IV) /**and concern for each other**. (V)

(I) The endless chattering on GDP growth

(II) miss the cardinal aspects

(III) of the country's cherished ideal and vision

(a) Only (II)

(b) Only (III)

(c) Both (II) and (III)

(d) All (I) , (II) and (III)

(e) No correction required

Q15. **The myth of an American military triumph** (I) /in Tet distract us (II) /from the raw fact where no victory (III) /in Vietnam was possible short (IV) /**of extermination of the populace**. (V)

(II) at Tet distracts us

(III) from the raw fact that no victory

(IV) on Vietnam would have possible short

(a) Only (II)

(b) Only (IV)

(c) Both (II) and (III)

(d) All (II) , (III) and (IV)

(e) No correction required

Directions (16-20) : **Rearrange the following six sentences (A) , (B) , (C) , (D) ,(E) , and (F) in the proper sequence to form a meaningful paragraph and then answer the questions given below.**

A. Be that as it may, how can one accept a dangerous game which is marked by cruelty, injury and much worse?

B. Leaning on tradition and culture to justify the practice does not carry any conviction.

C. Continuing the gene pool of country bulls can be done in other ways.

D. In a society which has advanced by leaps and bounds, following a sport bordering on barbarism is uncivilised and unacceptable.

E. Those in support of jallikattu need to be dispassionate and rational in their thinking.

F. As a lawyer, the writer has dealt with the subject exclusively as a legal subject.

Q16. Which of the following would be the **THIRD** sentence after rearrangement?

(a) A (b) B (c) C (d) D (e) F

Q17. Which of the following would be the **FIRST** sentence after rearrangement?

(a) D (b) F (c) A (d) C (e) E

Q18. Which of the following would be the **FOURTH** sentence after rearrangement?

(a) C (b) B (c) D (d) E (e) A

Q19. Which of the following would be the **SECOND** sentence after rearrangement?

(a) F (b) D (c) A (d) C (e) B

Q20. Which of the following would be the **LAST (SIXTH)** sentence after rearrangement?

(a) E (b) A (c) B (d) D (e) C

Directions (21-30) : **In the following passage, some of the words have been given in bold, each of which is indicated by a number. Find the suitable word from the options given against each number and fill up the blanks with appropriate words to make the paragraph meaningful.**

Unfortunately, smart-phones don't assign (**21**) some increased IQ upon the user. Infact there is no industry standard to measure (**22**) what is and what isn't a smart-phone. For some, it's a phone that takes (**23**) complete operating system software assisting (**24**) a standardized interface and platform for application developers. For others, a smart-phone is simply a phone with advanced features like e-mail, and view (**25**) to the Internet.

Even the definition of what a smart-phone is has changed (**26**) over time. According to David Wood, EVP at Symbian Ltd., "Smart phones conflict (**27**) from ordinary mobile phones in two fundamental ways: how they are maintained (**28**) and what they can do."

Other definitions put (**29**) different stresses on these two phases (**30**) .

Q21. (a) allot

(b) bestow

(c) facilitate

(d) agree

(e) No correction required

Q22. (a) define

(b) predict

(c) resolve

(d) settle

(e) No correction required

Q23. (a) works

(b) governs

**Section - IV**

(c) runs

(d) performs

(e) No correction required

Q24. (a) serving

(b) arranging

(c) regulating

(d) providing

(e) No correction required

Q25. (a) gain

(b) access

(c) acquaintance

(d) egress

(e) No correction required

Q26. (a) reversed

(b) modified

(c) covered

(d) designed

(e) No correction required

Q27. (a) varies

(b) confront

(c) differ

(d) contradicts

(e) No correction required

Q28. (a) thrived

(b) ended

(c) built

(d) loaded

(e) No correction required

Q29. (a) embark

(b) bets

(c) sets

(d) places

(e) No correction required

Q30. (a) purposes

(b) factors

(c) roles

(d) features

(e) No correction required

## Solutions (Mock Test – 03)

S1. Ans. (e)

Sol. We can infer from the passage that Arms trade Treaty is ratified to regulate the international trade in conventional arms, ensuring national and regional security and serving as an anti-terrorism toolbox. Hence all the given sentences are correct.

S2. Ans. (b)

Sol. Referring the first paragraph of the passage, we can conclude that sentence (b) cannot be inferred from the passage. "The past years didn't result in much progress; efforts to tighten arms transfer controls in the region seem to be at a stalemate."

S3. Ans. (d)

Sol. Refer the last few lines of the second paragraph "The treaty scope requires states to introduce legislation and establish comprehensive control systems to perform case-by-case risk assessments. To do so, states must have competent national licensing authorities that check relevant control lists of military items."

S4. Ans. (d)

Sol. In reference to the third paragraph, we can infer that option (a) and (c) are correct. As it has been mentioned that the ATT blueprint legislation published by Pacific Island Forum Secretariat, with the help of the government of New Zealand, had supported the Pacific states in their ambitions to ratify and implement the treaty framework. Hence option (d) is the correct choice.

S5. Ans. (d)

Sol. 'The Arms Trade Treaty in the Asia- Pacific' is the appropriate title.

S6. Ans. (d)

Sol. Refer the last paragraph of the passage "South Korea has viewed STC as an important security instrument, mainly preventing North Korea from acquiring products that may add to its conventional and unconventional weapons arsenal. After the Tokyo subway sarin gas attack in 1995, Japanese authorities started to give the overall topic of STC ever more emphasis and also began to promote the goal of establishing a tight regional network of sensitive items controls amongst their neighbors." Hence option (d) is the correct choice.

S7. Ans. (b)

Sol. Stalemate means a situation in which further action or progress by opposing or competing parties seems impossible. Hence it has similar meaning as 'impasse'.

S8. Ans. (a)

Sol. Connoted means imply or suggest (an idea or feeling) in addition to the literal or primary meaning. Hence it has same meaning as 'implied'.

S9. Ans. (e)

Sol. Illicit means forbidden by law, rules, or custom. Hence it has opposite meaning as 'authorised'.

S10. Ans. (b)

Sol. Acquiring means to buy or obtain (an asset or object) for oneself. Hence it has opposite meaning as 'forfeit'.

S11. Ans. (b)

Sol. Apart from the first and the fourth parts of the sentence, the second and the third parts of the sentence are also correct. These two parts do not require any correction as they are in the context of the correct grammar structure and thus following the syntax and adding proper meaning to the sentence. However, in the fifth part of the sentence, the expression "was the latest confused news emanates from the valley" should be replaced by "is the latest confused news emanating from the valley" to make the sentence grammatically and meaningfully feasible. The phrase "latest confused news" indicates that the expression would take the present form of the verb. Moreover, in terms of the sentence structure, the word "emanating" is the correct usage instead of "emanates". Hence option (b) is the correct choice.

S12. Ans. (d)

Sol. All the three parts of the sentence require the correction. In the first part, the word "desires" should be replaced by its singular "desire" as the singular verb "has" in the next part indicates that the subject it is referring to should be in the same form. In the fourth part, the verb "has undergoing" is incorrect which should be replaced by "has been undergoing" to make the sentence grammatically coherent. In the fifth part, the word "from" should be replaced by "for" as We use "For" when we measure the duration-when we say how long something lasts. Hence option (d) is the correct choice.

S13. Ans. (b)

Sol. Apart from the second and the fifth parts of the sentence, the first and the third parts of the sentence are also correct and they follow the correct grammar structure adding meaning to the sentence. Thus, they do not require any correction or replacement. However, in the case of the fourth part of the sentence, there is a minor error of determiner; the singular determiner "its" should be replaced by its plural "their" as the subject they are referring is in the plural form [people]. Hence option (b) is the correct choice.

S14. Ans. (e)

Sol. The given sentence is grammatically correct as none of the parts requires any correction or replacement. Hence option (e) is the correct choice.

S15. Ans. (c)

Sol. There are errors in both the second and the third parts of the sentence which can be rectified by replacing them by the given expressions. The expression, "in Tet distract us" should be replaced by "at Tet distracts us" as the subject is in singular form [The myth]; it should be followed by the singular verb "distracts". Similarly, in the case of the part (III) , the word "where" should be replaced by "that" to make the sentence grammatically viable. The other parts of the sentence are grammatically correct and do not require any correction. Hence option (c) is the correct choice.

For questions (16-20) : The correct sequence is **FABDCE**

S16. Ans. (b)

S17. Ans. (b)

S18. Ans. (c)

S19. Ans. (c)

S20. Ans. (a)

S21. Ans. (b)

Sol. 'bestow' is the correct choice as it means confer or present.

S22. Ans. (a)

Sol. 'define' is the correct word to be placed in the blank as the sentence is indicating the features or characteristics of the smart phone, for which 'define' is the correct word.

S23. Ans. (c)

Sol. Blank must be filled with the word that explains the feature of the smart phone. Hence 'runs' is the correct option.

S24. Ans. (d)

Sol. 'providing' best suits the blank as the sentence is giving the advantage of having complete operating system software running on the smart phone.

S25. Ans. (b)

Sol. 'access' is the correct word to be used here as 'access' as a noun is making the sentence meaningful.

S26. Ans. (e)

Sol. No correction is required here.

S27. Ans. (c)

Sol. 'differ' best suits the purpose as it is used to show the dissimilarity between the two things.

S28. Ans. (c)

Sol. 'built' is the correct word to be filled in the blank.

S29. Ans. (e)

Sol. No correction is required here.

S30. Ans. (b)

Sol. 'factors' is the correct word as 'factor' is a noun that is used for a circumstance or fact or influence that contributes to a result.

# Mock Test (Pre-Level) Set–04

**Directions (01- 10) : Read the following passage carefully and answer the questions given below them. Certain words/phrases have been printed in bold to help you locate them while answering some of the questions.**

The Chinese were among the first foreigners to do trade with the island of Sumatra. Six hundred years ago, villages would have been but infinitesimal specks in an inconceivably vast and sublime rain forest. In 1416, a Chinese report on Sumatra noted that "There are in the forests immense quantities of wild rhinoceroses, which the king lets catch by men." The rhinos, the author goes on to explain, would be sent to China as "tribute" to the emperor. Later, in the midst of compiling a list of agricultural products and minerals to be found in Sumatra, the author's mind drifts back to something even more valuable, and he abruptly ends his list by reminding his Chinese reader: "Besides, there are rhinoceroses."

There are still rhinoceroses in Sumatra today, perhaps as few as 30, and they are still hunted. According to that 15th century Chinese account, as well as the testimony of early European visitors and explorers, rhinoceroses once **swarmed** on the island. Yet their population has all been but wiped out. What happened? The answer is pretty straightforward: They were hunted and slaughtered for their horns. Many of those horns were sent to China, where they were used in so-called traditional medicine. The trend continues to this day, and it will continue until the last rhino has been hunted out of Sumatra's protected areas.

A similar story can be told about another species of Asian megafauna: Tigers. In the 19th century vast swaths of Sumatra and Java were "infested" with tigers, which would pick off mailmen and laborers wandering around the backroads and the edges of plantations and carry them off into the jungle for dinner. Natives built high spiked palisades around their dwellings to keep tigers out. During the clearing of the forests and swamps of what is now Singapore, it is said that a person would be carried off daily by tigers. In the 1930s, French Captain Henry Baudesson, overseeing the construction of a railway in southern Vietnam, wrote that the tiger's "supremacy has hardly yet been seriously challenged" in the hinterlands, adding, "In Indo-China the tiger is the hunter and man the hunted. It is estimated that there were 100,000 tigers in the wild in 1900; today their numbers are down to about 3,200. The Javan tiger was declared extinct in the 1980s; the last tiger of China's Yunnan province was **snared** and eaten by a poacher in 2009.

Asian elephants have been **ruthlessly** slaughtered for their ivory across Asia for years, and their numbers are declining. Habitat destruction is probably the key driver for this megafauna's **demise**, and their African cousins have it worse due to the fact that their tusks are much bigger and therefore more valuable, but Asian elephants have it bad too. There is thought to be just one or two wild herds remaining in Vietnam, numbering no more than 60 individuals, and several elephants across the border in Cambodia's Mondulkiri province have been found dead with their tusks sawed off in what might be a troubling new trend in the Kingdom. In the eastern Thai provinces of Rayong and Changseao, local media report almost daily on human-elephant conflicts, and in Myanmar wild elephants are being killed for their skin, which is used to make clothing, jewelry, and, of course, traditional medicine. These products are sold in the border town of Mong La and virtually all of the customers are from China. Elephants were once found as far north as the outskirts of Beijing, but Chinese farmers and elephants don't get along, and the pachyderms were pushed south or simply killed. In Mark Elvin's brilliant The Retreat of the Elephants, mention is made of Chinese recipes for barbecued elephant trunk.

Q1. Why the author drifted reader's mind by mentioning the phrase "Besides, there are rhinoceroses."?

(a) The author wanted to end his report abruptly.

(b) The author wanted to give the description of island of Sumatra.

(c) The author wanted to divert the reader's mind towards the condition of rhinoceros.

(d) Both (a) and (b)

(e) All are correct.

Q2. What causes the increase in level of poaching of rhinoceros on the island of Sumatra?

(a) The poaching of the Rhinoceros is the latest trend in the North Eastern countries.

(b) The decorative material used by the rhino's horns is the cause of their hunting and poaching.

(c) The horns of Rhino, which is a keratin material is used as medicine in China

(d) The parts of the rhino are imported and exported for reasonably high price.

(e) All of the above.

Q3. What does the term 'infested' suggests in reference to the passage?

(a) Hunting and poaching of tigers for their skin, whiskers, fur.

(b) The danger for tigers of being extinct

(c) Area of Sumatra and Java covered with Tigers

(d) The damage caused by the Tigers of the Sumatra and Java

(e) All of the above

Q4. Which of the following is the appropriate title of the passage?

(a) Imbalance of ecosystem

(b) Clearing of forests

(c) The continuing trend: Hunting

(d) China Decimating the Wildlife

(e) Endangered Species

Q5. How it can be inferred that African Elephants' condition was worse than Asian elephants'?

(I) African elephants are more poached for there are more dangerous

(II) The clothing, jewelry and medicine made of African elephants' skin are more valuable.

(III) The tusks of African elephants are more valuable and big than Asian elephants'.

(a) Only (I)

(b) Only (III)

(c) Both (I) and (II)

## Section - IV

(d) Both (II) and (III)

(e) All are correct

Q6. Which of the following sentence(s) cannot be inferred from the passage?

(a) The slaughtering of elephants is done through destroying their habitats.

(b) Myanmar elephants are killed for skin while African elephants for tusks.

(c) In the 20th century, the number of Javan tigers got extinct.

(d) China is the top importer of clothes, jewelry made of elephant's skin.

(e) All are correct

Direction (07-08) : **Choose the word which is MOST SIMILAR in meaning to the word printed in bold as used in the passage.**

Q7. **Snared**

(a) perplexed

(b) relinquished

(c) hunkered

(d) rant

(e) entrap

Q8. **Demise**

(a) admirable

(b) enticing

(c) callous

(d) decease

(e) unsparing

Direction (09- 10) : **Choose the word which is most opposite in meaning to the word printed in bold as used in the passage.**

Q9. **Swarmed**

(a) enthralled

(b) refined

(c) scattered

(d) tempted

(e) exalted

Q10. **Ruthlessly**

(a) concurrently

(b) inseparably

(c) abundantly

(d) collectively

(e) compassionately

Directions (11-15) : **In the following paragraph, there is a set of four highlighted words against each number indicated in bold in the beginning of the sentences. One of the given set of words may or may not fit into the statement. Choose the word which is not suitable in the context of the paragraph. If all the four words are correct and feasible, choose (e) i.e. "No error" as your answer.**

(**11**) When **electricity** first began to be used in the US, **generating** systems were built in order to power and **capture** mines, factories and other commercial **establishments**. (**12**) These were "private" power plants **building** on site to meet the specific energy **requirements** of a business. In those days, only the very **wealthy** could afford to have their homes **powered** by electricity. (**13**) There was no standardization **under** all the various companies manufacturing these private **generators**. As a result, every power plant **operated** at different voltages or at distinct rates of **oscillation** depending on whether they were DC or AC systems. **(14)** In the 1890s, Chicago alone was **home** to 40 different electric companies, each **offering** power at 100 to 2,000 volts with their own **system** of wires crisscrossing **overhead** across town. **(15)** It was only when America's first large-scale power plant **were** built at the Niagara Falls that **thought** was **given** to standardizing the **output**.

Q11. (a) electricity

(b) generating

(c) capture

(d) establishments

(e) no error

Q12. (a) building

(b) requirements

(c) wealthy

(d) powered

(e) no error

Q13. (a) under

(b) generated

(c) powered

(d) oscillation

(e) no error

Q14. (a) home

(b) offering

(c) system

(d) overhead

(e) no error

Q15. (a) were

(b) thought

(c) given

(d) output

(e) no error

Directions (16-18) : **In each of the questions given below three sentences are given which may or may not be grammatically or contextually correct. Find the sentences which is/are grammatically or contextually incorrect. If all the sentences are grammatically incorrect choose option (e) as your choice.**

Q16.

(i) If I was told earlier I would have certainly helped you.

(ii) Leaning on tradition and culture to justify the practice does not carry any conviction.

(iii) No sooner did the teacher enter the class when the students stood up.

(a) Only (i)

(b) Both (i) and (iii)

(c) Both (i) and (ii)

(d) Both (ii) and (iii)

(e) All are incorrect.

Q17.

(i) The company is negotiating new store launches at nearly half the rent.

(ii) Intense fear blocks both to the generation and expression.

(iii) The challenge of decentralization and distributed management is affecting other utilities as well.

(a) Only (i)

(b) Both (i) and (iii)

(c) Only (ii)

(d) Both (ii) and (iii)

(e) All are incorrect

Q18.

(i) Since we are living in Bangalore for five years, we are reluctant to move to another city.

(ii) No sooner has she agreed to marry him than she started having terrible doubts.

(iii) The increasing mechanization of life have led us farther away from daily contact with nature and the crafts of the farm.

(a) Only (i)

(b) Both (i) and (iii)

(c) Only (ii)

(d) Both (ii) and (iii)

(e) All are incorrect

Directions (19-20) : **In each of the questions given below two sentences are given with a blank which must be filled with one of the options given below. Choose the option which fits both the blanks appropriately.**

Q19.

(i) A former soldier, Jim is not ____________ to picking up a weapon to defend himself and his family.

(ii) Because we all know Betty is ________________ to heights, we were shocked when she took up skydiving.

(a) Hostile

(b) Averse

(c) Detrimental

(d) Adverse

(e) Anxious

Q20.

(i) The way the project evolved was a __________ of organic reality.

(ii) This _____________ of democracy has shaken the loyalty of people who've been in the party for a long time.

(a) Tragedy

(b) misfortune

(c) Paradigm

(d) travesty

(e) Version

Directions (21-25) : **In the following questions, there is a statement divided into five parts, when arranged properly forms a coherent sentence both grammatically and contextually. The first part of the statement is given in bold to help you rearrange the other parts accordingly. Choose the best alternative among the five options given below each statement as your answer.**

Q21. **Post-Doklam**, / indeed, in regions farther afield (A) / India's standing as a credible regional player (B) /has risen in the eyes of (C) /the South-east Asian leaders as, (D)

(a) BADC

(b) BCDA

(c) DACB

(d) CDBA

(e) No rearrangement required

Q22. **The unprecedented participation** /of 10 heads of ASEAN governments (A) / of India in international affairs (B) / was a landmark development in the expanding role (C) / as guests of honour at the Republic Day parade (D)

(a) ADCB

(b) BCDA

(c) CBDA

(d) DABC

(e) No rearrangement required

Q23. **The major issue** /for which a resolution (A) /or a common approach (B) /would always elude Asean is (C) /unanimity in its approach to China (D)

(a) DBCA

(b) ACDB

(c) BACD

(d) ADBC

(e) No rearrangement required

Q24. **The Chinese government** / which was intended (A) /to be opened by the end of 2017 (B) / recently announced (C) /an ambitious carbon trading market (D)

(a) DBAC

(b) CBAD

(c) CDAB

(d) ABDC

(e) No rearrangement required

Q25. **Amongst the most avid Budget-trackers/** will be the great Indian middle class — largely salaried taxpayers (A) /in whose hearts, despite a long history (B) /of having hopes dashed Budget after Budget, (C) / hope appears to spring eternal (D)

(a) BDCA

(b) CABD

(c) ABDC

(d) BACD

(e) No rearrangement required

Directions (26-30) : **Rearrange the following sentences (A) , (B) , (C) , (D) , (E) , (F) in the proper sequence to form a meaningful paragraph; then answer the questions given below them.**

(A) Over 80 days after its introduction, the GST Network, its online backbone, is struggling to keep pace with the millions of invoices and returns being filed electronically by businesses across the country.

(B) But even those filing returns well before the last date have struggled.

(C) The government has extended the deadline for filing GST returns for July, the first month of the GST era, twice.

(D) For a reform that was cracked up to be India's biggest tax overhaul since Independence, the roll-out of the goods and services tax is off to a less-than-desirable start

(E) It is clear that the network had not been fully tested for chinks before July.

(F) And Finance Minister Arun Jaitley has reiterated an appeal to taxpayers to not wait till the last day, to avoid burdening the GSTN.

Q26. Which of the following should be the first sentence after rearrangement?

(a) B

(b) D

(c) A

(d) F

(e) C

## Section - IV

Q27. Which of the following should be the third sentence after rearrangement?

(a) A

(b) D

(c) F

(d) E

(e) C

Q28. Which of the following should be the fourth sentence after rearrangement?

(a) B

(b) E

(c) A

(d) F

(e) D

Q29. Which of the following should be the last sentence after rearrangement?

(a) D

(b) E

(c) A

(d) B

(e) C

Q30. Which of the following should be the second sentence after rearrangement?

(a) C

(b) A

(c) B

(d) D

(e) E

# Solutions (Mock Test – 04)

S1. Ans. (c)

Sol. With respect to the first paragraph of the passage, the author wanted to emphasise on the condition of rhinoceros which is here termed as 'valuable' end.

S2. Ans. (c)

Sol. Referring the second paragraph of the passage, we can infer that option (c) is correct. As China is using the horns of the Rhino for traditional medicine.

S3. Ans. (d)

Sol. In reference to the passage, the word 'infested' refers to damage caused by Tigers by killing the people wandering around the backroads and the edges of plantations. Hence only option (d) is correct.

S4. Ans. (d)

Sol. The whole passage revolves around the theme of China's involvement in trade with the island of Sumatra and Java. Hence option (d) is the correct choice.

S5. Ans. (b)

Sol. Sentence (III) is the correct choice. Refer the first few lines of last paragraph "Habitat destruction is probably the key driver for this megafauna's demise, and their African cousins have it worse due to the fact that their tusks are much bigger and therefore more valuable, but Asian elephants have it bad too."

S6. Ans. (e)

Sol. All of the given sentences can be inferred from the passage.

S7. Ans. (e)

Sol. Snared means catch or trap. Hence it has a similar meaning as 'entrap'.

S8. Ans. (d)

Sol. Demise means death or destruction, which is similar in meaning to decease.

S9. Ans. (c)

Sol. Swarmed means move somewhere in large numbers. Hence it has the opposite meaning of scattered.

S10. Ans. (e)

Sol. Ruthlessly means without pity or compassion for others, which is opposite in meaning to compassionately.

S11. Ans. (c)

Sol. Option (c) is the correct choice. All the other given words except option (c) i.e., capture fits appropriately in the theme of the paragraph. The paragraph is describing about the availability and usage of power sources for various establishments. However, the usage of the word "capture" is incorrect as the correct word required here is "illuminate". Since the sentence is describing about the production of electricity which is to be used in various factories and mines, the correct word that shall provide the sentence a coherence is "illuminate" which means to light something and make it brighter; or something similar in meaning.

S12. Ans. (a)

Sol. Option (a) is the correct choice. The sentence is in the past tense thus the usage of the word "building" is grammatically incorrect. To make the sentence grammatically and contextually correct the word sould be other V3 or past participle form of the verb build which is "built". All the other given words in the sentence of the paragraph are correct and make it logical and comprehensible.

S13. Ans. (a)

Sol. Option (a) is the correct choice. All the other words given in bold are correct except for option (a), a the preposition "under" used here is incorrect. Under is used as a preposition, it is similar to below. We use under to talk about something that is below or lower than something else. However, the correct word required here is "across". Across can be used as a preposition or an adverb. When used as a preposition, it is followed by a noun. Here, "across" is used as a preposition and the noun "companies" acts as its object. Thus, with the help of the given rationale it is clear that the usage of the word "under" is incorrect and should be replaced by "across" making option (a) the correct answer choice.

S14. Ans. (e)

Sol. Option (e) is the correct choice. The theme of the paragraph is about the generation, distribution and utilization of energy sources such as electricity. Therefore, all the given words in the sentence are precise to the context of the paragraph making option (e) of no error a viable choice.

S15. Ans. (a)

Sol. Option (a) is the correct choice as in the given sentence the subject "America's first large-scale power plant" is singular which requires a singular verb with the rule of subject-verb agreement. Therefore, to make the sentence grammatically correct, replace "were" with its singular form "was". All the other given words fit aptly into the theme of the paragraph.

S16. Ans. (b)

Sol. (i) – Use 'had been told' in place of 'was told' because the use of 'earlier' represents past time and for unreal situation of past clause we use this:

IF + SUBJECT + HAD +V3

(iii) Use 'than' in place of 'when' as after 'No sooner' the conjunction we use is 'than'.

S17. Ans. (c)

Sol. Only (ii) is grammatically incorrect.

(ii) - 'to' will not be used after 'both' as block is a 'transitive verb' which directly takes the object.

S18. Ans. (e)

Sol. (i) Use 'since we have been living' instead of 'Since we are living' because of the use of 'for five years' as 'for/since+ time' is generally used in present continuous tense.

(ii) - Generally following structure is used:

'No sooner+ did+ subject+ verb'

Or

'No sooner+ had + subject+ verb'

Therefore 'No sooner had she agreed' will be used in place of 'No sooner has she agreed'

(iii) - Use 'has' in place of 'have' as the subject of the sentence "The increasing mechanization" is singular and therefore singular verb is required.

S19. Ans. (b)

Sol. Adverse and averse are not similar in meaning.

Adverse means harmful or unfavorable.

Averse refers to feelings of dislike or opposition.

S20. Ans. (d)

Sol. There may be some confusion in the actual meaning of travesty.

Incorrect meaning: A tragedy or something unfortunate.

What it really means: A mockery or parody.

Eg. You've heard people call 9/11 a travesty. Truth be told 9/11 was a tragedy. A travesty is actually a mockery or a parody.

S21. Ans. (b)

Sol. The correct sequence to arrange the sentence properly and meaningfully is BCDA. The expression "India's standing as a credible regional player has risen in the eyes of" gives a contextual meaning to the sentence. Hence option (b) is the correct choice.

"Post-Doklam, India's standing as a credible regional player has risen in the eyes of the South-east Asian leaders as, indeed, in regions farther afield."

S22. Ans. (a)

Sol. The correct sequence to arrange the sentence properly and meaningfully is ADCB. It is to be noted that the expression "The unprecedented participation of 10 heads of ASEAN governments" gives a meaningful sense to the sentence which when followed by the parts D, C and B respectively make the sentence meaningful. Hence option (a) is the correct choice.

"The unprecedented participation of 10 heads of ASEAN states/governments as guests of honour at the Republic Day parade was a landmark development in the expanding role of India in international affairs."

S23. Ans. (e)

Sol. The given statement doesn't require any rearrangement as it already gives a contextual meaning to the sentence. The expression "would always elude Asean is unanimity in its approach to China" gives the required structure to the sentence. Hence the correct sequence is ABCD.

"The major issue for which a resolution or a common approach would always elude Asean is unanimity in its approach to China."

S24. Ans. (c)

Sol. The correct sequence to arrange the sentence properly and meaningfully is CDAB. This can be verified by the expression "which was intended to be opened by the end of 2017" which gives a coherent meaning to the sentence. Hence option (c) is the correct choice.

"The Chinese government recently announced an ambitious carbon trading market which was intended to be opened by the end of 2017."

S25. Ans. (e)

Sol. The sentence doesn't require any reshuffling as all the parts are accordingly arranged giving a contextual meaning to the sentence. Hence option (e) is the correct choice with ABCD being the proper sequence.

"*Amongst the most avid Budget-trackers will be the great Indian middle class — largely salaried taxpayers in whose hearts, despite a long history of having hopes dashed Budget after Budget, hope appears to spring eternal.*"

S26. Ans. (b)

Sol. The correct sequence after rearrangement of the sentences is **DACFBE**.

S27. Ans. (e)

Sol. The correct sequence after rearrangement of the sentences is **DACFBE**.

S28. Ans. (d)

Sol. The correct sequence after rearrangement of the sentences is **DACFBE**.

S29. Ans. (b)

Sol. The correct sequence after rearrangement of the sentences is **DACFBE**.

S30. Ans. (b)

Sol. The correct sequence after rearrangement of the sentences is **DACFBE**.

# Mock Test (Pre-Level) Set–05

Directions (01-06) : **Read the following passage carefully and answer the questions given below it. Certain words have been printed in bold to help you locate them, while answering some of the questions**.

First, AOL and Time Warner announced their intention to combine. Then came Time Warner/ EMI and Tribune / Times Mirror. Even more significant, however, has been the speculation that these mergers have caused. If these transactions are consummated, a large number of additional media mergers are expected. There is even the possibility of a nightmare scenario- a wave of media mergers so large that within a decade most of our information will be supplied by perhaps six of these huge conglomerates and a fringe of much smaller firms.

It's time to ask two critical questions. Is this kind of media oligopoly what we, as a society, want? And if not, can the antitrust laws effectively prevent the threatened merger wave? The answer to the first question is clear. We do not want a media oligopoly. The answer to the second question, however, is far less certain. We should distrust a media oligopoly because it would give undue control to a small number of individuals. This need not manifest itself in a price rise for the daily newspaper or AOL's monthly fee. Rather, it could consist of a change in editorial viewpoints a shift and the relative prominence of links to certain websites or a decision not to cover certain topics, because they are not "newsworthy". These problems could exist without any improper intent on the part of the media barons. Even if they try to be fair and objective, they will necessarily bring their own worldview to the job. And in time, some of these **conglomerates** may be controlled by people who are to fair or objective.

At first it might appear that the antitrust laws are of little help in grappling with the issues presented by large media mergers. The anti- merger laws are commonly understood as protecting price competition and a relatively small number of firms- to greatly oversimplify let's say at most half a dozen – are normally though to be enough to keep a market price –competitive . In industry after industry, firms merge until there is only a handful left, and the antitrust enforcers are normally unable to do anything to prevent this. (In former years mergers were governed by an "incipiency "standard that prevented mergers and merger wave's well before they would have led to very large or likely anti- competitive problems.) Even if a handful of firms are enough to ensure effective competition in most industries, would six conglomerate media firms be sufficient for the diversity of viewpoints necessary to democracy? Would we be reassured if they could somehow guarantee that they would sell their magazines and internet advertisements at competitive prices?

I am hopeful that the antitrust laws, if correctly and vigorously interpreted are adaptable enough to meet this challenge. This is because antitrust is not exclusively about price. It is essentially about choice- about giving consumers a competitive range of options in the marketplace so that they can make their own, effective selection from the market's offerings. Consumers should be able to make their choice along any dimension important to them- including price, variety and editorial viewpoint.

Competition in terms of editorial viewpoint or gate-keeping can be guaranteed only by ensuring that a media market contains a significantly larger number of firms than is required for price competition in other, more conventional markets. It is unclear, however, whether this interpretation of the anti-trust laws will be applied by the enforcement agencies and the courts. What is needed therefore is a much more careful look at the challenges that will be raised by future media mergers.

Q1. A wave of media mergers could

(a) Be a threat to democracy

(b) Result in limiting editorial viewpoints

(c) Result in misuse of certain laws

(d) Both (a) and (b)

(e) None of the above

Q2. According to the passage what could be the most significant outcome of media oligopoly?

(a) An increase in the cost of newspapers

(b) The fact that in the long run, there will be a shift of power to people who might not be balanced and fair in the way they deal with the media

(c) Certain websites may get more prominence than others

(d) There will be no competition among the newspapers

(e) None of the above

Q3. Which of the following statements, according to the author, are true?

A. Half a dozen firms are enough to keep the market price – competitive

B. Half a dozen companies are not enough to provide a democratic media

C. Enforcement agencies may not interpret the anti- trust laws correctly

D. Half a dozen companies will be inadequate to meet the consumer demand for product diversity

(a) A and B

(b) A, B and C

(c) All of the above

(d) B, C and D

(e) None of the above

Q4. The current anti- trust laws

(a) Are not sufficient to deal with issues relating to large scale media mergers

(b) Can prevent mergers from happening

(c) Will be effective if properly interpreted

(d) Favour a particular company or group of companies

(e) None of the above

Q5. To get a clear picture of the challenges posed by media mergers, the author recommends:

(a) Creation of strict laws

(b) Strengthening the enforcement agencies

(c) Creation of a study committee by the congress

(d) None of the above

(e) All of the above

Q6. Choose the word which is most nearly similar in meaning to "**Conglomerates**" as used in the passage.

(a) solitaries

(b) mortals

(c) distinctive

(d) amalgamation

(e) asunder

Directions (07-10) : **Read the following passage carefully and answer the questions given below it. Certain words have been printed in bold to help you locate them, while answering some of the questions**.

In regard to propaganda the early advocates of universal literacy and a free press envisaged only two possibilities: the propaganda might be true, or it might be false. They did not foresee what in fact has happened, above all in our Western capitalist democracies- the development of a vast mass communications industry, concerned in the main neither with the true nor the false, but with the unreal, the more or less totally irrelevant. In a word, they failed to take into account man's almost infinite appetite for distractions.

In the past, most people never got a chance of fully satisfying this appetite. They might long for distractions, but the distractions were not provided. Christmas came but once a year, feasts were "solemn and rare", there were few readers and very little to read, and the nearest approach to a neighborhood movie theatre was the parish church, where the performances, though infrequent, were somewhat monotonous. For conditions even remotely comparable to those now prevailing we must return to imperial Rome, where the populace was kept in good humour by frequent, gratuitous does of many kinds of entertainment- from poetical dramas to gladiatorial fights, from recitations of Virgil to all-out boxing. From concerts to military reviews and public executions. But even in Rome there was nothing like the non-stop distraction now provided by newspapers and magazines, by radio, television and the cinema. In Brave New World non-stop distractions of the most fascinating nature (the feelies, orgy porgy, centrifugal bumble pupply) are deliberately used as instruments of policy, for the purpose of preventing people from paying too much attention to the realities of the social and political situation .The other world of religion is different from the other world of entertainment: but they resemble one another in being most decidedly "not of this world." Both are distractions and, if lived in too continuously, both can become, in Marx's phrase, "the opium of the people" and so a threat to freedom. Only the vigilant can maintain their liberties, and only those who are constantly and intelligently on the spot can hope to govern themselves effectively by democratic procedures. A society, most of whose members spend a great part of their time, not on the spot, not here and now and in the calculable future, but somewhere else, in the irrelevant other worlds of sport and soap opera, of mythology and metaphysical fantasy, will find it hard to resist the encroachments of those who would manipulate and control it.

In their propaganda today's dictators rely for the most part on repetition, suppression and rationalization – the repetition of catchwords which they wish to be an accepted as true, the suppression of facts which they wish to be ignored, the arousal and rationalization of passions which may be used in the interests of the party or the state.

As the art and science of manipulation came to be better understood, the dictators of the future will doubtless learn to combine these techniques with the non-stop distractions which, in the West are now threatening to drown in a sea of irrelevance the retinal propaganda essential to the maintenance of individual liberty and the survival of democratic institutions.

Q7. The author would be most likely to agree that propaganda

(a) Can serve a vital function in democracy

(b) Is concerned mainly with the irrelevant

(c) Is now combined with entertainment

(d) Is universally recognized as a danger

(e) None of the above

Q8. The "early advocates of universal literacy" are mentioned as

(a) Advocates of propaganda

(b) Opponents of an idea that the author thinks is correct

(c) Proponents of an idea that the author wishes to counter

(d) People who made wrong predictions about freedom of the press

(e) None of the above

Q9. The author refers to "Brave New World" as a fictional example of a society in which

(a) Non-stop distractions are the main instrument of government policy

(b) People are totally unaware of political realities

(c) Entertainment is used to keep people from full awareness of social realities

(d) Entertainment resembles religion in its effects on the masses

(e) None of the above

Q10. By "***intelligently on the spot***" the author apparently means

(a) Alert to the dangers of propaganda

(b) In a particular society at a particular time

(c) In a specific time and place

(d) Conscious of political and social realities

(e) None of the above

Directions (11-20) : **In the following passage there are blanks, each of which has been numbered. These numbers are printed below the passage and against each, five words/ phrases are suggested, one of which fits the blank appropriately. Find out the appropriate word/phrase in each case.**

The Right of Children to Free and Compulsory Education (RTE) Act, 2009, which came **(11)** effect in April this year, is meant to transform the education sector and take India closer to the goal of universal schooling. But with admissions to the new academic session just **(12)** the corner, it is fast becoming clear that **(13)** well intentioned ideas into **(14)** will take some doing. For a start, the guidelines for admissions under the RTE prohibit schools from conducting any sort of student profiling. The stress on a random yet justifiable admission process means that schools will have to resort to something as quirky as a lottery system. However, leaving admission to a good school to pure **(15)** will only incentivise manipulations, defeating the very essence of RTE. The main problem facing the education sector is that of a resource crunch. The provisions for ensuring universal access to education are all very well, **(16)** we have the infrastructure in place first. Brick and mortar schools need to precede open admission and not the **(17)** way around. In that sense, legislators' assessment of ground realities is **(18)** target when they endorse the closure of tens of thousands of low-cost private schools for not meeting the minimum standards of land plot, building specifications and playground area as laid out in the RTE Act. Instead of bearing down **(19)** on private schools for failing to conform to abstract bureaucratic criteria, efforts to bring about universal education should focus on upgrading and expanding the existing government school infrastructure to accommodate all. Only then can we ensure the much needed supply-demand **(20)** in the education sector.

Q11. (a) with

(b) for

(c) on

(d) into

(e) in

Q12. (a) around

(b) near

(c) into

(d) about

(e) reaching

Q13. (a) forming

(b) translating

(c) having

(d) taking

(e) framing

Q14. (a) affect

(b) ideas

(c) practice

(d) concept

(e) procedure

Q15. (a) benefit

(b) merit

(c) chance

(d) basis

(e) method

Q16. (a) unless

(b) until

(c) executed

(d) provided

(e) exercised

Q17. (a) other

(b) any

(c) two

(d) differ

(e) after

Q18. (a) on

(b) of

(c) often

(d) taken

(e) off

Q19. (a) soft

(b) more

(c) less

(d) only

(e) hard

Q20. (a) need

(b) equilibrium

(c) expectation

(d) attempt

(e) aspects

Directions (21-25) : **Read each sentence to find out whether there is any grammatical or idiomatic error in it. The error, if any, will be in one part of the sentence. The number of that part is the answer. If there is 'No error', the answer is 5) . (Ignore errors of punctuation, if any.)**

Q21. Distance and hectic (A) / work schedules made it hardly (B) / possible for the family to visit (C) / each other outside of holidays. (D) / No error. (E)

(a) A

(b) B

(c) C

(d) D

(e) E

Q22. Because his family traveled (A) / from place to place, (B) / so, Cesar Chavez attended more than (C) / thirty schools as a child. (D) / No error. (E)

(a) A

(b) B

(c) C

(d) D

(e) E

Q23. Some Hindu and some Muslim leaders (A) / are bent on strengthening (B) / communalism to achieve their(C) / political goals. (D) / No error. (E)

(a) A

(b) B

(c) C

(d) D

(e) E

Q24. Tom was unsure what (A) / Mary would be like and he wondered (C) / weather she would get (C) / along with his friends. (D) / No error. (E)

(a) A

(b) B

(c) C

(d) D

(e) E

Q25. Mary asked Tom that(A) / what he thought of her dress, (B) / but he knew better than to tell (C) / her what he really thought. (D) / No error. (E)

(a) A

(b) B

(c) C

(d) D

(e) E

Directions (26-30) : **In these questions, four alternatives are given for the idiom/phrase**

**given in bold in the sentence. Choose the alternative which best expresses the meaning of the idiom/phrase given in bold.**

Q26. My father **strained every nerve** to enable me to get settled in life.

(a) worked very hard

(b) spent a huge amount

(c) tried all tricks

(d) bribed several persons

(e) None of these

Q27. The class did not **keep a straight face** on hearing the strange pronunciation of the new teacher.

(a) remain serious

(b) remain unaffected

(c) remain silent

(d) remain indifferent

(e) None of these

Q28. Though he has a lot of money, yet all his plans are **built on sand**.

(a) based on inexperience

(b) resting on immature ideas

(c) resting on cheap material

(d) established on insecure foundations

(e) None of these

Q29. Sunil thought his skill would match up to Keshav's bulk, but in the fight he was beaten **neck and crop**.

(a) softly

(b) completely

(c) swiftly

(d) profoundly

(e) None of these

Q30. He was **in a brown study** and did not seem to catch my point.

(a) in his study room

(b) absorbed in reading

(c) absent-minded

(d) in a state of shock

(e) None of these

## Solutions (Mock Test – 05)

S1. Ans. (d)

Sol. The author talks about the necessity of diversity of viewpoints being essential for democracy. Therefore a lack of it could be a threat to democracy. So (a) can be inferred. Choice (b) is clearly mentioned in the passage. Choice (c) cannot be inferred from the passage. Hence Choice (d) is the correct answer.

S2. Ans. (b)

Sol. In the last line of the third paragraph the author voices the contents of choice (b) as the serious threat to medical oligopoly. While the author refers to the possibility of only six conglomerates, he uses the number six figuratively and not factually.

S3. Ans. (c)

Sol. In the third paragraph, the author answers that media mergers may not result in prices increasing. Statement (A) is mentioned. In the same paragraph, he clearly puts forth the case that the oligopoly will not be able to provide a democratic media. And in the sixth paragraph, the author mentions statement (C) and (D) . Hence all are true.

S4. Ans. (c)

Sol. In the first line of the fifth paragraph, the author mentions that the existing antitrust laws, if interpreted properly, are adequate to meet the media merger challenge.

S5. Ans. (c)

Sol. The last paragraph of the passage provides a clear suggestion. Choice C is correct.

S6. Ans. (d)

Sol. Conglomerates means a thing consisting of a number of different and distinct parts or items that are grouped together and amalgamation means the action, process, or result of combining or uniting.

S7. Ans. (a)

Sol. The last sentence tells us that rational propaganda is "essential to the maintenance of individual liberty and the survival of democratic institutions." This clearly suggests that answer (a) is correct.

S8. Ans. (c)

Sol. The "early advocates envisaged two possibilities; the propaganda could be concerned with the true or the false. The author wishes to show that their ideas were limited and that propaganda today is mainly concerned with the "Unreal". In other words that author only mentions these ideas so that he can knock them down and thus to form an introduction to the idea that he wishes to discuss.

S9. Ans. (c)

Sol. The non-stop distractions in Brave New World are used "for the purpose of preventing people from paying too much attention to the realities of the social and political situation". This is paraphrased in option (c) .

S10. Ans. (d)

Sol. The author uses the phrase 'on the spot' twice. In the second instance he amplifies thus: not here and now and in the calculable future, but somewhere else, in the irrelevant other worlds of sport and soap opera, of mythology and metaphysical fantasy. It is obvious he means the phrase to relate to an awareness of the actual and potential real as opposed to the unreal.

S11. Ans. (d)

Sol. into

S12. Ans. (a)

Sol. around

S13. Ans. (b)

Sol. translating

S14. Ans. (c)

Sol. practice

S15. Ans. (c)

Sol. chance

S16. Ans. (d)

Sol. provided

S17. Ans. (a)

Sol. other

S18. Ans. (e)

Sol. off

S19. Ans. (e)

Sol hard

S20. Ans. (b)

Sol. Equilibrium

S21. Ans. (d)

Sol. The error lies in part (D) of the sentence. To make the sentence grammatically feasible replace "each other" with "one another". The phrase "each other" is known as a reciprocal pronoun because it shows a bidirectional action. It is used to refer two people; however, "one another" is used while talking about more than just two people, we should use a different reciprocal pronoun: one another. Hence, option (d) becomes the most suitable choice.

S22. Ans. (c)

Sol. The error lies in part (C) of the sentence. Words like 'because, since, as' are conjunctions of reason. Since, the sentence already consists "because" which is a conjunction used 'to express a reason that; since' thus, usage of words like 'so/therefore' in such sentences are superfluous. Hence, the most suitable answer choice is option (c) .

S23. Ans. (e)

Sol. All the parts of the sentence are correct thus, forming a grammatically correct and contextually meaningful sentence. Hence, option (e) is the most feasible choice.

S24. Ans. (c)

Sol. The error lies in part (C) of the sentence. To make the sentence contextually meaningful and grammatically correct "weather" should be replaced with "whether" as 'weather' means the state of the atmosphere at a particular place and time as regards heat, cloudiness, dryness, sunshine, wind, rain, etc. Whereas 'whether' is a conjunction which means expressing a doubt or choice between alternatives. Hence, option (c) becomes the most suitable answer choice.

S25. Ans. (a)

Sol. The error lies in part (A) of the sentence. The usage of the determiner 'that' is incorrect as in an indirect narration of a sentence words like 'where/how/when/what' should not follow any conjunction. This is because if the reporting Speech is having interrogative words like who, when, how, why, when, what, then neither IF is used nor any other word is added. Therefore as, the error lies in part (A) of the sentence, option (a) becomes the most feasible answer choice.

S26. Ans. (a)

Sol. 'Strain every nerve' means 'make all possible efforts'. 'Worked very hard' comes closest in meaning to it.

## Section - IV

S27. Ans. (a)

Sol. A 'straight face' is one intentionally expressionless, especially avoiding smiles though amused. Option (a) suits this meaning best.

S28. Ans. (d)

Sol. 'Built on sand' means 'unstable'. So 'established on insecure foundations' will be the best answer as the foundations' may be anything- ideas, material, etc.

S29. Ans. (c)

Sol. 'Neck and crop' means 'headlong' (precipitately, impetuously) . 'Swiftly' is closest in meaning to this.

S30. Ans. (c)

Sol. 'In a brown study' refers to being 'in a reverie' or 'too intent on one's thoughts to observe what is passing'. Though 'absent-minded' does not exactly convey this meaning, it comes closest to this.

# Mock Test (Mains Level) Set–06

Directions (01-10) : **Read the following passage carefully and answer the questions given below it. Certain words/phrases have been printed in bold to help you locate them while answering some of the questions**.

The problem with science is that so much of it simply isn't. Last summer, the Open Science Collaboration announced that it had tried to **replicate** one hundred published psychology experiments sampled from three of the most prestigious journals in the field. Scientific claims rest on the idea that experiments repeated under nearly identical conditions ought to yield approximately the same results, but until very recently, very few had bothered to check in a systematic way whether this was actually the case. The OSC was the biggest attempt yet to check a field's results, and the most shocking. In many cases, they had used original experimental materials, and sometimes even performed the experiments under the guidance of the original researchers. Of the studies that had originally reported positive results, an astonishing 65 percent failed to show statistical significance on replication, and many of the remainder showed greatly reduced effect sizes.

Their findings made the news, and quickly became a club with which to bash the social sciences. But the problem isn't just with psychology. There's an ¬unspoken rule in the pharmaceutical industry that half of all academic biomedical research will ultimately prove false, and in 2011 a group of researchers at Bayer decided to test it. Looking at sixty-seven recent drug discovery projects based on preclinical cancer biology research, they found that in more than 75 percent of cases the published data did not match up with their in-house attempts to replicate. These were not studies published in fly-by-night oncology journals, but blockbuster research featured in I, and the like. The Bayer researchers were drowning in bad studies, and it was to this, in part, that they attributed the **mysteriously** declining yields of drug pipelines. Perhaps so many of these new drugs fail to have an effect because the basic research on which their development was based isn't valid.

When a study fails to replicate, there are two possible interpretations. The first is that, unbeknownst to the investigators, there was a real difference in experimental setup between the original investigation and the failed replication. These are colloquially referred to as "wallpaper effects," the joke being that the experiment was affected by the color of the wallpaper in the room. This is the happiest possible explanation for failure to reproduce: It means that both experiments have **revealed** facts about the universe, and we now have the opportunity to learn what the difference was between them and to incorporate a new and subtler distinction into our theories. The other interpretation is that the original finding was false. Unfortunately, an ingenious statistical argument shows that this second interpretation is far more likely. First articulated by John Ioannidis , a professor at Stanford University's School of Medicine, this argument proceeds by a simple application of Bayesian statistics. Suppose that there are a hundred and one stones in a certain field. One of them has a diamond inside it, and, luckily, you have a diamond-detecting device that advertises

99 percent accuracy. After an hour or so of moving the device around, examining each stone in turn, suddenly alarms flash and sirens wail while the device is pointed at a promising-looking stone. What is the probability that the stone contains a diamond?

Most would say that if the device advertises 99 percent accuracy, then there is a 99 percent chance that the device is correctly discerning a diamond, and a 1 percent chance that it has given a false positive reading. But consider: Of the one hundred and one stones in the field, only one is truly a diamond. Granted, our machine has a very high probability of correctly declaring it to be a diamond. But there are many more diamond-free stones, and while the machine only has a 1 percent chance of falsely declaring each of them to be a diamond, there are a hundred of them. So if we were to wave the detector over every stone in the field, it would, on average, sound twice—once for the real diamond, and once when a false reading was triggered by a stone. If we know only that the alarm has sounded, these two possibilities are roughly equally probable, giving us an approximately Fifty percent chance that the stone really contains a diamond.

This is a simplified version of the argument that Ioannidis applies to the process of science itself. The stones in the field are the set of all possible testable **hypotheses**, the diamond is a hypothesized connection or effect that happens to be true, and the diamond-detecting device is the scientific method. A tremendous amount depends on the proportion of possible hypotheses which turn out to be true, and on the accuracy with which an experiment can discern truth from falsehood. Ioannidis shows that for a wide variety of scientific settings and fields, the values of these two parameters are not at all favorable.

Q1. According to the passage, which of the following is/are true about Open Science Collaboration?

(i) It had tried to repeat many published psychology experiments

(ii) The OSC was the biggest attempt yet to check a field's results

(iii) It was in tandem with the earlier researches and findings.

(a) Only (i)

(b) Only (ii)

(c) Both (i) and (ii)

(d) Both (ii) and (iii)

(e) All of these

Q2. According to the author what is the problem with science?

(a) It changes with time.

(b) It is very rigid.

(c) It's not what it looks like.

(d) It's a virtual concept

(e) None of these

Q3. What according to the passage is an ¬unspoken rule in the pharmaceutical industry?

(a) The basic research on which a drug's development is based is not valid

(b) So much of it simply isn't

(c) Published data never matches up with their in-house attempts to replicate

(d) The Bayer researchers drown in bad studies

(e) Half of all academic biomedical research will ultimately prove false

Q4. According to the given passage, which of the following is/are the possible interpretations that can be made if a study fails to replicate?

(a) There was a difference in experimental setup between the original investigation and the failed replication

(b) The original finding was false

(c) We have the opportunity to learn what the difference was between them

(d) Both (a) and (b)

(e) All (a) , (b) and (c)

Q5. According to the given passage, what is the actual probability that the stone contains a diamond?

(a) 75 percent

(b) 65 percent

(c) 1 percent

(d) 99 percent

(e) 50 percent

Q6. Oncology is the study of

(a) Tumors

(b) Stones

(c) Probability

(d) Drugs

(e) Diseases

Directions (07-08) : **Choose the word/group of words which is most nearly the SAME in meaning as the word given in bold as given in the passage.**

Q7. **Mysteriously**

(a) Knowingly

(b) Comprehensibly

(c) Apprehensively

(d) Bafflingly

(e) Fathomable

Q8. **Replicate**

(a) Spurn

(b) Repulse

(c) Imitate

(d) Reject

(e) Nix

Directions (09-10) : **Choose the word/group of words which is most nearly the OPPOSITE in meaning as the word given in bold as given in the passage.**

Q9. **Hypotheses**

(a) Assumption

(b) Bicker

(c) Argument

(d) Hyperactive

(e) Fact

Q10. **Revealed**

(a) Disclosed

(b) camouflaged

(c) Imparted

(d) Unwrapped

(e) Repudiated

Directions (11-15) : **In each of the following questions, various sentences are given and you have to choose the one which has some or any grammatical error in it.**

Q11. (a) Immediately after boarding the bus Mahesh asked the conductor that if he knew where the museum was.

(b) Then I knelt down and opened my heart to her and poured out all the affection that was suffocating me.

(c) She was decidedly pretty, but it is surprising, monsieur, how much prettier women seem to us when the day is fine at the beginning of the spring.

(d) One morning on waking I saw from my window the blue sky glowing in the sun above the neighbouring houses.

(e) My neighbour raised her eyes again, and this time, as I was still looking at her, she smiled decidedly.

Q12. (a) No longer able to bear with her anguish she surrendered her life to the ocean.

(b) She experienced the summer grass beneath her feet and wore shoes that carried her over rocky terrain.

(c) Since then many a seafarer has told stories of his encounters with the mermaid.

(d) The success of our efforts depend upon the number of people who actually use the new methods.

(e) She lost her love to as much greed as any man could acquire, greed for luxury, greed for temporary pleasure and greed through self-absorbed advancement.

Q13. (a) By the Time he reaches his ship, time has crept ten-fold and he soon finds himself a crippled old man, unable to board his ship and escape.

(b) For Time is a treasure we rarely give credit to.

(c) Hardly had he threw the ball when it fell on the ground.

(d) Love no longer had value to him, her time meant little and her heart was no longer enough to offer him happiness.

(e) And the journey from the cavern back to his ship would prove to be futile.

Q14. (a) We can earn our gold and silver, we can lose it all and earn it back.

(b) Shyam is working in our organization for the last few years in the publication department.

(c) In a state of anguish she travelled alone across miles of ocean until she reached the Island of Alchemy.

(d) The morning starts with a bang or one bang after another, a series, a chorus–the same sound that lulled me to sleep the night before.

(e) A vital strong man would soon find the treasure he carries become a little harder to hold, and each step he makes him age.

Q15. (a) They talked for a while and then they will continue to play the game till tomorrow morning.

(b) In any case, it would take me very little persuasion to accept a Chungwah though I often refuse others, and perhaps make secret enemies.

(c) Anyway, I walk out and out the compound that houses the teachers and oficials' residences, looking for a place to get some chow.

(d) I walk down the four flights of the hotel building where I and others of my ilk are housed.

(e) I sit and spend the morning thus, making friends and losing some and finally decide lunch can wait no longer.

Directions (16-20) : **The questions below have a paragraph given with one sentence missing at the end. From among the answer choices given, select the sentence that can fill the blank to form a coherent paragraph.**

Q16. I am sometimes attacked for imposing 'rules'. Nothing could be further from the truth. I hate rules. All I do is report on how consumers react to different stimuli. I may say to a copywriter, "Research shows that commercials with celebrities are below average in persuading people to buy products. Are you sure you want to use a celebrity?" Call that a rule? Or I may say to an art director, "Research suggests that if you set the copy in black type on a white background, more people will read it than if you set it in white type on a black background." (________________)

(a) Guidance based on applied research can hardly qualify as 'rules'

(b) Thus, all my so called 'rules' are rooted in applied research

(c) Suggestion perhaps, but scarcely a rule

(d) Such principles are unavoidable if one wants to be systematic about consumer behaviour.

(e) Fundamentally it is about consumer behaviour–not about celebrities or type settings

Q17. Relations between the factory and the dealer are distant and usually strained as the factory tries to force cars on the dealers to smooth out production. Relations between the dealer and the customer are equally strained because dealers continuously adjust prices–make deals–to adjust demand with supply while maximizing profits. This becomes a system marked by a lack of long-term commitment on either side, which maximize feelings of mistrust. In order to maximize their bargaining positions, everyone holds back information–the dealer about the product and the consumer about his true desires. (________________)

(a) As a result, 'deal making' becomes rampant, without concern for customer satisfaction

(b) As a result, inefficiencies creep into the supply chain

(c) As a result, everyone treats the other as an adversary, rather than as an ally

(d) As a result, fundamental innovations are becoming scarce in the automobile industry

(e) As a result, everyone loses in the long run

Q18. The Time Traveler (for so it will be convenient to speak of him) was expounding a recondite matter to us. His grey eyes shone and twinkled, and his usually pale face was flushed and animated. The fire burned brightly, and the soft radiance of the incandescent lights in the lilies of silver caught the bubbles that flashed and passed in our glasses. Our chairs, being his patents, embraced and caressed us rather than submitted to be sat upon, and there was that luxurious after-dinner atmosphere when thought roams gracefully free of the trammels of precision. (________________)

(a) And slowly and steadily, the atmosphere grew stale and lost all the vibrancy it had

(b) And he put it to us in this way—marking the points with a lean forefinger—as we sat and lazily admired his earnestness over this new paradox (as we thought it) and his fecundity

(c) We sat like toddlers do in a nursery, eagerly anticipating the show the Time Traveler would put on for us

(d) We sat benumbed by the proceedings, for the radiance of the Time Traveler was unimaginable and unbearable

(e) None of these.

Q19. Age has a curvilinear relationship with the exploitation of opportunity. Initially, age will increase the likelihood that a person will exploit an entrepreneurial opportunity because people gather much of the knowledge necessary to exploit opportunities over the course of their lives, and because age provides credibility in transmitting that information to others. However, as people become older, their willingness to bear risks declines, their opportunity costs rise, and they become less receptive to new information. (________________)

(a) As a result, people transmit more information rather than experiment with new ideas as they reach an advanced age

(b) As a result, people are reluctant to experiment with new ideas as they reach an advanced age

(c) As a result, only people with lower opportunity costs exploit opportunity when they reach an advanced age.

(d) As a result, people become reluctant to exploit entrepreneurial opportunities when they reach an advanced age

(e) As a result, people depend on credibility rather than on novelty as they reach an advanced age

Q20. Most people at their first consultation take a furtive look at the surgeon's hands in the hope of reassurance. Prospective patients look for delicacy, sensitivity, steadiness, perhaps unblemished pallor. On this basis, Henry Perowne loses a number of cases each year. Generally, he knows it's about to happen before the patient does: the downward glance repeated, the prepared questions beginning to falter, the overemphatic thanks during the retreat to the door. (________________)

(a) Other people do not communicate due to their poor observation

(b) Other patients don't like what they see but are ignorant of their right to go elsewhere

(c) But Perowne himself is not concerned

(d) But others will take their place, he thought

(e) These hands are steady enough, but they are large

Directions (21-30) : **In the passage given below there are blanks which are to be filled with the options given below. Find out the appropriate pair of words in each case which can most suitably complete the sentence without altering the meaning of the statement. Both the pairs must fill the blank.**

Police reform in India has been ___________ **(21)** with political ___________ **(22)** ever since the landmark Supreme Court judgement, in 2006, on the subject. The focus should really be on reorganising criminal ____________ **(23)** .

The annual ___________ **(24)** of the National Crime Records Bureau (NCRB) , "Crime in India 2016", which was released recently, presents a ______**(25)** picture of the key performance statistic with only 47% convictions in Indian Penal Code (IPC) crimes at the national level.

Delhi provides an interesting case study, where there is no political interference and the Police Commissioner reports to the Lieutenant Governor, and not the Chief Minister. With a population smaller than Mumbai, it has two times the number of police stations. Yet, in Delhi, while 1,90,876 persons were sent to trial last year, there were only 9,837 IPC __________**(26)** in the year. In Delhi only 58% of those _________**(27)** were chargesheeted, while in Mumbai, more persons were chargesheeted than were arrested for IPC crimes. In Delhi, 13,803 crimes against women were reported and no charge sheets filed in 4,371 cases (32%) ; in Mumbai with 5,128 crimes reported against women, final reports were filed in only 15% of cases. The key __________**(28)** of police performance is not ___________**(29)** correct reporting and recording but chargesheets and convictions, as this impacts on criminal __________(**30**) .

Q21.

(a) uninvolved / dispassionate

(b) interested / disturbed

(c) concerned / solicitude

(d) worried / appreciated

(e) attentive / troubled

Q22.

(a) factors / invasion

(b) hassle / disregard

(c) reforms / policies

(d) interference / intervention

(e) opposition / arrest

Q23

(a) records / administration

(b) government / officials

(c) authority / jurisdiction

(d) management / supervision

(e) account / history

Q24

(a) opinion / relief

(b) release / publicity

(c) notice /display

(d) analysis / undercover

(e) publication / issue

Q25

(a) worrisome / boring

(b) pleasant / engaging

(c) horrible / evil

(d) agreeable / civilized

(e) dismal / horrid

Q26

(a) convictions /judgments

(b) sentences / culprits

(c) hearings / discriminations

(d) victims / punishments

(e) condemns / sanction

Q27.

(a) unrestrained / liberated

(b) arrested / seized

(c) captured / advocated

(d) released / freed

(e) held / punished

Q28.

(a) role / affair

(b) evidence / data

(c) process / factor

(d) statistic / feature

(e) circumstance / accomplishment

Q29.

(a) rarely/only

(b) Impartially/ incorrectly

(c) scantly/ slender

(d) merely/ just

(e) Impetuously/ imprudently

Q30.

(a) behaviour / psychology

(b) performance / mindset

(c) administration / records

(d) philosophy / values

(e) data / results

Directions (31-35) : **Each question below has two each blank indicating that something has been omitted. Choose the set of words for each**

## Section - IV

**blank that best fits the meaning of the sentence as a whole.**

Q31. It is said when you __________ a rural woman, you in turn make a complete family socially and economically ____________.

(a) authorise, absolute

(b) empower, independent

(c) allow, sovereign

(d) revoke, free

(e) charge, liberated

Q32. The rural system has its own customs, traditions and social implications and thus ____________ of self-help group is ____________ an easy task.

(a) composition, always

(b) establishment, forever

(c) constitution, no way

(d) creation, consistently

(e) formation, never

Q33. Hindustan Zinc ____________ a large corporate also has large ____________ of these products.

(a) actually, damage

(b) having, destruction

(c) presently, loss

(d) being, consumption

(e) really, depletion

Q34. Churchill did not and could not ____________ that Ballia would ignite the fire that would ______________ and destroy colonial rule both in India and beyond.

(a) anticipate, engulf

(b) await, envelop

(c) figure, plunge

(d) assume, bury

(e) forecast, deluge

Q35. When the British Company established __________ in the name of trade in 18th-century India, its officers trebled the taxes local peasants were ______________ to pay.

(a) bridle, urged

(b) authority, contracted

(c) control, obliged

(d) charge, indebted

(e) command, pledged

## Solutions (Mock Test – 06)

S1.Ans. (c)

Sol. In the first paragraph, it is given that 'it had tried to replicate one hundred published psychology experiments'. For this, we can conclude that (i) is true. Now, it's also given that 'The OSC was the biggest attempt yet to check a field's results, and the most shocking.' Hence (ii) is true and (iii) is not. Therefore, (c) is the correct option.

S2.Ans. (c)

Sol. From the first statement of the passage (The problem with ¬science is that so much of it simply isn't) we can conclude that (c) is the correct option.

S3.Ans. (e)

Sol. It is clearly given in the second paragraph of the passage that 'There's an unspoken rule in the pharmaceutical industry that half of all academic biomedical research will ultimately prove false' Hence, (e) is the correct option.

S4.Ans. (d)

Sol. According to the third paragraph of the given passage, two interpretations that can be made if a study fails to be replicated are 'there was a real difference in experimental setup between the original investigation and the failed replication' and 'the original finding was false.' Hence, (d) is the correct option.

S5.Ans. (e)

Sol. it is given in the second last paragraph of the passage that there is 'approximately Fifty percent chance that the stone really contains a diamond'. Hence (e) is the correct option.

S6.Ans. (a)

Sol. Oncology is the study of 'tumours'. Hence, (a) is the correct option.

S7.Ans. (d)

Sol. 'Mysteriously' means 'in a manner which is difficult or impossible to understand, explain, or identify.'. Hence 'Bafflingly' is the word which is most nearly the same in meaning to it.

S8.Ans. (c)

Sol. 'Replicate' means 'make an exact copy of'. Hence 'Imitate' is the word which is most nearly the same in meaning to it.

S9.Ans. (e)

Sol. 'Hypotheses' means 'a supposition or proposed explanation made on the basis of limited evidence as a starting point '. Hence 'Fact' is the word which is most nearly the opposite in meaning to it.

S10.Ans. (b)

Sol. 'Revealed' means 'make (something) known '. Hence 'camouflage' is the word which is most nearly the opposite in meaning to it.

S11. Ans. (a)

Sol. 'that' will not be used before 'if' as this is an interrogative sentence of indirect speech in which that is replaced by 'if/ whether'.

Ex. He asked me if/ whether I was ready.

S12. Ans. (d)

Sol. 'depends' will be used in place of 'depend' as the subject of the sentence 'success' is singular.

S13. Ans. (c)

Sol. 'thrown' will be used in place of 'threw' as 'have/ has/ had/ having + V3' is used.

Ex. Having taken breakfast, he went out.

S14. Ans. (b)

## Section - IV

Sol. 'has been working' will be used in place of 'is working' as the sentence is in present perfect continuous tense syntax 'for+ time'.

S15. Ans. (a)

Sol. 'will talk' will be used in place of 'talked' as two actions that will happen in future are described here.

Ex. He will go to his sister and then he will go to his friend.

S16.Ans. (c)

Sol. In the above question, the first three sentences of the paragraph establish the purpose for which the paragraph has been written. Then the writer provides certain example situations. Under option (c) , the writer tells us what his 'alleged' rules are while the writer does not assert even his explanation with undue vigor in the last sentence. Option (a) is contrary to the main purpose of the paragraph as 'guidance based on applied research' makes his actions more binding on others than are rules. Options (b) and (d) are also eliminated because of the same reason. Option (e) talks about one of the examples but it is not related to the purpose of the paragraph. Hence, option (c) is the right answer choice.

S17.Ans. (e)

Sol. In this question, 'As a result' indicates that one needs to discover the immediate consequences of the details given in the paragraph. Option (d) is not a consequence at all and hence directly gets eliminated. Options (a) and (b) are not consequences but may currently exist; as explained in the paragraph. Option (c) brings in 'adversary' and 'ally' and hence cannot be fully justified according to the details given in the paragraph. The direct consequence has been stated briefly in option (e) , bringing the paragraph to a smooth closure. Hence, option (e) is the right answer choice.

S18.Ans. (b)

Sol. In the given case, the author gives a positive portrayal of the time traveler and the scene in concern. Options A and D are rejected as they introduce negative sentiments. Option C is rejected as no show is being put on in the given case. Option B is the best match, as it gels well with the tone and narrative of the paragraph. Also, you should try to see how the tone of option B matches the rest of the paragraph and makes it the most appropriate one in the given context.

S19.Ans. (d)

Sol. One needs to establish the purpose of the paragraph by looking at the first and the last sentences given. ('Age has ...' and 'however, as people become older...') . Options (c) and (e) can be eliminated easily. None of the given options is a consequence of the curvilinear relationship between age and exploitation of opportunity. Option (d) includes all this and is specific to the ideas presented in the paragraph. Hence, option (d) is the right answer choice.

S20. Ans. (c)

In this question, option (a) moves away from the core idea of the paragraph i.e losing patients. Option (e) does not provide for enough data to explain the importance of hands being large. There is no logical continuity in option (d) . Option (c) provides a logical finish to the paragraph by showing that inspite of the losing patients, Perowne is not concerned. While option (b) states that observations of other patients are also negative and those who stay with Perowne do so out of ignorance of available alternatives. This is not in continuation of the main idea expressed in the paragraph. Hence, the option (c) is the right answer choice.

S21. Ans. (c)

Sol. Solicitude means anxiety or concern.

Option (c) is the correct choice as both the words best fits the theme of the paragraph.

S22. Ans. (D)

Sol. Option (D) is the correct choice.

Invasion means to enter for conquest or plunder.

Hassle means a heated often protracted argument.

S23. Ans. (a)

Sol. Both the words of option (a) are aptly justifying the sense of the paragraph. Further, it is mentioned about the publication of these criminal records in the passage.

S24. Ans. (e)

Sol. Option (e) is the correct choice.

S25. Ans. (e)

Sol. Option (e) is the correct choice.

Dismal means depressing.

Horrid means dreadful.

S26. Ans. (a)

Sol. Option (a) is the right choice.

Conviction means a declaration that a person is guilty of an offense.

Convictions and judgments both the words satisfactorily fill the blank.2

S27. Ans. (b)

Sol. Option (B) is the correct choice.

Seized means to capture or to take into custody.

S28. Ans. (d)

Sol. Option (d) is the correct choice.

Here, the word statistic is used in reference with a numerical fact or datum required to compute and calculate the performance of the police department.

S29. Ans.(d)

Sol. Option (d) is the correct choice.

Merely means just; only.

S30. Ans. (a)

Sol. Option (a) is the correct choice.

Here, the words behaviour and psychology are representing the general mindset of criminals.

S31. Ans. (b)

Sol. 'empower, independent' is the correct use.

Empower- give (someone) the authority or power to do something.

Independent- free from outside control.

S32. Ans. (e)

Sol. 'formation, never' is the correct use.

S33. Ans. (d)

Sol. 'being, consumption' is the correct use.

Consumption- the action of using up a resource.

S34. Ans. (a)

Sol. 'anticipate, engulf' is the correct use.

Anticipate- to expect or predict.

Engulf- powerfully affect (someone) .

S35. Ans. (c)

Sol. 'control, obliged' is the correct use.

Obliged- make (someone) legally or morally bound to do something

# Mock Test (Mains Level) Set–07

Directions (01-07) : **Read the following passage carefully and answer the questions given below it. Certain words are printed in bold to help you locate them while answering some of the questions**.

Throughout human history the leading causes of death have been infection and trauma. Modern medicine has scored significant victories against both, and the major causes of ill health and death are now the chronic degenerative diseases, such as coronary artery disease, arthritis, osteoporosis, Alzheimer's, macular degeneration, cataract and cancer. These have a long latency period before symptoms appear and a diagnosis is made. It follows that the majority of apparently healthy people are pre-ill.

But are these conditions **inevitably** degenerative? A truly preventive medicine that focused on the pre-ill, analysing the metabolic errors which lead to clinical illness, might be able to correct them before the first symptom. Genetic risk factors are known for all the chronic degenerative diseases, and are important to the individuals who possess them. At the population level, however, migration studies confirm that these illnesses are linked for the most part to lifestyle factors—exercise, smoking and nutrition. Nutrition is the easiest of these to change, and the most versatile tool for affecting the metabolic changes needed to tilt the balance away from disease.

Many national surveys reveal that malnutrition is common in developed countries. This is not the calorie and/or micronutrient deficiency associated with developing nations (Type A malnutrition) ; but multiple micronutrient depletion, usually combined with calorific balance or excess (Type B malnutrition) . The incidence and severity of Type B malnutrition will be shown to be worse if newer micronutrient groups such as the essential fatty acids, xanthophylls and flavonoids are included in the surveys. Commonly ingested levels of these micronutrients seem to be far too low in many developed countries.

There is now considerable evidence that Type B malnutrition is a major cause of chronic degenerative diseases. If this is the case, then it is logical to treat such diseases not with drugs but with multiple micronutrient repletion, or "pharmaco-nutrition'. This can take the form of pills and capsules—'nutraceuticals', or food formats known as 'functional foods'. This approach has been neglected hitherto because it is relatively unprofitable for drug companies—the products are hard to patent—and it is a strategy which does not sit easily with modern medical interventionism. Over the last 100 years, the drug industry has invested huge sums in developing a range of subtle and powerful drugs to treat the many diseases we are subject to. Medical training is couched in pharmaceutical terms and this approach has provided us with an exceptional range of therapeutic tools in the treatment of disease and in acute medical emergencies. However, the pharmaceutical model has also created an unhealthy dependency culture, in which relatively few of us accept responsibility for maintaining our own health. Instead, we have handed over this responsibility to health professionals who know very little about health maintenance, or disease prevention.

One problem for supporters of this argument is lack of the right kind of hard evidence. We have a wealth of epidemiological data linking dietary factors to health profiles / disease risks, and a great deal of information on mechanism: how food factors interact with our biochemistry. But almost all intervention studies with micronutrients, with the notable exception of the omega 3 fatty acids, have so far produced conflicting or negative results. In other words, our science appears to have no predictive value. Does this invalidate the science? Or are we simply asking the wrong questions?

Based on pharmaceutical thinking, most intervention studies have attempted to measure the impact of a single micronutrient on the incidence of disease. The classical approach says that if you give a compound formula to test subjects and obtain positive results, you cannot know which ingredient is exerting the benefit, so you must test each ingredient individually. But in the field of nutrition, this does not work. Each intervention on its own will hardly make enough difference to be measured. The best therapeutic response must therefore combine micronutrients to normalise our internal physiology. So do we need to analyse each individual's nutritional status and then tailor a formula specifically for him or her? While we do not have the resources to analyse millions of individual cases, there is no need to do so. The vast majority of people are consuming suboptimal amounts of most micronutrients, and most of the micronutrients concerned are very safe.

Accordingly, a comprehensive and universal program of micronutrient support is probably the most cost-effective and safest way of improving the general health of the nation.

Q1. Type-B malnutrition is a serious concern in developed countries because

(a) developing countries mainly suffer from Type-A malnutrition.

(b) it is a major contributor to illness and death.

(c) pharmaceutical companies are not producing drugs to treat this condition.

(d) national surveys on malnutrition do not include newer micronutrient groups.

(e) None of these

Q2. Why are a large number of apparently healthy people deemed pre-ill?

(a) They may have chronic degenerative diseases.

(b) They do not know their own genetic risk factors which predispose them to diseases.

(c) They suffer from Type-B malnutrition.

(d) There is a lengthy latency period associated with chronically degenerative diseases.

(e) All of the above

Q3. The author recommends micronutrient-repletion for large-scale treatment of chronic degenerative diseases because

(a) it is relatively easy to manage.

(b) micronutrient deficiency is the cause of these diseases.

(c) it can overcome genetic risk factors.

(d) it can compensate for other lifestyle factors.

(e) All of the above.

Q4. Tailoring micronutrient-based treatment plans to suit individual deficiency profiles is not necessary because

(a) it very likely to give inconsistent or negative results.

(b) it is a classic pharmaceutical approach not suited to micronutrients.

(e) most people are consuming suboptimal amounts of safe-to-consume micronutrients.

(d) it is not cost effective to do so.

(e) None of these

Directions (05-06) : **Choose the word which is most nearly the same in meaning as the word printed in bold as used in the passage.**

Q5. **Subtle**

(a) abject

(b) tenuous

(c) adamant

(d) emulate

(e) Travesty

Q6. **Invalidate**

(a) servile

(b) Inane

(c) equivocal

(d) hapless

(e) refute

Directions (07) : **Choose the word which is most opposite in meaning as the word printed in bold as used in the passage.**

Q7. **Inevitable**

(a) bereft

(b) avertable

(c) Amenable

(d) callous

(e) alacrity

Directions (08-15) : **Read the following passage carefully and answer the questions given below it. Certain words are printed in bold to help you locate them while answering some of the questions.**

Fifty feet away three male lions lay by the road. They didn't appear to have a hair on their heads. Noting the color of their noses (leonine noses darken as they age, from pink to black) , Craig estimated that they were six years old — young adults. "This is wonderful!" he said, after staring at them for several moments. "This is what we came to see. They really are maneless." Craig, a professor at the University of Minnesota, is arguably the leading expert on the majestic Serengeti lion, whose head is mantled in long, thick hair. He and Peyton West, a doctoral student who has been working with him in Tanzania, had never seen the Tsavo lions that live some 200 miles east of the Serengeti. The scientists had partly suspected that the maneless males were adolescents mistaken for adults by amateur observers. Now they knew better.

The Tsavo research expedition was mostly Peyton's show. She had spent several years in Tanzania, compiling the data she needed to answer a question that ought to have been answered long ago: Why do lions have manes? It's the only cat, wild or domestic, that displays such ornamentation. In Tsavo she was attacking the riddle from the opposite angle. Why do its lions not have manes? (Some "maneless" lions in Tsavo East do have partial manes, but they rarely attain the regal glory of the Serengeti lions.) Does environmental adaptation account for the trait? Are the lions of Tsavo, as some people believe, a distinct subspecies of their Serengeti cousins?

The Serengeti lions have been under continuous observation for more than 35 years, beginning with George Schaller's pioneering work in the 1960s. But the lions in Tsavo, Kenya's oldest and largest protected ecosystem, have hardly been studied. Consequently, legends have grown up around them. Not only do they look different, according to the myths, they behave differently, displaying greater cunning and aggressiveness. "Remember too," Kenya: The Rough Guide warns, "Tsavo's lions have a reputation of **ferocity**." Their fearsome image became well-known in 1898, when two males stalled construction of what is now Kenya Railways by allegedly killing and eating 135 Indian and African laborers. A British Army officer in charge of building a railroad bridge over the Tsavo River, Lt. Col. J. H. Patterson, spent nine months pursuing the pair before he brought them to bay and killed them. Stuffed and mounted, they now glare at visitors to the Field Museum in Chicago. Patterson's account of the leonine reign of terror, The Man-Eaters of Tsavo, was an international best seller when published in 1907. Still in print, the book has made Tsavo's lions notorious. That annoys some scientists. "People don't want to give up on mythology," Dennis King told me one day. The zoologist has been working in Tsavo off and on for four years. "I am so sick of this man-eater business. Patterson made a helluva lot of money off that story, but Tsavo's lions are no more likely to turn man-eater than lions from elsewhere."

But tales of their **savagery** and wiliness don't all come from sensationalist authors looking to make a buck. Tsavo lions are generally larger than lions elsewhere, enabling them to take down the predominant prey animal in Tsavo, the Cape buffalo, one of the strongest, most aggressive animals of Earth. The buffalo don't give up easily: They often kill or severely injure an attacking lion, and a wounded lion might be more likely to turn to cattle and humans for food.

And other prey is less abundant in Tsavo than in other traditional lion haunts. A hungry lion is more likely to attack humans. Safari guides and Kenya Wildlife Service rangers tell of lions attacking Land Rovers, raiding camps, stalking tourists. Tsavo is a tough neighborhood, they say, and it breeds tougher lions.

But are they really tougher? And if so, is there any connection between their manelessness and their ferocity? An **intriguing** hypothesis was advanced two years ago by Gnoske and Peterhans: Tsavo lions may be similar to the unmanned cave lions of the Pleistocene. The Serengeti variety is among the most evolved of the species — the latest model, so to speak — while certain morphological differences in Tsavo lions (bigger bodies, smaller skulls, and maybe even lack of a mane) suggest that they are closer to the **primitive** ancestor of all lions. Craig and Peyton had serious doubts about this idea, but admitted that Tsavo lions pose a mystery to science.

Q8. The sentence which concludes the first paragraph, "Now they knew better", implies that:

(a) The two scientists were struck by wonder on seeing maneless lions for the first time.

(b) Though Craig was all expert on the Serengeti lion, now he also knew about the Tsavo lions.

(c) Earlier, Craig and West thought that amateur observers had been mistaken.

(d) Craig was now able to confirm that darkening of the noses as lions aged applied to Tsavo lions as well.

(e) None of these

Q9. According to the passage, which of the following has **NOT** contributed to the popular image of Tsavo lions as savage creatures?

(a) Tsavo lions have been observed to bring down one of the strongest and most aggressive animals- the

Cape buffalo.

(b) In contrast to the situation in traditional lion haunts, scarcity of non-buffalo prey in the Tsavo makes the Tsavo lions more aggressive.

(c) The Tsavo lion is considered to be less evolved than the Serengeti variety.

(d) Tsavo lions have been observed to attack vehicles as well as humans.

(e) All of these

Q10. Which of the following, if true, would weaken the hypothesis advanced by Gnoske and Peterhans most?

(a) Craig and Peyton develop even more serious doubts about the idea that Tsavo lions are primitive.

(b) The maneless Tsavo East lions are shown to be closer to the cave lions.

(c) Pleistocene cave lions are shown to be far less violent than believed.

(d) The morphological variations in body and skull size between the cave and Tsavo lions are found to be insignificant.

(e) All of the above

Q11. The book Man-Eaters of Tsavo annoys some scientists because

(a) it revealed that Tsavo lions are ferocious.

(b) Patterson made a helluva lot of money from the book by sensationalism.

(c) it perpetuated the bad name Tsavo lions had.

(d) it narrated how two male Tsavo lions were killed.

(e) All of the above

Directions (12-13) : **Choose the word which is most nearly the same in meaning as the word printed in bold as used in the passage.**

Q12. **Intriguing**

(a) denigrate

(b) enthralling

(c) debacle

(d) Cogent

(e) Circumvent

Q13. **Savagery**

(a) concomitant

(b) viciousness

(c) duress

(d) disparate

(e) Cognizant

Directions (14-15) : **Choose the word which is most opposite in meaning as the word printed in bold as used in the passage.**

Q14. **Ferocity**

(a) Enervate

(b) elicit

(c) covet

(d) tame

(e) ebullient

Q15. **Primitive**

(a) neoteric

(b) Exigent

(c) onerous

(d) paucity

(e) Evince

Directions (16-18) : **In each of the following sentence there are three blank spaces. Below each sentence there are five options and each option consists of three words which can be filled up in the blanks in the sentence to make the sentence grammatically correct.**

Q16. With inflation-targeting as its main __________ the consensus position that was articulated when the RBI Act was amended in May 2016 was that "price stability is a __________ precondition to sustainable growth" — the Monetary Policy Committee (MPC) has opted yet again to keep interest rates __________.

(a) confirmation, primary, modified

(b) uphold, assured, unrelieved

(c) mandate, necessary, unchanged

(d) support, radical, stabile

(e) consent, inherent, endured

Q17. Ultimately, though, the central bank has once again __________ a word of circumspection to fiscal authorities: taken together, the farm loan waivers __________ by some States, the partial reduction of excise duty and VAT on petroleum products and the GST rate cuts could __________ in fiscal slippage with accompanying consequences for price stability.

(a) inflicted, provided, neglect

(b) proffered, implemented, result

(c) imposed, generated, occur

(d) expected, assembled, transpire

(e) intended, managed, appear

Q18. Our recent victory in the hotly contested election to the International Court of Justice seems to have lifted our __________ as a nation. We are justifiably proud of our success and of the skill and __________ with which our diplomacy was __________.

(a) conceit, sobriety, dissipated

(b) caprice, timidity, eliminated

(c) propensity, valuation, dispensed

(d) spirits, determination, deployed

(e) nature, judgment, mobilized

Directions (19-20) : **In the question given below few sentences are given which grammatically correct and meaningful. Connect them by the word given above the statements in the best possible way without changing the intended meaning. Choose your answer accordingly from the options to form a correct, coherent sentence.**

Q19. **NEVERTHELESS**

A. Ankara continues to defiantly say it doesn't need EU money or membership.

B. It is trying to develop ties with individual EU members, which seems to represent a search for another kind of relationship with Europe.

C. Turkey-EU ties are currently marked by mutual resentments and appear to be going nowhere.

D. It claims that it doesn't need EU membership, Ankara refuses to end this bid unilaterally.

(a) Only A-B

(b) Only B-C

(c) Only A-D

(d) Both A-B and A-D

(e) None

Q20. **WHEREAS**

(A) BJP has been routed in these elections having managed to win mere 18.7% of all seats

(B) The opposition, especially independent candidates, have walked away with flying colours.

(C) If Independents were a party they would have got a thumping majority in these elections.

(D) Out of 16 Mayoral positions they have captured 14 and that is the end of their success story.

## Section - IV

(a) Only C-D

(b) Only A-B

(c) Only D-A

(d) Only B-C

(e) None

Directions (21–25) : **In the following questions a sentence has been given with some of its part bold. To make the sentence correct you have to replace the bold part with the correct alternative given below. If the sentence is correct as it is, please give (e) as your answer, i.e. No correction required**.

Q21. A nation cannot progress when the elected representatives of the people are often seen **loading the cart in contrary directions**.

(a) loading the cart in all directions

(b) placing the cart in diverse areas

(c) pulling the cart in different directions

(d) fighting the cart in confusing directions

(e) No correction required

Q22. A nation like India that has **been suffering centuries of foreign subjection** has every right to strengthen its defence.

(a) for long suffered from foreign subjection of centuries

(b) been suffering for the centuries of foreign subjection

(c) to suffer with centuries of foreign subjection

(d) suffered centuries of foreign subjection

(e) No correction required

Q23. People seem to be developing **an attitude of dislike** towards the whole class of politicians.

(a) a disliking attitude

(b) an attitude for disliking

(c) some attitude of dislike

(d) some attitude for dislike

(e) No correction required

Q24. Food security for the ever-increasing population is **one of the most serious problem** world is facing.

(a) one of the serious problems

(b) one problem with seriousness

(c) amongst the serious problems

(d) one major serious problems

(e) No correction required

Q25. Instead of **showing up a front of unity** the politicians hurl allegations and counter – allegations at each other.

(a) gearing up a unity front

(b) bearing for a front with unity

(c) marking above a united front

(d) presenting a united front

(e) No correction required

Directions (26-30) : **Each of the following questions has a paragraph from which one sentence has been deleted. From the given options, choose the one that completes the paragraph in the most appropriate way**.

Q26. The government launched the "Housing For All by 2022" programme in 2015, with the Pradhan Mantri Awas Yojana (Pmay) as a key anchor scheme. ____________. Global examples indicate that affordable housing activities generate direct and indirect employment in the medium term and sustained consumption in the long term. A 2014 study by the National Council of Applied Economic Research indicates that every additional rupee of capital invested in the housing sector adds Rs1.54 to the gross domestic product (GDP) and every Rs1 lakh invested in residential housing creates 2.69 new jobs in the economy.

(a) Pmay envisages building 20 million urban units by 2022.

(b) On the demand side, while overall economic growth will create the right enablers to stimulate demand, loans need to be provided at affordable rates.

(c) By building a strong support system and hand-holding the real estate entrepreneurs, we could create an ecosystem of quality developers.

(d) The lending institutions and credit rating agencies need to design new frameworks/rating scales that benchmark companies on such new capabilities.

(e) For a national housing dream of such a magnitude to fructify, the entire housing ecosystem needs to be well developed and all the stakeholders need to share a unified vision.

Q27. Young and aspirational, the millennial generation that makes up about 40% of India's population has long been regarded as the saviour and driver of future economic growth. Yet, the gap between the productive labour force and the employment and entrepreneurial opportunities available to them continues to widen. The fourth Industrial Revolution has already made its mark on certain sectors. ______________________.

(a) Fulfilling the great expectations set for the MSDE seems unlikely unless certain changes are made.

(b) To be fair, policymakers recognize the problem and have taken steps to combat it.

(c) As technology continues to surge forward in leaps and bounds, both blue- and white-collar jobs will become increasingly sparse.

(d) Much of India's workforce is already hampered with outdated and irrelevant skills.

(e) The economic turmoil that could be brought on by further large-scale disruption should be a cause of concern.

Q28. In the past few years, the slowdown in exports could be attributed at least in part to tepid global growth and falling trade intensity. However, this year, the global economy has seen a strong cyclical upturn across geographies and sectors, driven by stronger growth in investment, trade and industrial production. As per S&P Global estimates, global GDP is expected to reverse a two-year slowdown and grow 3.6% in 2017, higher than the 3.1% logged in 2016. ______________________. In particular, the US and the euro area—India's largest export destinations—are expected to grow by 70 basis points (bps) and 30 bps higher than in 2016, at 2.2% and 2.3%, respectively.

(a) The impact shows in the exports of labour-intensive sectors, which mainly comprise SMEs.

(b) The pickup is expected to be broad-based, across both advanced and emerging market economies.

(c) The fastest growth in exports was achieved when the rupee was strengthening against the dollar.

(d) Clearly, India has not been able to take advantage of the improving global environment, especially compared with its Asian peers.

(e) Revival in global investment, which has a high import content, further helped boost trade.

Q29. Land and housing rights have been a contentious topic in Kyrgyzstan since the country achieved independence following the collapse of the Soviet Union in 1991. Although under Kyrgyz law the state is supposed to provide a free plot of land to every citizen, as Eurasianet notes, "In reality, a land-allocation process thick with corruption and bureaucratic obstacles awaits anyone attempting to claim his share." As a result, while elites and those with access to them have acquired more than their fair share of land for housing and construction projects, the majority of the population has been left to fend for themselves, vulnerable to elite power plays and manipulation. ______________________________________________.

(a) In this context, land rights and housing issues have long been at the center of political controversy, particularly at times of upheaval

(b) This is especially true in and around Bishkek, where prime land is very attractive and expensive due to plot scarcity and services availability.

(c) In exchange for their support at crunch time for the then newly installed interim government, they expected to be rewarded with the same land for housing.

(d) To this day, however, it has been impossible to establish exactly how many people participated in this scheme and the total sum that was collected.

(e) Land rights and housing issues have long been at the center of political controversy, particularly at times of upheaval.

Q30. On October 8, 2005, a magnitude 7.6 earthquake rocked Kashmir, resulting in nearly 75,000 deaths, injuring more than 100,000 people, and causing extensive damage. Although the epicenter was on the border between the Pakistani- and Indian-administered portions of Kashmir, the quake and its aftershocks were felt across the region from Central Asia to China. The tremors of Kashmir also created volatility in the region's already precarious security structure. ______________________________________________.

(a) The two countries nearly came to war in 1986-1987 and have engaged in numerous smaller border confrontations.

(b) This is due to the overlapping territorial claims of India, Pakistan, and China.

(c) Currently, Pakistan occupies about 78,114 sq. km and China about 42,685 sq. km (Aksai Chin) , including 5,180 sq. km controversially ceded by Pakistan to China (Shaksam Valley) in 1964.

(d) The planned corridor enters at the Gilgit-Baltistan region of Kashmir, which is controlled by Pakistan, but claimed by India.

(e) The two countries nearly came to war in 1986-1987 and have engaged in numerous smaller border confrontations.

Directions (31-35) : **Rearrange the following six sentences/group of sentences (A) , (B) , (C) , (D) , (E) and (F) in the proper sequence to form a meaningful paragraph; then answer the questions given below.**

A. Some of my most cherished memories are of my puppies fighting with cushions, the sun playing hide 'n' seek with the clouds, or me racing for that last bite of the dessert.

B. Photos are a return ticket to memories otherwise lost. Much like a forgotten song on the radio or a specific scent, photographs help us travel back in time.

C. They help me smile on a bad day and laugh out loud on a good one. One thing they most certainly do is turn your home into a cosy haven of love and joy.

D. These moments stay captured through the lens of my old Polaroid. I've framed them, stuck them on the refrigerator and inside cupboard doors.

E. The most beautiful things in life are rarely just things. Instead, they are people, places, memories, and pictures – odd selfies and awkward angles included.

F. I call myself a 'click-happy' person. My thumb is permanently placed on the click button, lest the crazy grin on my son's face disappears.

Q31. Which of the following should be the **FOURTH** sentence after the rearrangement?

(a) D (b) F (c) A (d) E (e) C

Q32. Which of the following should be the **SECOND** sentence after the rearrangement?

(a) A (b) D (c) F (d) B (e) E

Q33. Which of the following should be the **FIRST** sentence after the rearrangement?

(a) E (b) B (c) D (d) C (e) F

Q34. Which of the following should be the **SIXTH (LAST)** sentence after the rearrangement?

(a) A (b) D (c) F (d) E (e) C

Q35. Which of the following should be the **FIFTH** sentence after the rearrangement?

(a) E (b) D (c) B (d) C (e) F

## Solutions (Mock Test – 07)

S1. Ans. (b)

Sol. Refer to the first sentence of the fourth paragraph "There is now considerable evidence that Type B malnutrition is a major cause of chronic degenerative diseases."

S2. Ans. (d)

Sol. Refer to the last two sentences of the first paragraph "These have a long latency period before symptoms appear and a diagnosis is made. It follows that the majority of apparently healthy people are pre-ill."

S3. Ans. (a)

Sol. Refer to the last sentence of the second paragraph "Nutrition is the easiest of these to change, and the most versatile tool for affecting the metabolic changes needed to tilt the balance away from disease."

S4. Ans. (c)

Sol. Refer to the second last sentence of the passage ". The vast majority of people are consuming suboptimal amounts of most micronutrients, and most of the micronutrients concerned are very safe. "

S5. Ans. (b)

Sol. Subtle meaning so delicate or precise as to be difficult to analyse or describe. Hence it has same meaning as tenuous.

Abject means experienced or present to the maximum degree.

Adamant means impervious to pleas, persuasion, requests, reason.

Emulate means strive to equal or match, especially by imitating.

S6. Ans. (e)

Sol. Invalidate means make or prove (an argument, statement, or theory) unsound or erroneous. Hence it has same meaning as refute.

Servile means having or showing an excessive willingness to serve or please others.

Equivocal means open to two or more interpretations.

Hapless means unfortunate and deserving pity.

Inane means devoid of intelligence.

S7. Ans. (b)

Sol. Inevitable means certain to happen; unavoidable. Hence it has opposite meaning as avertable.

Alacrity means liveliness and eagerness.

Amenable means disposed or willing to comply.

Bereft means sorrowful through loss or deprivation.

Callous means emotionally hardened.

S8. Ans. (c)

Sol. Refer to the second last sentence of the first paragraph ". He and Peyton West, a doctoral student who has been working with him in Tanzania, had never seen the Tsavo lions that live some 200 miles east of the Serengeti."

S9. Ans. (c)

Sol. The statement "The Tsavo lion is considered to be less evolved than the Serengeti variety." do not contribute to the popular image of Tsavo lions as savage creatures.

S10. Ans. (c)

Sol. Tsavo lions are believed to be extremely ferocious. So if they are made close to Pleistocene lions and if option (c) is true, then the fact of their ferocity would be negated.

S11. Ans. (c)

Sol. Refer to the last part of the third paragraph "The zoologist has been working in Tsavo off and on for four years. "I am so sick of this maneater business. Patterson made a helluva lot of money off that story, but Tsavo's lions are no more likely to turn man-eater than lions from elsewhere."

S12. Ans. (b)

Sol. Intriguing means arousing one's curiosity or interest; fascinating. Hence it has the same meaning as enthralling. Circumvent means surround so as to force to give up. Cogent means powerfully persuasive. Debacle means a sudden and violent collapse. Denigrate means charge falsely or with malicious intent.

S13. Ans. (b)

Sol. Savagery means the quality of being fierce or cruel. Hence it has the same meaning as viciousness. Cognizant means having or showing knowledge or understanding or realization.

Concomitant means following or accompanying as a consequence.

Disparate means fundamentally different or distinct in quality or kind.

Duress means compulsory force or threat.

S14. Ans. (d)

Sol. Ferocity means savagely fierce, cruel, or violent. Hence it has opposite meaning as tame.

Covet means wish, long, or crave for.

Ebullient means joyously unrestrained.

Elicit means call forth, as an emotion, feeling, or response.

Enervate means weaken mentally or morally.

S15. Ans. (a)

Sol. Primitive means relating to, denoting, or preserving the character of an early stage in the evolutionary or historical development of something. Hence it has opposite meaning as neoteric.

Evince means give expression to.

Exigent means demanding immediate attention.

Onerous means not easily borne; wearing.

Paucity means an insufficient quantity or number.

S16. Ans. (c)

Sol. 'mandate, necessary, unchanged' is the correct set of words making the sentence meaningful.

S17. Ans. (b)

Sol. 'proffered, implemented, result' is the correct set of words making the sentence meaningful.

Proffered means hold out or put forward (something) to someone for acceptance.

Inflicted means cause (something unpleasant or painful) to be suffered by someone or something.

S18. Ans. (d)

Sol. 'spirits, determination, deployed' is the correct use.

S19. Ans. (a)

Sol. "nevertheless" means "however" connects statement A and statement B in the most appropriate manner.

Ankara continues to defiantly say it doesn't need EU money or membership; nevertheless, it is trying to develop ties with individual EU members, which seems to represent a search for another kind of relationship with Europe.

S20. Ans. (b)

Sol. "Whereas" is used while taking a fact into consideration.

BJP has been routed in these elections having

managed to win mere 18.7% of all seats whereas the opposition, especially independent candidates, have walked away with flying colours.

S21. Ans. (c)

Sol. Replace 'loading the cart in contrary directions' with 'pulling the cart in different directions'.

S22. Ans. (d)

Sol. Replace 'been suffering centuries of foreign subjection' with 'suffered centuries of foreign subjection'.

S23. Ans. (e)

Sol. No correction required.

S24. Ans. (a)

Sol. Replace 'one of the most serious problem' with 'one of the serious problem'.

S25. Ans. (d)

Sol. Replace 'showing up a front of unity' with 'presenting a united front'.

S26. Ans. (a)

Sol. The paragraph is about the programme "Housing For All by 2022" launched by government along with Pradhan Mantri Awas Yojana (Pmay) , generating direct and indirect employment as indicated by the National Council of Applied Economic Research. Hence the blank must be filled with the sentence that tells more about the scheme as mentioned in the above sentence of the blank. After reading all the sentences, we can conclude that sentence (a) talking about the Pmay scheme that envisions building 20 million urban units by 2022, is making the paragraph more complete and meaningful than other sentences. Hence option (a) is the best choice.

S27. Ans. (e)

Sol. In this paragraph, future economic growth has been discussed, which depends on the young generation. The sentences before the blank talks about the wide gap between productive labour force and the employment and entrepreneurial opportunities available. The success of the fourth Industrial Revolution has also been discussed. Hence the blank must be filled the sentence related to the economic condition. Going through all the sentences, we can infer that sentence (e) goes correctly with the paragraph that talks about the large-scale disruption causing economic turmoil. Hence sentence (e) is the correct choice.

S28. Ans. (b)

Sol. Here the theme of the paragraph revolves around the global economy depending upon the investment, trade and industrial production. The sentences before the blank is about the statistics of GDP growth in 2017 from 2016 whereas the sentences after the blank talks about the expected growth of export from previous year. Hence the blank must be filled with the sentence related to this economic growth. After reading all the sentences, we find that sentence (b) goes in agreement with the passage talking about the pickup of GDP, as discussed in its above sentence, which is expected to be broad based across both advanced and emerging market. Hence option (b) is the correct choice.

S29. Ans. (b)

Sol. The paragraph talks about the unavailability of land to the Kyrgystan's citizens, that is supposed to be provided free to every citizen under Kyrgyz law. Hence the blank must be filled by the sentence related to this theme. Going through all the sentences, we can conclude that sentence (b) goes in harmony with the paragraph talking about the attractive and expensive land because of plot scarcity in Bishkek. Hence option (b) is the correct choice.

S30. Ans. (b)

Sol. The paragraph is about the earthquake occurred on October 8, 2005 that has affected Kashmir and its aftershocks been felt from across the region from Central Asia to China. The sentence before the blank talks about volatility created in Kashmir hence the blank must be filled by the sentence related to these arguments. Sentence (b) that talks about the reason behind the volatility in Kashmir is going appropriately with the paragraph. Hence option (b) is the correct choice.

Directions (101-105) : The correct sequence to form meaningful paragraph is **EBFADC**.

S31. Ans. (c)

S32. Ans. (d)

S33. Ans. (a)

S34. Ans. (e)

S35. Ans. (b)

# Mock Test (Mains Level) Set–08

**Directions (01- 07) : Read the following passage carefully and answer the questions given below it. Certain words are given in bold to help you locate them while answering some of the questions.**

To remake the world (including Nature) , Fourier mobilized: an intolerance (for Civilization) , a form (classification) , astandard (pleasure) , on imagination (the 'scene') , a discourse (his book) , all of which pretty well defined 'the action of the signifier or the signifier in action. This action continually makes visible on the page a glaring lack, that of science and politics, that is, of the signified. What Fourier lacks (for that matter voluntarily) points in return to what we ourselves lack when we reject Fourier: to be ironic about Fourier is always–even from the scientific point of view–to censure the signifier. Political and Domestic (the name of Fourier's system) , science and Utopia, Marxism and Fourierism, are like two nets whose meshes are of different sizes. On the one hand, Fourier allows to pass through all the science that Marx collects and develops; from the political point of view (and above all since Marxism has given an indelible name to its shortcomings) . Fourier is completely off to one side, unrealistic and immoral. However, the other, facing, net allows pleasure, which Fourier collects, to pass through. Desire and Need pass through, as though the two nets were alternatively superimposed, playing at topping hands. However, the relationship of Desire and Need is not complementary (were they fitted one into the other, every-thing would be perfect) , but supplementary: each is the excess of the other. The excess: what does not pass through. For example, seen from today (i.e., after Marx) , politics is a necessary purge; Fourier is the child who avoids the purge, who vomits it up.

The vomiting of politics is what Fourier calls Invention. Fourierist invention ("For me, I am an inventor, and not an orator") addresses the absolutely new, that about which nothing has yet been said. The rule of invention is a rule of refusal: to doubt absolutely (more than did Descartes, who, Fourier though, never made more than a partial and misplaced use of doubt) , to be in opposition with everything being done, to treat only of what has not been treated, to stand apart from "literary agitator", Book People, to preach what opinion holds to be impossible. It is in sum for this purely structural reason (old/new) and through a simple constraint of the discourse (to speak only where there has not yet been speech) that Fourier is silent understood in the modem sense: Fourier repudiates the writer, i.e. the certified manager of good writing, of literature, he who guarantees decorative union and thus the fundamental separation of substance and form; in calling himself an inventor ("I am not a writer, but an inventor") , he places himself at the limit of meaning, what we today call Text. Perhaps, following Fourier, we should henceforth call inventor (and not writer or philosopher) he who proposes new formulae and thereby invests, by fragments, immensely and in detail, the space of the signifier.

Q1. According to the author

(a) Fourier does not say anything about modern politics.

(b) Fourier speaks volumes about modern

politics.

(c) The author makes a good commentary on modern politics.

(d) The author is silent about modern politics.

(e) None of these

Q2. Which is the most appropriate title for the above passage?

(a) Philosopher and writer

(b) Inventor, not writer

(c) Writer, not inventor

(d) Inventor and writer

(e) only Inventor

Q3. Which of the following is the author of the statement, "For me, I am an inventor, and not an orator".

(a) The author of the passage

(b) Karl Marx

(c) Fourier

(d) Descartes

(e) A political leader

Q4. According to the passage

(a) political and domestic belong to the same category.

(b) science and Utopia belong to the same category.

(c) Marxism and Fourierism belong to the same category.

(d) science and Utopia belong to different categories.

(e) All of these

Q5. According to Fourier

(a) one who creates a text is a writer.

(b) one who creates a text is an inventor.

(c) a writer calls himself an inventor.

(d) a philosopher calls himself an inventor.

(e) None of these

Q6. According to the author of the passage

(a) desire and need perfectly fit into each other.

(b) desire and need do not fit into each other.

(c) desire is a necessary purge.

(d) Fourier is the child of the purge.

(e) All of these

Q7. According to the passage

(a) Fourier thought that Descartes made only a partial use of doubt.

(b) Descartes thought the Fourier made only a partial use of doubt.

(c) the author of the passage made only a partial use of doubt.

(d) Descartes made full use of doubt.

(e) All of these

Directions (08- 15) : **Read the following passage carefully and answer the questions given below it. Certain words are given in bold to help you locate them while answering some of the questions.**

Have you ever come across a painting, by Picasso, Mondrian, Miro, or any other modern abstract painter of this century, and found yourself engulfed in a brightly-coloured canvas which your senses cannot interpret? Many people would tend to **denounce** abstractionism as senseless trash. These people are disoriented by Miro's bright, fanciful creatures and two-dimensional canvases. They click their tongues and shake their heads at Mondrian's grid works, declaring that the poor guy played too many scrabble games. They silently shake their heads in sympathy for Picasso, whose gruesome, distorted figures must be a reflection of his mental health. Then, standing in front of a work by Charlie Russell, the famous western artist, they'll declare it a work of God. People feel more comfortable with something they can relate to and understand immediately without too much thought. This is the case with the work of Charlie Russell. Being able to recognize the elements in his paintings — trees, horses and cowboys — gives people a safety line to their world of 'reality'. There are some who would disagree when I say abstract art requires more creativity and artistic talent to produce a good piece than does representational art, but there are many weaknesses in their arguments.

People who look down on abstract art have several major arguments to support their beliefs. They feel that artists turn abstract because they are not capable of the technical drafting skills that appear in a Russell: therefore, such artists create an art form that anyone is capable of and that is less time consuming, and then parade it as artistic progress. Secondly, they feel that the purpose of art is to create something of beauty in an orderly, logical composition. Russell's compositions are balanced and rational: everything sits calmly on the canvas, leaving the viewer satisfied that he has seen all there is to see. The modern abstractionists, on the other hand, seem to compose their pieces irrationally. For example, upon seeing Picasso's Guernica, a friend of mine asked me, "What's the point?" Finally, many people feel that art should portray the ideal and real. The exactness of detail in Charlie Russell's work is an example of this. He has been called a great historian because his pieces depict the lifestyle, dress, and events of the times. His subject matter is derived from his own experiences on the trial, and reproduced to the smallest detail.

I agree in part with many of these arguments, and at one time even endorsed them. But now, I believe differently. Firstly, I object to the argument that abstract artists are not capable of drafting. Many abstract artists, such as Picasso, are excellent draftsmen. As his work matured, Picasso became more abstract in order to increase the expressive quality of his work. Guernica was meant as a protest against the bombing of that city by the Germans. To express the terror and suffering of the victims more **vividly**, he distorted the figures and presented them in a black and white journalistic manner. If he had used representational images and colour, much of the emotional content would have been lost and the piece would not have caused the demand for justice that it did. Secondly, I do not think that a piece must be logical and aesthetically pleasing to be art. The message it conveys to its viewers is more important. It should reflect the ideals and issues of its time and be true to itself, not just a flowery, glossy surface. For example, through his work, Mondrian was trying to present a system of simplicity, logic, and rational order. As a result, his pieces did end up looking like a **scrabble** board.

Miro created powerful, surrealistic images from his dreams and subconscious. These artists were trying to evoke a response from society through an expressionistic manner. Finally, abstract artists and representational artists maintain different ideas about 'reality'. To the representational artist, reality is what he sees with his eyes. This is the reality he reproduces on canvas. To the abstract artist, reality is what he feels about what his eyes see. This is the reality he interprets on canvas. This can be illustrated by Mondrian's Trees series. You can actually see the progression from the early recognizable, though abstracted Trees, to his final solution, the grid system.

A cycle of abstract and representational art began with the first scratchings of prehistoric man. From the abstractions of ancient Egypt to representational, classical Rome, returning to abstractionism in early Christian art and, so on up to the present day, the cycle has been going on. But this day and age may witness its death through the camera. With film, there is no need to produce finely detailed, historical records manually; the camera does this for us more efficiently. Maybe, representational art would cease to exist. With abstractionism as the victor of the first battle, maybe, a different kind of cycle will be touched off. Possibly, sometime in the distant future, thousands of years from now, art itself will be physically non-existent. Some artists today believe that once they have planned and constructed a piece in their mind, there is no sense in finishing it with their hands; it has already been done and can never be duplicated.

Q8. The author believes that people feel comfortable with representational art because

(a) they are not engulfed in brightly-coloured canvases.

(b) they do not have to click their tongues and shake their heads in sympathy.

(c) they understand the art without putting too much strain on their minds.

(d) painting like Guernica do not have a point.

(e) All of these

Q9. In the author's opinion, Picasso's Guernica created a strong demand for justice since

(a) it was a protest against the German bombing of Guernica.

(b) Picasso managed to express the emotional content well with his abstract depiction.

(c) it depicts the terror and suffering of the victims in a distorted manner.

(d) it was a mature work of Picasso, painted when the artist's drafting skills were excellent.

(e) Both (c) and (d)

Q10.The author argues that many people look down upon abstract art because they feel that

(a) modern abstract art does not portray what is ideal and real.

(b) abstract artists are unskilled in matters of technical drafting.

(c) abstractionists compose irrationally.

(d) Both (b) and (c)

(e) All of the above

Q11. The author acknowledges that Mondrian's pieces may have ended up looking like a scrabble board because

(a) many people declared the poor guy played too many scrabble games.

(b) Mondrian believed in the 'grid-works' approach to abstractionist painting.

(c) Mondrian was trying to convey the message of simplicity and rational order.

(d) Mondrian learned from his Trees series to evolve a grid system.

(e) None of these

Q12. The main difference between the abstract artist and the representational artist in matters of the 'ideal' and the 'real', according to the author, is:

(a) How each chooses to deal with 'reality' on his

or her canvas.

(b) The superiority of interpretation of reality over reproduction of reality.

(c) The different values attached by each to being a historian.

(d) The varying levels of drafting skills and logical thinking abilities.

(e) All of these

Directions (13-14) : **Choose the word/group of words which is most SIMILAR in meaning to the word/group of words printed in bold as used in passage.**

Q13. **Denounce**

(a) candid

(b) allure

(c) sublime

(d) proscribe

(e) splendid

Q14. **Scrabble**

(a) Rummage

(b) ascribe

(c) murky

(d) rebuke

(e) rife

Direction (15) : **Choose the word/group of words which is most OPPOSITE in meaning to the word/group of words printed in bold as used in passage.**

Q15. **Vividly**

(a) reprehend

(b) disparage

(c) berate

(d) cavil

(e) indeterminate

Directions (16-20) : **Read each sentence to find out whether there is any grammatical or idiomatic error in it. The error, if any, will be in one part of the sentence. The number of that part is the answer. If there is 'No error', the answer is (5) . (Ignore errors of punctuation, if any.)**

Q16. (1) The award recognizes her fiction works / (2) which have illuminated the Indian-American experience / (3) in beautifully wrought narratives / (4) of estrangement and belonging. / (5) No error

Q17. (1) We strongly believe in motivating the students / (2) and give them the opportunities / (3) to explore their potential / (4) and understand the importance of team work. / (5) No error

Q18. (1) A team of researchers has developed / (2) an inexpensive, secure method / (3) named SafePay prototype system / (4) to prevent mass credit card fraud. / (5) No error

Q19. (1) The marketing programme focuses / (2) on the challenges any management faces / (3) in developing and implementing / (4) a successful marketing programme. / (5) No error

Q20. (1) Group Discussion and Personal Interviews / (2) will hold in all important centres / (3) across the country / (4) depending on the need. / (5) No error

Directions (21-23) : **In each of the following sentence there are three blank spaces. Below each sentence there are five options and each option consists of three words which can be filled up in the blanks in the sentence to make the sentence grammatically correct.**

Q21. Even as the Supreme Court judgment ________________ on the powers of the elected government in Delhi, the Lt Governor's office has ______________ chief minister Arvind Kejriwal to the ______________ of an official.

(a) is awaited, demoted, status

(b) has been anticipated, busted, report

(c) is awaiting, broken, prestige

(d) counted on, ruled out, sphere

(e) looked for, written off, rank

Q22. Climate negotiators ______________ a dramatic charge in the 2015 Paris ______________, asking world leaders to ______________ to keep global temperatures at just 1.5 degrees Celsius above pre-industrial levels.

(a) enclosed, deal, repress

(b) involved, rapport, laze

(c) inserted, accord, strive

(d) stuck in, acquiesce, yield

(e) sponsored, pact, squirm

Q23. This is a story of a young financial-sector professional who ______________ on the economic boom of the past few years, but lost his job when the wave of the global credit ______________ hit India after the ______________ of the Wall Street investment bank Lehman Brothers.

(a) cruised, crisis, creation

(b) managed, crux, success

(c) endured, jinx, cross

(d) rode, crunch, collapse

(e) guided, pickle, flop

Direction (24-25) : **In questions given below there are two statements, each statement consists of two blanks. You have to choose the option which provides the correct set of words that fits both the blanks in both the statements appropriately and in the same order making them meaningful and grammatically correct.**

Q24.

(1) However ______________ and dictatorial Mr. Mugabe's regime had been, a coup will remain a coup irrespective of what the plotters call it, raising questions of ______________ about the new government.

(2) When change in the court is made rapidly, and when attacks on the court become a bad habit of this ______________ government, the court loses ______________.

(a) inept, legitimacy

(b) inferior, inquisition

(c) consummate, licitness

(d) incompetent, Ingenuity

(e) Pertinent, lawfulness

Q25.

(1) We must declare that, in our deliberate judgement, no man ought to be admitted into a participation in civil privileges with ourselves, who dares, contrary to our opinion of the ______________ of such ______________, to invoke, in his closet, the intercession of saints between himself and his makers.

(2) The spirit of Vedic worship is pervaded by a devout belief in the ______________ of ______________ and sacrificial offering.

(a) contemplation, citation

(b) Plausibility, incursion

(c) malaise, intercession

(d) potency, bestiality

(e) efficacy, invocation

Direction (26) : **There are four sentences given in the following question. Find the sentence(s)**

**which is/are grammatically correct and mark your answer choosing the best possible alternative among the five options given below each question. If all sentences are correct, choose (e) as your answer.**

Q26. (I) The GST Council, at its 23rd meeting in Guwahati last week announced major GST rate cuts by shifting 177 items—ranging from shaving creams to wristwatches—from the highest slab of 28% to the 18% slab.

(II) The government has procured 2 million tonnes of pulses by ensuring minimum support price or market rates, whichever is higher, directly from the farmers and this has been the highest ever procurement of pulses.

(III) Globally, firms across industries are cutting their spending on legacy work such as application maintenance, and ploughing the savings on newer projects into areas such as data analytics and cyber security solutions.

(IV) TCS, India's largest software services firm, maintains that it is the company's DNA to build technologies and groom leaders to take against senior roles, even if implementing this strategy means the company has to sacrifice some growth in the short term.

(a) Only (I) is correct

(b) Only (IV) is correct

(c) Both (I) and (II) are correct

(d) Only (I) , (II) and (III) are correct

(e) All are correct

Direction (27) : **The following question consists of a sentence which is divided into three parts which contain grammatical errors in one or more than one part of the sentence, as specified in bold in each part. If there is an error in any part of the sentence, find the correct alternatives to replace those parts from the three options given below each question to make the sentence grammatically correct. If the given sentence is grammatically correct or does not require any correction, choose (e) , i.e., "No correction required" as your answer.**

Q27. **In the biggest revamp of the GST tax structure**, the GST Council last week removed 178 items (I) /from the highest 28 per cent category **while cutting the tax on all restaurants** outside starred-hotels (II) /to 5 per cent but withdrawing input credit **facility for them**. (III)

(I) To revamp the biggest GST tax structure

(II) by cutting the tax from all restaurants

(III) facilities to them

(a) Only (I)

(b) Only (III)

(c) Both (I) and (III)

(d) All (I) , (II) and (III)

(e) No correction required

Direction (28) : **In the question given below, there are four sentences. Choose the sentence which is grammatically incorrect as your answer. If all the given sentences are grammatically correct and do not require any correction, choose (e) i.e. "All are correct" as your answer.**

Q28. (a) Owing to the rampant change in the lifestyle of the majority of Indian populace, it is vital to understand lifestyle diseases, including and especially diabetes.

(b) The Union Cabinet on Thursday approved setting up of the anti-profiteering authority under the Goods and Services Tax (GST) regime to be composed of a chairman and four technical members.

(c) Less than half of Indian households has access to a proper toilet and as a consequence many people defecate in public spaces.

(d) Once a regional breadbasket, Zimbabwe saw its economy collapse after the seizure of white-owned farms in the early 2000s, followed by runaway money-printing that catapulted inflation to 500 billion percent in 2008.

(e) All are correct.

Direction (29) : **There are three sentences given in the following question. Find the sentence(s) which is/are grammatically correct and mark your answer choosing the best possible alternative among the five options given below each question. If all the sentences are correct, choose (e) as your answer.**

Q29. (I) In recent months, Mr Modi's Clean India programme to provide access to sanitation has received international attention and even praise from people like Bill Gates who has commended the fact that the Modi government has said that the problem will not exist by the year 2019.

(II) As researchers Diane Coffey and Dean Spear point out in their recently released book Where India Goes, the issue of why most Indians do not use toilets was less than a problem of the unavailability of proper toilets and more to with having social behaviour and religious beliefs.

(III) If Pakistanis want a better future for their children, if they want to ensure that so many of them do not perish because of entirely preventable illnesses, this attitude of stubborn denial will have to change.

(a) Only (II) is correct

(b) Both (I) and (III) are correct

(c) Both (I) and (II) are correct

(d) Both (II) and (III) are correct

(e) All are correct

Direction (30) : **Rearrange the following sentences to form a meaningful paragraph and then answer the questions that follow.**

Q30. If the sentence (C) , "The multiple terror attacks that killed at least 200 people in Afghanistan last week has set alarm bells ringing in Kabul." is the first sentence of the paragraph, then what is the sequence of other sentences after rearrangement?

(A) That the attacks occurred at a time when the United States was putting to work its new strategy to stabilise Afghanistan underscores the resolve of the militants to stay the course of insurgency.

(B) On Friday, bombings in two Shia mosques killed more than 80 people, mostly Shias, for which the Islamic State has claimed responsibility.

(C) The multiple terror attacks that killed at least 200 people in Afghanistan last week has set alarm bells ringing in Kabul.

(D) If the government faced only one major armed insurgency till a couple of years ago, now it has to fight on many fronts.

(E) Most of these attacks were carried out by the Taliban.

(F) The security situation in Afghanistan is increasingly worsening.

(a) FBEDA

(b) AEBDF

(c) DABEF

(d) ADFEB

(e) AEBFD

Direction (31-35) :**Below in each questions**

## Section - IV

**some sentences are given, find the sentence which is not really contributing to the main theme and OUT of the passage or find the odd sentence and rearrange the remaining sentences to make a coherent paragraph.**

**Q31.**

A. This has proven a boon for the aerospace industry. Globally, in the next two decades, more than 41,000 aircraft are expected to be produced, with a value of over $6.1 trillion.

B. Across the globe, rising wealth and the advent of discount airlines have made air travel more of a mass proposition than ever before.

C. This bounty will flow not only to plane manufacturers but also to a range of supporting parts and service suppliers.

D.A monthly cap of Rs10,000 for each means users may only use them for such use cases as utilities, telephone bills and so forth.

E. At the same time, the boom in electronic and mobile commerce has increased air-freight volumes as consumers order goods across borders, demanding speedy delivery.

(a) BCEA

(b) DBCA

(c) BEAC

(d) EADC

(e) EABC

**Q32.**

A. These are the electrodes that record the impulses of individual cells, ideally simultaneously with lots of others, in order to try to work out how networks of cells process information.

B. Until the invention of the microscope, microbiology did not exist. Neuroscience, too, has advanced recently on the back of some powerful tools, particularly techniques for scanning whole brains.

C. But the devices that look at the nitty-gritty of how nerve cells themselves work are still Heath-Robinson affairs.

D. For example, since the 2016 edition, the indicator on ease of getting electricity began to include indicators on reliability of supply, price of electricity, and transparency of tariffs.

E. Science is a mixture of the intellectual and the practical. And the practical requires tools. Until the invention of the telescope, astronomy had been stuck in a rut for millennia.

(a) BCDA

(b) CAED

(c) DBCA

(d) BACD

(e) EBCA

**Q33.**

A. He speculated that both types of sounds were important for sending signals to others, but was unsure If this was true. In the years that have passed since his death, ornithologists have proved time and again that birds' songs, squawks and shrieks are used for sending signals to their kin, their rivals and sometimes even their predators.

B. Such quick fixes may even be effective, but will only remain under the glare of the media.

C. In "The Descent of Man and Selection in Relation to Sex" he devoted equal space to both the sorts of sounds that emerge from birds' beaks and the more percussive noises that they make with other parts of their bodies, such as their feet and feathers.

D. In contrast, their more percussive sounds

have received almost no attention at all . A study published in Current Biology by Trevor Murray at the Australian National University, in Canberra, however, suggests that is a mistake. At least one bird creates a specific, audible warning with the flapping of its wings.

E. CHARLES DARWIN was fascinated by bird communication.

(a) DCAB

(b) CABD

(c) ECAD

(d) ECAB

(e) CAED

**Q34.**

A. They have also taken to flirting with deep science to achieve a part of this vision.

B. The common refrain is that IT services firms are not original enough, and seek to profit only on the deep technology advancements made by other firms, usually based in Silicon Valley.

C. However, to be fair, Infosys Ltd and some of the other firms in this category such as Wipro Ltd and Tata Consultancy Services Ltd (TCS) have actually been hard at work to retool their operations to allow for the creation of new technology "products" such that these become an increasingly important part of their eventual go-to-market propositions.

D. Information technology (IT) services providers are often faulted for not having any "original" product ideas.

E. Meanwhile, private industry can't justify investment in expensive research that doesn't yet have clear commercial potential.

(a) DBAC

(b) DBCA

(c) EDCB

(d) BCEA

(e) BDEC

**Q35.**

A. Another part of the flawed start can be explained by poor incentive design.

B. The overdue transition to the new goods and services tax (GST) has started off on the wrong foot.

C. One part of the flawed start can be explained by political realities. The complicated federal bargaining in the GST council led to a system of five tax rates, along with a special rate for gold, as well as cesses that go against the very basic principles of value-added taxation.

D. The three main problems have been the complicated tax structure that can create distortions, onerous compliance procedures that have created working capital stress in many smaller companies, and technical glitches in the GST network.

E. This widened the trade deficit to $14.01 billion, the highest level since $14.08 billion in May 2017.

(a) BCAD

(b) ECBA

(c) DABC

(d) BDCA

(e) EABD

## Solutions (Mock Test – 08)

S1. Ans. (a)

Sol. Refer to the fifth sentence of the first paragraph "from the political point of view ..........................................off to one side", hence option (a) is the correct choice.

S2. Ans. (b)

Sol. Refer to the last few sentences of the second paragraph "I am not a writer, but an inventor", hence option (b) is the correct choice.

S3. Ans. (c)

Sol. Refer to the first sentence of the second paragraph.

S4. Ans. (d)

Sol. Refer to "political and domestic......... science and utopia...are like two nets" (first paragraph) .

S5. Ans. (a)

Sol. Refer to the second last sentence of the passage. "the certified manager of good writing, of literature, he who guarantees decorative union and thus the fundamental separation of substance and form; in calling himself an inventor ("I am not a writer, but an inventor") , he places himself at the limit of meaning, what we today call Text." Hence option (a) is correct.

S6. Ans. (b)

Sol. Refer to the third last sentence of the first paragraph "However, the relationship of Desire and Need is not complementary (were they fitted one into the other, every-thing would be perfect) , but supplementary: each is the excess of the other."

S7. Ans. (a)

Sol. Refer to the second sentence of the second paragraph "Descartes, Who, Fourier thought,.... use of doubt." Hence option (a) is the correct choice.

S8. Ans. (c)

Sol. Refer to the fourth last sentence of the first paragraph "People feel more comfortable with something they can relate to and understand immediately without too much thought".

S9. Ans. (b)

Sol. Refer to the eighth sentence of the third paragraph "If he had used representational images and colour, much of the emotional content would have been lost and the piece would not have caused the demand for justice that it did."

S10. Ans. (d)

Sol. Refer to the first few sentences of the second paragraph "People who look down on abstract art have several major arguments to support their beliefs. They feel that artists turn abstract because they are not capable of the technical drafting skills that appear in a Russell: therefore, such artists create an art form that anyone is capable of and that is less time consuming, and then parade it as artistic progress."

S11. Ans. (c)

Sol. Refer to the last two sentences of the third paragraph "This can be illustrated by Mondrian's Trees series. You can actually see the progression from the early recognizable, though abstracted Trees, to his final solution, the grid system."

S12. Ans. (a)

Sol. Refer to the fourth paragraph.

S13. Ans. (d)

Sol. Denounce means publicly declare to be

wrong or evil. Hence it has same meaning as proscribe.

Splendid means magnificent, very impressive.

Candid means truthful and straightforward, frank.

Sublime means of very great excellence or beauty.

S14. Ans. (a)

Sol. Scrabble means an act of scratching or scrambling for something. Hence it has the same meaning as rummage.

Rebuke means express sharp disapproval or criticism of (someone) because of their behaviour or actions.

Ascribe means regard something as being due to (a cause) .

Rife means abundant.

Murky means dark and gloomy, especially due to thick mist.

S15. Ans. (e)

Sol. **Vividly** means strongly. Hence it has the opposite meaning of indeterminate.

Cavil means make petty or unnecessary objections.

Berate means scold or criticize (someone) angrily.

Disparage means regard or represent as being of little worth.

S16. Ans. (1)

Sol. Replace 'fiction' with 'fictional'

S17. Ans. (2)

Sol. Replace 'give' with 'giving'

S18. Ans. (1)

Sol. Replace 'has' with 'have'

S19. Ans. (5)

Sol. No correction required.

S20. Ans. (2)

Sol. Replace 'will hold' with 'will be held'

S21. Ans. (a)

Sol. "is awaited, demoted, status" is the correct set of words that fill perfectly into the blanks provided in the sentence. Hence (a) is the correct choice.

**Demote** means move (someone) to a lower position or rank, usually as a punishment.

**Busted** means been caught in the act of doing something wrong.

**Count on** means bank on; rely.

**Look for** means attempt to get.

S22. Ans. (c)

Sol. "inserted, accord, strive" is the correct set of words that fill perfectly into the blanks provided in the sentence. Hence option (c) is the correct choice.

**Accord** means an official agreement or treaty.

**Strive** means make great efforts to achieve or obtain something.

**Rapport** means a close and harmonious relationship in which the people or groups concerned understand each other's feelings or ideas and communicate well.

**Repress** means subdue (someone or something) by force.

**Laze** means spend time in a relaxed, lazy manner.

**Stuck in** means introduced.

**Acquiesce** means accept something reluctantly but without protest.

**Squirm** means show or feel embarrassment or shame.

**Section - IV**

S23. Ans. (d)

Sol. "rode, crunch, collapse" is the correct set of words that fill perfectly into the blanks provided in the sentence. Hence (d) is the correct choice.

**Crunch** means a severe shortage of money or credit.

**Cruise** means sail about in an area without a precise destination, especially for pleasure.

**Crux** means the decisive or most important point at issue.

**Jinx** means a person or thing that brings bad luck.

**Pickle** means a difficult situation.

S24. Ans. (a)

Sol. **Inept** means having or showing no skill; clumsy.

**Pertinent** means relevant or applicable to a particular matter; apposite.

**Legitimacy** means ability to be defended with logic or justification; validity.

**Inquisition** means a period of prolonged and intensive questioning.

**Consummate** means showing great skill and flair.

S25. Ans. (e)

Sol. **Efficacy** means the ability to produce a desired or intended result.

**Invocation** means the action of invoking someone or something.

**Bestiality** means savagely cruel or depraved behavior.

**Malaise** means a general feeling of discomfort, illness, or unease whose exact cause is difficult to identify.

S26. Ans. (d)

Sol. All the sentences, except (IV) , are grammatically correct. In the case of sentence (IV) , the phrasal verb "***take against***" should be replaced with "***take up***" to impart a meaningful sentence. The phrasal verb "***take against***" means to begin to dislike (someone) , often for no strong or obvious reason, which is irrelevant to the context of the sentence. The phrasal verb "***take up***" means to accept an offer or challenge, which adds meaning to the sentence. Thus except (IV) , all the other sentences are grammatically correct. Hence option (d) is the correct choice.

S27. Ans. (e)

Sol. The sentence is grammatically correct which means that all the three bold parts in the sentence do not require any replacement or correction. Hence option (e) is the correct choice.

S28. Ans. (c)

Sol. There is a grammatical error in the sentence (c) , the singular verb "***has***" should be replaced by its plural "***have***" as the subject it signifies is in plural form [*Less than half of Indian households*]. The other sentences are grammatically correct. Hence option (c) is the correct choice.

S29. Ans. (b)

Sol. There is an error in the sentence structure of sentence (II) , the later part of the sentence "***was less than a problem of the unavailability of proper toilets and more to with having social behaviour and religious beliefs***" should be replaced with "***is less a problem of the unavailability of proper toilets and more to do with social behaviour and religious beliefs***" to make the sentence both logically and contextually correct. Moreover, it is to be noted that the sentence is in Present Tense, so the use of the verb "***was***" is incorrect. The correct structure of the sentence should be –

"***As researchers Diane Coffey and Dean Spear point out in their recently released book Where India Goes, the issue of why most Indians do not use toilets is less a problem of the unavailability of proper toilets and more to do with social behaviour and religious beliefs.***", which is both grammatically and meaningfully correct. The other two sentences are grammatically correct and do not require any correction. Hence option (b) is the correct choice.

S30. Ans. (e)

Sol. If (C) is the first sentence, the correct sequence of other sentences after rearrangement should be **AEBFD**. The first two sentences (C) and (A) make a clear connection with each other ["*multiple terror attacks*" in the first case can be connected with "*that the attacks occurred at*" in the second case]. Similarly, the sentence (E) follows the sentence (A) . The sentence (D) clearly suggests that it should be the concluding sentence. Thus sentences in the sequence of **CAEBFD** form a coherent paragraph which is about the multiple terror attacks in Afghanistan that happened recently. Hence option (e) is the correct choice.

S31. Ans. (c)

Sol. Correct Choice is option (c) . Statement B is most likely the starting sentence. Now that we know statement B is the starting statement A and C gets eliminated as the second sentence. Statement E follows B, which is then followed by A and C.

Now that we can see Sentence D has no correlation with aerospace industry, and its business, we can rule out Sentence D.

S32. Ans. (e)

Sol. Correct Choice is option (e) . Statement B logically initiate the discussion, followed by B, which further elaborates the idea introduced in E. Subsequently A explains C. Hence EBCA is the apt choice.

Hence we can rule out Option D as it does not contribute to a coherent meaning.

S33. Ans. (c)

Sol. Correct Choice is option (c) . Statement E starts the discussion, followed by C , 'He' is the hint . Here 'He' refers to CHARLES DARWIN. Then comes statement A, which elaborates "types of sounds", which is referred in statement C. Statement D is the concluding statement. B is ruled out as it is out of context.

S34. Ans. (b)

Sol. Correct Choice is option (b) .

Statement D initiates the discussion, followed by B and C. Statement A concludes the statement.

Statement E is out of context.

S35. Ans. (d)

Sol. Correct Choice is option (d) .Statement E is out of context.

Correct choice is BDCA.

# Mock Test (Mains Level) Set–09

Directions (01- 08) **: Read the following passage carefully and answer the questions given below it. Certain words are given in bold to help you locate them while answering some of the questions.**

It sounds pretty obvious: life is all a game. Charles Lamb (1775-1834) put it rather elegantly: "Man is a gaming animal. He must always be trying to get the better in something or other." What John Harsanyi and other economists did was to apply mathematical Logic to this human urge and make game theory, as it is called, part of their tool kit. At its humblest level, game theory is useful in saving the players from going mad. In devising a strategy you know that your rival may know what you are planning, and he knows that you know he knows, and soon.... even skilled chess players can feel mentally wounded.

In chess and comparable real-life games, each side has basic information about the other. The problem of Charles Lamb's gaming animals is that they usually have imperfect knowledge about their opponents. They guessed, or relied on "intuition" or, as Napoleon said of his favorite generals, they were lucky. Until quite recent items, this was the way countries and great companies dealt with their rivals.

Mr. Harsanyi's contribution to game theory was to show that such games need not be played in a fog, or at least not much. It was possible to analyze such games and provide guidance about the probable moves and their outcomes. This advanced game theory was employed, at least by the Americans, in their negotiations with the Soviet Union on arms control. Kennedy and Khrushchev used game theory in their **tussle** over Cuban missiles in 1962.

Game theory is widely used in commerce, as happened this year when, with great success, the British government sold licenses for mobile phone services in an auction designed by an Oxford economist. Paul Kemmerer. Some economists are watching with fascination the contest between the European Central Bank and the currency market over the future of the Europe, which has at least the look of an exercise in game theory. A Dutch team of economists applied the theory to international football and concluded that a bad team playing at home is more likely to score than a good one playing away. One effect of game theory is to make economists seem quite human.

As often happens when an idea becomes fashionable, there has been some argument about who first thought to game theory. Mr. Harsanyi, who shared a Nobel Prize in 1994 with two other economists in the same field, John Nash and Reinhardt Selten, was happy to acknowledge that game theory had been around in some form for a longtime. Players of poker, and of course chess, had been using game theory without calling it that. Philosophy has a claim: it seeks to rationalize the behaviour of people with conflicting interests. As a young man in Budapest, Mr. Harsanyi had studied philosophy and mathematics and, to please his parents who ran a pharmacy, he added chemistry.

What triggered his interest in game theory appears to have been the work of John von Neumann and Oskar Morgenstern, who in 1944 published a book entitled "The Theory of Games and Economic Behaviour". Von Neumann was an

American mathematician who, by coincidence, had also been born in Hungary and had attended the same school as Mr. Harsanyi. He and Morgenstern may have been the first to show how the philosophical idea of rational behaviour could be applied to economics. They did not develop the idea. In his short life, von Neumann especially had much other interest, including work on quantum theory and the design of the first electronic computers. In paper after paper, Mr. Harsanyi and his colleagues took the theory further. It is still being polished.

The philosopher in John Harsanyi saw in game theory means of improving the human condition. He promoted the idea that the rightness or wrongness of an action depended on its consequences, an ethical theory known as utilitarianism. The connection between game theory and ethics is a complex one. His book on this theme, Essays on Ethics. Social Behaviour and Scientific Explanation", is a hard read, just as game theory itself demands lots of tricky mathematics. No one would blame you for sticking to Charles Lamb.

Q1. What is the author meaning to convey when he says, "even skilled chess-players can feel mentally wounded"?

(a) it saves the players from going mad

(b) the mathematical logic of the game theory leaves even skilled players wounded

(c) that the theory is very complicated

(d) chess players find the theory hard to comprehend

(e) All of the above

Q2. The author feels that prior to game theory, companies and countries:

(a) relied on guess work when dealing with each other

(b) relied on luck rather than scientific analysis

(c) made imperfect decisions

(d) had no idea how to deal with each other

(e) None of these

Q3. The main contribution of Mr. Harsanyi to game theory is:

(a) it made economists seem quite human

(b) games need not be played in fog now

(c) it provided guidance about the probable moves of opponents

(d) it was employed by Americans in dealing with the Soviet Union.

(e) All of the above

Q4. Why does the author say that one effect of the game theory is to make economists seem quite human?

(a) because complicated theory could now be applied to real life situations

(b) because game theory was used in diverse fields like football and politics

(c) because it brought economics closer to the masses

(d) because it was a way of adding human element to complicated theories

(e) All of the above

Q5. How did game theory originate?

(a) from the works of Harsanyi

(b) from John Nash and Rein hard Selten

(c) from John Von Neumann and Oskar Morgernoten

(d) from games like chess and poker

(e) None of these

## Section - IV

Q6. The passage is a/an:

(a) review of a book written by Mr. Harsanyi

(b) assessment of the work of Mr. Harsanyi

(c) summation of the game theory

(d) explanation of the game theory

(e) None of these

**Directions (07) : Choose the word/group of words which is most SIMILAR in meaning to the word/group of words printed in bold as used in passage.**

Q7. **Tussle**

(a) disdain

(b) candor

(c) dissuade

(d) skirmish

(e) rugged

**Directions (08- 15) : Read the following passage carefully and answer the questions given below it. Certain words are given in bold to help you locate them while answering some of the questions.**

Among those who call themselves socialists, two kinds of persons may be distinguished. They are, in the first place, those who plan for a new order of society, in which private and individual competition are to be superseded and other motives to action substituted, are on the scale of a village community of township, and would be applied to an entire country by the multiplication of such self-acting units; of this character are the systems of Owen, of Fourier, and the more thoughtful and philosophic socialists generally. The other class, which is more a product of the continent than of Great Britain and may be called the revolutionary socialists, has people who propose to themselves a much bolder stroke. Their scheme is the management of the whole productive resources of the country by one central authority, the general government. And with this view some of them **avow** as their purpose that the working classes, or somebody on their behalf, should take possession of all the property of the country, and administer it for the general benefit.

Whatever may be the difficulties of the first of these two forms of socialism, the second may evidently involve the same difficulties and many more. The former, too has the great advantage that it can be brought into operation progressively, and can prove its capabilities by trial. It can be tried first on a select population and extended to the rest as their education and cultivation permit. It need not, and the natural order of things would not, become an engine of subversion until it has shown itself capable of being also a mean of reconstruction. It is not so with the other: the aim of that is to substitute the new rule for the old at a single stroke, and to exchange the amount of good realized under the present system, and its large possibilities for a plunge without any preparation into the most extreme form of the problem of carrying on the whole round of the operations of social life without the motive power which has always hitherto worked the social machinery. It must be acknowledged that those who would play this game on the strength of their own private opinion, unconfirmed as yet by any experimental verification-who would forcibly deprive all who have now a comfortable physical existence of their only present means of preserving it, and would brave the frightful bloodshed and misery that would ensue if the attempt was resisted-must have a serene confidence in their own wisdom on one hand and the recklessness of other peoples' suffering on the other, of which, Roberspierre and St. Just, were hitherto the typical instances, scarcely came up to. Nevertheless, this scheme has great elements of popularity which the more cautious and reasonable form of socialism has not; because what it professes to do, it promises to do quickly and holds out hope to the enthusiasts of seeing the whole of their aspirations realised in their own time and at a blow.

Q8. Who among of the following is not a socialist?

(a) Robespierre

(b) Fourier

(c) Owen

(d) All are socialists

(e) All

Q9. Which of the following, according to the author, is true?

(a) The second form of socialism has more difficulties that the first

(b) The second form of socialism has the same difficulties as the first

(c) The second form of socialism has less difficulties than the first

(d) The author has not compared the difficulties of the two

(e) None of these

Q10. According to the author, the difference between the two kinds of socialists is that

(a) one consists of thinkers and the others are active people

(b) the first have a definite philosophy and the second don't have any definite philosophy

(c) the first believe in gradual change while the others believe in revolutionary change

(d) the first are the products of Britain, while the other are products of Russia

(e) None of these

Q11. Which of the following were characteristics of St. Just and Robespierre?

(a) Unconcern for other's suffering

(b) Full confidence in their own wisdom

(c) Both (a) and (b)

(d) Neither (a) nor (b)

(e) Only (a)

Q12. Which of the following according to the author, may not be the result of not verifying the desirability of socialism experimentally first?

(a) Bloodshed

(b) Deprivation of current comfortable existence

(c) Corruption in high places

(d) Misery caused by resisting the change

(e) All

Q13. According to the philosophy of revolutionary socialism,

(a) the government takes over the villages first, and then gradually the whole country.

(b) the government takes over all productive resources of the country at one stroke.

(c) the government declares a police state and rules by decree.

(d) there is no government as such: the people rule themselves by the socialist doctrine.

(e) All are correct.

Q14. The word **'avow'** in the context of the passage means

(a) proclaim

(b) vow

(c) confirm

(d) deny

(e) affirm

Q15. It may be inferred from the passage that the author's sympathies are for

(a) neither side.

(b) the side of the socialist doctrine.

(c) the second type of socialism.

(d) the first type of socialism.

(e) All

Directions (16-20) **: In each question, there is a pair of words/phrases that highlighted. From the highlighted word(s) /phrase(s) , select the most appropriate word(s) /phrase(s) to form correct sentences. Then, from the options given, choose the best one.**

Q16.

I. "So tonight, we are **respectfully**(a) / **respectively**(b) asking the candidates to try to put aside the talking points," he says.

II. The rivers become so **turbid**(a) /**turgid**(b) that they turn a chocolate brown color.

III. It's taken nearly nine years, but large-scale commercial redevelopment of the World Trade Center **site** (a) /**sight**(b) is tantalizingly close to taking off.

(a) bba

(b) aab

(c) baa

(d) aba

(e) aaa

Q17.

I. I just took my shoes off at midnight and found that I have little, **turbid**(a) /**turgid**(b) toes!

II. It is impossible to tell if there is a specific **breech**(a) /**breach**(b) of any conflict of interest laws

III. **Eminent**(a) / **imminent**(b) domain laws generally allow for the confiscation of private property if taking it is judged to serve a larger public good.

(a) bbb

(b) abb

(c) bba

(d) aba

(e) aaa

Q18.

I. Thinking about the **etymology**(a) / **entomology**(b) of these words made me think about exactly why we, as designers, were originally inspired by these ideas.

II. Charming and gregarious with a **flair**(a) / **flare**(b) for grand gestures, he was haunted by drug addiction.

III. In our textbooks, there are photos of physicians a century ago performing autopsies with their **bear**(a) /**bare** (b) hands.

(a) aba

(b) aaa

(c) aab

(d) bba

(e) bab

Q19.

I. Anaklet says we›re going to surprise some **guerilla** (a) /**gorillas** (b) eating breakfast.

II .Starbucks announced last summer it would start retailing flavored **instance** (a) /**instant** (b) coffee, and here it is.

III. An **insidious** (a) /**invidious** (b) new email

virus infiltrated high-profile US companies Thursday.

(a) abb

(b) baa

(c) bab

(d) bbb

(e) bba

Q20.

I. **The alternative** (a) /**alternate**(b) jersey will have an interlocking SD on the left chest.

II. The current council will **formerly**(a) / **formally** (b) disband within the next few days.

III. Their report was **titled**(a) /**entitled**(b) : "Euro zone: Thinking the unthinkable?

(a) bab

(b) bbb

(c) bba

(d) aba

(e) bbb

Direction (21-23) : **Select the phrase/connector (STARTERS) from the given three options which can be used to form a single sentence from the two sentences given below, implying the same meaning as expressed in the statement sentences.**

Q21. (1) A person can be charged with sedition only if he incites violence or intends to create disorder through speech or writing.

(2) The Constitutional Bench of the Supreme Court in the Kedarnath case came up with the judgment.

(I) If a person is charged with...

(II) According to the judgment of the...

(III) In the Kedarnath case...

(a) Only (I) is correct

(b) Only (II) is correct

(c) Both (I) and (III) are correct

(d) Both (II) and (III) are correct

(e) All are correct

Q22. (1) Mr. Debroy said that the only good way to obtain satisfactory jobs data is through household surveys and that the previous National Sample Survey was released in 2011, and the next one will release data only in 2018.

(2) He stressed that there is no good data regarding jobs, employment and unemployment.

(I) Stressing that there is no...

(II) In defiance of good way to...

(III) To obtain satisfactory jobs...

(a) Only (I) is correct

(b) Only (III) is correct

(c) Both (I) and (II) are correct

(d) Both (II) and (III) are correct

(e) All are correct

Q23. (1) Germany saw its position enhanced, albeit obliquely via the tradition of having a European head of the IMF.

(2) Japan's frustrations led it to create the Asian Development Bank as its major channel of development funding.

(I) Creating the Asian Development ....

(II) While Germany did see its...

(III) Regardless of Japan's frustrations...

(a) Only (I) is correct

(b) Only (II) is correct

(c) Both (I) and (II) are correct

(d) Both (I) and (III) are correct

(e) All are correct

## Section - IV

Direction (24-25) : **Rearrange the following sentences to form a meaningful paragraph and then answer the questions that follow.**

Q24. If Sentence (C) , "India's surge in the latest World Bank report on "the ease of doing business" around the world — from the 130th position last year to the 100th — could not have come at a better time for the government."is the first sentence, what is the order of other sentences after rearrangement?

(A) He reiterated the commitment to pursue more reforms, especially in areas where the Index still rates India poorly among 190 countries.

(B) Specific steps to cut red tape seem to be paying off, with the Bank recognising India as one of the top 10 countries that have made improvement over the past year, and the only large country to see a significant shift.

(C) India's surge in the latest World Bank report on "the ease of doing business" around the world — from the 130th position last year to the 100th — could not have come at a better time for the government.

(D) Prime Minister NarendraModi has set for his government the target of entering the top 50 in the Bank's index, from the 142nd rank India was placed at in 2014 soon after he assumed office.

(E) The introduction of the new insolvency and bankruptcy resolution process, simplifications in the payment of statutory dues such as provident fund contributions and corporate taxes and easier access to credit are among the key changes that spurred India's latest ranking.

(F) Facing sustained criticism of late over its handling of the economy, it was not entirely surprising that Finance Minister ArunJaitley held a press conference just to discuss the findings of the Bank's report.

(a) FADBE

(b) ABDEF

(c) DEABF

(d) BDFEA

(e) DFBAE

Q25. If sentence (D) , "The number of deaths and the incidence rate have been falling both globally and in India." is the last sentence of the paragraph, then which of the following sentences does not fit into the paragraph formed after rearranging other sentences?

(A) Incidence estimates for India are considered interim, pending a national TB prevalence survey scheduled for 2017-2018.

(B) Notably, domestic funding (74%, $387 million) for anti-TB work has been more than that from international sources (26%, $124 million) .

(C) There is a glimmer of hope with India registering a slight drop in the number of new tuberculosis cases and TB deaths in 2016 compared with 2015.

(D) The number of deaths and the incidence rate have been falling both globally and in India.

(E) In terms of mortality, the drop was from 0.51 million in 2015 to 0.43 million in 2016.

(F) From an estimated 2.84 million new cases in 2015, the number dropped marginally to 2.79 million in 2016, according to the World Health Organisation's Global tuberculosis report, 2017.

(a) A

(b) C

(c) E

(d) B

(e) F

**Directions (26-30) : In the questions given below, find out which of the phrases (I) , (II) , (III) given below should replace the phrase given in bold in the following sentence to make the sentence grammatically correct. If the sentence is correct as it is and no correction is required, mark (e) as the answer.**

Q26. I was in the middle of a sentence, and he **hang around** on me! How rude.

I. Hang on

II. Hang out

III. Hung up

(a) Only I

(b) Only I and II

(c) Only II

(d) Only III

(e) No change required

Q27. He **checked over** the old car to see if it was worth buying.

I. check up on

II. check through

III. check with

(a) Only I

(b) Only I and II

(c) Only II

(d) Only III

(e) No change required

Q28. You need to **think** this **up** carefully before you make a decision.

I. think through

II. think over

III. thing on

(a) Only I

(b) Only I and II

(c) Only II

(d) Only III

(e) No change required

Q29. My boss really **stuck it to** me when I arrived late to work for the third time this week

I. stick to

II. stick up for

III. stick down

(a) Only I

(b) Only I and II

(c) Only II

(d) Only III

(e) No change required

Q30. I **run out** of my English teacher at the movies last night. She›s so nice!

I. run off

II. ran into

III. run down

(a) Only I

(b) Only I and II

(c) Only II

(d) Only III

(e) No change required

Directions (31-35) : **Five alternative summaries are given below each text. Choose the option that best captures the essence of the text.**

Q31. There is good news for small investors as the new changes announced in the transaction tax will increase their choice as far as their personal finance decisions are concerned. On the overall issue of investing in equity, the changes do not impact the long term investors who take delivery of their shares. The transaction tax rate has been maintained at 0.15% for this category.

## Section - IV

At the same time the Finance Minister has stuck to his decision to abolish long-term capital gains exemption and lower the short term capital gains tax to 10%.

(a) The benefit received by investors on the capital front has meant that long term investors have decided to invest in equity. The Finance Minister's decision on long and short term capital gains tax has been welcomed.

(b) The benefit received by investors on capital gains front will be tremendous, according to the new transaction tax. Investors will have a wider option to invest in and the Finance Minister has stuck to his decision to abolish certain exemptions.

(c) The Finance Minister has introduced some promised tax exemptions which have been welcomed by the tax-payer. Smaller investors are over joyed at the overall issue of investing in equity.

(d) The Finance Minister's decision on long and short term investments had made small investors invest in a number of equity funds. They are overjoyed as this has been a welcome move on the point of the Finance Minister.

(e) The new changes announced regarding the transaction tax and the decision taken by the Finance Minister in this regard have done a world of good especially for the long term investors as the interest rate has been slashed by more than half of the existing one.

Q32. ING Vysya Bank has finished the first quarter which ended on June 30, 2004 with a net loss of Rs. 20 crore. The result is in direct contrast to quarter I of FY '03 when the bank had a net profit of Rs.33.09 crore. The loss in quarter I of the current fiscal year is attributable to a record Rs.43.96 crores of other operating expenses and Rs.40.34 crore worth of payments / provisions for employee cost. The other operating expenses also included provisions for non-performing assets and standard assets as per RBI guidelines. Against the total income of Rs.297.04 crore, the amount of interest expended stood at Rs.163.07 crore.

(a) ING Vysya Bank has suffered heavy losses against some previous profits. The loss in quarter II has been attributed to high attrition rate along with provisions for employee cost.

(b) ING Vysya Bank was in the red in the first quarter of this year. The second quarter was comparatively better although the company registered a net loss of Rs.20 crores.

(c) ING Vysya Bank is in the black. In the second quarter of this year as the bank expended a lot of money on overheads and other miscellaneous expenses which went up to a few crores.

(d) ING Vysya Bank is in doldrums owing to its record expenditure on operating expenses against the norms laid down by the RBI. This eventually has resulted in heavy losses.

(e) ING Vysya Bank is in the red in the quarter of this year due to the heavy overheads. Expenses were high which included provisions for non-profitable assets; interest spent was also very high.

Q33. The unseemly spectacle of a police team searching the residence of Union Coal and Mines Minister Shibu Soren, accused in a murder case, with an arrest warrant, today pushed the ruling congress led establishment into a politically embarrassing corner. In what is seen as the first of its kind, police officials searched Mr. Soren's residence with the minister going into hiding, they were forced to paste a copy of the arrest warrant on the gates of the residence. This was removed within minutes of the team's departure by Mr. Soren's supporters. Sources said that the minister has gone into hiding in the jungles of Chaibasa.

(a) An embarrassed Congress led government has ordered the searching of the residence of Union Coal and Mines minister Shibu Soren for having committed a murder. Mr. Soren is absconding but his supporters removed the arrest warrant pasted on the gate by the police.

(b) The police team searching the house and pasting an arrest warrant on the gates of the Union Coal and Mines Minster's house was a treat to sore eyes. Shibu Soren, the accused has caused great embarrassment to the congress led government.

(c) The Congress party hung its head in shame when Shibu Soren, the Union Coal Minister refused to surrender after being accused of murder. His supporters removed the arrest warrant pasted on the gates of his house immediately after the police's departure.

(d) The Union Coal and Mines Minister, Mr. Shibu Soren is absconding after being accused of murder. The police have had no choice but to paste a copy of the arrest warrant on the gates of his house but the copy was immediately removed by his supporters.

(e) The residence of the Union Coal and Mines minister who is accused of a murder, was searched by the police team which had to paste the arrest warrant on the gates of his residence as the minister was at large.

Q34. Viruses make their stealthy march forward, finding newer and newer targets of infection. After the cabis virus which was the first to infect mobile phones running the symbian OS, now we have a virus of the pocket PC, running Microsoft pocket PC OS. The virus is named WINCE4 dust. This virus does nothing harmful, rather it is a very polite virus, asking you for permission to spread. If the user clicks on yes in response to the message, the virus proceeds to infect flies — else it quits. The virus seems to have been written by someone called Ratter, who is part of a hacker group called 29A, and produced the Cabis virus for mobile phones.

(a) A unique virus, written by Ratter, a member of hacker group is slowly but surely spreading among pocket PCs. The virus although not detrimental had earlier invaded mobile phones and was called the Cabis virus.

(b) This unique virus is polite and modifies the virus code with a polite request for permission to infect and replaces it by a malicious code.

(c) This is a unique virus which seeks permission before it actually spreads. Ratter, a member of a hacker group, who has written this virus is not a first timer for the pocket PC as he had done the same for mobiles as well.

(d) The virus which is stealthily marching forwards to be all pervasive among pocket PCs is a safe virus, unable to spread independently and incapable of crippling a business.

(e) A unique virus, polite enough to seek permission before infecting, has been produced by a person called Ratter exclusively for pocket PC. The best thing about this is that the user has a choice to protect his PC.

Q35. The government has made strenuous efforts to inculcate the saving and banking habit amongst the masses since independence. But the tempo of savings that has developed over almost five decades ended in a fiasco after the recent, drastic interest rate cuts. Rates fell to "pre-sixties"! levels, despite inflation and a steep fall in the rupee value. Savings and borrowings via official channels have thus become anathema for the masses, who have again fallen prey to money lenders, taken to hoarding or investing in the unorganized sector. Banks also have been deprived of a perennial source of stable deposits from almost 50% of the population.

(a) The banking industry is in a turmoil due to the Government's decision to encourage the masses to save and invest. Interest rates are at an all time low forcing people to make a bee-line to private money-lenders and financiers.

(b) India is a country where interest rates have dipped despite the Government's encouragement. People are flocking to private money lenders and financiers, much to the chagrin of bankers.

(c) A severe dip in interest rates has seen investors, lenders and financiers scurrying to the ones who offer a much higher rate of interest because in India we do not have free medical aid, social security or any other safety net.

(d) A severe dip in interest rates in banking sector has seen investors turning to money lenders and financiers. This has brought down deposits in banks by almost half although the Government has spared no effort to encourage the saving and banking habit among people.

(e) The failure of the Government to inculcate the banking habit among masses has forced it to go for drastic interest rate cuts despite inflation. This has prompted the customers to invest in unorganised sectors.

## SOLUTIONS (MOCK TEST – 09)

S1. Ans. (c)

Sol. The author means to say that the game theory strategized by John Harsanayi is so tricky that it can take the mind of even skilled chess players.

S2. Ans. (a)

Sol. Explained in the second paragraph "They guessed, or relied on "intuition" or, as Napoleon said of his favorite generals, they were lucky. Until quite recent items, this was the way countries and great companies dealt with their rivals." Hence option (a) is the correct choice.

S3. Ans. (c)

Sol. Refer to the second sentence of the third paragraph. "It was possible to analyze such games and provide guidance about the probable moves and their outcomes. "

S4. Ans. (a)

Sol. Explained in the fourth paragraph. "A Dutch team of economists applied the theory to international football and concluded that a bad team playing at home is more likely to score than a good one playing away. One effect of game theory is to make economists seem quite human."

S5. Ans. (d)

Sol. Refer to the fifth paragraph "Players of poker, and of course chess, had been using game theory without calling it that".

S6. Ans. (b)

Sol. The whole passage revolves around the work of Mr. Harsanyi and how he applied mathematical Logic to human urge to improve the condition of human.

S7. Ans. (d)

Sol. Tussle means a vigorous struggle or scuffle, typically in order to obtain or achieve something. Hence it has the same meaning as skirmish.

S8. Ans. (d)

Sol. According to the passage, all of the above have been mentioned as socialists. Hence, option (d) is the right choice.

S9. Ans. (a)

Sol. Refer to the line from paragraph 2...,"Whatever may be the difficulties of the first of these two forms of socialism, the second must evidently involve the same difficulties and many more" which explains that option (a) is the right answer choice.

S10. Ans. (c)

Sol. The answer to this question can be found in paragraph 1 of the passage. It explains that the first believe in gradual change while the others believe in revolutionary change. Option (c) is the right choice.

S11. Ans. (c)

Sol. According to the passage, both have been mentioned as the characteristics of the two. Option (c) is the right answer. Refer to the lines: It must be acknowledged that those who would play this game on the strength of their own private opinion, unconfirmed as yet by any experimental verification-who would forcibly deprive all who have now a comfortable physical existence of their only present means of preserving it, and would brave the frightful bloodshed and misery that would ensue if the attempt was resisted-must have a serene confidence in their own wisdom on one hand and the recklessness of other peoples' suffering on the other, of which, Roberspierre and St. Just, were hitherto the typical instances, scarcely came up to. Now you might be tempted to read the last four words of the above extract (scarcely came up to) in continuation with the last bit and assume that Roberspierre and St. Just scarcely come up to these values. But in reality, the sentence should be read as: It must be acknowledged that those who would play this game on the strength of their own private opinion, unconfirmed as yet by any experimental verification... scarcely came up to. Considering this, option (c) is the correct answer in this case.

S12. Ans. (c)

Sol. This is an easy question. Option (c) does not find a mention in the passage.

S13. Ans. (b)

Sol. It is directly given in the passage that the aum of revolutionary socialism is to take over everything and then things in one go. This makes option (b) the correct answer.

S14. Ans. (a)

Sol. Refer to the sentence: And with this view some of them avow as their purpose that the working classes, or somebody on their behalf, should take possession of all the property of the country, and administer it for the general benefit. Avow means: assert or confess openly Proclaim means: State or announce.

S15. Ans. (a)

Sol. The author does not exhibit sympathy for any one side in particular. He adopts a descriptive approach in the passage.

S16. Ans. (e)

Sol. Respectfully- To show respect is to show how you admire something or someone, to show deference or obedience. Therefore, when you do something respectfully, you're being polite because you do it with full of respect.

Respectively, on the other hand, means in a manner that treats several things individually, one by one, in a sequence.

turgid- swollen and distended or congested.

turbid- (of a liquid) cloudy, opaque, or thick with suspended matter.

Cite is a verb to mean to quote, to summon officially, to mention formally, or even to compliment.

site -an area of ground on which a town, building, or monument is constructed.

sight- the faculty or power of seeing, the action or fact of seeing someone or something

S17. Ans. (c)

Sol. breach- A breach is a break — whether it's a breach in contract or a breach in a dam.

A breech, double "e," is an opening at back of the gun.

eminent-(of a person) famous and respected within a particular sphere.

immanent–existing or operating within; inherent.

imminent-about to happen

S18. Ans. (c)

Sol. Entomology-the branch of zoology concerned with the study of insects.

etymology-study of the origin of words and the way in which their meanings have changed throughout history.

Flair is a noun meaning an aptitude or eagerness for something or a distinctive style.

Flare -a sudden brief burst of bright flame or light. bare–(of a person or part of the body) not clothed or covered. bear-(of a vehicle or boat) convey (passengers or cargo) .

S19. Ans. (e)

Sol. A gorilla is a type of large African ape. A guerrilla, on the other hand, is a fighter who's a part of a rebellious group that's battling a government or other authority and likes to raid and ambush.

instance- an example or single occurrence of something; cite (a fact, case, etc.) as an example.

Instant-happening or coming immediately; prepared quickly and with little effort.

insidious -proceeding in a gradual, subtle way, but with very harmful effects.

invidious-(of an action or situation) likely to arouse or incur resentment or anger in others.

S20. Ans. (c)

Sol. Alternate–occur in turn repeatedly, change repeatedly between two contrasting conditions.

Alternative -(of one or more things) available as another possibility or choice. Alternative can be an adjective or noun, too. As an adjective, it describes something available as another choice, including alternative lifestyles. As a noun, it means one of two or more choices.

Former is at the root of formerly, referring to something that occurred earlier. If you changed your name, you'd be referred to as formerly known as whatever-your-name-used-to-be. At the root of formally is formal, an adjective that describes something as following custom, regulations, or ceremonies. You might speak formally during your speech but chat casually with everyone after. Formally describes something official.

entitle-give (someone) a legal right or a just claim to receive or do something.

titled-(of a person) having a title indicating high social or official rank.

S21. Ans. (d)

Sol. Both the starters (II) and (III) are correct to frame the meaningful sentence. The first one is incorrect as it would alter the meaning of the sentence.

(II) According to the judgment of the Constitutional Bench of the Supreme Court in the Kedarnath case, a person can be charged with sedition only if he incites violence or intends to create disorder through speech or writing.

(III) In the Kedarnath case, the Constitutional Bench of the Supreme Court came up with the judgment that a person can be charged with sedition only if he incites violence or intends to create disorder through speech or writing.

S22. Ans. (a)

Sol. Among the given three starters, only (I) is correct enough to fulfill the required purpose. The other two would alter the meaning of the sentence.

(I) Stressing that there is no good data regarding jobs, employment and unemployment, Mr. Debroy said the only good way to obtain satisfactory jobs data is through household surveys and that the previous National Sample Survey was released in 2011, and the next one will release data only in 2018.

S23. Ans. (b)

Sol. Starter (II) provides a meaningful and common sentence. The third one is incorrect as it doesn't have the correct structure to start a sentence.

(II) While Germany did see its position enhanced, albeit obliquely via the tradition of having a European head of the IMF, Japan's frustrations led it to create the Asian Development Bank as its major channel of development funding.

S24. Ans. (a)

Sol. As mentioned in the question, if sentence (c) is the first sentence then the correct order of other sentences after rearrangement is FADBE.

S25. Ans. (d)

Sol. Upon reading the sentences we can easily observe that CFAED forms a coherent paragraph as it talks about the statistics of the drop in number of cases of Tuberculosis in India as compared to previous year while sentence (d) which fails to connect with other sentences talks about the funding for anti TB work. Hence option (d) is the correct choice.

S26. Ans. (d)

Sol. Hang up — To end a call on the phone, especially if it's before the other person is ready.

Hang out — To spend time with someone, casually.

Hang on — To keep something.

S27. Ans. (e)

Sol. check over -closely examine the condition of something

check out of–leave a hotel, hospital

check through- send luggage through (to a destination) investigate someone or something

check with- ask a person for confirmation

S28. Ans. (a)

Sol. think through–consider carefully

Think up–create or invent a false story

Think over-consider

'Think something over' means 'consider'. For example:

'It was an interesting proposition, but I didn't want to decide straight away. So I asked my boss if I could have a few days to think it over'.

'Think something through' means separate something out into its individual parts and stages. This might involve envisaging a plan of action, and deciding what you might do first, and what you would do if things were to go wrong.

Thinking something over means you'll consider it in a general way, whereas thinking something through suggests you'll consider it more carefully, step by step, logically.

Hence think through is correct

S29. Ans. (e)

Sol. stick it to–severely criticize a person (inf.)

stick to–persevere, keep trying

stick up for–defend oneself or opinions

S30. Ans. (c)

Sol. run into–meet unexpectedly

run off–make leave

run off- reproduce (photocopies)

run off leave quickly

run out of–not have any more of something

run down- loose power, be very tired

S31. Ans. (b)

Sol. The text contains the following key ideas.

(1) Small investors now have wider choice.

(2) The new transaction tax.

(3) The Finance Minister's decision.

Only 'B' captures all there elements

S32. Ans. (e)

Sol. The text contains the following key ideas.

(1) ING Vysya Bank incurred losses in the first quarter.

(2) The main reason for incurring losses is its high expenses.

Only 'E' captures all these elements.

S33. Ans. (d)

Sol. The text contains the following key ideas.

(1) The union Coal and Mines Minister is absconding after being accused of murder.

(2) The police have raided his house.

(3) The police have pasted an arrest warrant which his supporters have removed.

Only 'D' captures all these elements.

S34. Ans.(c)

Sol. The text contains the following key ideas.

(1) There is a unique virus, which actually seeks permission before its spreads.

(2) Ratter, the producer of Cabis virus has produced this virus for mobiles as well.

Only choice 'C' captures there points.

S35. Ans. (d)

Sol. The text contains the following key ideas.

(1) Interest rates in banks have fallen.

(2) Investors are investing with money-leaders.

(3) Deposits in banks have come down.

Only 'D' captures all these elements.

Section - IV

# Mock Test (Mains Level) Set–10

Directions (01-10) : **Read the following passage carefully and answer the questions given below. Certain words/phrases have been printed in bold to help you locate them.**

It is frequently said by top managers that were they ever inclined to ask themselves if there might be problems or opportunities deserving their attention other than those continuously arising from the daily round, they would at once send for some reputable firm of business consultants-company doctoral management professors, experts from Boston, confidential advisors, and so forth. The Idea that what might be lacking is something personal to the top managers themselves, something, moreover, that they alone might one day be able to put right, would strike them as very strange. It would be even stranger to them to suggest that, not only were they themselves alone in being able to put things right, but that only they, too, could discover the **avenues** to successful amendment, But since there can be no learning without action and no action without learning, If change is to be brought about by the purchased services of outsiders, independently of any involvement at a personal level of the top managers who commission those outsiders, then there can be no learning-that is, no preparation among those at present in charge to meet the recurrent challenges of the future. The enterprise will therefore become dependent upon its external advisors until it can no longer afford to meet their fees and expenses-a condition now frequently encountered. Nor is this all, the external consultant generally claims expertise in such-and-such a field, and, on this account, will diagnose the **affliction** (or interpret the hope) of his client management in terms of it; for a month or more everything will go as he predicts, the pattern uncovered will fit the forecast already made, and the plan of action will build upon the personal enthusiasms of members of the host management. The outside consultants who have prepared the plan-not seldom by piecing together fragments of their past prescriptions to other clients-will gradually '**phase themselves out**', leaving those on the spot to implement what still needs to be done. With their wide connections across a fast professional culture, the itinerant experts are able quickly to find the super-specialist needed (it might seem) to advice upon some highly technical obstruction to success…

The assignment of a visiting fellow from another enterprise also anxious to do something about its more **obstinate** and ill-structured embarrassments has battle in common with the engagement of professional experts. Were the fellows of the Inter University Programme to carry visiting cards to widen their possibilities of future employment, they would endorse them in red capitals: '**Our strength, just like your own, lies in our ignorance of your troubles**.' For, while the expert may pretend that his first desire is to see the problem as it is seen by the management that needs to do something about it, he is in his particular business for quite a different reason; the visiting fellow, on the other hand, is clearly another manager in fact, anxious to interpret the trouble as a manager among managers, and to learn from his hosts as much as they are to learn from him. He does not seek to prolong his engagement with his hosts, or to withhold unpleasant advice that may prejudice the willingness of his clients to meet their financial obligations-since there are none. He is not hoping, as are many consultants that he may be offered an appointment in the firm he is setting out to help, so that his advice will not be coloured by quite adventitious possibilities having nothing to do with the original reasons for his being in the action learning programme at all. Faced with a temporary check, the visiting fellow has no headquarters office he may ring for instant support from another **itinerant** expert; he will need to open up some fresh line of questioning with his hosts. Unlike the professional consultant, he will not be spending a lot of his time trying to find out what the most powerful person in the receiving organization believes the problem to be in order to present to him a solution based upon that interpretation; the visiting fellow will, laboriously and with little thanks, be trying to reconcile the myriad views and experiences of large numbers of his new colleagues in such a manner that these now start to suggest to him what might be going on and how it may be improved upon. While in practice the expert consultant is desperately striving to use every interview he conducts as a means of assembling every shared of an idea from others into what he will claim as his own solution, he must be very cautious about creating the impression that he is circulating as the thirstiest of learners; his official status is a teller of others, an instructor of babes, a guide to the foolish, an enlightened dispelling the darkness, a leader of the blind, and so forth, He must be extremely cautious about giving an impression that there is anything he has to learn. The visiting fellow, on the other hand, gets his authority to help his new colleagues from his own eagerness to learn by recording the explanations of what they themselves imagine to be wrong, as the supreme non-expert, he is, at least at the outset, in no position to question what they say, nor to stem their desire to say it-and hence to learn from what they are trying to tell him about that which, they feel, seems to pass their own understanding, As Saint Paul reminded us all. 'Let no man **deceive** himself. If any man among you seemed to be wise in this world, let him become a fool that he may be wise.' It is one of the texts upon which action learning is founded, but rarely seen on the Christmas cards from experts.

Q1. According to the writer, the top managers send for the outside experts to put things right as-

(a) They do not believe in the capability level of their company staff.

(b) It appears to them, as the waste of time to get their own company staff involved.

(c) They do not wish to get themselves shouldered with such involvements and personal responsibilities in such situations.

(d) They think that outside companies/firms have better skilled expertise in the area.

(e) None of these.

Q2. As per the passage, it would be better in the interest of the company –

(a) If the top managers are not involved in such situations of putting the right, as it might distract them from their other important role.

(b) If the job of correction and putting the things right is handled by the staff of the host company, with an active involvement of top managers, to enable them to have proper knowledge & skills. It will gear them up to face the problems which might arise later on.

(c) If the job of putting things right is given to outside companies, within the fixed time frame since they have better expertise.

(d) To award the jobs of putting things right to outside companies as the charges paid to the outside companies are much less than those that might be incurred on own experts.

(e) None of these.

Q3. Which of the following messages does the writer desire to convey by using the phrases **"Our strength, just like your own, lies in our ignorance of your troubles"**?

(a) The host company is full of ignorant people, it would be better to put them to action learning programmed.

(b) The visiting expert is equally ignorant but cunning enough to buy time and getting the things put right by gathering knowledge from the host company.

(c) The expert from outside company is also a manager and can very well put the things right with his knowledge & skill.

(d) The visiting expert would be making strenuous efforts to get things right in order to get a job in the company, he is visiting.

(e) None of these.

Q4. – **'Phase themselves out'** as described in the passage means –

(a) The ignorance and working style of outside consultants might put the host company in trouble.

(b) The expert company/firm will prolong the work to buy time only.

(c) The work will ultimately have to be managed by the host team whole the visiting expert will move out of the role.

(d) Right from the beginning, the outside expert will not be of much help and the entire work will be accomplished by the employees of Host Company.

(e) None of these.

Q5. The writer firmly believes that –

(a) The managers at the top level should not be involved in action learning programmes.

(b) It is better to have the knowledge & skill from outside agencies than involving the own staff.

(c) The managers & operational staff of the host company must go for operational learning to face recurring problems and is critical of outside agencies.

(d) The visiting expert will solve the problem without wasting the time of host company managers, thus avoiding the trouble of their personal responsibilities.

(e) None of these.

Directions (06-08) : **Choose the word which is most nearly the SAME in meaning as the word printed in bold as used in the passage.**

Q6. **Avenue**

(a) Method

(b) Refusal

(c) Dissent

(d) Rejection

(e) Veto

Q7. **Affliction**

(a) Advantage

(b) Delight

(c) Hope

(d) Blessing

(e) Hardship

Q8. **Obstinate**

(a) Amenable

(b) Pliant

(c) Soft

(d) Adamant

(e) Flexible

Directions (09-10) : **Choose the word which is most OPPOSITE in meaning of the word printed in bold as used in the passage.**

Q9. **Itinerant**

(a) Roving

(b) Afoot

(c) Floating

(d) Nomadic

(e) Settled

Q10. **Deceive**

(a) Assist

(b) Beguile

(c) Betray

(d) Fake

(e) Hoodwink

Directions (11-15) : **Read the following passage carefully and answer the questions given below it. Certain words have been printed in bold to help you locate them while answering some of the questions.**

The Global Nutrition Report (GNR) and India Health Report on Nutrition, 2015 (IHR) , offer a critical analysis of the state of nutrition in India. The first report, the India Health Report: Nutrition 2015(IHR) , provides easy-to-understand, State-wise data dashboards that give a comprehensive view of nutrition and its determinants. It looks at disparities in these outcomes and their multiple determinants across geographical regions, socio-economic classes, and demographic groups to help identify strategic choices for policy-making at the State level.

In turn, GNR assesses progress in reducing malnutrition for all 193 countries. It concludes that while India is on track to meeting only two of the eight global targets on nutrition, it has significantly improved its nutrition performance in the past 10 years. GNR notes that there has been a big increase in the number of countries on track to meet global nutrition targets, and encourages countries, including India, to establish specific and time-bound targets for malnutrition reduction that are consistent with the new Sustainable Development Goals. Together, these reports paint several pictures about India, a data-poor country. They portray one of great progress in improving nutrition across India; stunting among children, a marker of the most **persistent** types of malnutrition, has declined rapidly in the last ten years. And this decline has been faster than in many other countries. But as we dig deeper, there are **diverse** pictures about the life conditions of Indian children—positive stories about children's lives and futures in Goa, Kerala, Manipur and Tamil Nadu, but dismal ones in Bihar, Jharkhand and Uttar Pradesh. What cannot be debated is the reality of deep, systemic inequality; of inequality in the circumstances that children are born into, that they live and grow in. For those of us who are worried about India's economic growth, these are also pictures of inequality that point to how well these children will be able to contribute to India's economic growth and their own prosperity. Their poor nutrition stunts more than their bodies. It stunts their well-being, and, consequentially, that of their home States and their nation. Two other things, both related to inequality, stand out as well in the data. First, the data point to tremendous variability across States in delivering what should be universal, rights-based and already **mandated** health and nutrition services. For example, sample this for intra-State disparity. Food provided by the Integrated Child Development Services reaches barely 1 in 5 children in Uttar Pradesh but over 90 per cent in Odisha. Less than 33 per cent of children in Nagaland are fully immunised; in Goa, it is more than 90 per cent. Close to 80 per cent defecate in the open in Odisha; barely 2 per cent do so in Kerala. Why?

These are disparities across States that operate in the same national framework, and there is, let's face it, no good reason for this other than an inability or an unwillingness to invest in changing ground realities, for everyone and everywhere. This is not an insurmountable challenge and it's certainly an area where States can, if they want it, make dramatic change in short timeframes. Examples abound from within India. The data in the reports show that, clearly, the **imperative** for introspection, and looking within for solutions was never clearer. No child should go without basic health care, food security and things like water and a toilet. Indeed, no adult should either. No society should **condone** such inequalities in the basics. And no society has progressed without addressing these basics.

Q11. What are the disparities that states are facing in the national framework?

I.Health and nutirition services

II.Variable food services

III.Inequality in education

(a) III

(b) II & III

(c) I & II

(d) I,II & III

(e) None of the above

Q12. The Global Nutrition Report focuses mainly on the

(a) Sustainable Development Goals

(b) comprehensive view of nutrition and its determinants

(c) India's economic growth

(d) Intra-State variability

(e) Progress in reducing malnutrition

Q13. Which of the following would be the suitable title?

(a) State of nutrition in India

(b) Global nutrition targets

(c) Nutrition and its determinants

(d) Progressive India

(e) Inequality: A big challenge

Q14. According to author what is the biggest challenge that India is facing?

(a) Reducing progress in malnutrition

(b) Inability to invest in education and health services

(c) unwillingness and inability to invest in basic facilities

(d) High global nutrition targets

(e) None of these

Q15. What is **NOT TRUE** according to the above passage?

I. Food provided by ICDS reaches to only few children in UP.

II. Nearly 80 percent defecate in open in West bengal.

III. Less than 33 percent children in Nagaland are immunised.

(a) III & II

(b) I,II & III

(c) I & II

(d) I & III

(e) II only

Directions (16-20) : **In each of the following questions four words are given of which two are most nearly the same or opposite in meaning. Find the two words which are most nearly the same or opposite in meaning and find the number of the correct letter combination.**

Q16. (A) Slack

(B) Confusing

(C) Strenuous

(D) Light

(a) B-C

(b) A-D

(c) B-D

(d) A-C

(e) C-D

Q17. (A) Harmony

(B) Accord

(C) Concord

(D) Melody

(a) B-C

(b) A-D

(c) B-D

(d) A-C

(e) C-D

Q18. (A) Enthralling

(B) Respecting

(C) Projecting

(D) Alluring

(a) A-B

(b) B-C

(c) C-D

(d) A-D

(e) B-D

Q19. (A) Swoop

(B) Perturb

(C) Plump

(D) Boil

(a) A-D

(b) B-C

(c) A-C

(d) B-D

(e) C-D

Q20. (A) Concise

(B) Elegant

(C) Indifferent

(D) Indecorous

(a) B-C

(b) A-C

(c) A-B

(d) C-D

(e) B-D

Directions (21-25) : **Read each sentence to find out whether there is any grammatical or idiomatic error in it. The error, if any, will be in one part of the sentence. The number of that part is the answer. If there is 'No error', the answer is (e) ) . (Ignore errors of punctuation, if any.)**

Q21. One Indian virtue that has impressed me

greatly and touched me deeply was the Indian people's freedom of rancor.

(a) One Indian virtue that has impressed me greatly

(b) and touched me deeply

(c) was the Indian

(d) people's freedom of rancor

(e) No error

Q22. When we reached at the station I fought my way through people and luggage and secured a place next to the window.

(a) When we reached at the station

(b) I fought my way through

(c) people and luggage

(d) and secured a place next to the window

(e) No error

Q23. The parents are happy to know that a number of summer programmes have been arranged for the benefit of their children.

(a) The parents are happy to know

(b) that a number of summer programmes

(c) have been arranged

(d) for the benefit of their children

(e) No error

Q24. The teacher asked his students if they had gone through either of three chapters included in the prescribed text.

(a) The teacher asked his students

(b) if they had gone through

(c) either of three chapters

(d) included in the prescribed text

(e) No error

Q25. Mother tongue is as natural for the development of man's mind as mother's milk is for the development of the infant's body.

(a) Mother tongue is as natural

(b) for the development of man's min

(c) as mother's milk is for the development

(d) of the infant's body

(e) No error

Directions (26-30) : **In each of the following questions a short passage is given with lastline in the passage missing and represented by a blank. Select the best out of the four answer choices given, to make the passage complete and coherent. If none follows, choose (e) as your answer.**

Q26. It's August, and Americans by the millions are cramming themselves into coach-class seats as they embark on their summer vacations. Airlines are sparing no expense these days to enlarge, upgrade and increase the price of their first-class and business-class seating. As the space and dollars devoted to the front of the planes increase, something else has to be diminished, and, as multitudes of travellers can attest, it's the experience of flying coach. ______________

(a) But people fly airlines because the fares are what they can afford.

(b) They are in a rush to squeeze as much money as possible out of business travellers willing to pay thousands of dollars for a premium seat.

(c) The joys of air travel — once common to all who flew — have been redistributed upward and are now reserved for the well-heeled few.

(d) If you're an average American who travels, this is not good news.

(e) None of these.

Q27. According to Clayton Christensen's theory of "disruptive innovation," an industry becomes ripe for disruption once it begins super-serving its best, most affluent customers and ignoring the rest. Each stage in the maturation of a company or industry inevitably pushes it to embrace its best, most profitable customers. However, in the process, the companies fighting over the "best" customers gradually cede the low end of the market to new entrants. ____________

(a) Over time, new technologies introduced for the low end of the market climb the price-performance curve and. start to surpass the technologies at the high end.

(b) So, it's game over for the market leaders forever.

(c) They are too big to react quickly to a new era of innovation.

(d) This should be a clear sign that the industry is headed for a period of peak disruption.

(e) None of these.

Q28. Till 1969, India's major banks, other than the State Bank of India and its subsidiaries, were directly or indirectly controlled by big business, resulting in the capture of a dominant share of the nation's savings by large firms to the exclusion of small borrowers and the agricultural sector. Seizing the ownership of these banks and bringing them into the public sector established social control. ____________

(a) But public ownership stalls innovation and adversely affects customer service.

(b) Public ownership of the State Bank of India subordinates the profit principle to other development goals.

(c) The result is a more stable banking sector.

(d) In the two decades that followed, India's banking sector, judged by behaviour or social performance indicators, went through a dramatic transformation.

(e) None of these.

Q29. Scientists have unveiled plans to genetically engineer a lethal strain of bird flu to understand how it could mutate in nature and trigger a catastrophic pandemic. The controversial experiments are expected to make the H7N9 virus more virulent and increase its ability to spread between people. But researchers argue the work is crucial for public health because it will drive research into drugs and vaccines, and help identify dangerous mutations to watch out for in the wild. ____________

(a) Scientists already track mutations in bird flu viruses found in patients, but this kind of surveillance does not give health authorities time to respond if they find a pandemic strain.

(b) But the details of the experiments, if leaked, could help terrorists create lethal viruses as bio weapons.

(c) "The pandemic risk rises exponentially should these viruses acquire the ability to transmit readily among humans," they say.

(d) The work will be done in high-security laboratories to minimize the risk of the modified viruses escaping and causing precisely the kind of devastation the W.H.O. aims to prevent.

(e) None of these.

Q30. A leader who is truly humble, and is perceived as being so by others, ultimately will have far more authority than an arrogant leader. Self-knowledge is the first and foremost expression of humility. People who are humble neither overestimate their virtues nor disparage themselves. Having high self-esteem does not make them pretentious. They constantly evaluate themselves, and realise that they are not infallible. This self-awareness includes recognizing what they owe to others. Humble individuals do not take credit for all of their strengths and achievements. ____________

(a) Humility often goes hand in hand with other virtues, such as objectivity, simplicity, the desire to learn and patience with others.

(b) Instead they value and appreciate the help they receive from others.

(c) They don't boast about their strengths, but they don't deny or conceal them either.

(d) They seek praise from others and feel hurt by criticism.

(e) None of these.

Directions (31-35) : **In each of the questions below, four different ways of writing a sentence are indicated. Choose the best way of writing the sentence which is both grammatically and meaningfully correct. If none follows, choose (e) as your answer**.

Q31. (a) It could be argued that the most significant virtue of a popular democracy' is not the right to participate in the selection of leaders, but rather that it is an affirmation of our importance in the scheme of things.

(b) It could be argued that the most significant virtue of a popular democracy is not the right to participate in the selection of leaders, but rather that if affirms our importance in the scheme of things.

(c) It could be argued that the most significant virtue of a popular democracy is not the right to participate in the selection of leaders, but rather it's affirmation in terms of our importance in the scheme of things.

(d) It could be argued that the most significant virtue of a popular democracy is not the right to participate in the selection of leaders, but instead of that, its affirming that our importance in the scheme of things.

(e) None of these.

Q32. (a) Long popular among the connoisseurs of Indian music, Ravi Shankar first impressed Western listeners with his phenomenal technical virtuosity, but it soon occurred that they appreciated his artful music as an expression of an older culture's musical insight.

(b) Long popular among the connoisseurs of Indian music, Ravi Shankar first impressed Western listeners with his phenomenal technical virtuosity, but they soon came to appreciate his music as an artful expression of an older culture's musical insight.

(c) Long popular among the connoisseurs of Indian music, Ravi Shankar first impressed Western listeners with his phenomenal technical virtuosity, but soon this was surpassed by an appreciation of it as an artful expression of an older culture's musical insight.

(d) Long popular among the connoisseurs of Indian music, Ravi Shankar first impressed Western listeners with his phenomenal technical virtuosity, which was soon surpassed by an even deeper appreciation of it as an artful expression of an older culture's musical insight.

(e) None of these.

Q33. (a) No officer had ought to be put into a situation in which he has to choose between his love for his family and the responsibilities accompanying his duty.

(b) No officer had ought to be put into a situation where he has to choose between his love for his family and the responsibilities accompanying his duty.

(c) No officer should be put into a situation where he has to choose between his love for his family and the responsibilities accompanying his duty.

(d) No officer ought to be put into a situation in which he has to choose between his love for his family and the responsibilities accompanying his duty.

(e) None of these.

Q34. (a) Since he was a realist, the detective could not accept the statement of the accused that UFOs had caused the disturbance.

(b) Being a realist, the detective could not accept the statement of the accused that UFOs had caused the disturbance.

(c) Being that he was a realist, the detective could not accept the statement of the accused that UFOs had caused the disturbance.

(d) Realist that he was, the detective could not accept the statement of the accused that UFOs had caused the disturbance.

(e) None of these.

Q35. (a) Ever since the sting operation, there has been much opposition from they who maintain that it had been an unauthorized act.

(b) Ever since the sting operation, there has been much opposition from they who maintain that it was an unauthorized act.

(c) Ever since the sting operation, there has been much opposition from those who maintain that it was an unauthorized act.

(d) Ever since the sting operation, there has been much opposition from those maintaining that it was an unauthorized act.

(e) None of these.

## Solutions (Mock Test – 10)

S1. Ans. (c)

Sol. Read the passage carefully. Refer to the first paragraph of the passage. It can be easily implied that they do not wish to get themselves shouldered with such involvements and personal responsibilities in such situations.

S2. Ans. (b)

Sol. "If the job of correction and putting the things right is handled by the staff of the host company, with an active involvement of top managers, to enable them to have proper knowledge & skills. It will gear them up to face the problems which might arise later on." is the correct choice as it can be inferred from the second paragraph of the passage.

S3. Ans. (b)

Sol. Read the first few sentences of the second paragraph. It can be inferred from there that the visiting expert is equally ignorant but cunning enough to buy time and getting the things put right by gathering knowledge from the host company. Hence (b) is the correct option.

S4. Ans. (c)

Sol. "The work will ultimately have to be managed by the host team whole the visiting expert will move out of the role." explains the phrase appropriately.

S5. Ans. (c)

Sol. After reading the whole passage it can be easily inferred that the writer believes that the managers & operational staff of the host company must go for operational learning to face recurring problems and is critical of outside agencies.

S6. Ans. (a)

Sol. **Avenue** means a way of approaching a problem or making progress towards something. Hence **'avenues'** and **'method'** are similar in meanings.

S7. Ans. (e)

Sol. **Affliction** means a cause of pain or harm. Hence **'affliction'** and **'hardship'** are similar in meanings.

S8. Ans. (d)

Sol. **Obstinate** means (of an unwelcome situation) very difficult to change or overcome. **Adamant** means refusing to be persuaded or to change one's mind. Hence **'obstinate'** and **'adamant'** are similar in meanings.

S9. Ans. (e)

Sol. **Itinerant** means travelling from place to place. Hence **'settled'** and **'itinerant'** are opposite in meanings.

S10. Ans. (a)

Sol. **Deceive** means (of a thing) give (someone) a mistaken impression. Hence **'assist'** and **'deceive'** are opposite in meanings.

S11. Ans. (c)

Sol. Refer to last part of second paragraph of the passage.

S12. Ans.(e)

Sol. Refer to second paragraph of the passage. 'GNR assesses progress in reducing malnutrition for all 193 countries.'

S13. Ans. (a)

Sol. State of nutrition in India

S14. Ans. (c)

Sol. Refer to the last paragraph of the passage, 'no good reason for this other than an inability or an unwillingness to invest in changing ground realities, for everyone and everywhere.'

S15. Ans. (e)

Sol. II statement is not true. Refer to last sentence of second paragraph.

S16. Ans. (e)

Sol. **Strenuous** means requiring or using great effort or exertion. Hence '**strenuous**' and '**light**' are opposite in meanings.

**Slack** means not taut or held tightly in position; loose.

S17. Ans. (d)

Sol. **Concord** means agreement or harmony between people or groups. Hence '**harmony**' and '**concord**' are similar in meanings.

S18. Ans. (d)

Sol. **Enthralling** means capturing and holding one's attention; fascinating. Hence '**enthralling**' and '**alluring**' are similar in meanings.

S19. Ans. (d)

Sol. **Perturb** means make (someone) anxious or unsettled. Hence '**perturb**' and '**boil**' are similar in meanings.

S20. Ans. (e)

Sol. **Indecorous** means not in keeping with good taste and propriety; improper. Hence '**elegant**' and '**indecorous**' are opposite in meanings.

S21. Ans. (c)

Sol. Replace 'was' with 'is'.

S22. Ans. (a)

Sol. Remove 'at', the verb 'reach' is not followed by the preposition 'at'.

S23. Ans. (e)

Sol. The given sentence is grammatically correct.

S24. Ans. (a)

Sol. Use 'any' in place of 'either'. 'Either' is used in case of two alternatives.

S25. Ans. (d)

Sol. Use 'an' in place of 'the'.

S26. Ans. (c)

Sol. The passage suggests that flying coach-class is what the average American does. When airlines are enlarging and upgrading first-class and business-class seating at the cost of coach-class, the joys of air-travel are taken away from the average American as mentioned in Option (c) . This option is well related to 'the experience of flying coach' in the penultimate sentence. So option (c) is the most suitable concluding sentence. 'Affording the fares' is not the central point here, so (a) can be eliminated. Option (b) may be a point related to the paragraph, but it has no connection with the preceding sentence. Option (d) also does not go with the penultimate sentence. It is too general and means any kind of travel.

S27. Ans. (a)

Sol. The passage says that when companies start super-servicing the best customers, they give up the low end customers to new entrants in the long run. The best conclusion to this line of argument could be option A, which explains the reason. Option B is absurd as it says, it's game over for the market leaders forever. C is also unrelated as it talks about the size of the industry to react. D is also irrelevant because there is no precedent to 'this' in D.

S28. Ans. (d)

Sol. The reference here is to nationalisation of banks. The penultimate sentence says that bringing the banks into the public sector established social control. Option D gives the passage continuity, mentioning social indicators and concludes by saying these banks went through a dramatic transformation. Option A mentions another point and has no connection to the penultimate sentence. (B) is too specific and related only to S.B.I. 'Stability' in C is not mentioned in the paragraph.

S29. Ans. (c)

Sol. The passage talks about the scientists' attempt 'to make the H7N9 virus more virulent and increase its ability to spread between people' and the justification they give for continuing with their research. Option C best suits as the concluding sentence as it is a continuation of the argument in the previous sentence. Option A is unrelated to the preceding sentence. B is a different point. Option D, though related to the topic, has no relevance to the preceding sentence and the W.H.O. occurs nowhere in the passage.

S30. Ans. (b)

Sol. The idea expressed in option B (Instead they value and appreciate the help they receive from others) is a sequence to the penultimate sentence which says they do not take credit for all of their strengths and achievements, and therefore is the concluding sentence. Choice A is a new point. D and C are unrelated to the preceding sentence.

S31. Ans. (a)

S32. Ans. (d)

Sol. 'But' should be replaced with 'what' because the sentences are not contradictory.

S33. Ans. (d)

Sol. "had ought to" should be replaced by either should or ought to; with situation "in which" sounds better.

S34. Ans. (b)

Sol. The given sentence is correct.

S35. Ans. (c)

Sol. In place of "from they", "from those" is correct.

NOTE